CAROL JUDD has been an editor with the *Dictionary of Canadian Biography* and a historian with Parks Canada.

ARTHUR RAY is a member of the Department of Geography at York University, author of *Indians in the Fur Trade*, and co-author of '*Give Us Good Measure.*'

Fur trade scholarship has changed considerably in recent years. The tempo of research has quickened and the field has become more multi-disciplinary, bringing together scholars in archaeology, economics, ethnohistory, geography, history, and anthropology. The papers in this volume reflect recent developments in several specific areas of research: mapping, native cultures, social and labour history, personalities, the Pacific coast, and economics.

The moving of the Hudson's Bay Archives from London to Winnipeg in 1974 has patriated an incredibly rich source of information on many aspects of Canadian history, and the effects of this superb collection being available to Canadian scholars are just beginning to be felt. In this volume we can see that the history of the fur trade in Canada is not merely the story of the world's first great multi-national – the Hudson's Bay Company – but a study of a complex society during a period of more than two centuries. Languages, customs, transportation, personalities, marriage, and even sex are looked at in the wide-ranging papers in this book.

Edited by
CAROL M. JUDD and
ARTHUR J. RAY

Old Trails and New Directions: Papers of the Third North American Fur Trade Conference

UNIVERSITY OF TORONTO PRESS
Toronto Buffalo London

© University of Toronto Press 1980
Toronto Buffalo London
Reprinted in paperback 2017
ISBN 978-0-8020-5468-5 (cloth)
ISBN 978-1-4875-9216-5 (paper)

Canadian Cataloguing in Publication Data

North American Fur Trade Conference, 3d, Winnipeg,
   Man., 1978.
   Old trails and new directions

Bibliography: p.
ISBN 978-0-8020-5468-5 (bound) ISBN 978-1-4875-9216-5 (pbk.)
1. Fur trade – Canada – Congresses. 2. Fur trade –
United States – Congresses. I. Judd, Carol M.
II. Ray, Arthur J., 1941– III. Title.
HD9944.A2N6 1978   338.3'72'90971   C79-094744-7

This book has been published with the
assistance of a grant from the Publications Fund of
University of Toronto Press.

Contents

vi   Contents

Foreword

The Third North American Fur Trade Conference, held in Winnipeg, Manitoba, in May 1978, was by general agreement a success. The degree of success is affirmed by the published papers of the conference in this volume. At the same time those who attended the conference will remember the growing sense of comradeship, the excitement of effort in a common cause which made the conference the rewarding experience it was.

The program of the conference was, as the following papers confirm, much wider than the term 'fur trade' suggests. It dealt with people, European and native, with women in the fur trade, with crops, seasons, and weather. Its concerns were those of an entire way of life, as complete in itself as most human existence. This catholicity of interest is, of course, a reflection of the Hudson's Bay Company Archives in Winnipeg, which covers the many facets of company enterprise and contacts, and is used by researchers in many fields – climatology, botany, ornithology, and so on – besides those of the fur trade and native life.

There have now been three fur trade conferences: in St Paul (1965) and in Winnipeg (1970 and 1978). There was general agreement at the 1978 conference that there should be another. The Minnesota Historical Society and fur trade historians have decided to organize and sponsor the fourth conference.

The 1978 conference was made possible by generous financial grants from the Canada Council, the City of Winnipeg, the Government of Manitoba, the Hudson's Bay Company, Parks Canada, Ottawa, and Parks Canada, Winnipeg. The sponsorship of the Manitoba Historical Society, the Manitoba Museum of Man and Nature, the University of Brandon, and the University of Winnipeg is also acknowledged. The organizing committee warmly thanks these good friends.

As advisory chairman, I would like to praise and thank the members of the active committees for much often delicate and difficult work. The success of the conference was a result of the careful preparation they made in the choice of topics and of speakers. The committee members were: Carol Judd, historian, Parks Canada, Ottawa (conference chairman); Arthur Ray, associate professor, York University, Toronto (program chairman); Charles A. Bishop, professor, State University of New York, Oswego; John Bovey, provincial archivist of Manitoba, Winnipeg; Robert V. Oleson, public relations officer (history), Hudson's Bay Company, Winnipeg; Frits Pannekoek, chief, historical research, prairie region, Parks Canada, Winnipeg; Shirlee Anne Smith, Hudson's Bay Company Archivist, Provincial Archives of Manitoba, Winnipeg. Professor Glyndwr Williams suggested the title of this book.

The careful editing of the papers by Carol Judd and Arthur Ray has completed the work of the conference. They have together done a superb job of making the conference not only a great, but also a complete success.

On behalf of the contributors to this volume I would like to thank the Hudsons's Bay Company for granting them permission to consult and quote from its records.

W.L. MORTON
Advisory chairman

Abbreviations

ANQM Archives nationales du Québec à Montréal
BM   British Museum
EGL   Edmonton Genealogical Library, Church of Jesus Christ of
      Latter-Day Saints
GAI   Glenbow-Alberta Institute, Calgary
HBCA Hudson's Bay Company Archives, Provincial Archives of Man-
      itoba, Winnipeg
OA   Archives of Ontario, Toronto
PABC Provincial Archives of British Columbia, Victoria
PAC   Public Archives of Canada, Ottawa
PRO   Public Record Office, London, England
SRO   Scottish Record Office, Edinburgh

OLD TRAILS AND NEW DIRECTIONS

Introduction

Fur trade scholarship, traditionally preoccupied with lauding the heroic efforts of European explorers and other officials of fur companies, has changed considerably in recent years. The tempo of research has quickened and become more interdisciplinary: its field of investigation is wider, new questions are being asked, and new theses are being developed. To reflect these new perspectives in fur trade research the fur trade conference committee invited a cross-section of both young and established scholars from several academic fields: archaeology, economics, ethnohistory, geography, history, and anthropology. We believe this volume, the end product of the conference, illustrates the increasing depth, breadth, and multi-disciplinary nature of current fur trade scholarship.

Only two papers originally presented at the fur trade conference have not been included in the selection which follows. One of these, 'Authorship and Illiteracy: Did John Sayer Write the Diary of Thomas Connor?' by Douglas Birk of the Minnesota Historical Society, is being published by that society. The other, an excellent selection of slides with commentary, 'The Discovery of Artifacts of the North West Company from Otter Falls, Winnipeg River, Manitoba' by Andrew Lockery, University of Winnipeg, was best suited to oral delivery.

Because the conference sessions were consciously designed to introduce recent developments in several specific research themes, we decided to divide this book as much as possible along the same lines. Hence, we have grouped the papers according to the following themes: mapping, native societies, social history, personalities, the Pacific coast, and economics.

The first section, on maps, covers a topic not examined in detail at previous conferences. Included is a paper by Malcolm Lewis, a historical geographer from Sheffield, England, who is engaged in a project dealing with Indian contributions to the cartographic history of North America. In the other paper, based largely on surviving maps, Richard Ruggles considers early cartographic efforts of the Hudson's Bay Company. These two papers, each based on several years of research, add considerably to our knowledge of the historical geography of Canada.

The papers about native societies address an old theme but employ new approaches, adopt fresh perspectives, and in one instance, deal with an area previously ignored. The setting for Toby Morantz's paper, the eastern James Bay region, for instance, has received very little attention in historical literature. Her paper, an outgrowth of a research project on the history of the James Bay Cree, considers the Cree impact on the fur traders as well as the changes in aboriginal practices that resulted from contact. The papers by Cornelius Jaenen and Calvin Martin also consider contact and its results, but focus their attention on its influence on European and Indian attitudes. Jaenen reconsiders the popular notion that the French perceived the Indians as either noble savages or as degenerate beings. Martin looks beyond the traditional economic explanation for changes in the Indian attitudes toward game that resulted from contact.

The section of social history also considers a subject area that has received relatively little systematic attention until recently. The papers by Trudy Nicks, John Nicks, and Carol Judd break new ground in Canadian labour history. Judd's paper investigates the ethnic composition of the Hudson's Bay Company recruits in the nineteenth century, while John Nicks's paper concentrates on one of these groups, the men from the Orkneys. Trudy Nicks delves into a relatively unexplored chapter of western Canadian history – the role of the Iroquois in the northwest. These three papers are based on long-term projects that still continue. Sylvia Van Kirk's paper reviews recent developments in the study of fur trade society and highlights some of the issues that currently engage the interests of social historians. Jennifer Brown's paper exposes problems in language and method that will have to be confronted in order to understand better the society generated by the fur trade.

Individual members of fur trade society have always been of considerable interest. The section on fur trade personalities, however, departs from tradition in not focusing on leading explorers or traders. Hilary Russell discusses a first-rank officer of second-rank calibre, who, like many others, had to make the transition in 1821 from being an associate of the North West Company to becoming an officer of the new Hudson's Bay

Company. Charles Bishop, in contrast, devotes his paper to a discussion of a very successful Indian leader. Written from an anthropological perspective, Bishop provides an understanding of the problems that native leaders faced in dealing with two cultural worlds.

Fur trade studies have commonly focused on the activities of the English and the French. However, on the Pacific coast, Russians also played an important role. Stephen Johnson considers the interaction of the Russians with the English by revealing the relationship between Baron Ferdinand von Wrangel of the Russian-American Company and Sir George Simpson of the Hudson's Bay Company. James Gibson, while also investigating the competition among Russian, British, and American traders, contrasts the Russian maritime trade with the Siberian trade. Mary Cullen considers the inland aspect of the Pacific coast fur trade by concentrating on the transportation system of the Hudson's Bay Company. She suggests many areas for further research, pointing out that this aspect of the trade has received little systematic attention.

The closing section explores several topics of increasing interest in the past few years. Arthur Ray's paper examines the role of the Indian in the fur trade, considering his behaviour as a consumer and the implications that this behaviour had for European merchants. Wayne Moodie's paper explores this theme further within the context of the relationship between fur trading and agricultural activities. He points out that the Indians of central Canada, the Ojibwa, adopted and expanded agriculture in response to opportunities they perceived the fur trade offered to them. The final paper, by Irene Spry, considers the very topical question of the relevance of Innis' fur trade studies for our understanding of the nature of many of Canada's current economic problems. In doing so, Spry also helps put into general perspective the importance of fur trade research to an understanding of the political, social, and economic development of Canada.

The epilogue by Glyndwr Williams, former editor of the Hudson's Bay Record Society and currently head of the Department of History, Queen Mary College, University of London, provides a fresh, outside view of the papers presented at the conference and of work by other North American scholars during the past decade. He raises a number of thoughtful questions about the paths future research might take, possibilities for quantitative history, and the need to explore the hitherto largely untapped resources of the Hudson's Bay Company Archives for the period after 1870.

Taken in their entirety the papers in this volume are more significant than any of their separate parts. Frequently one paper develops a theme another mentions only in passing. At the same time, because of the solitary nature of research, some scholars seem not to be aware of the work of others which might have significance for their own work. Such is the nature of research. A reflection of its time, it inches forward in uneven measure, following similar lines and often touching the same issues but not always reaching identical conclusions.

CAROL JUDD
ARTHUR RAY
Ottawa 1979

PART I ✧ MAPS

Indian Maps

G. MALCOLM LEWIS

From the late sixteenth century onwards traders and trappers were among the most active Europeans in that ill-defined and shifting transition zone between 'terra cognita' and 'terra incognita': the 'terra semicognita.' Europeans made increasingly frequent incursions into the latter while seeking territorial control and its incorporation into their terra cognita. During the more than three centuries of their active involvement, fur traders were probably more important in this exploration and absorption than any other group: soldiers, missionaries, miners, agricultural settlers, sportsmen, or government-sponsored explorers. At various periods fur traders were in perhaps four-fifths of the continent, in search of either fur-bearing animals or routes of access to their habitat areas. As individuals, fur traders and trappers tended to have longer and wider experience of the terra semicognita than most other European 'frontiersmen.' At any one time their composite terra semicognita tended to be more extensive and more remote than that of any other group. They thus played a very important role in the geographical exploration of North America.

This paper is concerned with an aspect of the exploration process hitherto overlooked: the transmission by Indians to traders and trappers of information in map-form about the terra semicognita and the terra incognita beyond.

Communication between native peoples and aliens is always beset by problems: cultural differences, suspicion, ill will, linguistic differences, and sometimes the absence of a written native language. These problems are particularly acute when the newcomers are unable to verify the information given – for example, where it relates to their terra semicognita. Native people in this zone sense, realize, and store information about the environment according to their own cultural values. In transmitting information to aliens they will always subconsciously and almost always consciously suppress, amplify, and mix elements prior to coding them in oral, sign, or graphic form. On receiving such messages the newcomers reverse the procedure by first attempting to decode them, next amplifying or suppressing certain elements therein, then mixing them with others already at hand, before finally memorizing, physically recording, rejecting, or forgetting them. Much that is recorded or memorized is subsequently lost by accident, death, or failure to retransmit. Much that is received is wrongly decoded; much that is correctly decoded is misconceived in the subconscious process of cultural re-evaluation or consciously rejected as redundant. Hence, the potential within the system for loss and misunderstanding of information is tremendous.

Furthermore, the system itself is inefficient. Links operate only intermittently and usually only between a few atypical members of each group. The quantity of information transmitted is small, and the aliens have, to begin with, little control over content or quality. In the absence of adequate 'mental maps' into which the aliens can integrate new information, a high proportion seems redundant or is wrongly appraised.

The meagre content of the aliens' image of the terra semicognita inevitably lacks clear structures. In the absence of a system of geographical co-ordinates or a reasonably reliable map, information on the spatial arrangement of phenomena can be conveyed either as statements of the distance and direction of places reported from places which are known (in practice a route traverse or distance with bearing) or by means of sketch maps. The first method is unsatisfactory, especially when distances are great and routes tortuous. 'A route traverse when carefully made is admirably adapted to illustrate the account of a journey and to enable future travellers to follow the same route ... [but even when carefully observed and recorded] it is altogether wrong to suppose that anything in the nature of a satisfactory map can be made by combining a number of these ... [because each] is a zigzag line, which may have been stretched by error in estimating distances, and distorted by errors in the mean bearing of tortuous tracks.'[1] When route traverses are made by native people, subject to consistent bias (randomly distributed errors can result in remarkably good results), estimated without the aid of a compass, and with travel time substituted for absolute distance, they are utterly useless for conveying spatially structured information. Sketch maps, providing that they show networks and are not merely representations of single routes (in which case they are no better than the route traverses from which they were derived), are somewhat better in this respect.

In the past, throughout much of the world, aliens have obtained from native peoples information in map form about the terra semicognita. The term 'cartographic device' is used for the several forms of artifact by which such information was transmitted; unlike modern maps they were not drawn to scale, not constructed according to particular projections, and not consistent in the representation of *all* phenomena in a given class above a given threshold size.

Scholars have recently given little theoretical attention to this class of information. A century of interest among German geographers was initiated by Alexander von Humboldt in 1836,[2] reached its peak with monographs by Dröber and Adler in 1903[3] and 1910[4] respectively, and terminated with a significant contribution from Friderici in 1936.[5] During the twentieth century few North American scholars have shown continuing interest in the cartographic devices of the continent's native peoples, though some individuals have made contributions to our knowledge and understanding of them.

North American Indians and Inuit used cartographic devices for a variety of purposes. Three uses were particularly important: the recording and reconstructing of past events, such as tribal migrations and the routes of war parties; for messages, left prominently displayed at major points on routeways to inform those following behind of the direction in which the preceding persons had gone, the circumstances of the journey, and the distance to the intended destination; and as instructional aids used by those who had once followed a particular route or travelled in a particular area to brief others who were about to do so for the first time. They were inscribed, painted, modelled, or carved in or on skin, bark, mats, stone, bone, or wood or inscribed in ephemeral materials such as sand, silt, snow, and wood ash.

In one form or other they appear to have been used in every part of the continent at the time of virtually all early European-Indian contacts; and petrogylphs seem to suggest that in at least some parts of the continent they may have been used long before. With or without modification in technique they were also used by the Indians in communicating information to the Europeans. The most frequent modifications of technique were the use of crayons, pencils, and paper instead of indigenous materials, and of maps supplied by Europeans of their terra cognita on which to add information about the adjacent terra semicognita and perhaps about their terra incognita beyond.

Surviving examples of cartographic devices produced for indigenous use are harder to locate than those used in communicating with Europeans. There are several reasons for this dearth: their purpose was usually short lived; surviving examples are sometimes not recognized for what they are (as when incorporated in petroglyphs); some are effectively lost in museum collections; and others (many incorporated on sacred scrolls) are still secretively treasured by their owners.

Examples of cartographic devices used to communicate with Europeans are more numerous, but rarely survive in their original form, usually having been transcribed, incorporated with cartographic information derived from elsewhere, or even printed. Because of the manner in which collectors and custodial institutions have segregated printed, manuscript, and artifact materials and have separated maps from the sources with which they originated, locating such cartographic devices and tracing their origins are difficult. Many are known, however, and of these a significant proportion have descended to us through the activities of fur traders.

The earliest devices predate the emergence of the fur trade as a distinctive economic activity. Perhaps the earliest record of native peoples providing spatially arranged information in sketch form in North America is in Fernando Alarchon's relation of his second attempt to ascend the Colorado River in 1540. He successfully persuaded an elderly native to 'set me downe in a charte as much as he knew concerning that River, and what manner of people those were which dwelt upon the banckes thereof on both sides.'[6] In the following year Jacques Cartier ascended the St Lawrence River, intending to go as far as Hochelaga 'to view and understand the fashion of the Saults of water, which are to be passed to go to Saguenay' via the Ottawa River route. Near the site of modern Montreal he reached the limit of his unsuccessful attempt to pass the rapids. Here he inquired of the natives how much further it was and how many more saults there were before he would reach the kingdom of Saguenay. They replied by placing sticks on the ground to represent the St Lawrence and by placing other sticks across them to represent the rapids.[7]

Sixty-two years later, and in the same area, natives drew on the deck of Samuel Champlain's vessel rude plans of the lakes and rapids on the St Lawrence upstream from his furthest point of penetration.[8] Two years later, having sailed down the coast of Maine and New Hampshire, Champlain himself drew on paper with a crayon the coast as far south as Cape Ann. On presenting the map to the natives they added Massachusetts Bay, which Champlain had not then seen, and the Merrimack River, the mouth of which Champlain had passed but not seen because of its bay bar. They also placed pebbles on the map to show the locations of 'six chiefs and tribes.'[9]

A map of the east coast of North America from Labrador to Cape Fear (North Carolina), was sent to Philip III of Spain in 1611 by Don Alonso de Velasco, the Spanish ambassador in London. It shows in blue outline certain rivers and lakes 'done by the relations of the Indian.'[10] Whether these were communicated orally, graphically, or by sign is not known; but the features outlined in blue include the upper parts of several of the west-bank rivers of Chesapeake Bay, what is apparently the Mohawk River, the St Lawrence River above Montreal, the eastern part of Lake Ontario, and what would appear to be a misplaced, oversized, and wrongly oriented Lake Champlain.

A Dutch account of a few years later affords an example of how such information may have been collected. At an Oneida town somewhere between present-day Utica and Syracuse, a factor of the Dutch West India Company at Fort Orange describe how he and his companion questioned the Indians on 31 December 1634 'concerning the situation [of the places] in their castle and their names, and how far they were away from each other. They showed us with stones and maize grains, and Jeronimus [de Lacroix] then made a chart of it. And we counted all in leagues how far each place was away from the next. The savages told us that on the high land which we had seen by that lake [Oneida] there lived men with horns on their heads; and they told us that a good many beavers were caught there, too, but they dared not go so far because of the French savages.'[11] This is an early surviving example of information in cartographic form gained by fur traders from Amerindians. The expedition from Fort Orange (now Albany, NY) was made to verify complaints made by Seneca and Mohawk Indians, who came to trade at the fort, that they received less from the Duth in exchange for their skins than did their near neighbours who traded with the French. In the course of their journey they traded for more than thirty beaver skins but the collection of information in the form of a cartographic device was for longer-term strategic purposes rather than immediate profit.

In 1687, while seeking to establish French control of the southern access to the fur resources of the Ohio and upper Mississippi valleys, La Salle reached the great Cenis village in what is now northeast Texas. Through their allies, the Choumans, the Cenis claimed to have indirect contact with the Spaniards to the west. La Salle 'made them draw on bark a map of their country, of that of their neighbors and of the river Colbert, or Mississippi, with which they are acquainted. They reckoned themselves six days' journey from the Spaniards, of which they gave us so natural description, that we no longer had doubts on that point.'[12] La Salle's brother described the map of the 'neighbouring rivers and nations' as 'very exact' and stated that the Cenis also 'depicted' Spanish clothing.[13] These brief quotations embody three of the characteristics of this technique for sensing the terra semicognita: graphical representation of the spatial arrangement of a few selected types of phenomena; selected distances expressed in travel time; and verification by questioning the Indians about phenomena of which the Europeans already had some reliable knowledge (in this case the characteristics of the Spaniards' dress).

The use of these simple techniques was not restricted to the French. In 1699, Francis Nicholson, then governor of Virginia, actively encouraged the Indian trade beyond the Appalachians, hoping to restrict French activity in the lower Mississippi valley. Writing to Governor Blake of South Carolina he expressed the opinion that should the French 'Seal that River it would be a very great Prejudice to the Crown of England.'[14] He urged Blake to submit a scheme to the king for restricting French influence in the area, to support this with geographical information obtained on oath from English traders, and to compare the information thus obtained with that in the first English edition of Hennepin's *A New Discovery of a Vast Country in America* (of which he sent Blake a copy.)[15] Nicholson also urged Blake to obtain accounts of the country from 'Indians which you can rely upon, and [to] lett them draw out the Country as Hennepin says one of the Shauanee Indians did for him for I think at least 400 leagues wch he found to be true.'[16]

Five years earlier, while governor of Maryland, Nicholson had received this type of information from a Lawrence van den Bosh – almost certainly Laurent van den Bosck, at one time an ordained Anglican priest in interior Carolina and hence probably having some involvement in the fur trade. Bosh's information included an original sketch map of the lower Mississippi valley and a statement that he had received the information about the area west of the river 'from a French Indian.'[17] Whether Governor Blake (who died in 1701) sought information from the Indians in map form is not known.

Soon after becoming governor of South Carolina in 1720 Nicholson himself forwarded to London transcripts on paper of two examples which had been presented to him on deer skin by Indian caciques.[18] One of these is remarkable for the extent of the area shown, from the Gulf coast almost to the Greak Lakes and from the southern Atlantic seaboard to well west of the Mississippi River, in all perhaps as much as one tenth of the continent.[19] It uses circles to show the locations of Indian tribal areas and of French and English settlements, the range of diameters of which suggests a proportional technique for showing relative quantities or sizes (in this case probably tribal populations). In this respect it is similar to an Indian cartographic device representing part of New Mexico which was drawn in 1602 and shows the population of pueblos in proportion to those of better known places in Mexico (Mexico, Zacatecas, and Sombrerete)[20] and to two cartographic devices drawn in 1737 by Chickasaw Indians, one of which shows the location of their villages and the other of both friendly and hostile nations.[21]

The representation on the cacique's cartographic device of paths as straight lines and of rivers and coastlines by a combination of straight lines and high radius curves likewise has much in common with those of New Mexico and the world of the Chickasaws. These characteristics indicate that they were each drawn according to topological rather than Euclidean principles. In topology the properties of distance, angle, area (and hence shape) are of no concern. The interest is in those properties of enclosed shapes, networks, and locations which remain unchanged when these 'absolutes' are disregarded. (It is sometimes popularly referred to as 'rubber sheet geometry.') The cacique's map could be transformed into a fairly accurate Euclidean representation. The amount and nature of the required transformation would vary from one part of the area to another and would be greatest in the west. There the cacique reached the edge of the deerskin and swung what would seem to be the Red and Arkansas rivers clockwise through almost ninety degrees in order to accommodate them. Topological properties were characteristic of virtually all Indian maps and failure to recognize this must have led to many false interpretations by Europeans. Two examples collected in the course of the fur trade serve to illustrate this.

About 1728, Pierre Gaultier La Vérendrye obtained from a group of Cree Indians at Lake Nipigon a series of cartographic devices showing the waterways from the western end of Lake Superior to Lake Winnipeg and beyond. The originals have not survived, but they were collated onto a manuscript map which has.[22] The manuscript map was apparently based on four originals (the most easterly perhaps European in origin) and its four different bar scales suggest the Crees must have attempted to convey some idea of relative distance. The bar scales refer to different parts of the route between Lake Superior and the 'River of the West': from Lake Superior to Lake Tecamamiouen (now Rainy Lake); then to Lake of the Woods; from there to the 'River of the West'; and finally along the 'River of the West.' The smallest of the four scales is less than one-fifteenth of the largest and none states the units of distance. There are no indications as to exactly where one scale ends and the next begins, whether the scales are supposed to apply in directions transverse to those in which they are oriented, or how such apparently precise information was obtained from the Crees.

Yet someone produced a derivative from the composite map which achieved a single scale in leagues by retaining the essential shapes and relative sizes of the main lakes along the route but altering the lengths of the connecting waterways.[23] This in turn was incorporated in a number of engraved maps of the continent, in so doing placing Lake Winnipeg far too far west and locating the source of the 'River of the West' too near the Pacific coast.[24] Topological analysis of the western part of the first collation in relation to the known hydrological features of interior North America reveals how valid topological information was transformed into a false geometrical statement which became a powerful myth when communicated in the apparently authentic maps of French commercial cartographers of the stature of Jean Baptiste D'Anville and Philippe Buache.[25]

A second example of misinterpretation arose from the Hudson's Bay Company's renewed interest during the 1760s in a long-reported source of copper to the north. In 1762 Moses Norton sent two Indians to observe and report on the supposed source area.[26] They were away for five years but on their return to Churchill in 1767 he reported that they had 'brought me a draught.'[27] This has survived and shows a remarkably straight coastline between the mouths of the Churchill and Coppermine rivers, paralleled for much of its length by an almost equally straight ornamented line which seems to have been intended to mark the inner edge of the coastal plain.[28] Inland from this are a dashed line representing 'The leaders track in coming to ye fort' (from the Coppermine River to Fort Churchill) and a faint pencil or charcoal line marking the boundary between the tundra and forest. The latter, like the inner edge of the coastal plain, is shown parallel to the coast except at either end.

In 1771–2, Matonabbee, one of the two Indians who had presented this draft to Norton, was to lead Samuel Hearne on his third and ultimately successful attempt to reach the lower Coppermine River.[29] The draft, or a version thereof, was presumably available to Hearne prior to his two earlier and unsuccessful attempts of 1769 and 1770, as on both occasions he had been briefed by Moses Norton. He failed on the first attempt in part because he had kept too far to the east (and hence found himself exposed on the tundra in winter). This error was perhaps due to his interpreting Matonabbee's draft just as he would have a European map.

His own manuscript map, presented to the governor and committee of the company soon after the return from his successful mission, presents the same forest-tundra boundary, essentially the same route between the Churchill and Coppermine rivers, and the coasts near Churchill and the mouth of the Coppermine.[30] However, the geometry is markedly different. Hearne was a good surveyor and he made clear for the first time the Euclidean relation between features and places hitherto known to the company only through Indian reports. Like two earlier cartographic devices of the same area still in the company's possession, Matonabbee's was correct in its topology, but grossly misleading.[31] Because of the secretive policy of the company, these maps were not generally known and thus, unlike those drawn by the Cree Indians for La Vérendrye, did not generate false popular images.

Many examples could be cited of the use made by those in the fur trade of cartographic devices obtained from Indians and half-breeds. In 1744 Arthur Dobbs, in his unsuccessful attempt to break the monopoly of the Hudson's Bay Company, published *An Account of the Countries Adjoining to Hudson's Bay* ... with a map attributed to a description by Joseph la France, a half-breed trader.[32] It was drawn first as a cartographic device in chalk on the floor of the dining room of the Golden Fleece in New Bond Street, London. The account of its construction is somewhat ambiguous but apparently Dobbs and his friend Bowman listened to an oral account by La France, then drew on the floor their impression of the country which he had described, in the process of which the half-breed was encouraged to make corrections.[33]

A chart dating from about 1779 by Philip Turnor of the Hudson's Bay Company shows the Nelson, Saskatchewan, and upper Athabasca drainage systems, but clearly distinguishes the surveyed areas from those for which the detail was obtained from 'Canadian and Indian information.'[34] Areas for which unsurveyed information is shown include the South Saskatchewan above the Forks, the North Saskatchewan beyond Hudson's House, the Beaver River country, and the Peace River.

In 1789, while descending the Mackenzie River and hoping to learn of a route to the Pacific Ocean, Alexander Mackenzie promised beads to an Indian if he would 'describe the circumjacent country upon the sand. This singular map he immediately undertook to delineate, and accordingly traced out a very long point of land between the rivers ... at the extremity of which, as he had been told by Indians of other nations, there was a ... White Man's Fort.'[35] Mackenzie assumed the fort to have been that founded by the Russians on the Aleutian island of Unalaska, in which case the 'very long point of land' was intended to represent the whole of the Alaskan peninsula.

Peter Fidler recorded in his journals for 1801, 1802, and 1806 numerous sketch maps done by Indians. Most of these were for the upper Saskatchewan and upper Missouri country but one example drawn for him by a York Fort Indian in 1809 is of interest: it shows certain geological and ecological boundaries inland from Hudson Bay.[36] William Clark made at least sixteen copies of Indian cartographic devices in the course of his journeys to and from the lower Columbia River in 1804-6. Many of these were of areas well away from his route and ultimately they provided the bases for much of his unpublished 'A Map of part of the Continent of North America ...'[37]

A less well known map (on paper) which can be dated 1801 was probably copied by a member of the North West Company and once belonged to Simon McGillivray.[38] Although endorsed 'Indian Chart. Rocky Mountains' the title is a misnomer. It covers an area to the east of the mountains, including the upper Athabasca, Churchill, North and South Saskatchewan, Red, and Assiniboine valleys. Later in the nineteenth century soldiers, missionaries, scientists, and government officials tended to replace fur traders as collectors of cartographic devices. In 1869 a Chilkaht chief drew for the Californian scientist George Davidson a sketch map of an extensive area now within southeastern Alaska and the western part of the Yukon to show his route in 1852 when he had marched several hundred miles to burn the Hudson's Bay Company post at Fort Selkirk. The original, 110 × 69 cm, took the chief and his two wives two or three days to complete, but has not survived though a printed version indicates something of its scope and detail.[39]

Indian cartographic devices are potentially significant sources of data for cultural anthropology, the history of cartography, historical geography, the history of Indian-European relationships, and perhaps even developmental psychology. They afford useful data to supplement and structure spatially the toponymy, settlement patterns, routeways, and other significant components of the environment during the early period of contact. Cautious use of them can improve our understanding of terrae semicognitae of the past. They are of even greater potential significance as records of the known world of the Indian. All give insight as to how native peoples chose objects and places as significant, and how they organized their perception of space.

It should be possible to re-interpret some of the strange geographies and perceptions of fur traders in the early contact period as Euclidean interpretations of topological information. The highly selective content of their cartographic devices reveals much about Indian understanding of the natural world. For example, river systems often appear to intersect in a manner unknown in nature: they were mapped not as hydrological systems but as routeways, in which portages across watersheds, being integral parts of the routes, were barely if at all distinguished from river channels. Arrows, automatically interpreted by European cartographers, if not by fur traders, as indicating direction of stream flow, were probably intended to show the direction of trade or movement.

Language in general, confusion over prepositions in particular, and lack of appreciation of the Indians' geographical perspective made it difficult to know for example, whether a river flowed *from* the west or constituted a route *to* the west. The 'River of the West' on the composite map derived from the cartographic devices which La Vérendrye collected from the Crees at Lake Nipigon in 1728 or 1729 (see above) has usually been interpreted as the Saskatchewan; it may have been the Nelson River, which flows to the north east from Lake Winnipeg, but leads to the west from the perspective of the Crees at York Fort. To these Crees the quartzites and schists exposed where the Nelson River cuts through an ancient dyke and associated metamorphic aureole above and below Pipestone Lake could have been the 'Mountains of Bright Stones,' located well up but not at the head of their 'river to the west.' Where transportation networks consisted of a mixture of trails and waterways it is often difficult to distinguish between the two. Lakes, which were usually easy to cross, were often shown schematically as circles; but rapids, which presented obstacles to travel by canoe, were usually located with relative precision. Because they marked the end of the Indian's world, sea coasts were usually shown schematically. Conversely, because they separated different but equally important worlds, the much more elusive transitions from prairie to forest and from forest to tundra were drawn quite well.[40] Lack of ornamentation and the absence of keys frequently led to confusion, as when Alexander Dalrymple interpreted a boundary line between the prairies and forest to have been an Indian trail.[41]

Until we locate and record more examples of Indian cartographic devices, relate them to associated documents, understand more about their descent, learn to recognize their different states, and begin to understand their distinctive geometries we are unlikely to realize their significance for re-evaluating Indian influences on the spatial perceptions of fur traders.

The research upon which this article is based was supported by financial assistance received at various times from the University of Sheffield

Research Fund, the Newberry Library, the British Academy, and the Social Science Research Council (UK).

NOTES AND REFERENCES

1 Hinks *Maps and Surveys* 72–3
2 Von Humboldt *Kritische Untersuchungen uber die historische Entwickelung der geographischen Kenntnisse von der Neuen Welt* ... I 297–8
3 Dröber *Kartographie bei den Naturvölkern*
4 Adler 'Karty Piervobytnyh Narodov' [Maps of Primitive Peoples] 162–71
5 Friederici *Der Charakter der Entdeckung und Eroberung Amerikas durch die Europiäer* 158–61
6 Alarchon 'The relation of the Navigation and discovery which Captaine Fernando Alarchon made' 438
7 Cartier 'The Third Voyage of Discovery' 235
8 Parkman *France and England in North America* I 220
9 Champlain *Voyages of Samuel de Champlain* 65
10 Untitled ms map of the east coast of North America sent by Don Alonso de Velasco, the Spanish ambassador in London, to Philip III in March 1611; Archivo General de Simancas, Estado. Leg. 2588, f22
11 Anon. 'Narrative of a Journey into the Mohawk and Oneida Country 1634–1635' 149–50
12 Douay 'Narrative of La Salle's Attempt to Ascend the Mississippi in 1687' 204
13 Delanglez tr and ed *The Journal of Jean Cavelier* 104
14 Letter from Francis Nicholson, governor of Virginia, to Joseph Blake, governor of South Carolina, dated Jamestown, 25 Sept. 1699, in *Plantations* (a leather bound office ms book containing reports, letters, queries, etc. relating to the English colonies in America), Newberry Library, Chicago, Ayer Collection No. 339
15 Ibid
16 Hennepin *A New Discovery of a Vast Country in America* ... Hennepin describes an occasion near Fort Crèvecoeur in 1680 in which an Illinois warrior 'took a piece of Charcoal, and drew a Map of the Course of that [Mississippi] River, which I found afterwards pretty exact' (111). The Indian claimed to have gone down the Mississippi in a canoe to near where it 'falls into the great Lake; for so they call the sea' (111).
17 Copies made at the time of map and letter (both now lost) sent by Lawrence van den Bosh to Francis Nicholson, dated North Sassifrix, 19 Oct. 1694; described in Clara A. Smith *List of Manuscript Maps in the Edward E. Ayer*

Collection (Chicago 1927) map #59, 25. The map is reproduced in Cumming et al *The Exploration of North America 1630–1776* (London 1974) 151, figure 226.

18 'A Map Describing the Situation of the several Nations of Indians between South Carolina and the Massisipi; was copyed from a Draught Drawn upon a Deer Skin by an Indian Cacique and Presented to Francis Nicholson Esqr. Governour of Carolina' ms map on paper, PRO CO700, North America Colonies General No. 6 (2), Map Room. 'This Map describing the Scituation of the Several Nations of Indians to the N.W. of South Carolina was coppyed from a Draught drawn and painted on a Deer Skin by an Indian Cacique and presented to Francis Nicholson Esqr. Governour of South Carolina by whom it is most humbly Dedicated To His Royal Highness George Prince of Wales' BM Sloane Mss 4723. Nicholson was appointed governor of South Carolina in 1720 and knighted in the same year. Therefore both maps presumably date from that year or 1721 at the latest.

19 'A Map Describing ... South Carolina and the Massisipi ...'

20 A 'picture map' of New Mexico drawn in 1602 by an Indian named Miguel as part of the official inquiry made by the factor, Don Francisco de Valverde, by order of the Count of Monterrey, concerning the new discovery undertaken by Governor Don Juan de Oñate toward the north beyond the Provinces of New Mexico; Archivo General de las Indias, Seville, Patronato, Est. 1, Caj 1, Leg. 3/22, Ramo 4) tr in Hammond and Rey 'Don Juan de Oñate Colonizer of New Mexico 1595–1628' 836–77

21 'Plan et Scituation des Villages Tchikachas' and 'Nations Amies et Ennemies des Tchikachas,' ms copies made by Alexander de Batz of two cartographic devices drawn by Chickasaw Indians and dated Mobile, 7 Sept. 1737; Archives des Colonies, Paris, C13 A22, ff 67 and 68

22 The better known of the two extant ms versions of this collection carries an inscription at the extreme lower right, 'Reduction de la Carte copieé sur celle qui a été par le Sauvage Ochagach et autres' and nearby 'B. Janr. 1750', Dépôt des Cartes et Plans, Service Historique de la Marine, Paris, 4044 B, no 16. It may have been copied from a larger, somewhat cruder, untitled, and apparently earlier ms which contains somewhat more information, of which there is a photographic copy, PAC Map Collection H2/902–19 (1728–1729).

23 'Cours des Rivieres, et fleuve a Louest du nord du Lac Superieur, suivant la Carte faite par le Sauvage Ochagac et autres ...' Dépôt des Cartes et Plans, Service Historique de la Marine, Paris, 4044 B, no 84

24 In 1730 Guillaume De l'Isle pasted a small-scale copy of the composite map onto an untitled ms map of North America; Département des Estampes, Bibliothèque Nationale, Paris, série vd, vol 22. An example of a printed variant of this is Georges L. Le Rouge *L'Amérique Suivant Le R. P. Charlevoix Jée.* (Paris 1746).

Hudson's Bay Company Mapping

RICHARD I. RUGGLES

In 1752 James Isham, the chief factor at York, received his annual official letter from the committee[1] in London, encouraging him to explore, measure, and sketch the environs of the fort, but 'without breaking into the necessary Business of the Factory.'[2] While such activities were significant to its operations, the Hudson's Bay Company was a commercial enterprise; its chief concern was to secure the highest possible return from the trade. The company paid some employees to survey and map, purchased instruments and supplies, and paid for the repair of instruments. But the company's purpose was not to promote surveying and cartography or to advance geographical knowledge among the learned public, but to aid its senior servants in making decisions in the conduct of their business.

Over the centuries of its activities the Hudson's Bay Company has amassed one of the largest private collections of maps in Canada.[3] It consists of two main segments: maps prepared by company servants or drawn by commercial cartographers at the request of the company for its use; and printed maps purchased from publishing houses and placed with the other maps in the head office for the use of members of the company's committee.

Most of the original maps prepared for the company were drafted before 1870. I have chosen as the terminal date for this analysis the year 1821, when Peter Fidler, one of the greatest of the mapping servants, drew his last map just before his death. The most crucial period of company activity in cartography was over by this date. That year also saw the company's union with its great rival, the North West Company.

Original maps were treated as company commercial documents, and were not available to anyone other than its own officials up to about 1790. The maps and plans were prepared principally for the executive group, the committee, which included the governor, deputy governor, committee members, and other officers of the company. The cartographic documents were stored in chests or mounted and placed upon rollers in the London central office. Some may have hung on office walls. The committee referred to them during the autumn, winter, and spring, when preparing its decisions to be transmitted in official letters to the company's resident officers in the field.

Newly received maps were usually examined critically by various members of the committee for the new information provided. The committee often acknowledged receipt of maps, assessing their utility (and sometimes extending its thanks or a monetary award). Approval was withheld if the map or sketch was thought to be prepared from insufficient data, or based on a journey which was suspect. Charts and maps drawn by or for the ships' officers were kept under the careful control of the captains, and were apparently turned in to the central office upon completion of voyages.

The committee believed that maps were of considerable use to the factors in Hudson Bay. Copies were made by servants at some of the main posts for local use. The executive had copies of certain of their maps prepared, and purchased both maps and globes which were sent to the chief factors to aid them in making decisions for their seasonal activities. However, the general rule was that all new maps, plans, and sketches drafted overseas should be sent on the next ship back to London.

The Hudson's Bay Company gradually came to recognize that it required precise measurements and maps for several reasons. The captains of its trading ships needed the most up-to-date hydrographic charts of the north Atlantic, Hudson Strait, and Hudson and James bays for navigational purposes. Detailed knowledge of river-estuary harbours, including shore configuration, marine hazards, water depths, and bottom characteristics for anchorage was imperative. Moreover, the committee wished to have accessible the plans of the various trading posts and their immediate locales. As the company became increasingly involved in the interior of its territory, and as the complexity of the waterways network became apparent, it was vital to determine the precise longitude and latitude of its posts and of the main lineament of the hydrographic network. Such information was essential for making intelligent decisions on trading tactics and the opening and closing of trading posts, and for assessing the strategic position of its trading structure vis-à-vis its competitors. Maps were also drafted to clarify the character of trade routes, including comparative distances, the shapes and dimensions of water bodies, the location of rapids and waterfalls which necessitated portages, and so on. There was also a genuine interest in the geography of the north of the continent, particularly in the possibility of a water passage from Hudson Bay to the Pacific.

An inventory of the production of maps through 1821 has been compiled through a detailed search of company journals, letters, official correspondence, minute books, account books, and other similar material. I followed up all maps referred to as requested, drafted, dispatched to London, or received in London. From 1669 to 1821 there were at least 213[4] individual maps and sketches drawn by employees (not including plans), and 22 maps ordered to be made for company use from commercial cartographers. Moreover, in the extant journals[5] of Peter Fidler, there are some 383 separate sketches made by him on his travels. These segment sketches depict the shores of lakes and rivers, and include distance and direction data. He employed these, along with his latitude and longitude observations and written descriptions in the logs of his journeys, in compiling several large maps of sections of the west and North of Canada.[6]

The Hudson's Bay Company Archives now house only a portion of the maps and sketches attributable to company servants or contracted for from commercial cartographers. Many maps have not survived, or are not in the collection. Nearly one-quarter of the map documents drawn by or for the company (if one excludes the Fidler sketches) are missing. For the period before 1778 when the first official surveyor-cartographer, Philip Turnor, was appointed, only about forty-five per cent of the material has survived. Several examples of maps gone astray will indicate the quality of the lost material.

The first map noted as having been made for the small pre-charter 'Company of Adventurers' was of Hudson and James bays by one Norwood, who was paid two pounds in 1669; it is not in the archives.[7] Also unavailable are two maps which apparently resulted from the epic journey of Anthony Henday in 1754 into the Battle and Red Deer River region – one was a copy made by James Isham 'taken from Henday's original.'[8] Such treasures would have been invaluable for the reconstruction of his cross-country travels. Early river journeys in the Albany and Moose river basins were undertaken in 1776 and 1777 by Edward Jarvis and George Donald, who reported that they had prepared 'draughts' of their courses. The chief factor of Moose Fort reported his pleasure in receiving Donald's Moose map,[9] and the Jarvis sketch from Albany Fort to Michipicoten on Lake Superior is noted as having been copied by John Hodgson, a young apprentice at the Fort.[10] Not one has survived.

Why have these documents been lost? Deterioration due to use, imperfect housing, and normal degradation of the materials are obvious causes. There was probably not a conservationist attitude prevalent in the company offices. Certainly the wear and tear on the marine charts during their use on sea voyages must have been high. The demand for more up-to-date versions would have rendered older charts obsolete, and they were perhaps discarded. Committee members perhaps borrowed items for home perusal, and may have lost them. The Arrowsmith firm became a constant user of the collection after 1790 for its first and later North American maps; there are reasons for believing they may have failed to return some of the maps. There is an unfortunate tendency among cartographers, to destroy compilation materials once the fair copy of a new map has been completed. Perhaps some maps were not sent from the bay, or did not reach London. In some cases an annual post journal or journal of a journey with a map inserted has vanished, along with the map. A factor who stated in a letter or post journal that a draft was to be sent home may have forgotten to do so, and the document may have vanished. The committee did not acknowledge receipt of every map stated to have been forwarded to them, making the historian's job even more difficult.

The executive officers of the Hudson's Bay Company encouraged their field personnel to engage in coastal and interior exploration, to make notes on the landscape and the native peoples, and to prepare maps of the routes followed. The first statement of such a policy was made by the committee in a letter of instruction, dated 29 May 1680. A young man, Bryan Norbury, was introduced to Governor Nixon as one who could be useful to the business if he proved a diligent employee. This new man had 'been entred in the Mathematicks, and ... [had] a peculiar Genius for making of Landskips.'[11] There is no evidence that he used this facility to make any drafts, although he served successfully for seven years with the new company. But a significant number of personnel did prepare cartographic materials over the years as a result of company policy and incentive.

The complex development, organization, and operation of the trading enterprise over the years required maps which the company invited, urged, or ordered to be made for its use. The annual directives to the chief

factors, in turn transmitted to the post officers, rarely missed the opportunity to encourage coastal and inland travel and mapping. The earliest
example is Henry Kelsey, who responded to the committee's request for
young men to move from the bay shore with inland Indians. In 1742
George Howy was rewarded with five guineas for his 'diligence' in preparing 'draughts ... done to great exactness' of the Moose River mouth,
and urged to continue his good work in other areas.[12] Numerous annual
letters to the chiefs at Churchill from the 1740s through the 1760s required the resident sloop masters to be sent north up the coast, searching
the coves, noting their suitability for harbourage, describing the land, the
tides, and so on, and to make 'a Draft of every Cove Bay or Inlet'[13] that
they might enter.

Andrew Graham, the York factor, wrote in his instructions to Henry
Pressick, going inland in 1761 to winter with the Plains Indians, that it was
the company's order that no person willing to go to the interior be
hindered, and moreover he said 'You have paper etc by you to observe the
course you take, Daily setting down such ... daily keep a Draught of the
Rivers you pass, Remarkg the names of the Bays, Bluffs etc both up and
down.'[14] Such references exemplify the committee's continuing policy of
supporting exploration and mapping, in order that its members 'may be
better enabled to form a Proper Judgement thereof'[15] for decision-
making purposes.

Maps, or as they were more commonly called, 'draughts' or 'sketches,'
were drawn over the years for the company by at least fifty-four servants,
and six commercial map makers. The period of greatest production was
after 1778, notably from 1791 to 1821. A large proportion of those who
contributed maps were responsible for only one. Eighteen servants produced two or three maps, and the rest four or more.

Peter Fidler was the most prolific of all, drawing some nineteen separate
maps, sixty-seven sketches based on information provided by native
people and fellow servants, and finally, several hundred sectional sketches
entered into his journals under difficult circumstances while out in the
wilderness. John Hodgson was involved with seven or more maps, although his major contribution was as a draftsman compiling other
people's data, or making fair copies of very rough sketches. Producing
five or six maps each were Philip Turnor, James Clouston, Captain William Coates, and Joseph Howse.

Commercial cartographers were of direct service to the company,
mainly in the first forty years of its existence, and the committee purchased from them navigational charts and instruments for its captains.

The shops of such artificers as John Seller, John Thornton, and Samuel Thornton provided maps of Hudson and James bays and Hudson Strait, and the adjacent regions. Later, in 1748, R.W. Seale designed a map privately for the company, which was printed, with a number of copies run off.[16] Its unusual rendition of the unexplored northwest of the continent made it useless for the company's purposes.

The Hudson's Bay Company developed a program for the hiring and training of men to undertake surveying and cartographic tasks. Only a handful of those so selected became experienced surveyors or draftsmen. Most were untrained, though all were literate and most learned to make basic measurements. The company proposed to hire 'three or more Persons well skilled in the Mathematicks & in making Astronomical Observations ... to travel Inland with the Title of Inland Surveyors.' This message was expressed in a letter of 26 March 1778 from the secretary of the company to William Wales, mathematical master of the Blue Coat School, Christ's Hospital, London, whom the company officers knew through the Royal Society.[17] Wales recommended Philip Turnor of Laleham, Middlesex, twenty-seven years of age, and a trained land surveyor; but the other professionals desired were not obtained.

Turnor began his task in the autumn of 1778. He came into contact over the years with another group of employees who had been hired by the committee because of their educational experience. These were young mathematical apprentices, bound over from the Grey Coat School, London.[18] Between 1766 and 1799, eleven of these boys aged fourteen or fifteen years were placed at factories or assigned to company ships. The mathematical boys all had studied – besides reading, writing, and grammar – basic mathematics, practical navigation, and the elements of cartography. Most of the boys in such classes entered the Royal Navy or the merchant fleet, but at least five, apprenticed to the company, came under the tutelage of Philip Turnor for part of their careers.

In 1778, Joseph Hansom[19] and George Hudson[20] accompanied Turnor into the north Saskatchewan River valley; in 1780, John Hodgson[21] was his assistant while Turnor was mapping the Albany River up to Gloucester House; in 1781 and 1782 George Donald[22] spent much time with the inland surveyor in the Moose and Abitibi basins; and finally, David Thompson,[23] incapacitated with a broken leg, spent the winter of 1789–90 recuperating at Cumberland House, and being re-introduced to surveying methods by Turnor. Thompson wrote proudly to the committee in an autumn letter that he had greatly improved his knowledge of the theory and practice of practical astronomy.[24]

In addition to the young apprentices, Turnor was instrumental in the training of two other young servants, Peter Fidler[25] and Malcolm Ross.[26] Fidler became the most versatile and effective of all the local men as an explorer, surveyor, and mapper. Neither had the background of the hospital apprentices in such activities, but being intelligent and active young men, they accomplished a great deal.

The committee also turned for aid in exploring and mapping its territory to another type of employee – ship captains, and the sloop masters who maintained the connections between the bayside posts. The captains had a considerable amount of navigational training and experience, and the sloop masters could use the sextant, compass, quadrant, and lead line, and were usually able to prepare at least rough charts illustrating their findings. Some fourteen or more of both types were involved, the best known being Captain Henry Hanwell, sr, a 'Grey Coat' boy, and captains William Coates and John Marley. Naturally, their expeditions were mainly along the Hudson Bay and James Bay shores, but several sloop masters also aided in inland movement.

The company was also fortunate in obtaining a number of servants who, though without surveying or cartographic training or geographical education, had natural inclinations in these directions, and expressed an interest in the morphology of the interior regions. Jarvis at Albany, Kitchin at Moose, and Isham and Graham at York are good examples. Moreover, the last two were notable observers and collectors of flora and fauna, and kept notes on the culture and mores of the native inhabitants of the bay area.[27]

The company apparently did not furnish a mapping room in London beyond the map chests at company headquarters, and no special facilities were provided in Rupert's Land. At best a drawing board might have been made by the fort carpenter. A considerable array of equipment, mathematical tables, and associated almanacs and books arrived in the territory on the ships. These supplies were distributed from the main factories, usually under the control of the chief factors, but sometimes assigned to specific workers. The officers' and servants' ledgers also reveal a considerable outlay of personal funds for surveying and mapping equipment. The committee periodically requested an inventory of equipment held at the posts, or being used in the field; similarly it admonished servants who misappropriated such company property. On one occasion the committee acknowledged young David Thompson's efforts and eagerness by making a personal gift of instruments for his own use.

The records indicate that Peter Fidler accumulated the largest personal collection of equipment, tables, nautical almanacs and technical books of any of the servants. From 1792 to 1799 alone, the ledgers show that he had had more than £70 debited to his account for such items.

A normal complement of instruments available to more experienced personnel might include sextant, watch, compass, quadrant, telescope, Gunter's scale, mathematical drawing instruments, parallel ruler, and protractor. Most maps would have been drafted using drawing paper (normally Whatman's), transparent paper, black lead pencils, India ink block, a marble grinding plate for inks, India rubber, and in some instances, water colours. Goose quills were available for inking, but metal nibs became more common.

In 1778 the company decided to hire a chief inland surveyor, to provide him with mapping apprentices, and to encourage other servants to explore, survey, and map. This policy was consistent with the committee's earlier resolution to develop a more open policy of limited co-operation with the Royal Society in scientific matters, and with some authors, such as Hearne, in preparing manuscripts for publication. Although the committee must have agreed to such a change in policy, Samuel Wegg, committee member, deputy governor, and governor from 1760 to 1799, was probably the influential instrument of change.[28] While Wegg was a senior official of the company he was also for thirty-seven years treasurer of the Royal Society and for forty-two years a participant in the society's dining and conversation club, in which many contacts were possible among the world's leading practitioners and amateurs of the pure, natural, and geographical sciences.

By 1790 the committee, as a direct result of Wegg's more enlightened attitude to commercial public relations, had agreed to allow several reputable persons, such as the cartographers Alexander Dalrymple and Aaron Arrowsmith, to use its map collection as sources for the compilation of new maps of northern North America. Since map documents had previously been sequestered in the company's files, the profusion of novel geographical intelligence which had accumulated there, unsurpassed by any other source, had been a latent resource held back from the map publishing world. This can easily be observed by comparison of the company's maps with printed North American maps from British and European map publishers, for the century and more of operations.

The maps of the Hudson's Bay Company have many similarities as a group. Almost all are manuscript, since they were drawn not for publication, but as in-house documents. Almost all were drawn on paper; a few are on parchment, especially those drawn earlier by professional cartographers. There was little use of hand-applied colour – almost all of them being drafted with black Indian ink. John and Samuel Thornton applied bright water colours, as was the practice among commercial map makers of the seventeenth and early eighteenth centuries. Fidler, Hodgson, Thompson, and Turnor, among others, emphasized lake, river, and sea patterns by applying a grey ink wash as a band along the adjacent land. The overall design of the maps is simple and unadorned, dominated, as could be expected, by a single-line drafting of the hydrographic network. Symbols are limited in range since water routes were of central concern and there had been little cultural imprint upon the landscape. Features most crucial to the trade are emphasized: waterfalls, rapids or other portage sites, direction of water flow, cliffs, bathymetric depths, navigational features in harbours, and sand bars and other hazards. Cultural detail is largely confined to fur post symbols and cross country trails.

The maps were of five main types, each relating to different strategies and operational policies:

About a dozen regional and coastal marine charts survive. These were drawn as navigational guides, and there are references to, and examples of such charts from the Norwood map of 1669 to 1812, when Henry Hanwell, sr. drafted a chart of Strutton's Sound in James Bay.[29] The first extant map by a company employee is a chart (about 1678) of the west side of James Bay,[30] similar to other charts of the period. It was drawn by Thomas Moore, a sailor on a company ship, apparently to secure advancement with the company. It was not presented to the company, and instead ended in the British Museum collection. Most of these maps were prepared by company mariners. Unfortunately over half of the charts have not survived.

Related to the former are maps of varied stretches of the sea shores, concerned particularly with the configuration of the coasts, islands, passages, shoals, and bottom soundings. Included are the charts of the large bights, such as Chesterfield and Rankin inlets, Whale Cove, and Richmond Gulf, which puncture the bay coastline. At least seventeen maps from 1749 to 1811 are involved. All were the outcome of coastal forays by servants responding to the persistent pressure of the committee to examine the entire coast of the bay for commercial advantage and for the Northwest Passage. Approximately one-third of the group has disappeared, half of them for each side of the bay.

Large-scale maps of many river mouths on the bay shores and of the vicinities of some inland fur posts encompass about twenty items. Since the search for ideal sites continued constantly, maps of post sites were requested from the factors through the years. The records extend from

1703, when Captain Michael Grimington, 'a skilfull coaster,' produced details of the Albany River mouth[31] to 1818, when George Gladman detailed the locale of the lead mine operations between the mouth of the Little Whale River and the site of Richmond Post.[32] Most of these maps exist, and are useful supplements to the detailed plans of the post buildings themselves. The lower junction of the Nelson and Hayes rivers at York Fort, more than any other locale, received the attention of the surveyors and mappers; this factory had a dominant role in the trading system, and these rivers were major routes to and from the continental interior.

About 120 maps and the Fidler sketches of segments of the hydrographic network, at intermediate scales, delineate parts of the river courses and interconnections between river basins. Such a concentration of maps of this type is understandable: they were the product of exploration by traders searching for advantageous routes to their customers, and of the imposition of a trading lattice over the complex hydrography of the interior. Later in the period, with the establishment of a system of trading districts, maps of these new operational regions were requested, to accompany the annual district reports.

There is periodical variation in the production of this fourth and large group of maps. Inland wintering commenced in 1754, and the Henday-Isham sketches resulted immediately, although they have not survived. Before 1774, when the company began to expand inland, little mapping was done by wintering servants – only a few were able to prepare adequate journals and maps. Perhaps 18 men were involved in two decades, and Samuel Hearne alone contributed to the cartographic files maps which still survive. Of the three he sent to the company, only one, that of the full transect from Churchill to the Coppermine, is in the map archives.

In 1774 the company began to expand inland, and in 1778 a new inland surveyor was appointed. Two maps per year on average appeared from this time on, with the greatest productivity in the 1790s, from 1806 to 1811, and from 1815 to 1820. The 1790s saw intense activity on several fronts. The carrying of trade into the Mackenzie River basin across Methye Portage was matched by the expansion of effort in the Churchill-Nelson interconnecting waterways, and by the upstream mobility of the company on the Albany and Moose rivers and tributaries, and over the divide to Lake Superior.

Fidler was the most prolific of the regional mappers in the first two decades of the nineteenth century – maps and sketches flowed from his pen. Characteristically, he made special efforts to learn about the geography of the interior by quizzing native people and his fellow servants, who were familar with particular sections of the West. He would ask them to make and annotate sketches which he would copy into his journals, giving credit to his informants. In the Fidler journals about 35 maps are based on Indian information, and another 32 are credited to various trade companions. Whenever possible, Fidler would attempt to verify the maps and obtain precise measurements of these areas if he later travelled through them.

Movement inland from the Eastmain coast occurred much later than into the West. Wintering did not take place in the eastern part of Rupert's Land until the nineteenth century, even though the committee repeatedly urged the post factors to outfit men and to arrange Indian guides to lead them into the inland lakes which they had heard about on many occasions. The post-1800 maps have sustained few losses compared with the previous several decades.

The final category consists of various smaller-scale renditions of larger areas. These maps mirror the expanding knowledge of the geography of the interior, gained from Indian conceptions of their land and from the traders' actual and imaginative topographical knowledge. How valuable such documents would have been to the European cartographers and geographers if they had been made public! Perhaps two dozen maps were of this type, and most are still available to the researcher. The first map depicting most of northern Canada reached the committee in 1760, and was therefore the pioneer 'British' map of this vast area. It had been transposed by Moses Norton, the York factor, from sketches by northern Indians.[33] Although its directional distortions hindered full understanding of the geography of the region, it was probably a considerable stimulus and a visual aid to the committee, and to the York and Churchill chiefs in their preparation for the Barren Ground crossing to the copper mines a decade later. A re-oriented version of this map indicates the surprisingly realistic integration of the rivers of the area.

Among the other maps in this group I believe four were of great significance to the company in its evolving knowledge of its trade territory. These are Graham's map of about 1774,[34] the Donald McKay–Jarvis map of 1791,[35] the Hudson or Hodgson map of about 1791,[36] and Turnor's 'magnum opus' of 1794.[37] This last map predated by one year the great printed map of Aaron Arrowsmith,[38] who obtained the details from the company's map files, by its permission, and reproduced much of Turnor's map. This magnificent commercial map was the first public printing of a compendium of the company's geographical information, painstakingly gathered by its servants.

It is difficult, without more specific documentation, to evaluate the role of surveying and mapping in the company's operations, and to identify those decisions which were based primarily upon data from maps. Detailed minutes of committee meetings would have been a vital source but unfortunately they do not exist. However, maps and plans, supplemented by the post journals, annual letters of instruction, official letters between London and the bay, and other types of records of company operations are rich sources for historians of cartography, who have only begun to appreciate and use them.

NOTES AND REFERENCES

1 The company's executive group, elected annually by the stockholders
2 HBCA A 6/8 f 96d
3 They are lodged in HBCA.
4 It is impossible to ascertain exact figures since the HBCA do not contain all the documents from this period.
5 HBCA E 3/1, 3/2, 3/3, 3/4; B 39/a/5^b, 49/a/32^b, 104/a/1
6 For example, HBCA G 1/28, G 2/21
7 HBCA A 14/1, fs107 & 108
8 HBCA A 11/114, f197, York Fort
9 HBCA A 11/44, f64, Moose Fort
10 HBCA A 11/4, f28, Albany Fort
11 HBCA A 6/1, f7
12 HBCA A 6/7, f4d
13 HBCA A 6/8 f71
14 HBCA B 239/a/48, f47
15 HBCA A 6/8, f120 d
16 HBCA G 4/20
17 HBCA A 5/2, f32
18 At the Grey Coat Hospital, Westminster. For discussion of the hospital and its mathematical school, see Ruggles 'Hospital Boys of the Bay' 4–11.
19 Apprenticed 25 April 1769 to Moses Norton at Churchill Factory; most of his career spent at this factory, and later at Cumberland House; drowned at the Great Falls on the Lower Saskatchewan River, 17 June 1779, when canoe overturned
20 Apprenticed 15 May 1775, and assigned to York Fort; the larger part of his career centred at Cumberland House; died suddenly there on 19 April 1790
21 Apprenticed 10 May 1774; Albany Fort and Henley House his main centres of

service until 1810, when discharged from the company as chief factor at Albany.

22 Apprenticed 10 May 1774, and assigned to Moose Factory; in this district until 1791, after which at York and then Churchill Factory; returned to London after several years of illness

23 Apprenticed 20 May 1784; under Samuel Hearne at Churchill; for most of company service was stationed out of York Factory in the Saskatchewan region and the middle Churchill River area; 21 May 1797 joined North West Company

24 HBCA A 11/117 f54

25 Born 1769, and hired as labourer in 1788; died in company service at Fort Dauphin in 1822 at the age of 53; his career largely in the interior plains, and the Churchill River–Athabaska area

26 Entered company service as labourer in 1774; drowned after falling overboard in a rapid in 1779; bulk of his service spent in the Saskatchewan, Churchill, and Athabaska regions

27 See *James Isham's Observations on Hudsons Bay 1743* and *Andrew Graham's Observations on Hudsons Bay 1767–91*.

28 For detailed discussion of Governor Wegg's role, see Ruggles 'Governor Samuel Wegg "The Winds of Change" ' 10–20; and Ruggles 'Governor Samuel Wegg, Intelligent Layman of the Royal Society, 1753–1802.'

29 'Strutton Sound Surveyed by Henry Hanwell Junr. in the Winter 1811 & 1812' HBCA G 1/162

30 BM Add. Mss. 5027A, f64. For discussion of map see Thorman 'An Early Map of James Bay' 18–22.

31 HBCA A 11/2 f7d

32 Two sketches, HBCA B 77/e/2[b]

33 'Moses Nortons D[rt.] of the Northern Parts of Hudsons Bay laid down on Ind[n.] Information & brt Home by him Anno 1760' HBCA G 2/8

34 'A Plan Of Part Of Hudson's Bay & Rivers, Communicating With York Fort & Severn' HBCA G 2/7

35 ['A Map of Hudsons Bay and interior Westerly particularly above Albany. 1791 J. Hodgson'] HBCA G 1/13

36 'An Accurate Map of the Territories of the Hudson's Bay Company in North America' HBCA G 2/28

37 '... Map of Hudson's Bay and the Rivers and Lakes Between the Atlantick and Pacifick Oceans ...' HBCA G 2/32

38 'A Map Exhibiting all the New Discoveries in the Interior Parts of North America...' 'Published Jan 1, 1795 by A. Arrowsmith, Charles Street, Soho Square'

PART II ❖ NATIVE SOCIETIES

The Fur Trade and
the Cree of James Bay

TOBY MORANTZ

To discuss the impact of the fur trade on the Indians without analysing their influence on it or examining the trade within the context of its social setting is to present only a partial view of what transpired. The early fur trade analyses were in this regard seriously deficient because anthropologists abandoned the field to historians whose training had not prepared them to analyse the fur trade from an Indian perspective. This paper is not a pioneering work in making this correction; Arthur Ray, Charles Bishop, and John Foster[1] have already identified and discussed many of the shortcomings in fur trade studies and this work proceeds from theirs.

The dominant theme in the historical analyses of the relationship between European and Indian is Indian dependence. This term implies that the Indians were under the domination of the Europeans, that they lacked the ability to direct and control their lives. Such a conclusion shows not only a lack of understanding of the principles of social change but also ignores the reciprocal basis of most Indian-European relations.

This paper examines two issues – the degree of reliance of the Indians on the Europeans and the control the Indians were able to exert over the fur trade. In an attempt to correct the imbalance in the literature, I examine principally the Indian involvement in the fur trade rather than the European one.

It must be emphasized that the Indians were affected by the fur trade but that the effects were neither monolithic nor total. Different groups of Indians with different life-styles chose to participate in the trade in varying degrees and thus were influenced by it in different ways. However even its main producers were not entirely dependent in any sense on their 'earnings' from the fur trade. Furthermore the control the Indians exercised over the conduct of the fur trade during this period was considerable. Their position in the fur trade was considerably more autonomous than has usually been allowed in historical writings.

This analysis focuses on the role of the James Bay Cree in the fur trade. The territory of these people is the eastern James Bay region, today part of Nouveau Québec. The data are drawn almost entirely from the archival records of the Hudson's Bay Company and cover roughly the period from 1700 to 1870.

It is both popular and scholarly convention that the arrival of the Europeans quickly revolutionized the material culture of the Indians. This is usually stated as though instantly their lives were radically transformed. As recently as 1967, E.E. Rich reiterated this position. He claimed that on contact a process of rapid technological change was set in motion: 'European supplies were necessities, not luxuries, for the Indians who traded to the Bay, and to many times that number of Indians living inland. Within a decade of their becoming acquainted with European goods, tribe after tribe became utterly dependent on regular European supplies. The bow and arrow went out of use, and the Indian starved if he did not own a serviceable gun, powder, and shot.'[2] Interestingly, in a paper written seven years earlier, Rich was the first historian to argue that the fur trade practices were fashioned to a very large extent by the Indians' values and notions of gift exchange, ritual, property, and limited consumer demands.[3] However, Rich did not apparently consider that this 'independence' could be extended to other aspects of Indian-European relations for in both papers he portrayed them as economically subservient.

The evidence from the records of the James Bay trading activities indicates that Rich's claim is greatly exaggerated. Although the Indians of eastern James Bay readily incorporated the use of metal and firearms into their technological arsenal they did not become entirely dependent on them. An examination of the data in the Hudson's Bay Company account books tends to refute the claim of Indian wholesale dependence on European manufactured goods.

Table 1 sets out all the goods traded on the Eastmain from 1700 to 1704 – the earliest years for which these data are available. Trade in those years was conducted by the Hudson's Bay Company from a ship sent from Albany each fall to winter on the eastern James Bay coast. Consequently the kind and number of European goods brought for trade would have been decided beforehand by traders at Albany, not by people far removed in England. The year 1700 does not mark the beginning of trade with the eastern Cree for by then many had already been involved in direct trade with the French or English for some thirty years. The table shows the quantity remaining of each trade good after trading occurred as well as the quantity of each item actually traded to the Indians. The annual value of furs traded, expressed in the standard of the day, 'made beaver,' is also given to demonstrate the total volume of trade in each of those years. The traders, when they left Albany each autumn, would not have known how extensive the coming trade would be, though the men in charge must have had an idea of the maximum that could be expected.

The category of goods that most readily lends itself to an examination is guns and ammunition (the first arrangement of goods in table 1). According to the data a large portion of the guns, particularly the preferred shorter ones,[4] were traded. By contrast, both gunpowder and shot do not show nearly the same level of consumption by the Indians. Gunpowder, a rather dangerous item to transport, particularly on a ship, would not have been brought in such large quantities unless there was the expectation it would be traded. Presumably the amount of gunpowder and shot brought over for the trade would have been calculated on the basis of the expected needs of the anticipated number of hunters. That the number of Indians coming to trade was never greatly overestimated is clear from the comparatively low number of other essential goods remaining after trading, namely hatchets, knives, chisels, twine, etc. It seems reasonable to conclude from the evidence that although guns were traded, their use by the Indians was limited.

They did not, for many reasons, become the all-purpose hunting tool as has been claimed by historians. Discounting the coasters who lived close to the post, most of the James Bay hunters of the eighteenth century lived inland and managed to journey to the post only once a year. Although French and later North West Company posts were established inland the distances were still too great for most hunters to manage more than an annual visit. Furthermore, guns were not entirely reliable, often 'bursting,' as it is phrased in the records.[5] They could not be repaired or replaced until brought back to the post. If the gunpowder supply ran out or was damaged, it could not be replenished until the annual trading visit. Moreover a full year's supply of ammunition would have been a bulky, heavy item to carry around.

That the Indians did not, in fact, depend entirely on the new European technology is evident from statements in the archival sources. James Hester, the master at Eastmain in 1776, noted that: 'Few or no Partridges for the Indians to get they not being able to afford Powder & shot & the

TABLE 1
Number of goods traded at Eastmain

R = Remaining T = Traded	Year and number of furs traded in made beaver				
	1700	1701	1702	1703	1704
	(1528MB)	(2435MB)	(1432MB)	(3242MB)	(2796MB)
Items	R/T	R/T	R/T	R/T	R/T
Fire steels	29/20	16/32	80/20	170/30	53/47
Flints	743/177	405/395	676/324	860/640	170/830
Gunpowder, lbs	406/144	252/298	224/280	343/329	214/346
Guns, 4½ ft	7/9	4/3	9/9	6/3	0/2
Guns, 4 ft	0/2	3/15	3/9	16/31	0/10
Guns, 3½ ft	0/13	0/15		0/3	0/10
Gunworms	23/9	20/10		72/28	30/18
Horns, powder	0/12	10/18	54/6	40/20	5/25
Shots, lbs	1334/346	972/820	863/369	1132/660	836/788
Arrowheads					43/5
Awls	148/52	102/46	84/60	100/188	0/100
Chisels	6/30		3/21	12/24	0/30
Files	1/0				
Hatchets	83/55	3/76	0/40	35/105	5/75
Kettles	62/26	0/41	3/37	33/43	20/35
Knives	29/189	5/273	40/360	0/324	2/334
Lines, net	20/30	6/26	18/12	16/44	10/2
Needles				140/60	90/110
Scissors				24/0	
Scrapers		8/4	24/12	12/12	8/16
Spoons			12/0		2/10
Sword blades		3/9		0/12	2/16
Tin skows	12/0	13/0		23/1	34/2
Twine, skein	55/95	18/136	3/6	0/201	1/79
Baize, yds			0/16		9/67
Blankets	0/10	2/10	4/2	9/42	14/36
Caps		0/6	5/19		
Cloth, broad, yds	24/35	4/75	6/14		26/143
Cloth, kersey, yds	16/0	18/0			9/0
Coats, plain, men's	0/10	1/6		6/19	0/10
Coats, laced, men's	1/4				
Coats, youths, men's	0/6	0/10	0/10		
Coats, cargo, men's		6/0	0/3	0/10	
Duffle, yds	94/23	42/61	4/23	5/1	26/26
Gloves, pr		22/0		24/0	11/1
Handcuffs			10/2	20/4	
Shirts, blue	12/0	8/4			
Shirts, white		6/0	1/0	22/2	13/7
Shoes, pr.	12/0	12/0		9/3	10/2
Stockings, pr.		16/5	3/3	40/4	12/12

TABLE 1 (*concluded*)

R = Remaining *T* = Traded	Year and number of furs traded in made beaver				
	1700 (1528MB) *R/T*	1701 (2435MB) *R/T*	1702 (1432MB) *R/T*	1703 (3242MB) *R/T*	1704 (2796MB) *R/T*
Items					
Tobacco, Brazil	202/85	12/188	68/95	91/197	46/208
Tobacco, roll		101/3	89/20	48/129	8/22
Beads	0/10			4/25	0/8
Bells, hawk	19/89	45/63	384/16	60/140	0/200
Boxes, tobacco	0/6	0/6		14/10	2/10
Boxes, painted				0/24	4/20
Combs	9/27	0/25		0/60	2/46
Glasses, looking		4/8		48/0	30/6
Rings, gilt				36/12	42/18
Tongs, tobacco				32/4	40/8
Vermilion, oz.	2/1	2/4	3/2	7/3	5/5

Sources: B3/d/11, 16b; B3/d/12, 12; B3/d/13, 12; B3/d/13, 63d; B3/d/14, 10 HBCA

scarcity of Partridges has been such they could not get any with their Bows & Arrows.'[6] Another discussion of the relative merits of the gun comes from Joseph Normandin, a surveyor for New France, who journeyed in 1732 overland from Quebec to Chamouchouane, northwest of Lake St Jean. The Indians he met along the way used bows and arrows to hunt, preferring to conserve their supply of powder; guns were to be used on caribou and beaver, although they also killed these animals with bows and arrows.[7]

The account books also provide another argument against representing the Indians as having a great dependence on European technology. No matter how poor his production of furs was any year, the James Bay hunter always took a significant portion of his credit in non-essential goods: tobacco, alcohol, beads, and so on. If ammunition, cloth, and other items were absolute necessities then one would expect he could not have afforded to trade every year for these other goods. In a study made of the percentage of total furs 'spent' on selected trade goods at Eastmain House, and as seen in Table 2, it was found that in the years 1730–65, some 9 to 15 per cent of the furs traded annually by the Cree were used to barter for brandy and tobacco. In the subsequent years to 1780, during the rivalry with the North West Company, this percentage jumped to 20 to 26 per cent. In only about seven of the fifty years examined did the percentages fall below the minimums given above and these were not

TABLE 2
Percentage of total furs 'spent' on selected essential* and non-essential items, Eastmain House, 1730–80

Year	Total fur trade in made beaver	Percentage 'spent' on guns and ammunition	Percentage 'spent' on brandy and tobacco	Year	Total fur trade in made beaver	Percentage 'Spent' on guns and ammunition	Percentage 'spent' on brandy and tobacco
1730	2522	29.4	11.3	1756	1732	15.4	13.3
1731	3684	25	10.3	1757	1905	12.8	16.2
1732	3077	30.1	9.6	1758	2116	13.7	11.5
1733	3613	25.5	11.4	1759	2125	21.5	12.9
1734	2403	28.4	15.8	1760	2209	16.9	16.1
1735	2382			1761	2404	19.7	13.5
1736	2194	28.3	12.7	1762	3640	16.8	11.8
1737	2307	17	9.9	1763	2555	16.5	15.8
1738	1646	20.6	11.4	1764	1848	16.5	19.5
1739	2311	21.9	11.3	1765	2092	19	8.6
1740	1685	21.7	13.1	1766	1823	19.2	22.6
1741	1413	21.7	9.7	1767	1482	16.2	22.5
1742	1841	20.9	9.3	1768	1242	15.8	23.5
1743	2611	24.3	9.6	1769	1305	22	24.2
1744	3271	20	8.8	1770	1492	21	21
1745	2654	17.1	13.1	1771	2271	24.2	20.2
1746	2263	20.3	11	1772	1901	18.8	20.5
1747	2970	22.4	13.9	1773	2351	6.5	18.5
1748	3772	18.5	11.1	1774	2410	21.5	25
1749	1419	25.2	11	1775	2798	25	26.5
1750	1655	22.3	10	1776	2988	25	14
1751	2196	20	8.2	1777	2471	26.5	22
1752	2596	17.5	11.9	1778	2617	19	26.5
1753	3299	19	11.6	1779	3686	17.5	25
1754	2983	17.3	5	1780	5170	18	16
1755	2839	18.7	10.4				

*Items essential for subsistence

Source: HBCA B.3/d/38–88; Francis and Morantz *Partners in Furs* 94, 102

years of poor fur returns. For instance, in 1754, only 5 per cent of the furs traded were spent on brandy and tobacco. This was the lowest of any year, yet the volume of furs traded that year was above average. In 1768, when the annual fur trade at Eastmain reached its lowest point in the fifty years examined, the percentage of these furs devoted to so-called luxury goods was high, as 23 per cent. Therefore, items not directly related to subsistence continued to be obtained at a relatively consistent level, regardless of the size of the year's fur harvest.

The Hudson's Bay Company continuously endeavoured to find ways of bringing into the trade the most northern of hunters, today referred to as the Naskapis. These people subsisted, in the main, on caribou and remained aloof from the fur trapping business, picking up from time to time a few European-made goods from other Indians they chanced to meet. Their steadfast refusal, along with the Inuit, to be lured into the trade until the middle of the nineteenth century demonstrates that one cannot generalize about Indian involvement in, and dependence on, the trade. But these northern peoples were not the only ones who treated rather casually the presence of the English in their midst. There were numerous complaints by the traders in the Eastmain journals that when the caribou abounded the Indians ignored their 'fur hunting.' Apparently the situation continued into the nineteenth century. One of many examples is Joseph Beioley's Rupert House journal of 1834 in which he tries to explain why several inlanders brought very few furs: 'The reason they assign is that Deer were so numerous on their land that they had attended principally to Deer Hunting.'[8]

I am not denying that the Indians used European goods – Any device which was labour- and time-saving was welcome. However it is clear that the Indians did not become slaves to the new technology; other life-styles and interests could, and did, take precedence.

Richard Glover's assessment of the impact of European trading ventures on the life-styles of the Indians is similar to Rich's. He speaks of 'profound changes in Indian life' and 'old skills' dying out as a result.[9] Skills did not disappear, but in some cases raw materials changed. Snowshoes, canoes, toboggans, skin and bark tents, and skin clothing continued to be made. Clouston, travelling in Ungava in 1820, even came across a family using a birch-bark cooking vessel instead of the copper one which they also owned.[10] One would have expected this item, because of its relative inefficiency, to have disappeared long before.

Accounts of Indian material culture were not recorded by traders in their journals or correspondence. All the eastern James Bay records have yielded are references to arrow points being fashioned from old kettles and guns, chisels of caribou antlers, and nets of sinew.[11] However, one can imagine a host of essential items being fashioned by the Indians with the aid, in some but not all instances, of European-made tools and raw materials. Indeed, Edward Rogers[12] devotes more than a hundred pages to describing the home-made tools and other effects of the Mistassini Cree of only twenty-five years ago. These skills, except possibly for making fishing nets, were not learned from the English or French. They were carried on, with modifications, from traditions established by ancestors before the arrival of the Europeans.

Similarly, hunting methods and equipment did not become dramatically transformed with the arrival of the *Nonsuch* in James Bay. Ancient hunting techniques using deadfalls, snares, bows and arrows, to name but a few, are still in use today.[13] Not even the introduction of the steel trap revolutionized James Bay Cree beaver hunting practices. Its first appearance in the 'general charge' as a trade item appears in 1789: twelve were on hand; two were traded. The Eastmain account books terminate in 1814, but by then steel beaver traps were still not a favoured item, an average of only six per year having been traded at Eastmain.[14]

The popularly held notion that the coming of the European resulted in the Indians' utter dependence on European goods and in their casting aside old skills demonstrates either pure ethnocentrism or a great deal of naïveté. That the introduction of metal goods and the gun refined the Indians' hunting tools and methods is indisputable but it did not eliminate a technology already honed to the vicissitudes of the environment. 'Supplement' rather than 'supplant' would more appropriately describe the impact of the new technology.

Just as one must speak of various regional fur trades, one must also speak of their varying impact on different Indian groups. The fur trading companies did not administer their policies uniformly across their vast domain; even the sub-Arctic Algonquian peoples, sharing a similar cultural background, were affected in different ways. Furthermore, even within the hunting area of the James Bay Cree, local people and conditions influenced the consequences of this culture contact. I will look at three principal groups of James Bay Cree: coasters, mixed bloods, and inlanders, and their relations with the fur trade; and then examine the impact of the fur trade on the social organization of the coasters and inlanders.

The coasters, or Home Guard, as they were called in the eighteenth century, felt to a great extent the effects of the Hudson's Bay Company's presence. As their name implies, they were James Bay Indians who lived in the coastal regions. At various times of the year they worked for the maintenance of the Europeans: in the beginning supplying them with geese; later providing all types of provisions and even performing tasks about the post. Still later, they were employed as voyageurs for the inland posts. In effect, they were casual or seasonal employees of the post; for most of the year they were subsistence fishermen, and hunters and trappers (mainly of marten and fox). They did not reside in the post but lived relatively close by. Even when the company began voyaging operations to supply the inland posts, the families of the voyageurs camped some distance away from the post where a supply of fish could be secured for themselves and the Europeans. Summer residence at the establishments was a post-1870 development and not directly related to the fur trade.[15]

Whether coasters antedated the arrival of the Europeans is a matter to be determined in the future by archaeologists. What is important to this study is that these James Bay Cree were distinguishable from the inlanders or trading Indians by their variant life-style. Their life-style, combining a kind of wage employment with trading furs and subsistence hunting and fishing, was a distinct Cree adaptation to the fur trade operations. Thus, unlike the inland Indians, the coasters were directly and profoundly affected by their involvement in the fur trade. However, how many European customs and values were taken back to their camps is unknown. They consumed European goods at a higher rate than the inlanders to the extent that one can reasonably speak of their reliance on the post for these goods. William Falconer's comments, regarding the coasters in 1769 at Severn on the south-west coast of Hudson Bay, may be equally applicable to Eastmain: 'they being so much used to the gun ect [sic] that the use of the bows and arrows is so little practiced by the low-country Natives; they could not subsist by it alone; ... yet the uplanders, that can do very weel without us at present.'[16]

There is also a popular notion that the Indians, specifically the coasters, were dependent on food from the post.[17] The reading of the post journals shows this concept to be erroneous. The volume of food contributed by the coasters to the posts, on an almost daily basis, far exceeded whatever sustenance they received in dire times. For instance in 1757, a poor year for country provisions at Eastmain, twenty coasters during the period from February to June received help from the company in the form of 573 quarts of oatmeal. In the same year, eight company men at Eastmain consumed 976 salt geese, 190 pounds of dried caribou meat and at least 100 fish, all supplied by the Indians. In 1786 at Eastmain the coasters brought to the post: 1599 geese, 318 ducks, 1414 pounds of fish, 368 rabbits, the flesh of 20 beaver, 11 porcupines, 2 seals, etc.[18] In that excellent year for provisions, the coasters needed no help from the English.

The company supplied a limited quantity of food in recognition of its obligations to the coastal Indians for having restricted their movement. Thomas Mitchell, master at Eastmain, explained this in his journal entry of 20 March 1745: 'served ot to 36 Indians Small & great 6 lbs. of damidgd. flower = These Indians if thay where a 100 mile in Land thay might find supply a Nough But yt we should want them to kill geese.'[19] Most often, the coasters were in great need only during the late winter period when they could not venture too far afield lest they get caught in the spring thaw and miss the goose hunt. If one were to calculate the amount of food which flowed in each direction throughout the first two hundred years of the fur trade one would find that the flow of subsistence goods from the Indians to the Hudson's Bay Company men was overwhelmingly greater.

In many ways the Europeans, particularly those who lived for many years at the posts, must have modified their life-style, values, and worldview, in ways learned from the Cree, to accommodate to the demands of this harsh environment and their relations with the local people. A number of traders of French, English, and Orkney extraction had Indian wives and offspring who must have greatly influenced their lives.

Clearly the second group, the mixed-blood offspring, were heavily influenced by the Europeans. Even before it became company policy early in the 1800s to cultivate a 'small Colony of very Useful Hands' who would ultimately replace European-born servants,[20] sons of some British traders entered the service of the company. Not all did though; many chose to live an Indian life and settled among the coaster families. There are cases such as the Beads family where one brother (Thomas) joined the company while the other (Chizzo) remained a hunter.[21] Others such as the Atkinsons and Hesters vacillated between the two.

Initially the native servants performed general labouring tasks but by the 1840s they were involved in all aspects of the company's operations and formed the majority of the servants in James Bay. It is unlikely the inland posts would have succeeded without the special skills gained from their Indian heritage. Furthmore their lower salaries and greater abilities, according to the records, produced higher profits for the company than at other posts in the southern department.[22]

It was this group, with its allegiances to both sides, which was most useful to the company in mediating and negotiating with the inland Indians. Little is said about the life-style of these mixed-blood servants except that they hunted to provide for the post and for their families who often did not live at the post but camped near it. Beginning in 1806 and lasting to 1826, there can be found in the records a list of those baptized at the post by the chief trader. The first Christian minister to preach amongst the eastern James Bay people did not arrive until 1840, but included in the school-books sent to the bay in 1810 were bibles, hymn books, scriptures, and moral sketches. That the Europeans accepted mixed bloods as their own is evident from their writings and the fact that not only their children but their grandchildren were buried in the 'European burial ground' rather than in the Indian one at Eastmain.[23]

Aside from the often short-lived influence of their fathers, their brief period of schooling, and their work experience, most other aspects of their lives would have been heavily influenced by their mother's family. The men married either coasters or mixed-blood women like themselves. Some practiced polygamy. A few of them were criticized by other Hudson's Bay Company employees for their strong Indian affiliations. George Atkinson II, who had visited England, told his mixed-blood friends they were being cheated and advised them not to hunt furs or geese until they were better paid for them. It was recommended that Thomas Cooper be withdrawn from service because he divulged too much of the company's business to the Indians at Mistassini in 1840. Most, however, seemed to identify their interests with those of their employer. Some of the native servants retired, under pressure from the company, to the Red River Colony or Lake Superior.[24] (This was a precautionary measure to remove them from the fur trade arena in order to prevent them from joining the opposition or trading independently.) Many, however, remained at the bay and rejoined their coaster relatives. Of the three groups of Indians in James Bay this was the group whose life-style had strayed the farthest from the traditional Indian one and yet they and their children could be re-incorporated into it.

The third group of James Bay Cree who maintained a distinctive life-style were those who inhabited the interior of the James Bay region. They were referred to, by the Europeans, by a variety of geographical designations such as 'inlanders,' 'uplanders,' 'easterners,' and 'northerners.' Their acquaintance with the activities at the post was limited to a total of about three days each June or July when they arrived in trading parties of anywhere from four to twenty men. Women and children were seldom involved. The inlanders did not all arrive at the same time. In fact, it was rare for more than two or three trading groups to meet at the post. On their arrival they were greeted by the chief trader and given presents of brandy and tobacco which they used that day in their feasting and celebrating at their encampment beyond the post. The following day they traded, and on the third they usually departed. Unlike many of the Indians going to York Factory, the James Bay Cree inlanders were hunters and only rarely middlemen.

This, in the most general terms, represents the inlanders' direct contact with the fur trade complex. Its impact on them unlike the other Cree groups, was strictly one that emerged from the exchange of furs for European manufactured goods. These goods created among them a consumer demand that could only be met by devoting some of their time to hunting for exchange purposes. However, the Cree of the eighteenth and nineteenth centuries were not full-time trappers. Subsistence hunting was still, by far, their most important and time-consuming pursuit for they depended entirely on the resources of the land. Unlike the coasters they were too far away from the posts to be able to secure oatmeal in times of starvation. Even when inland posts were established, there were barely enough European provisions to sustain the employees and certainly extremely little was ever provided for the hunters. In fact, if the country resources were poor that year, both the Indians and the post employees suffered.

The consumer demand of the Indians for European manufactured goods throughout this period remained more or less constant. One can show, using the account books of the James Bay posts, that from the mid-eighteenth century to the mid-nineteenth century the Cree maintained a similar level of consumption of trade goods, roughly thirty to forty 'made beaver' of furs. The Hudson's Bay Company could never induce them to increase their consumer demands beyond what the hunters perceived as desirable.[25] Furthermore, as was demonstrated earlier, beaver trapping competed with caribou hunting – the latter the preferred activity. As well, there were groups of Indians, in Ungava particularly, who chose to remain on the fringes of the fur trade, content to trade every few years for only small quantities of ammunition and other necessities.

For most of the James Bay inlanders the fur trade not only aided in improving their technology but had some impact on their hunting strategies. At all times, subsistence activities were primary though animals, such as beaver, served both subsistence and exchange needs. However, when the country resources were sufficient that they could 'afford' to hunt animals for exchange purposes, they had to assess their needs with respect to European goods and use this as the basis for deciding where and what they hunted. Therefore the impact of the fur trade permeated beyond strictly their material culture, but the James Bay Cree, during this period, remained first and foremost subsistence hunters. Thus only moderate adjustments to their way of life were made as a result of their participation in the fur trade.

The social organization of the coasters and inlanders was undoubtedly affected by their involvement in the fur trade. What these effects were is difficult to determine, since we are not certain about the kind of social organization that antedated the coming of the Europeans. However, archaeologists have found evidence that the people camped in relatively small groups and had a diversified diet.[26] This seems consistent with conditions that existed during the first half of the nineteenth century when the records begin supplying more pertinent data.[27] One can only conclude that the fur trade had little effect on winter hunting group composition or small band affiliations. Family hunting territories and 'trading captains,' two important developments in social organization, are, however, attributable to the impact of the fur trade.

Family hunting territories, which became an important aspect of Cree social organization, are thought by many to have arisen solely as a result of the eastern Algonquians' involvement in the fur trade. Ethnographers, in the early years of this century, noticed that specific hunting territories seemed to be the preserve of individual families and they designated this form of land tenure a 'family hunting territory' system. This designation has persisted although we now know that the land is considered to belong to individuals rather than groups of kinsmen. Furthermore it is probably more accurate to view this phenomenon not as land that is owned but as rights to resources so that the territory is in reality 'a unit of management.' As well, both the current ethnographies and historical materials indicate that this land tenure system was highly flexible.[28]

Reduced to its most general terms, the consensus, so far, is that the fur trade, because of either its emphasis on sedentary fur bearers or its promotion of individualism, was the direct cause of the development of such a system of land tenure which came into being, at the earliest, by the mid-nineteenth century.

The Hudson's Bay Company records from the James Bay posts yield interesting data in this regard. Unlike northern Ontario or the lower north shore of the St Lawrence,[29] the James Bay area was not abundant in large migratory game such as caribou or moose so that dependence on a wide variety of animals, including sedentary fur bearers, was necessary. Furthermore, as earlier noted, the James Bay Cree were, by mid-eighteenth century, already producing furs in the same quantity as they were to do one hundred years later. It cannot be said that they were progressively being drawn into the fur trade during this period. The records also suggest that a system of family hunting territories perhaps existed much earlier than at present acknowledged. The extension of credit to the Indians by the Hudson's Bay Company, first mentioned when the Eastmain records begin in 1739 (although known to be practiced at Albany in 1696 and by the French, too)[30] is a strong indication that a sense of individual ownership operated among the Cree at an early period in Indian-European relations. Similarly, the notion of exclusive owner-ship of fur bearing (as opposed to food) animals is expressed in this remarkably clear discussion of trespass, related by Mitchell at Eastmain in his 1745 journal: 'Ever [sic] Indian hath a River or Part whear ya Resorts to ye winter season & in som are More fish yn others. But ya count it a Trespass to kill anything in one anothers Leiberty for Last winter one of our Indians did not kill one Martain & I asked him ye rason. He sade another Indian tould him all ye martains Be Longd to him so he sade he lived on dear & Som Rabbits.'[31]

Therefore, if a family hunting territory system did not exist in eighteenth-century James Bay, then the essential elements were in various stages of development, culminating with its emergence as a land tenure system by the early nineteenth century. This system may well have de-veloped in the early stages of the fur trade or already existed, in some form, prior to it. It is not unreasonable to suggest, however, that the needs of the fur trade imposed their own very significant stamp on the nature of the family hunting territory system, whatever its origin.

Trading captains (so called by the English) were an interesting, though short-lived, development in Algonquian leadership patterns, and clearly attributable to the impact of the fur trade.

Leaders naturally existed long before the arrival of the Europeans and one was there when they arrived in 1670.[32] As at the other posts to the west, the trading company began using this leadership system to advance its own ends. It rewarded a man who had influence or 'sway,' that is who could convince a number of men to accompany him to the post with their furs, by making him a trading captain. In some years a captain was able to command as many as twenty canoes, but the next year might bring only two or three canoes. Over the seventy-odd years of the trading captain

system at Eastmain the average was 4.97 canoes or nine to ten men.[33]
Unlike the trading captains to the west, the James Bay ones were not so
much middlemen as leaders of groups of men coming to trade.

By 1695 at Albany and by 1701 at the latest at Eastmain, company
officials began presenting coats, in addition to the usual gifts of tobacco
and gunpowder, but they later included whole outfits involving fine cloth,
lace, ruffles, shoes, stockings, etc. These special fancy uniforms, in addition to the large quantities of brandy and tobacco with which they were
freely provided to dispense amongst their followers, enabled the captains
to develop a unique status in a hitherto egalitarian society. The French
also created trading captains as did the North West Company after
them.[34]

The fierce competition between the Hudson's Bay Company and North
West Company enabled the trading captain system to flourish. For example, in 1771, two captains and one lieutenant visited Eastmain. By 1783
this number had tripled to five captains and four lieutenants.[35] The very
large number of leaders created, their inability to command the same
number of men each year, and the fact that what the Europeans considered leadership qualities probably were not Cree values[36] all suggest that
at least some of these trading captains held no other status in Cree society
than that created by the fur trade. Others would have been heads of
co-residential groups or local bands. When trading ended, all trading
captains probably resumed their usual roles and held no special distinction until the following trading season.

An interesting aspect of this phenomenon is that no matter how few
pelts the captains and their followers brought, the company continued to
present them with lavish gifts of brandy, tobacco, and clothing. These
gifts sometimes represented as much as half the value of the furs brought,
though more usually about one-fifth.[37] Obviously the James Bay Cree
were exploiting, and benefiting from, the fierce rivalry between the two
fur trading companies.

Though the Europeans initiated the trading captain system based on
the traditional leadership system of the Indians, its form and peculiarities
were developed by the Indians. However, the system was eventually
phased out by the English company when its inland posts were taking
root, making long trading journeys to the coast unnecessary. This also
coincided with the North West Company's diminishing control over the
fur trade. By 1818 the trading captain system in James Bay had all but
disappeared. Thereafter the records only refer to 'leading' or 'principal'
Indians, those who were heads of large family groups and acknowledged

by the hunters as having some influence over them. They, unlike the trading captains, held no particular role as representatives of their people. In the final analysis, however, the trading captain system likely had little effect on the underlying traditional Cree social order which continued to respond to the subsistence needs of the people. It was purely a specific response to a particular era of the fur trade.

The impact of the fur trade on the Indians and vice versa cannot be simply stated for it depends on which group of James Bay Cree in what period and which aspects of the fur trade are being analysed. It is difficult to separate the influences of the two cultures, since the Indian-European relationship in the fur trade of 1700 to 1870 can only be described as 'interdependent.' There are many aspects of the James Bay Cree involvement in the fur trade that demonstrate they did not consider themselves, and should not be considered, dominated by the Europeans. For example, the Indians exerted a great deal of control over the trade in terms of their economic relationship with the Europeans. The Indians were discriminating 'shoppers,' a quality the Hudson's Bay Company men quickly recognized. The Indians of the eighteenth century also exercised a considerable influence in fashioning the trading policies of the company. Trade rituals, giving of presents, value of goods traded and their quality, respect of the factor toward the Indians, and the expansion of trade were all affected. The Indians had the upper hand for they could always take their furs to the opposition. It was a weapon they knew how to use well to their own advantage.

The Indian impact on the fur trade was not confined to the eighteenth century. One tends to think of the 1821 union of the two companies as the end of competition and therefore the end of whatever advantage the Indians had been able to wrest from the fur trade. Although changes occurred in eastern James Bay they were not nearly as dramatic as might be expected. Though resources declined, the account books and Simpson's reports show the Rupert's River and Eastmain districts continued to be valuable and profitable ones for the company.[38]

Actually one can distinguish three groups of James Bay trading Indians, each with a different relationship with the company in this post-1821 period. Still considered very independent were the Indians north of Fort George whose use of trade goods was only slight. The ones most directly influenced by the company were those who were attached to Rupert House. In that region the company instituted a vigorous campaign amongst the Indians, first to conserve the beaver and in the late

1830s to rear them on specifically designated beaver preserves, until their numbers had been replenished. At first the company had difficulty in launching both schemes but by adjusting their restrictions to the Indians' needs and compensating them for their loss in revenue, they were successful in their endeavours.[39] The third group were those people attached to the inland posts where the company did not initiate such measures. They fall somewhere between these other two groups.

After union, the company had increased expectations of being able to establish greater control over the trade by restricting the hunters to specific posts and by limiting the flow of presents and extension of credit. They were not very successful in this. The records of the inland posts are filled with accounts of the strategies and manoeuvres the Hudson's Bay Company officers employed to keep the James Bay people loyal. Operating to the Indians' advantage was the competition provided by the lessees of the former king's posts. These latter were receiving furs at double and triple the Hudson's Bay Company prices. This situation lasted until 1831 when the company gained control. During these years the company had to accede to any demands made by the inlanders – such as delivering their trade goods to them, increasing the value of the furs, and sending presents of rum and tobacco. Even new outposts were established to attempt to secure the trade of the Indians in the area. Rather than accept the company's lower prices or take their business to traders they did not like, the James Bay people were prepared to undertake long trading journeys. Some travelled to posts as far away as the Gulf of St Lawrence. As in the previous century, a number of families sent some members to the Hudson's Bay Company post and others to the competition.[40]

Though the rival traders were absorbed in 1831 this did not end the Indians' ability to continue to manipulate the conduct of the fur trade to their advantage. Try as it might, the company was unable to prevent them from going to other of their posts in the St Maurice and Lake St Jean districts. Goods were cheaper at the more eastern posts and alcohol was available there.[41] This attracted the hunters.

The supplying of the inland posts required the services of a large number of Cree each summer. Though the company paid them the equivalent of about one half the value of an average year's hunt, it had problems recruiting voyageurs. Those who finally agreed to go often deserted along the way. The work was arduous, and, besides, the Indians needed the summer to lay up a stock of dried fish for the winter.[42] The company was never able to depend on a smooth operation.

Exploration and travel were also dependent on the Indians' co-operation. In 1825, for instance, Clouston had to cancel a trip to Was-wanipi because the man whom he had contracted to take him deserted. This was not the only time Clouston had difficulties. In an earlier incident in 1820, Clouston commented that 'rather than a dissatisfied Indian going before me, in an unknown country, among savages, I considered it best to agree to these offers.'[43]

Throughout the period 1830 to 1870, although the Hudson's Bay Company enjoyed a near monopoly of the trade, they still were unable to direct the trade to their satisfaction. As throughout the history of their relations with the James Bay Cree, company officials continued to woo the Indians with presents. Many Indians, it was felt, were not exerting themselves to the fullest and were exhorted by the company to do better. The giving of debt also could not be curtailed as the traders recognized its importance for both the Indians and the fur trade itself. In 1839, the inland Indians were still considered 'untrustworthy' because the company officials could not predict where they would go to trade. In 1862 there was concern about 'a spirit of great discontent' having spread among the 'most valuable' of their hunters. As for how the James Bay people may have viewed their relations with the Hudson's Bay Company we have these comments by the chief trader of Rupert House in 1865. Bernard Ross, in discussing the giving of presents to the James Bay people, notes that: 'I do not believe that the natives ever consider these presents in the light of payment for anything, regarding them more as gift-offerings to their own importance and superiority.'[44]

James Bay Cree society was never the same after the Europeans arrived but it was not directly remodelled or dismantled. The Cree worked out their own adjustments, by and large, to those aspects of the fur trade they valued and wished incorporated. They were able to evolve mechanisms which enabled them to adjust from a society essentially producing for its own consumption to one that also produced for exchange. They were also able to exert considerable influence over their relations with the Europeans. They seem to have done so in the eighteenth century with relatively little cultural loss or social disintegration.

Besides failing to assess adequately the impact of the fur trade, earlier writers also seem to have used their particular conceptions of modern-day economically dependent Indian society as their model for the one created in the aftermath of the arrival of the European fur trade. The fur trade companies did not make concerted efforts to alter drastically the Indian life-style. It was not in their interest. However, in the last century the various Indian societies have had their ideological systems assaulted by the missionaries and their political authority thoroughly undermined by the government. Additional major alterations in the ecological system affecting their subsistence patterns and changes in the world fur markets were also extremely important factors, for *some* groups, in furthering the trend away from a hunting and trapping economy to greater economic reliance on the larger society. This process began perhaps in the middle of the nineteenth century, but its chief agents were these more recent encroachments on the integrity of the Indian cultures – not the fur trade.

A final lesson is this: When you compare developments among the James Bay Cree coasters and inlanders, the northern caribou hunters, the northern Ojibwa, and the parkland Indians of the prairies, the inescapable conclusion is that there was not one fur trade, but many.

I wish to express my gratitude to Direction de l'Archéologie et de l'Ethnologie, Ministère des Affaires Culturelles, Québec, for generously financing most of the research for this study.

I also wish to thank Professor Edward Rogers for his helpful comments on the paper read at the conference.

REFERENCES

1 Ray *Indians in the Fur Trade;* Bishop *The Northern Ojibwa and the Fur Trade;* Foster 'The Home Guard Cree and the Hudson's Bay Company: The First Hundred Years'
2 Rich *The Fur Trade and the Northwest to 1857*
3 Rich 'Trade Habits and Economic Motivation Among the Indians of North America'
4 HBCA B 3/d/3, 2 (1964)
5 HBCA B 59/a/29, 3d (1759)
6 HBCA B 59/a/35, 17d
7 Normandin 124
8 HBCA B 186/1/47, 34d
9 Glover, 'Introduction' to Davies ed *Letters from Hudson Bay, 1730–40* xxvi–xxvii
10 Davies ed *Letters from Hudson Bay* 57
11 HBCA B 77/a/5, 8 (1818), B 59/a/4, 33d (1740)
12 Rogers *Material Culture of the Mistassini*
13 Ibid 67
14 HBCA B 59/d/6–43
15 Francis and Morantz *Partners in Furs: A History of the Fur Trade in Eastern James Bay, 1600–1870* 232–34, 242
16 Falconer 32

17 Rich *Hudson's Bay Company* I 71
18 HBCA B 59/a/26, B 69/a/61
19 HBCA B 59/a/12, 20
20 HBCA A 6/17, 76 (1806)
21 HBCA B 186/a/58, 60 (1839)
22 HBCA D 4/92, 22d (1828), A 12/2, 214 (1843)
23 HBCA B 133/a/8, 16d (1825), B 59/z/1; PAC Methodist Missionary Society, MG 17, vol. 11, 271; HBCA B 59/z/2, 2, B 59/a/96, 35 (1817)
24 HBCA B 59/a/94, 21d (1816), B 77/e/5, 2, 5 (1823), B 186/b/41, 22, D 9/1, 639 (1867)
25 HBCA B 59/e/1, 5 (1814)
26 James Chism, personal communication
27 Morantz 'James Bay Cree Social Organization, 1730–1850'
28 Tanner 'The Significance of Hunting Territories' 105, 112; Morantz 'The Probability of Family Hunting Territories in Eighteenth Century James Bay: Old Evidence Newly Presented'
29 Bishop *Northern Ojibwa* 9; Leacock *The Montagnais 'Hunting Territory' and the Fur Trade* 24
30 HBCA B 59/a/4, 7, B 3/d/7, 7; Normandin 117
31 HBCA B 59/a/12, 17d
32 Oldmixon 'The History of Hudson's Bay' 38
33 Morantz 'James Bay Cree Social Organization, 1730–1850' 83
34 HBCA B 3/d/5, 16, B 3/d/12, 13, B 59/d/3, 30 (1786), B 135/a/14, 44 (1744), B 59/a/46, 30 (1774)
35 HBCA B 59/a/40, B 59/a/58
36 Morantz 'Trading Captains' 87
37 Ibid 85
38 HBCA D 4/91, 15d (1828), D 4/97, 46d (1830), B 135/z/2, 51ff (1843–70)
39 HBCA B 59/e/13, 5 (1828), B 135/k/1, 6d (1822), B 186/b/38, 42 (1839); Francis and Morantz *Partners in Furs* 195–8
40 HBCA B 59/a/108, 25 (1824), B 186/b/6, 4 (1823), B 135/a/9, 9–9d (1825), B 133/a/9, 5d (1825) and 18d, B 227/e/4, 3d (1825) and 23, B 133/e/2, 5 (1821), B 77/e/6, 6 (1824), B 133/a/9, 2, 23 (1825), B 59/a/46, 30 (1774), B 133/a/9, 4 (1825)
41 HBCA B 186/b/22, 2, B 186/b/64, 12d (1853), B 186/b/69, 60d (1864), B 186/b/56, 15 (1849)
42 HBCA B 186/b/2, 9d (1819), B 186/a/37, 3 (1828)
43 HBCA B 133/a/8, 15; Davies ed *Letters from Hudson Bay* 43
44 HBCA B 186/b/70, 48d (1865), B 186/b/55, 7 (1848), B 186/b/6, 4 (1823), B 186/b/41, 2, B 186/b/70, 17d and 48d

French Attitudes towards Native Society

CORNELIUS JAENEN

A long-held view of French contact with native peoples has asserted that the French excelled in exploration, evangelization, and indigenous relations, but that they were too impetuous to put down deep roots in the New World. In spite of apparently good relations with the native peoples, there were literary references as early as 1591 to the impatience and inconstancy which flawed the character of France overseas.[1] French historians, such as Deschamps, Leroy-Beaulieu, Vignon, Halot, Mury, and Hanotaux,[2] writing during the revival of French imperialism in the late nineteenth and early twentieth centuries, extolled the French génie colonial but also grappled with the 'problem' of the collapse of the First Empire of the ancien régime.[3]

French attitudes towards the native peoples were described in the seventeenth century by the Dominican missionary Du Tertre[4] as exemplary, compared to the conduct of the 'murderous' Spaniards and the 'cold-hearted' English. The French kept alive the 'Black Legend' of Spanish cruelty to the native American peoples while nurturing their own perception of superior sensitivity to indigenous customs and needs. This view is still expounded by twentieth-century French historians. Georges Hardy wrote that his countrymen 'have been delivered more quickly of primitive expansionism and we have from the beginning incorporated with our needs of colonial domination the scruples of civilized peoples and the concern of educators.' André Julien added that the 'French had without argument a gift for conciliating the aborigines that no other people possessed to the same degree.' Hubert Deschamps, in describing French colonial doctrines since the sixteenth century, stated that 'their gift of sympathy [for the aborigines], their facility of assimilation, their absence of racism were there from the beginning.'[5]

The English-speaking world since Edmund Burke has generally adopted the same thesis. Francis Parkman gave it eloquent expression in the memorable phrase, 'Spanish civilization crushed the Indian; English civilization scorned and neglected him; French civilization embraced and cherished him.'[6] Philip Means, writing in 1965, commended the 'singularly sympathetic and conciliating spirit which Frenchmen have always displayed toward races distinct from their own.'[7]

What, indeed, were the French attitudes toward native American peoples and cultures? Can these attitudes be separated from their concepts of the new world or of primitive peoples in general? To what extent were the attitudes expressed by Frenchmen the products of their social and cultural heritage and to what extent were certain attitudes the consequence of what Bishop Bossuet in 1681 called *convergences* or 'the important combination of events' which produce history?[8] How do the 'accepted views' as reported in our current historiography stand up to scholarly scrutiny?

In a brief paper, one is restricted to the methodological approaches and to an overview of the vast domain in order to come to some conclusion about the nature of French attitudes toward native society. Even the term 'native society' can pose a problem. The French rarely perceived a native society, an aboriginal collectivity, as distinct from individuals and agglomerations of natives. They wrote and spoke of 'nations' but it is not definite that they made distinctions beyond friendly or allied tribes as opposed to enemy tribes, beyond sedentary as opposed to nomadic tribes, or beyond trading partners as opposed to British subjects. La Condamine in the eighteenth century acknowledged there were many Indian languages and tribes but nonetheless assured his readers that all 'appeared to me to have certain traits of resemblance to one another ... I believe to have recognized in all of them a same basis of character'.[9]

Attitude is a central concept in social psychology. It would therefore seem pertinent to employ a model for the study of relations between groups.[10]

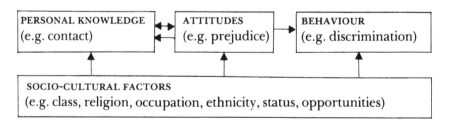

PERSONAL KNOWLEDGE (e.g. contact)	ATTITUDES (e.g. prejudice)	BEHAVIOUR (e.g. discrimination)

SOCIO-CULTURAL FACTORS
(e.g. class, religion, occupation, ethnicity, status, opportunities)

There is clearly no simple stimulus/response situation. Frenchmen who heard and thought about Indians, who saw them, or who came into direct contact with them in the new world did so with social and cultural baggage, a complex of ideas which conditioned (and even determined) their perception and their interpretation of what they perceived. The native peoples, however, were not passive recipients in this meeting of cultures but, as I have suggested elsewhere,[11] they were active participants with their own socially and culturally derived knowledge and attitudes. Therefore, in defining French attitudes towards native society let us consider the concepts and patterns of ideas contemporary with the period of contact being examined, insofar as these are known to us.

Where and how does one encounter these concepts and patterns of thought? The terminology itself suggests that we are concerned with a literate or professional élite which may (and in fact does) nevertheless express deeply held and felt views from the lowest social classes through to the dominant groups who give them literary and artistic expression. A reading of Olive Dickason's doctoral dissertation[12] will confirm that the works of illustrators, engravers, cartographers, and sculptors, of poets and playwrights, and literary works from travel journals and missionary propaganda to cosmographies and universal histories are a lodestone of concepts and constructs. They tell a trained historian virtually as much about writers and artists as they do about their supposed Indian subjects.

There is a danger of attempting to present a unifying theme of the new world and of French-Indian contact if one restricts oneself to this level of investigation. More about this later.

In the study of relations between groups it is not sufficient to remain at the level of the social and cultural factors which each participant brings to the contact. This level of prejudgments, values, and moral assumptions is basic information, to be sure, but it demands from the historian further consideration of the experience of contact.

Where personal knowledge is increased in exchanges between cultures, it is obvious that not only the character but also the attitudes of the participants are brought into play. The meeting itself is important, as Bossuet suggested centuries ago. It matters which cultural representatives of France come into contact with which representatives of Indians. Presumably a contact between a missionary and a sachem in the process of French evangelization will not produce the same attitudes and behaviour as would a contact between a French soldier and an Algonkian trading captain during a French exploratory mission.

Attitudes affect the perception of contact, but the realities of contact also reinforce or alter perceptions and attitudes. The realities of contact ('events') may also affect favourably or unfavourably certain social and cultural factors which originally shaped knowledge, attitudes, and behaviour. For example, the realities of contact may undermine the status of certain Indians (e.g. the medicine-man) or enhance a component (e.g. missions) in the French cultural complex. Behaviour may be viewed as reflecting attitudes, but behavioural patterns also act upon attitudes. The dominance of the fur trade in French-Indian contact, for example, especially in the absence of extensive white settlement in aboriginal territories, was a behavioural pattern which had far-reaching results for both French and Indian attitudes. The relationship between behaviour and attitude was so marked in this case that ethnic stereotyping resulted. This in some measure explains a prevalent Indian view of the Frenchman as a trader/soldier, dispenser of merchandise and brandy, and not as a farmer interested in land acquisition. Similarly, French views of Indians inclined to the skilful hunter/wary warrior stereotype rather than to the forest fiend who prevented the advance of the settlement frontier.

Other social science models may clarify the contact experiences. Doob, for example, identified three levels of change flowing from contact: causal: direct result of intrusion; consequential: consequence of some causal change(s); interactional: consequence of changes in one's own society, but also on changes in intruding society.[13] For example, the Indian use of and desire for brandy is causal; the annual supply of brandy to the pays d'en haut is consequential; and the introduction of brandy into the gift-giving ceremonies is interactional. In employing this set of definitions it must be kept in mind that intrusion may be initiated by Indian society too.

Thus, if we take Bishop's three categories of response to intrusion[14] and apply them to the French responses to contact with Indians we see that in some cases there was augmentation, or some modification of existing culture to incorporate new elements; in other cases there was replacement, or loss of traditional customs; and in still other cases there was reinterpretation, or the attribution of new meanings or functions to traditional practices. What is significant for our present purposes is that all these responses supported, in varying degrees, positive French attitudes towards native society.

Larrabee's concepts of themal interaction and sequence of cultural interaction are of particular interest.[15] He distinguishes between coincident themes, where Indian and European behaviour and concepts find a middle or 'common factor of interests and intentions,' and conflict themes, where there is no common ground. What emerges quite clearly for the historian of New France is that the nature of most French-Indian contacts made for more coincidental themes and fewer conflict themes in the French experience than in the Delaware-English contact studied by Larrabee.

Let us return to the question of concepts and patterns of thought which Frenchmen used to meet the two-fold challenge of understanding the new world and its inhabitants as observed by old world exploiters and explorers, and of describing or depicting them to compatriots who had no first-hand experience of them.[16] Proceeding on the hypothesis that the unknown, or recently known, is understood and communicated in terms of the well known, a content analysis of the major publications relating to the French experience with Indians should identify the significant images and attitudes. We have, accordingly, identified seven such ideas or organizing concepts.

First, there was the myth of the terrestrial paradise, the idyllic lost Eden, the Elysian Fields, Arcadia and Avalon of classical and mediaeval tradition which scholars as late as 1730 were still trying to locate geographically in the mysterious unknown west.[17] Peter Martyr so identified the areas of tropical America where the French made their initial colonizing ventures in the sixteenth century – the resplendent perfumed forests teeming with exotic flora and fauna and naked 'savages.' The image of the innocent natural man who inhabited this primeval garden was largely the creation of Ronsard, Rabelais, and Montaigne. Montaigne wrote: 'Those people are wild, just as we call wild the fruits that Nature has produced by herself and in her normal course; whereas really it is those that we have changed artificially and led astray from the common order, that we should rather call wild.[18]

The Jesuit relations of 1648 from Canada, where forests when robed in summer and autumn beauty could be assimilated to the image of the terrestrial paradise, said: 'It seems as if innocence, banished from the majority of the Empires and Kingdoms of the World, had withdrawn into these great forests where these people dwell. Their nature has something, I know not what, of the goodness of the Terrestrial Paradise before sin entered it. Their practices manifest none of the luxury, the ambition, the avarice, or the pleasures that corrupt our cities.'[19]

The nudity of the Indians continued in the eighteenth century to be interpreted by some as natural behaviour for innocent aborigines. The abbé Prévost wrote that 'the shame of being naked is not a natural sentiment,' but rather he thought it was 'a prejudice of education and the simple effect of custom.' Indians were somewhat indolent and improvident, according to this concept, because America represented a 'garden paradise of pleasure and a life of ease.'[20]

Second, there was the image of 'another world,' a truly new world, a more recently created and emerged 'infant world,' to borrow Montaigne's phrase. Within such a framework, the Indians were 'new men,' beings whose origins were as yet uncertain but of great importance. There ensued boundless speculation about the origins of the native peoples – migrations from every part of the old world were postulated, correspondence with every known ancient civilization was indicated. In 1647 Samuel Bochart argued in favour of a pre-Adamite origin and in 1655 Isaac de La Peyrère elaborated a thesis of concurrent creations. In the eighteenth century it was even postulated that the Indians were descendants of Adam, but not of Noah since the deluge had not touched the new world.[21]

The naturalist Buffon in developing his thesis of an inferiority of American fauna observed, almost in passing, that the Indian was 'no more than an animal of the first order, existing within nature as a creature without significance ... powerless to change nature or assist her.' When Cornelius De Pauw used Buffon's work to bolster a full-blown theory of complete colonial degeneracy (i.e. that plants, animals, men, and institutions degenerated in the new world), Buffon reacted with the assertion that 'Nature, far from being degenerate through old age there, is on the contrary recently born,' and the Iroquois, Huron, and Caribs had demonstrated superior endurance and strength to Europeans so it was impossible to conceive that 'beings just created can be in a state of decrepitude.' Buffon saw them, instead, as being in a state of infancy or caducity.[22] The Jesuit missionaries found this a useful image to explain the tutelage and wardship of the reservation.

Third, there was the concept of the utopian dream, the humanist vision of a better world for the downtrodden and oppressed of the old world. Lescarbot pictured Acadia as a refuge where an immigrant could 'pass his days at rest and without poverty,' while Denys wrote of Frenchmen being 'happier in that country than over here [France] begging their living.'[23] The poet Scarron eulogized his future abode in Guiana in 1653 in these words:

> I am going to America where peace reigns
> Without cold, without war, without taxes,

There, no Mazarin, no satraps
To confiscate revenues.[24]

The utopian vision was based on the premise that Europeans would be able to enjoy the same freedoms, equality, and toleration as were enjoyed by native societies. Lahontan's sauvage de bon sens and Charlevoix's Antillian tribesmen were the most humane, unpretentious, and happy people imaginable. Hennepin praised the Indians for their freedom and tolerance: 'They think every one ought to be left to his own Opinion, without being thwarted.' Montesquieu extended the traditional geographical view of the relationship of climate, latitude and human character to theorize that the natural cowardice of the peoples of Central and South America was responsible for the prevalence of slavery among them, while Canadian tribesmen fiercely retained their northern liberty. He also speculated that the fertility of the land made it possible to survive with a minimum of labour, hence the native peoples felt little inclination to better their condition.[25]

The utopian framework was closely related to a fourth idea – the four ages of mankind, with emphasis on the golden age. This cyclical view of history depicted four world empires – Babylon, Persia, Greece, Rome – as representing an earlier cycle of four stages in human development and as corresponding to ages of gold, silver, bronze, and iron. The golden age, a period of unsophisticated contentment and simplicity, was the greatest of these four ages. During that stage, gold was the chief metal worked by men and was neither over-valued nor lusted after. The fabulous wealth of Spanish America was well known in France and there was a Renaissance hope of the advent of another golden age. Just as gold was supposed to be a source of origins and of initial physical perfection, found at the centre of the world, so the native Americans might be the original men. Lafitau saw them as similar to the ancient old world tribes, the ancestors of the classical Greeks and Romans and of later Europeans. Fontenelle speculated that the Iroquois and early Greeks possessed cultural similarities, therefore 'there is cause to believe that the barbarians of America would in the end have come to think as rationally as the Greeks, if they had been allowed the time to do so.'[26] All men were one, but some were farther along the road of human development and progress.

A fifth concept was the myth of the millennial kingdom and the imminent end of the world. According to this mystical view, the church would be restored to its apostolic pristine purity, the lost tribes of Israel would be found and converted, the Jews would return to the holy land, the entire world would come under Christian domination (whether of the papacy or the Christian princes was still much debated) before Christ's second advent and the parousia. In this eschatological system the Indians could readily be identified with the lost tribes of Israel; their rapid conversion and their fervent piety could be expected. While Lafitau and Hennepin noted many similarities between Jewish and Indian customs, Cadillac went further and affirmed that the tribes around Michilimackinac were 'descended from the Hebrews and were originally Jews.'[27]

The religious zealots engaged in laying the temporal and spiritual foundations of New France readily saw the Indians as possessing 'the fervour of the first Christians of the Church.' Marie de l'Incarnation observed: 'Add to this spirit of simplicity [in the Amerindians] that of fervour, for we see in our Primitive Church, the zeal and ardour of the primitive Church converted by the Apostles.'[28] Father Le Jeune wrote in 1635: 'it seems as if God shed the dew of his grace much more abundantly upon this New France than upon the old, and that the internal consolations and the Divine infusions are much stronger here, and hearts are more on fire. The Lord knoweth who are his.'[29] This was the language of those who believed in the Third Age of the Holy Ghost.

Even those who did not share the optimism of the dévots might concede, as Jean Bodin had suggested as early as 1576, that 'all men have become brothers and share miraculously in the universal republic, as if they formed one same city.'[30] This was the earliest expression of the 'global village' which rejoiced that all God's children had been found and that the human family was now complete.

A sixth concept familiar to the French of the ancien régime was the 'chain of being,' according to which all creation was ranked in hierarchical fashion, beginning with the heavenly hosts at the top and running down to the human, animal, vegetable, and mineral states. The critical intervals were between the angelic and human, and between the human and bestial, because men could be raised to a superhuman level and could also fall to a sub-human and bestial state. This agreed well with the theological concepts of sainthood and depravity and with the folk beliefs concerning giants, Amazons, nymphs, unicorns, centaurs, werewolves, witches, and cannibals. Papal bulls of 1493, 1537, and 1639 reaffirmed that Indians were 'truly men,' rational beings, part of the Adamic creation and capable of receiving divine grace. There persisted, in other words, a counter view that Indians were sub-human, perhaps bestial. The missionary Allouez in 1683 said that the Illinois and Miamis resented the English because the latter 'look upon them only as beasts, and that Paradise is not for that sort of People,' whereas, according to the missionary, the French were known to 'look upon them as men, in whom he recognizes the image of God who has created them ... and who destined them to the same eternal bliss as the Europeans.'[31] The Huron had not felt the same sense of unity and kinship when the Jesuits refused to have European and converts' bones mingled with those of pagans at the feast of the dead.

The *Journal des Savants* for 1724 praised Lafitau for having given the lie to travel literature 'in which the Savages are represented as beasts.'[32] Numerous travel books stressed the inappropriateness of depicting Indians as dark, hairy forest-dwellers, like the homme sylvestre or wildeman of legend and literature. Later in the eighteenth century there were still French writers who portrayed the Indians as lacking familial love and a developed sense of moral obligation which could 'render them superior to the other animals,'[33] or who thought of them as possessing highly developed animal instincts for finding their way and their food in the wilds but also displaying 'stupid insensibility' and attenuated human emotions. 'Superior to the animals, because they use their hands and tongue, they are really inferior to the least of the Europeans. Deprived at once of intelligence and of perfectibility, they obey only the impulses of their instincts.'[34]

Finally, there was the monstrous world of the damned, the image of the part of the world still under satanic domination, nature gone wild and men unrestrained as yet by 'civility' – possessing, as the sixteenth-century phrase put it: ni foi, ni roi, ni loi. Thévet wrote of demons in the Gulf of St Lawrence, Cartier reported unipeds on the Saguenay, Champlain was forced to abandon an expedition because of the Gougou, and Lafitau in 1724 still included a man with his head in his chest among his Indians. Official correspondence from Quebec to Versailles long continued to maintain that among the Inuit there were men with tails and many children were born there with but one arm and one leg. The ultimate proof, however, of the monstrous and devilish nature of the aborigines was their resistance to the gospel preached by the missionaries, their practice of scalping, their cruel platform torture of prisoners, and their supposed cannibalism. Cornelius De Pauw[35] described the new world as weak and corrupt because it was inferior and degenerate, and the Indians as incurably lazy, idiot children incapable of any intellectual progress. Lafitau would have agreed to the extent that Indian religion was a degenerate form of the original religious revelation to all mankind. Charlevoix took an even more comprehensive view, asserting that the cultural differences and linguistic diversity of the native peoples were proofs of degeneration from an original state of cultural uniformity, man's pristine state before the Fall.[36]

The approach through concepts and organizing patterns is a fruitful one because none of the travel accounts, missionary letters, and cosmographies presents a consistent and coherent interpretation of native society. Within the work of a single author many different viewpoints are indicated, some contradicting each other. Such apparent inconsistencies and diversity are inevitable consequences of attempting to explain new information in terms of known frames of reference. No single idea or concept is sufficiently comprehensive to encompass America and its native peoples.

Attempts to present a unifying theme of French contact with the new world and attitudes towards Indians have not been lacking. Gilbert Chinard attempted to demonstrate that exoticism was this unifying theme. He ably documented the origins and development of the 'noble savage' myth in French literature. Later, Geoffrey Atkinson stressed the influence of travel literature upon ideas and focussed attention on the 'extraordinary voyages' as a literary and historical genre. Finally, in 1935, Arthur Lovejoy brought together these earlier studies in the single thesis of primitivism.[37]

In 1964, H. Mumford Jones in *O Strange New World* argued that all these themes – exoticism, extraordinary voyages, primitivism – were part of one cluster of concepts which he called the 'Adamic Myth.' He identified a dual construct: (a) the earthly paradise, land of the golden age, land of native felicity, which he called the 'Edenic image'; (b) the land of incredible terror and savage cruelty, which he called the counter-image. Jones also 'canonized' Peter Martyr of Anghiera as the source of this positive Edenic image of the new world and its peoples.[38]

Four years later, Bausum elaborated the theme of the two images of the terrestrial paradise in the Anglo-American context. He opposed the Peter Martyr image of 1555 and the John Smith image of 1624, the secular renaissance and the religious colonizing view respectively, 'each with its own distinctive and comprehensive view of the New World.'[39] He contended that the Martyr tradition of free, hospitable, innocent, healthy aborigines dominated all early accounts, but that as exploration and colonization progressed there emerged a revised image of slothful, cruel, barbarous, proud, and unsubmissive natives.

How do these attempts to find a unifying theme in European-Indian contact influence our efforts to identify French views of native society?

They reinforce our conviction that they explain only one level, albeit a basic and important stage, of contact and attitudes. Frenchmen in old France acquired their impressions and attitudes from their literary, philosophical, and theological tradition, from the oral tradition of the French Atlantic region, the writings of the time, the artistic representations of Indians, and from Indian visitors to France. But Frenchmen in New France also formed some opinions from face-to-face contact, from the colonial atmosphere, and from the written accounts originating in the colony and its upper country.

There is, therefore, a second level of direct contact – face-to-face contact and its impact – which must also be taken into account. Concepts and theories were transplanted to the colony too, but some new forms and versions emerged because French colonial society was not static after the 'fragment' took root in America. Indian society did not cease to be dynamic after the French intrusion. The attempt to find a unifying theme is a pleasant intellectual exercise, to be sure, but examination of specific sources will rapidly confirm that the authors do not conform to such patterns but draw on a wide range of different images and constructs. There is, at the same time, an extraordinary persistence of organizing patterns over the centuries, experience with the Indians in the new world notwithstanding.

Within the limits of this paper it is not possible to illustrate adequately the second major area of research into the origins and nature of French attitudes towards native society. This domain, using Berry's model,[40] concerns the attitudes which developed in contact itself. Allusion has already been made to French reactions to Indian forest skills, warfare, treatment of prisoners, and the like. One can think of French views of Indian child rearing, sexual mores, ideas of leadership, division of labour, and so on. The primary source materials also demonstrate that the Indians were often seen as little concerned about conservation of resources, incapable of resisting epidemic infections, dependent on French technology, and shrewd traders in matters of kinds, quality, and price of goods in a competitive situation. The cultural (not ethical) relativism of some of the missionaries helped in avoiding overtly aggressive approaches to native society, so that evangelization supported the symbiotic or mutually satisfactory economic relationship between French and Indians.

While the Iroquois, Fox, and Sioux were successively regarded as cruel and dangerous enemies, there was not a progressive and general adoption in New France of what Bausum called the religious colonizing view of ignoble savages. In fact, the Iroquois came to be more highly regarded in the eighteenth century than they had been at the end of the seventeenth century. Eighteenth-century Frenchmen continued to wonder, as Montaigne had done centuries before, if civilization might not corrupt l'homme naturel américain. One experienced missionary told the Propaganda Fide in Rome in 1765 that contact with the French was a 'contagion' to the Indians who 'become soft and can no longer stand up to the hard life required of them, when one spends the winter in the woods as they do.'[41] There is obviously an important level of French attitudes awaiting further investigation.

My tentative conclusion is that French attitudes towards native society were generally more positive than were the English attitudes of the same period[42]. Our examination does not indicate that differences in attitudes can be attributed largely to western European social and cultural factors – this was very much a shared European experience.[43] One is then left with the working hypothesis that the differentiation arises in good measure out of the North American experience of contact itself. Our research to date has tended to support this hypothesis. The approaches suggested would seem to provide a method to undertake the research still required.

It may be added that the French attitudes we have indicated for the period of early contact, during the ancien régime, do not necessarily project themselves beyond 1763. One need only consider Donald Smith's study of French-Canadian attitudes in the nineteenth and twentieth centuries to French-Indian contacts in the 'heroic period' of New France[44] to realize how inaccurate would be a retrospective interpretation of earlier French attitudes.

REFERENCES

1 Du Bartas *La Seconde sepmaine* vii, 86
2 Deschamps 'La Question coloniale en France' 366; Leroy-Beaulieu *De la colonisation chez les peuples modernes* 140–55; Vignon *L'Expansion de la France* 369; Halot 'Aptitude des Français à coloniser' 23; Mury 'Le Génie colonisateur de la France' 76; Hanotaux 'L'Amérique du Nord et la France' 796
3 Boucher 'The First French Empire: Reflections on an Old Issue' passim
4 Du Tertre *Histoire générale des Antilles habitées par les François* 1 1
5 Hardy *Histoire de la colonisation française* vii; Julien *Les Voyages de découvertes et les premiers établissements* 182; Deschamps *Les Méthodes et les doctrines coloniales de la France* 16

6 Parkman *The Jesuits in North America in the Seventeenth Century* I 131
7 Means *The Spanish Main* 197; quoted in Boucher 'The First French Empire'
8 Velat and Champailler eds *Oeuvres de Bossuet* 953
9 Hervé 'Débuts de l'Ethnographie au XVIIIe siècle (1701–1765)' 358
10 Berry 'Multiculturalism and Intergroup Attitudes' 27
11 Jaenen 'Amerindian Views of French Culture in the Seventeenth Century' passim
12 Dickason 'The Myth of the Savage and Early French Colonization in the Americas' passim
13 Doob *Becoming more Civilized: A Psychological Exploration* 18–19
14 Bishop *The Northern Ojibwa and the Fur Trade: An Historical and Ecological Study*
15 Larrabee 'Recurrent Themes and Sequences in North American Indian-European Culture Contact' 25–35
16 Jaenen 'Concepts of America, Amerindians and Acculturation' 1
17 Hardouin *Nouveau traité sur la situation du Paradis terrestre*
18 Frame *Montaigne's Essays and Selected Writings* 89
19 Thwaites *The Jesuit Relations and Allied Documents* XXXII 283
20 Prévost *Le Philosophe anglais* V 125; d'Avity *The Estates, Empires and Principalities of the World* 248
21 De La Peyrere *Praedamitae. Sive Exercitatio super Epistolae ad Romanos* passim; Engel *Essai sur cette question: Quand et comment l'Amérique a-t-elle été peuplée d'hommes et d'animaux*
22 Buffon *Œuvres complètes* XV 443–6; XII 434–49
23 Lescarbot *La Conversion des sauvages qui ont esté baptisez en la Nouvelle France* 33–4; Denys *Description geographique et historique des Costes de l'Amerique septentrionale* II 26
24 Magne *Scarron et son milieu* 254
25 Lahontan *Dialogues curieux entre l'auteur et un sauvage de bon sens* 133; Charlevoix *Histoire de l'isle Espagnole de S. Domingue* I 37–9; Hennepin *A New Discovery of a Vast Country in America* II 70; Montesquieu *Oeuvres* II 114, 133
26 Lafitau *Les Moeurs des sauvages amériquains comparées aux moeurs des premiers temps* I 89, 92; Fontenelle *Discours sur l'origine des fables* II 288–9
27 Quaife *The Western Country in the 17th Century. The Memoirs of Antoine Lamothe Cadillac and Pierre Liette* 53
28 Oury *Marie de l'Incarnation, Ursuline (1599–1672). Correspondance* 26–7, 119–39
29 Thwaites *Jesuit Relations* VIII 189
30 Mesnard *Jean Bodin: La Méthode de l'histoire* 198
31 Thwaites *Jesuit Relations* LXI 209–11
32 *Journal des Savants pour l'anée* MDCCXXIV 571
33 Levesque *L'Homme morale, ou l'homme considéré tant dans l'état de pure nature que dans la société* 5–19

34 De la Roche-Tilhac *Almanach Américain* 5
35 De Pauw *Recherches philosophiques sur les Américains* ii 102, 153–5
36 Charlevoix *Histoire et description générale de la Nouvelle-France* v 55–8, 63
37 Chinard *L'Amérique et le rêve exotique dans la littérature française au XVIIe et XVIIIe siècles* and *L'Exotisme américain dans la littérature française au XVIe siècle;* Atkinson *The Extraordinary Voyage in French Literature before 1700; Les Relations de Voyages du XVIIe siècle et l'evolution des idees;* and *Les Nouveaux Horizons de la Renaissance;* Boas and Lovejoy *Primitivism and Related Ideas in Antiquity;* Lovejoy *The Great Chain of Being*
38 Jones *O Strange New World*
39 Bausum 'Edenic Images of the Western World: A Reappraisal'
40 See note 10.
41 Archives of Propaganda Fide: Congressi, America Centrale, 1673–1775 428v.
42 For English attitudes see Jennings *The Invasion of America.*
43 Jones *O Strange New World*
44 Smith *Le Sauvage. The Native People in Quebec historical writing in the Heroic Period (1534–1663) of New France*

Subarctic Indians and Wildlife

CALVIN MARTIN

Long ago, at the dawn of creation, ' "all was man," ' the ethnologist Frederica de Laguna was told. 'In myth-time all creatures appeared as human beings, speaking and living like men, yet mysteriously possessing some distinctive animal qualities or occasionally donning animal guise.' This curious, unitary view of human and animal genesis prevails throughout the Canadian subarctic. Nearly a half century ago Robert Sullivan uncovered this conviction among the Koyukon, while more recently James VanStone, describing Athapaskans in general, declared that 'both men and animals ... possessed essentially the same characteristics' when the world was new. Frank Speck, writing of the Montagnais-Naskapi of the Labrador Peninsula, remarked: 'In the beginning of the world, before humans were formed, all animals existed grouped under "tribes" of their kinds who could talk like men, and were even covered with the same protection.' Because of this shared origin conjurors could declare to the game around them, ' "You and I wear the same covering and have the same mind and spiritual strength," ' acknowledging that after the passage of untold generations the two were still, after all, spiritually akin.[1]

At first, then, humans and animals were identical, superimposed on each other in some nebulous human-animal form. Only subsequently did the two become differentiated, or polarized, in their outward, physical nature. ' "The animals were once like the Indians and could talk as we do," ' a retired Mistassini shaman once confided in Speck. ' "But some of them were overcome by others while in some animal disguise and forced to remain as such. Others assumed animal shapes so much that involuntarily they became transformed permanently." '[2] Whatever the reasons, the change occurred: human and animal beings were no longer interchangeable, except in rare instances where certain Powerful shamans and particular animal species still seem capable of metamorphosis.[3] Under the new dispensation, 'animals still remain close to men, understanding what men say, aware of their acts, and ready to bestow good or bad fortune. They are full members of man's moral universe, though living outside the human circle of his campfire light.'[4]

The foregoing myth is a prerequisite to understanding the subarctic hunter's attitude toward game resources. Its message is clear: from time immemorial there has been a fundamental equation or sympathy between human persons and animal persons – a sympathy that pervades not just the hunt itself, but all of life's experiences. Of course it would be impossible to fit this origin myth within a particular time frame; it is sufficient to know that it is the bedrock upon which virtually all modern-day subarctic hunters construct their relationship with wildlife.

The relationship is a social one. In the words of Murray and Rosalie Wax, animals 'reside in lodges, gather in council, and act according to the norms and regulations of kinship. In [American Indian folktales] ... man and the animals are depicted as engaging in all manner of social and sociable interaction: They visit, smoke, gamble, and dance together; they exchange wisdom; they compete in games and combat; and they even marry and beget offspring.' Animals and humans, despite morphological differences, remain fundamentally similar. Diamond Jenness was told by Parry Island Potawatomi (nearly indistinguishable from their Ojibwa relatives) that animals have a tripartite nature, like man's: body, soul, and shadow (the shadow functioning as the 'eye' of the soul). And Julius Lips found Montagnais-Naskapi adhering to a similar principle: 'the game animal is gifted with a soul similar to that of man; its reactions and social organization are imagined as similar to those of its human brethren.' Earlier in this century, the ethnologist Alanson Skinner described the Eastern Cree as believing 'that all animals are speaking and thinking beings, in many ways not one whit less intelligent than human beings ... In some cases ... certain animals have a greater supernatural ability than the Indian. This is particularly true of the bear who is considered more intelligent and to have greater medicine powers in many ways than mankind. He walks upon his hind legs like a man, and displays manlike characteristics. In fact, some tribes regard the bear as an unfortunate man.'[5]

Animals thus allegedly think and behave as humans do. The chief distinction between the two beings, animal and human, is that they live in different dimensions. The world of animals is the spirit world – the 'manito world' – with the understanding that animals exist primarily as spirits who don fleshy robes from time to time for human benefit. 'The fox or other animal that one kills today is not the real animal,' confirmed de Laguna, 'but only its fleshy clothing. The real fox himself, his spirit or shadow or soul, is alive, watching the hunter. "His coat and dress, I get it," explained one old man; "his self over there," pointing to the bushes. "Himself, he listens, he sees ... That's why I take care nice, everything burn ... No treat right, no more kill."' The two realms, spiritual and physical, are separate and opposite and – most important – mediated by animals. In conjunction with this, the Copper River Ahtena interviewed by de Laguna were adamant that wildlife should never be domesticated (not a universal subarctic sentiment, incidentally): 'it is taboo to keep any wild animal or bird as a pet, to tie it up or bring it into the house ... For though animals and men live in the same social and religious world, still each must keep a respectful distance from the other.'[6] To domesticate animals evidently would destroy the integrity of this spiritual/physical relationship, with disastrous results for the devout.

Be that as it may, what is perceived, here, is a set of binary contrasts, or opposites (spiritual/physical), that have been effectively bridged through the goodwill of game animals. Subarctic Indians have a penchant for arranging life's experiences in terms of binary opposites; the spiritual/physical opposition is just one of many. Animals, so far as we can discern, serve as the chief reference point or transformation agent in all of the major dualities of life: spiritual/physical, male/female, outside/inside, clean/soiled, health/illness, luck-success-confidence/failure-bad luck-anxiety, Power/Powerlessness, feast-satiety-abundance/starvation-scarcity. There are undoubtedly more; these most readily come to mind. A number of the above bipolar groups are subsumed within broader, more comprehensive polarities. Nonetheless, in each case, whether dealing with superior or inferior sets of contrasts, animals appear to regulate the polar extremes.

Unlike our Western cosmology, which emphasizes the physical realm, the subarctic Indian cosmology is principally concerned with the spiritual world. 'To enter this world was to step *into*, not out of, the *real* world.'[7] The crucial point is that it was often game animals who ushered the individual, usually a male, into this esoteric dimension. Animals, in short, were the prime source of Power, endowing the supplicant with the supernatural force and wisdom necessary to traffic successfully in this other realm.[8] Visitation from some guide, generally in animal guise, came at puberty during the vision quest when the youth, at the urging of his elders, went out alone and begged the 'grandfathers' (in Ojibwa parlance) for their 'blessings.' Among those groups that did not have a guardian spirit complex, such as the Montagnais-Naskapi of the Labrador Peninsula, Power generally welled up from some inner source, one's soul-spirit, or 'Great Man,' as Speck was told.[9]

Whatever the source of Power, whether the inner (e.g., soul-spirit) or more common outer (animal guide) variety, its most common and acceptable use has been in subduing animal spirits in the chase. This is what Speck had in mind when he referred to hunting as a 'holy occupation': animal spirits are first subdued by the hunter's spirit before the incarnate form of the beast is actually slain. In a very real sense, the final bagging of the animal victim is a foregone conclusion. The hunter knows through scouting and various divinatory techniques – often scapulimancy, involving the extorting of information from an animal bone[10] – where the game awaits him on the appointed day of execution. He has been stalking the victim's spirit for perhaps days before and has managed, through the siren Power of his hunt songs and dreams, to secure its permission to be slaughtered.

Subarctic hunters thus traditionally have regarded game animals as *gifts*; in hunt dreams, the animal *surrenders* itself to be killed. This is hardly surprising among people who believe, as do the Montagnais-Naskapi, that the beaver, for example, 'embodies extraordinarily high spiritual endowments. It can transform itself into other animal forms, that of geese and other birds being specifically mentioned. The beaver can disappear by penetrating the ground, by rising aloft into the air, or by diving into the depths of lake or stream and remaining any length of time desired. In short, "he can escape or hide himself if he wishes to, so that he can never be taken"' – except with his 'amiable consent.'[11]

Animals who voluntarily sacrifice themselves to the needy hunter are regarded by Mistassini Cree, at least, as 'friends': 'The relationship of hunters to the animals may sometimes be likened to having friends among those animals which inhabit the particular region.' (One might suggest that friendship or its opposite – hostility – has always characterized the human-animal relationship throughout the Canadian subarctic. Mutual insensibility must have been rare or nonexistent.) Indeed, this conviction formed the basis of Eastern Cree–Montagnais concepts of land tenure. Game animals, Julius Lips was repeatedly told, 'were the true owners of the hunting-grounds.'[12]

Descendants of these people detailed a similar belief to Adrian Tanner: within the hunting group ownership of the territory derived from the fauna, who had a cordial relationship with the hunting-group leader. 'The most common use of this idea of friendship between a hunter and an animal,' Tanner found, 'is in stories about men who have the reputation of having killed a large number of animals of a particular species. Such a man is said to have a particular member of that species as a "friend." Sometimes this animal, which the man must never kill, is spoken of as being the man's "pet." Generally, the man who has such a reputation is already past the age of peak hunting abilities, so that while his reputation rests on past kills, the significance of his ability is that he is believed to be able to help the younger men of his group make kills of that particular species.' There was always an anxious moment right after the death of such a hunting leader, when it was feared his friends would follow him to the land of the dead – a clear sign that the remaining members of the species would elude future capture by the man's survivors. 'In such a case where an animal friend does stay in the group's area it is often said to be because someone else in the group has become a friend of that species.'[13]

Animal persons, as friends, were to be treated courteously. 'A central attitude in the conduct of hunting is that game animals are persons and that they must be respected.'[14] This meant they were usually addressed by some quaint title of endearment rather than by their common name; the hunter refrained from disclosing to associates his intention to pursue a particular animal species; inwardly ecstatic relatives and friends were subdued as they greeted the returning hunter, since animal shades took a dim view of noisy celebration;[15] and the carcass was disposed of according to a procedure thought pleasing to the slain beast's spirit.

It was once common throughout the subarctic to consume or otherwise use the entire carcass of at least certain economically and mythologically prominent species. Left-overs from the so-called eat-all feast were either burned or, more recently among the Mistassini Cree at least, wrapped up and hidden from the gaze of the animal shade. The concealed flesh would be eaten at some future time. As for the inedible remains, these were either made into useful or aesthetic objects, or decorated and prominently displayed – large-animal skulls are and were often placed in a tree, so as to enjoy the view. Moreover, certain bones of most, if not all, large game species are habitually returned to their natural element (terrestrial or aquatic) where eventually they will be re-clothed in flesh (at the whim of the 'game boss') in order to be hunted, once more, by the Indian.[16] Hunting is thus a cycle for the game species involved, a cycle whose chief ethical principle is *courtesy* – mutual courtesy – which is a mutual obligation.

Clearly, then, animals join the physical and spiritual realms in several contexts. 'The vision quest symbolically transforms the child's meat into spirit, and the hunt transforms the animal's spirit into meat,' observed

Robin Ridington.[17] The co-operation of animal persons is the essential catalyst in both transformation equations.

Continuing to think in structural terms, and limiting our attention strictly to the hunt, we might in sum characterize it as a spiritual/physical transaction mediated by game persons. There are included within this umbrella transaction several minor relationships, expressed as bipolar opposites, which likewise take their cue from animals. The hunt occurs in the bush, the 'outside,' spiritually 'clean' realm, which terms bespeak the place of animal spirits. Men, in general, are the only sex allowed to penetrate this outside space. At the other extreme, women function in the campsite, the 'inside,' spiritually 'soiled' realm – the place of animal carcasses.[18]

It is curious that certain Ojibwa appear to equate women with game animals. Irving Hallowell noted that 'the verb applied to the hunting of animals is commonly used by men when speaking of the pursuit of a girl. And this association between animal and woman appears in one of the dreams I collected. A hunter dreamed of a beautiful girl approaching him. Waking up, he interpreted this dream as meaning that an animal had been caught in one of his deadfalls. He went to the trap and, sure enough, he found a female fisher.' Moreover, there is an apparent parallel between a man's prerogatives with a woman and those he enjoys with game animals. Hallowell goes on to tell of an incident wherein a woman, thought to have been made ill through the sorcery of a rebuffed suitor, retaliated by making the man more ill than she. 'Her life had been threatened but she did not kill him, although she had the power to do so. This outcome is significant when considered in relation to the dominant role of men in this culture. What seems to be implied is the assumption that men have potential sexual *rights* over women that must always be respected.'[19] This relationship seems roughly analogous to that of the male hunter with the game: a man may harvest animals so long as he refrains from abusing them. The hunter who violates this principle is liable to be struck down by disease – disease originating with offended game spirits. Indeed, the animal theory of disease etiology is conspicuous throughout the subarctic. And here one discerns yet another set of binary contrasts brokered by game spirits: health and disease. Health results from a proper relationship with game; disease follows from a perverted one.[20] Likewise, an abundance of food (i.e. '"forest food," tantamount in meaning to "pure food" ')[21] derives from an amicable relationship with game, while famine is the result of disharmony between animals and man.

Wild game flesh is loaded with symbolic significance: it is a palpable sign of animal friendship; it represents physical nourishment; and it is medicine (prophylactic), since animal flesh is but an altered form of plant forage and 'the vegetable kingdom ... [is] the original source of medicine agency.'[22] Animal flesh may also serve as a sexual metaphor. Tanner has noticed that bear and beaver carcasses are laid out in the lodge along a sexual axis: the head and foreparts face the male half of the structure, the hind parts the female half. This positioning of the animal along a gender axis is often carried over into consumption ritual, by which women are restricted to eating the hind limbs and men the forelimbs. 'Eating both establishes the separate nature of men and women, and also makes possible the relationship between the two. It is the animal, which is a combination of sexual elements, which makes the establishment of sexual relations and reproduction possible.' Elsewhere Tanner declares: 'Bringing home an animal means for the hunter not only the end of the hunting cycle, but the start of a domestic one ... This reunion [of the hunter with his family] has a distinctly sexual aspect, and ... the animal itself becomes a symbolic mediator in the starting, or re-starting, of this sexual relationship.'[23]

One could explore further symbolic relationships between animals and humans. If it is true, as I believe, that animals are the linchpin holding together the paired contrasts of traditional subarctic Indian life, then it follows that the human-animal relationship must encompass far more than just the subsistence economy. Hunting, writ large, lends meaning and inspiration to life; as a way of living it gives participants their sense of identity. A proper, cordial relationship with animals becomes vital in maintaining that sense of identity – that sense of how the world functions and how humans are to conduct themselves within this larger sphere of existence. Animals instruct human beings, at least males, in the mysteries of life; by giving heed to animals and their ways – by making themselves receptive to their counsel – hunters learn how they must behave.[24] No wonder game is typically treated with exquisite respect.

The foregoing information has been gleaned from twentieth-century ethnographic sources which describe modern Indians living more or less traditionally. We must leave to the ethnohistorian the task of determining just where matters stood between human and animal persons back through the centuries of recorded time. In particular, historians should re-evaluate what the Canadian fur trade meant for the Indians involved. If animals were as vital to the Indian sense of identity and purpose during the catastrophic years of the trade, when furbearers and other game were hunted rapaciously, how did native hunters and trappers rationalize their destructive behavior? What *was* the human-animal relationship during the height of fur trade involvement?

Why is there a tendency in this century to treat animals, once more it seems, with deference? Has there been a re-emergence of an aboriginal hunting ethic – a revival of the traditionally courteous relationship between the hunter and hunted? My reading of the evidence leads me to believe there has indeed been such a revival. I have elsewhere made the case that the hunting ethic witnessed by twentieth-century ethnographers is essentially aboriginal, although it was suspended for much of the fur trade era, for reasons which cannot be explored here.[25] Why Indians overhunted game for purposes of trade is one obvious question to be considered, given the evidence for a cordial relationship between humans and animals in this century and the suspicion (at least) that this mutually courteous arrangement has prehistoric origins.

A more fundamental yet related question is, What did the European intrusion do to the structure of the Indian world? How was the balance of life's contrasting elements affected? Thinking in today's terms and bearing in mind that animals occupy a strategic position in binding together the basic contrasts of life, what have been the social and cultural ramifications of a decline in hunting as a way of life? As traditional hunting pursuits become increasingly impracticable and other life-styles take over, what is happening to these peoples' sense of identity and purpose? It strikes me that much that is distinctive about the traditional subarctic Indian way of life hinges, as it always has, on the peculiar relationship with game animals. To undermine that rapport, either deliberately (say, by government action) or inadvertently (through subtle pressures of assimilation), is to erode a people's confidence in who they are. They were originally kinsmen to animals; that many individuals remain so even today is a powerful and, to the chauvinistic Western world, rather deflating lesson in cultural resilience.

REFERENCES

1 De Laguna 'The Atna of the Copper River, Alaska: The World of Men and Animals' 19; Sullivan *The Ten'a Food Quest* 97; VanStone *Athapaskan Adaptations: Hunters and Fishermen of the Subarctic Forests* 61; Speck *Naskapi: The Savage Hunters of the Labrador Peninsula* 76

2 Speck *Naskapi* 55

3 See, for example, Hallowell 'Ojibwa World View and Disease' 271–2.

4 De Laguna 'Atna' 19

5 Wax and Wax 'The Magical World View' 181; Jenness *The Ojibwa Indians of Parry Island: Their Social and Religious Life* 18–20; Lips 'Notes on Montagnais-

Naskapi Economy' 6; Skinner 'Notes on the Eastern Cree and Northern Saulteaux' 73, 76; Landes *Ojibwa Religion and the Midewiwin* 27

6 Dewdney *The Sacred Scrolls of the Southern Ojibway* 37; de Laguna 'Atna' 22, 26

7 Dewdney *Sacred Scrolls* 37

8 Sullivan *Ten'a Food Quest* 75, 79, 121; Smith *Inkonze: Magico-Religious Beliefs of Contact – Traditional Chipewyan Trading at Fort Resolution, NWT, Canada* 12, 20

9 Hallowell *Culture and Experience* 361; Hallowell 'Ojibwa Ontology, Behavior, and World View' 45–7; Hallowell 'Ojibwa World View' 273–4, 283; Speck *Naskapi* 48, 41, 22–3

10 Speck *Naskapi* 20, 139

11 Ibid 112–13

12 Tanner 'Bringing Home Animals: Religious Ideology and Mode of Production of the Mistassini Cree Hunters' 246, 265–6, 272, 343; Lips 'Notes' 5–6; de Laguna 'Atna' 18; Smith *Inkonze* 12; VanStone *Athapaskan Adaptations* 59; Martin *Keepers of the Game: Indian-Animal Relationships and the Fur Trade*

13 Tanner 'Bringing Home Animals' 110, 192, 248, 250, 316, 335–8, 370

14 Ibid 230–1

15 de Laguna 'Atna' 20–1; Sullivan *Ten'a Food Quest* 123; Tanner 'Bringing Home Animals' 154, 275–6, 319

16 Speck *Naskapi* 91–3, 112, 122–3; Tanner 'Bringing Home Animals' 118–19, 230–1, 295–7, 306–7, 313–14, 324–5; Jenness *Ojibwa Indians* 23–5

17 Ridington 'Beaver Dreaming and Singing' 124–5

18 Landes *Ojibwa Religion* 7; Ridington 'Beaver Dreaming' 120–1; Tanner 'Bringing Home Animals' 20, 110–11, 118–19, 142, 187, 204, 295, 307–8

19 Hallowell *Culture and Experience* 295–6, 299; Bogoras 'Ideas of Space and Time in the Conception of Primitive Religion' 208–9

20 Ritzenthaler 'Chippewa Preoccupation with Health: Change in a Traditional Attitude Resulting from Modern Health Problems' 243; Hallowell *Culture and Experience* 268; Hallowell 'Ojibwa World View' 286; de Laguna 'Atna' 23–4; Smith *Inkonze* 12

21 Speck *Naskapi* 80; Tanner 'Bringing Home Animals' 39

22 Speck *Naskapi* 80–1

23 Tanner 'Bringing Home Animals' 125–6, 287–8, 319, 320–1, 324–5; Sullivan *Ten'a Food Quest* 87–8.

24 Ridington 'Beaver Dreaming' 122–4

25 For a fuller discussion see Martin *Keepers*.

PART III ✧ SOCIAL HISTORY

The Iroquois and the Fur Trade in Western Canada

TRUDY NICKS

The historiography of native participation in the fur trade in western Canada is dominated by accounts of the movements of major Indian tribal groups. This study focuses on a phenomenon of smaller scale – the participation of Iroquois in the Western Canadian trade. Of the eastern Indians who opted to go to the northwest in the late eighteenth century in order to maintain direct ties to a fur trade economy the Iroquois are most consistently and clearly identified in historic documents, and therefore the most useful group to study. This paper covers the period from 1794, the date Iroquois are first recorded in the West, to the end of competition between major fur companies in 1821. Four main questions are considered. What was the background of the Iroquois? How many Iroquois moved west? What roles did they play in the western fur trade? What relationships developed between Iroquois and local native groups?

The paper is based on research into the historical and demographic development of an Alberta population which was founded by immigrant Iroquois and local natives at the beginning of the nineteenth century, and therefore largely excludes consideration of the Iroquois who crossed the mountains to the Columbia and New Caledonia.

References to Iroquois in the West are widely scattered through fur trade documents and are usually limited to brief comments. The noteworthy exception is the extensive discussion of Iroquois in David Thompson's *Narrative*.[1] Unfortunately, his account has proven to be highly unreliable. Firsthand accounts, including his own daily journals, contemporaneous with many of the events he describes, show the *Narrative* to be inaccurate on several points and unverifiable on many others. In general, his account, written more than half a century after the fact, is considerably embellished and reflects a bias against the Iroquois.[2]

The Iroquois who moved west were in no way new to the business of trading furs. Iroquoian peoples were early associated with the fur trade in the east. Competition for access to fur-rich territories has been cited as a primary cause of warfare among Iroquoian tribes in the early period after contact.[3] The Iroquois converts to Christianity who settled near Montreal in the seventeenth century retained fur hunting as a preferred economic pursuit.[4] During the French regime in Canada the Jesuit mission of Caughnawaga, or Sault Saint-Louis, as it was then called, became the headquarters for an illegal trade which saw Canadian furs going south to Albany in exchange for British trade goods which the Indians preferred to French items.[5]

In the last decade of the eighteenth century, Iroquois from the Canadian villages of Caughnawaga, its offshoot St Regis, and the mission at the Lake of Two Mountains became participants in the fur trade in quarters far distant from their traditional, but largely depleted, hunting grounds. The 'Répertoire des engagements pour l'ouest' in the Archives judiciaires de Montréal indicates that between 1790 and 1815 approximately 350 men were hired from these three missions by Montreal fur companies or their agents. Over eighty per cent of these contracts were with the North West Company, and the majority of these were for Temiscaming and/or Abitibi, Fort Moose, Lac la Pluie, and the northwest.[6]

Documentary evidence for the number of Iroquois who moved to the West is ambiguous and probably incomplete. It is, however, possible to gain an impression of the magnitude of the Iroquois presence in the West and suggest some potential sources of confusion in the historical records.

The first Iroquois recorded in the northwest arrived near Sturgeon Post on the North Saskatchewan River in 1794 in the employ of David Grant, a former member of the North West Company.[7] Grant's venture failed in its second year, in part because the North West Company lured away several of his men, three of whom were Iroquois.

Alexander Mackenzie, in his *Journal of a Voyage to the Pacific Ocean*, refers to a 'small colony' of Iroquois from a 'Romish' missionary village near Montreal emigrating to the 'Saskatchiwine' river in 1799. They came, he wrote, to escape the 'improvements of civilization' in the east and to follow the mode of life of their forefathers.[8]

The largest single incursion of Iroquois is reported by William Tomison of the Hudson's Bay Company. In the summer of 1801, according to him, more than 300 'Eroquees' or Mohawk Indians were brought into the Saskatchewan district on three-year contracts by the North West and xy companies. These Mohawks, along with the 'many Bungee Tawau Mischelemacana (and) Eroquee Indians' who had followed the Canadians westward in previous years, were blamed by Tomison for stripping the district of its furs, so that by 1802 the fur returns of the Hudson's Bay Company were much reduced.[9] It seems certain that this large influx in 1801 is the same event which David Thompson remembered in his *Narrative*, and which Tyrrell, his first editor, errs in attributing to 1798. Specifically, Thompson reported that in one season a large number of Iroquois, Nipissings, and Algonkians came into the northwest. The number of Iroquois involved, depending on how one interprets Thompson's writing, may have been in excess of 250.[10] According to his journal entries, Thompson played a role in laying the groundwork for their acceptance by local Indians. In November of 1800 he visited two Peigan camps near the junction of the Highwood and Bow rivers and proposed to them a plan to bring Iroquois and Saulteaux from the east to hunt fur in the southern foothills area frequented by the Peigan.[11]

Between 1797 and 1803 the 'Répertoire' indicates 41 Iroquois were hired for the northwest by the North West Company and four were hired by the xy Company. In 1802 David Thompson met some of the xy Company employees on the Peace River.[12]

It is clear from available documents that the greatest concentration of Iroquois manpower in the West was from 1800 to 1804, the period during which the North West Company was following a policy of expansion in order to force its Montreal rival, the xy Company, to over-extend its resources in goods and manpower. The amalgamation of these companies in 1804 meant fewer posts and less manpower were needed, and new recruitment from the eastern villages virtually ceased. Indeed, many employees were released, including, no doubt, many of the Iroquois. Some of those released from contracts as voyageurs remained in the West to hunt on their own and possibly pick up seasonal contracts to hunt furs for the North West Company. In 1804–5 at least sixteen such contracts were signed between Simon Fraser and Iroquois at Fort Vermilion on the Peace River.[13]

When the Hudson's Bay Company moved into Athabasca in 1815 it had acquired a Canadian working force, a move which Colin Robertson had recommended as early as 1810.[14] A number of these servants were Iroquois.[15] Some of the Iroquois hired by the Hudson's Bay Company were former North West Company employees who had remained inland to hunt on their own; others were apparently hired at Montreal. Unfortunately, none of the Hudson's Bay Company contracts from these years appear to have been included in the 'Répertoire' and those of the North West Company also appear to be incomplete. In the absence of contracts between Iroquois and either the Hudson's Bay or North West companies, it is difficult to estimate the numbers of Iroquois coming to the northwest from 1815 to 1821. The number certainly seems to have been well below the figures quoted by Tomison at the beginning of the century.[16]

By 1810 the concentration of Iroquois east of the Rockies had moved from the Saskatchewan to the Athabasca and Peace River regions. In particular, Iroquois were trapping along the eastern slopes of the Rocky Mountains, along the Smoky River to its junction with the Peace, and in the area surrounding Lesser Slave Lake (but especially to the north and east). Probably members of these groups had begun spending summers across the mountains in New Caledonia before 1818.[17] The actual number of Iroquois in these districts cannot be ascertained with accuracy from existing documents, but the evidence indicates they were associated with several bands of free trappers, consisting on average of five to eight males related by blood or marriage, with their wives and families.[18]

The foregoing accounting of the numbers of Iroquois moving to the West in the period 1794–1821 is not comprehensive for two main reasons. First, records of contracts between Iroquois and fur companies are incomplete. Although the 'Répertoire' covers the entire period considered, it lists far fewer Iroquois engagés than accounts left by observers in the area suggest were present, particularly before 1802. Ouellet has suggested for an earlier period, 1760–90, that fur companies made private contracts with engagés in addition to those registered with legal authorities.[19] The same situation may well have prevailed during the period now being considered.

Secondly, there is also the possibility of Iroquois moving west on their own. The Mackenzie reference is ambiguous. It appears to suggest independent migration; however Mackenzie was probably aware of any Iroquois engagés heading west, as he appears as the representative for MacTavish, Frobisher & Co. on at least one contract for the northwest made with an individual from the Lake of Two Mountains in 1797.[20]

The discrepancy between the 'Répertoire' and the Tomison and Thompson accounts may also be due to Iroquois moving west without contracts. Tomison's reference to eastern natives following the Canadians westward before 1801 suggests Indians moving on their own initiative.[21] When David Thompson talked to the Peigan in 1800, he implied that the North West Company was doing a favor for the Iroquois and Saulteaux, who had asked the company to help them find new hunting grounds, their own country now being 'so very poor.'[22] The company's assistance may have involved some public relations work in the West, and help with transportation, but stopped short of actual contracts. While William

Tomison was on the Saskatchewan in 1801–2 and therefore in a good position to know something of the numbers who came inland in 1801, he was with the Hudson's Bay Company and may have been deliberately misled into believing they were under contract.

Attempts to assess numbers of Iroquois in the northwest at any one time are subject to even more confusion. Iroquois came for various lengths of time under contract and an indeterminable number of these stayed on after their contracts expired. Some of the latter occasionally signed short-term contracts in the northwest which might or might not lead to their return to Montreal.

The variety of roles fulfilled by Iroquois in the western fur trade can be defined, even if the numbers involved in each case are uncertain. The majority were voyageurs and fur hunters, but some also served as interpreters, guides, and provision hunters. The Iroquois fulfilling these roles might be under contract or free.

Those engaged as voyageurs by the North West Company signed a standard contract – most for the rank of milieu, a few as devant or gouvernail. Their skill in handling canoes seems to have earned them their greatest reputation. For example, Colin Robertson wrote in 1819: 'I have frequently heard the Canadian and Irroquois voyagers disputed as regards their merits, perhaps the former may be more hardy or undergo more fatigue, but in either a rapid or traverse, give me the latter, from their calmness and prescence of mind which never forsakes them in the greatest danger.'[23]

The Montreal contracts for the northwest were for terms of one to three years. Wages for milieu in 1797 were 500 livres; between 1800 and 1803 they ranged from 600 to 1000 livres, but most contracts were for 700 or 900 livres. The sample of original contracts consulted included only one contract for a gouvernail; his wages in 1803 were 1000 livres. Iroquois voyageurs were given 'double equipment.'[24]

Among the Montreal contracts was one with an Iroquois hired to go to the northwest as an interpreter.[25] The value of his linguistic skills to the North West Company is reflected in his high wages – 1200 livres for the first year and 1400 livres for the second – and in the fact that he was able to re-negotiate his contract before leaving Montreal. His first contract, signed in February 1800, was superseded in April of the same year. The new contract retained all wages and equipment granted him in the first, but in addition exempted him from carrying on portages and provided him with a new coat for each year of his contract.

In addition to contracts signed at Montreal, Iroquois also signed a variety of agreements with the North West Company at their inland establishments.[26] One type of agreement assigned an Iroquois to the rank of milieu, devant, or gouvernail while travelling between the Grand Portage or Lac la Pluie and Athabasca, but set him free in winter to hunt fur within the district to which he was assigned. Examples of these agreements were signed on the Peace River and at Grand Portage in 1804.[27] Terms of one or two years were specified although one contract appears to be open regarding the length of time it would be in effect. Wages were 400 or 500 livres per year. On some contracts equipment provided was specified and included a three-point blanket, a shirt, a pair of trousers or a pair of mittens, a handkerchief, tobacco, and sometimes knives or a bracelet. Other contracts simply specified 'double ordinaire' equipment.

Yet another category of North West Company agreements signed at Fort Vermilion in 1804 and 1805 was for hunting fur only.[28] The term of these contracts was one year, or, in several cases, one hunting season. A hunter received no wages, but the rates to be paid for beaver, both in and out of season, and otter pelts were stipulated. Special prices for goods and traps were sometimes quoted. Where wages were involved, compliance with the terms of a contract could be enforced by threat of loss of wages. On the hunting contracts the penalty for trading with opponents of the North West Company was ten beaver skins for each skin given or traded 'to be lawfully taken off' the offender's property. Similar arrangements with fur hunters may well have been made both before and after 1804–5. An 1802 McTavish, Frobisher & Co. document cited by Davidson refers to North West Company contracts with Canadian and Iroquois hunters who ranged free over the country 'wherever they find it convenient to hunt.'[29] There are also references by Hudson's Bay Company traders in the 1810s to the North West Company having a task force of fur hunters available to them.

The inland contracts contain the interesting stipulation that an Iroquois was not finally free until his return to Montreal. The hunting contracts contain no provisions for travel in the company's canoes, however, and the other contracts would take the engagé only as far as Lac la Pluie or Grand Portage. Perhaps this was an attempt to prevent the Iroquois from joining rival companies in the northwest. Should an Iroquois wish to make the return trip to Montreal he would probably have had to sign a contract to work for the company as a voyageur.

It was as fur hunters that the Iroquois provided the North West Company with an important competitive edge over the Hudson's Bay Company until about 1820. As an imported labour force of professional hunters the Iroquois applied themselves more single-mindedly to the business of trapping furs than any of the resident native groups on whom the Hudson's Bay Company relied for furs. Their use of steel traps likewise gave them a technological advantage over local native groups.

The value of these hunters to the North West Company is clear from Hudson's Bay Company records. In 1815 James Bird, master at Fort Edmonton, reported that the North West Company was able to 'procure several more Beaver and musquash than we can because they have sixteen freemen, Canadians [&(?)] Iroquois, Men partly worn out in their service whom they have, without making them quite free, permitted to go and Kill furs on their own account, and these people apply themselves to Killing Beaver with an application unknown to the Indians.'

In 1819 Francois Heron indicated in the Edmonton district report that the North West Company was obtaining nearly two-fifths of its fur returns 'from the Canadian and Iroqoi trappers they retain in their service, These trappers are of great service to the North West Company, and give them a great advantage over us, for wherever there are Beaver to be found, there they immediately dispatch their trappers to hunt them, who have now nearly destroyed all the Beaver in this quarter.'[30]

Overtrapping of fur resources was, of course, the other side of the coin. William Tomison's earlier complaint against eastern Indians who had depleted the Saskatchewan district of furs by 1802 has already been cited. In 1814, W.F. Wentzel, a North West Company bourgeois, wrote to Roderick Mackenzie that the Athabasca district was 'dwindling down to nothing,' and blamed the Iroquois for having ruined the country's beaver supply.[31]

Iroquois under contract to the Hudson's Bay Company in the Athabasca district after 1815 served as voyageurs and were also sent out on their own to make fur hunts in the winter months between trips to and from the east.[32]

Some Iroquois who remained in the West became freemen.[33] Technically, a freeman had completed his contract, or had been discharged by a company, and remained in the West to trade and hunt on his own account. In reality, for at least another ten years after 1804, nearly all of the Iroquois freemen were closely tied to the North West Company, probably through a combination of custom, as well as debts and gifts received from the company. George Simpson attributes the Hudson's Bay Company's early difficulties in obtaining a significant proportion of the trade of the Athabasca district to the fear local natives and freemen had of oppression by the North West Company should the Hudson's Bay venture fail. When free Iroquois did transfer their allegiances to the Hudson's Bay Company, usually leaving a sizable debt in skins and/or currency, the North West Company listed them as 'deserted' in their account book. The Hudson's Bay Company post master at St Mary's fort on Peace River complained that the North West Company had tried to prevent him from hiring two Iroquois who had been free for ten years. The North West Company argued that the Iroquois could not enter new agreements until after their return to Montreal. In one of these cases there was also an outstanding debt of one hundred dollars owed to the North West Company.[34]

The nomadic life-style of the Iroquois freemen, resulting from their constant search for food and furs, brought them into contact with many local native groups and also gave them a broader knowledge of the countryside than most of the traders possessed. Their experience made them valuable as guides and interpreters, especially where fur companies were expanding into new territories. Iroquois had been involved in the North West Company's move into the Columbia district following the union with the XY Company. A map prepared for David Thompson by Jean Findley included routes through the mountains pioneered by five Iroquois in 1806.[35] Iroquois freemen, some of whom had entered new contracts, provided contacts with local natives for the Hudson's Bay Company when it wished to move into New Caledonia in 1820–1.[36] George Simpson deemed their services so essential to this venture that, in February of 1821, he instructed Duncan Finlayson, master at St Mary's fort on Peace River that 'The Iroquois must be engaged without delay. I shall not limit you to terms, we absolutely need their services and you will therefore make the best bargain you can.'[37] It is clear from Simpson's Athabasca journal and report that the Iroquois freemen had also become an important source of provisions for the Hudson's Bay Company by 1820.[38]

The fur trade facilitated exchanges not only between European and Indian cultures, but also between different Indian tribes, which, prior to the fur trade, were widely separated by geography and cultural traditions. The Iroquois came from a sedentary, partly agricultural society and met nomadic hunters, gatherers, and trappers of the forests in the northwest. But these differences appear to have been relatively unimportant in determining the results of contact between Iroquois and western groups including Cree, Sekani, Beaver, Carrier, and some of the plains tribes. The important factor was that both sides were participants in a fur trade economy. This shared economic sphere provided the main avenue by which the Iroquois could enter into local native groups, and it also provided the basis for hostility between them. The following discussion outlines the major features of contact between Iroquois and northwestern native groups in the early nineteenth century.

The first impression gained from the documents is that the Iroquois were generally disliked by the natives in the West. Examples of hostility can be found between Iroquois and both plains and northern forest Indians. In 1802 Peter Fidler described an incident in which fourteen Iroquois and two Canadians were killed by the Gros Ventre near Chesterfield House at the junction of the Red Deer and South Saskatchewan rivers. This seems certainly to be the same event David Thompson described, with much elaboration, in his *Narrative*. The murder of the Iroquois, however, stemmed not from provocation on their part, as Thompson indicated, but from the frustration felt by the Gros Ventre after a year-long series of tragedies had beset them.[39] In the previous year, warfare with the Stonies and Crees had claimed 76 Gros Ventre lives, another 100 young people had succumbed to smallpox, and more died due to the severity of the winter of 1801–2. In addition, nearly 300 of their horses had been lost through snowstorms in the spring of 1801, or through theft by their enemies.

The Gros Ventre were in a mood to avenge themselves, and the Iroquois coming into Chesterfield House in the spring of 1802 proved a convenient target. Fidler's journal entries suggest the Gros Ventre may not even have known who the Iroquois were – they explained to Fidler that they had determined to kill them because 'they well knew from their hair and heads that they was not Europeans.'[40]

Clashes with Indians of the northern forests can be attributed directly to competition for fur hunting territories. The success of Iroquois freemen as fur hunters has already been cited. Their trapping methods resulted in rapid depletion of the stock of fur bearing animals in a region, and the search for new sources of fur occasionally brought them into conflict with others, as they encroached on territories frequented by local Indians. Daniel Harmon attributed the murder of an Iroquois and his family at the hands of Carrier Indians in New Caledonia in 1818 to the fact that Iroquois freemen had been encroaching on Carrier territory for several years. Local natives, probably Beaver Indians, in the Peace River district in 1822 made a firm stand against Hudson's Bay Company plans to send Iroquois to the Smoky River.[41]

These examples of hostility, however, represent relatively isolated incidents. Of the plains Indians, the Iroquois seem only to have run into difficulty with the Gros Ventre, a tribe with a history of hostility toward outsiders which also included burning, looting, and murder at Manchester House in 1793 and South Branch House in 1794. Although Beaver and Carrier Indians on occasion protested the presence of Iroquois freemen, there was not a consistent resistance which could keep Iroquois out of an area for more than a season or two. The murder in New Caledonia, for example, did not have the desired effect of keeping Iroquois away from the area. They were so well established, in fact, that the Hudson's Bay Company looked to them for assistance in gaining a foothold in the region in 1820.

There were few hostile encounters between Iroquois and western Indians because the Iroquois most often hunted in thinly populated areas or those not frequented by local Indians. This seems to have been the case for the eastern slopes area north of the Athabasca River and the area north of Lesser Slave Lake.

Iroquois who stayed on in the West as freemen intermarried with local native groups and in large measure adopted their life-style. Intermarriage between Iroquois males and local native women probably met few obstacles. Marriages outside the band or outside the tribe are common in numerically small hunting and gathering or hunting and trapping populations. The Iroquois routinely adopted into the tribe outsiders who thus became eligible marriage partners.

Iroquois freemen and their families followed a life-style similar in large measure to that of 'indigenous' native hunters and trappers. There were times when the traders saw the freemen becoming too similar to local Indians for their liking. William Connelly, in charge at Lesser Slave Lake for the 1822–3 season complained: 'Many of them are in the habit of passing whole winters along the Lakes where fish can be caught [and] as long as they have any thing to eat, trouble themselves but little about paying their Debts.'[42] In this the freemen and their families were wisely adapting to the aboriginal survival pattern, as trapping furs often meant a reduction in the time spent hunting for food, or working in areas poor in food resources. Starvation was a more than remote possibility for those who concentrated too heavily on fur trapping.

The freemen and their families did not, however, become submerged in the local native populations. From the daily journals of the traders, both before and after union in 1821, it is clear that freemen associated almost exclusively with other freemen, and with their families they formed and perpetuated their own bands.[43] These bands were distinguished from those made up of local Indians by greater concentration on fur trapping, and in consequence, greater wealth. The wealth was derived not only from the barter of furs, but, especially before 1821, through gifts, preferential prices, and easy credit made available by traders competing for their hunts. In 1819–20 the Hudson's Bay Company was charging freemen half the price Indians were required to pay for items such as tobacco and spirits. In addition, the company was bringing in several articles especially for trade with freemen: fine cloth, fine capots, trousers, stockings, handkerchiefs, and hats.[44]

After the union of the North West and Hudson's Bay companies in 1821 attempts were made to discontinue preferential treatment. At Lesser Slave Post in October of 1821, postmaster Connelly received his freemen 'rather Coolly ... presenting them with nothing more than each a foot of Tobacco and a dram ... (so that they would) feel at once that times have altered.'[45] The minutes of council for the northern department of Rupert's Land in 1825 directed that freemen, halfbreed, or Iroquois trappers paying for their supplies with hunts should be treated on the same footing as Indians.[46]

The change in company policy no doubt removed important incentives to hunt fur. This fact, along with the very real problems of periodic starvation, would have led the Iroquois freemen and other fur hunters to spend more time obtaining food, causing Connelly to complain. The policy change apparently did not alter the freemen's concept of themselves as a separate group. A sense of identity appears to have been maintained among descendants of the original unions between eastern men and local women, which was reinforced by patterns of intermarriage and co-residence within and between freemen bands. It was not a result of continuous addition of easterners to the group. In the case of Iroquois, at least, very few new recruits were hired in the east after 1821, and most of these returned to Canada after one or a few contracts.[47]

Very little of eastern Iroquoian culture that might serve both to link and distinguish Iroquois and their descendants in the West appears to have been carried over. The necessity of hiring an Iroquois interpreter at Montreal suggests that many Iroquois voyageurs initially spoke only their mother tongue. Those who remained in the West for any length of time learned local languages, with Cree the most likely language of common use.[48] The only major cultural difference carried over from their eastern background appears to have been their Roman Catholic religion.[49] Records at Lac Ste Anne, the first mission in the Alberta area, established in 1842, indicate that the Iroquois and their descendants adhered at least to the basic sacraments. Syncretism with local native beliefs also occurred, especially among descendants retaining a hunting and trapping life-style.

The establishment of the Lac Ste Anne mission west of Edmonton drew many Iroquois descendants back to the Saskatchewan River district, particularly from the eastern slopes area. Some settled permanently in the Lac Ste Anne region, eventually signing an adhesion to Treaty 6 in September 1878 and settling on the Michel Reserve near St Albert, Alberta. This band enfranchised in 1958 and former members have now largely entered the mainstream of Canadian culture.

Some descendants stayed in refuge areas such as the eastern slopes of the Rocky Mountains and the Peace River region of British Columbia, where, like the Iroquois described by Mackenzie in 1799, they might escape the 'improvements of civilization' to the east and follow the mode of life of their forefathers. Present industrial development is, however, rapidly encroaching on this option.

During the period of competition in the western fur trade, Iroquois from Canadian mission villages served as an important source of manpower, particularly for Montreal-based fur companies, but also for the Hudson's Bay Company. As voyageurs their role in the western fur trade was not different from that of the Canadian engagés or Hudson's Bay Company servants. As independent immigrants and freemen their experiences in the West no doubt parallel those of other Indians who left their eastern homelands to maintain a particular life-style among alien groups. The visibility of Iroquois in the historic record has particular advantages for the study of the development of descendant native populations in the West. In addition to the fur trade documentation, Iroquois and their descendants are identifiable in the records of the treaty and half-breed commissions of the late nineteenth century and church records from the last half of the nineteenth century into the twentieth century. Such documentation makes feasible studies of demographic development for native populations in the era of the fur trade and early settlement. The major role of Iroquois in the historiography of the Canadian West may therefore become that of a model of native population development for the period after initial contact.

This research was assisted by a grant-in-aid from the Boreal Institute for Northern Studies at the University of Alberta. The Hudson's Bay Company Archives was a major source of information for this paper.

NOTES AND REFERENCES

1 Glover ed *David Thompson's Narrative 1784–1812* 229–33
2 Problems with the Thompson *Narrative* will be dealt with at appropriate places in the text. The uncritical use of Thompson's descriptions of Iroquois and other documentary sources detracts from Frisch's 'Some Ethnological and Ethnohistoric Notes on the Iroquois in Alberta' 51–64.
3 Trelease 'The Iroquois and the Western Fur Trade: A Problem in Interpretation' 32–51
4 This preference is cited in Devine *Historic Caughnawaga*; see for example 137, 206, 212.
5 Lunn 'The Illegal Fur Trade out of New France 1713–60' 61–76
6 'Répertoire des engagements pour l'ouest conservés dans les archives judiciaires de Montreal' *Rapport de l'archiviste de la Province de Québec* (1942–43) 261–397; (1943–44) 335–444; (1944–45) 307–401; (1945–46) 225–340. Spelling variations make identification of repeat contracts uncertain, therefore the exact number of individuals represented is difficult to ascertain. Next to the North West Company, the Michilimakinac Company hired the largest number of men from these villages and sent them to Michilimackinac. The remaining men listed in the 'Répertoire' were hired by several companies for a variety of localities.

     In addition to the published lists, original contracts with Iroquois for the northwest and examples of contracts for other areas were obtained from ANQM. The author wishes to thank Mr Yves Puzo of the department of romance languages, University of Alberta, for assistance in the translation of these contracts.
7 Morton ed *The Journal of Duncan McGillivray of the North West Company at Fort George on the Saskatchewan, 1794–5* li, 49
8 Lamb ed *The Journals and Letters of Sir Alexander Mackenzie* 411. Iroquois, probably attached to the North West Company, visited the Hudson's Bay Company posts of Buckingham House on the North Saskatchewan river in 1797 and Greenwich House on Green Lake in March of 1800 (HBCA B 49/a/27b, B 24/a/4, B 104/a/1, respectively).
9 Johnson ed *Saskatchewan Journals and Correspondence Edmonton House 1795–1800. Chesterfield House 1800–1802* xci, xcii
10 Glover ed *Narrative* 229–31. There are several reasons for assuming this to be the same event reported by Tomison in 1801. The number of Indians involved is of the same order of magnitude. More importantly, however, other documents of the times including Thompson's own journals for 1798, the year

in which he made his visits to the Mandan villages, do not mention such an event. If the 1798 date for the *Narrative* account were accepted, by 1800 the Peigan would already have met a party of Iroquois on the plains and there would already have been a battle between Iroquois and Gros Ventre in which many of the eastern Indians were slain. Surely, had such events occurred within the previous two years, they would have come up in Thompson's discussions with the Peigan in 1800. The latter group also might not have responded as favourably as they did to the idea of Iroquois entering their territory. Finally, the clash with the Gros Ventre mentioned in the *Narrative* is very reminiscent of an event which occurred at Chesterfield House in 1802 and is discussed below.

11 Thompson 'Journey to the Bow River and Rocky Mountains Nov. 1800' *Journals of Travel and Observation in Canada 1790–1825*

12 Dempsey 'David Thompson on the Peace River, Part II' 17

13 North West Company Servants Contracts, 1803–1805 HBCA F 5/2. Only six contracts with Iroquois for the northwest appear in the 'Répertoire' after 1804.

14 Rich ed *Colin Robertson's Correspondence Book, September 1817 to September 1822* xxvii, liv, lv. The Hudson's Bay Company initially ignored Robertson's recommendation, but took it up in 1814.

15 This is evident in the journals for St Mary's fort on the Peace River, in particular; HBCA B 190/a/1; B 190/a/2; B 190/a/3.

16 An attempt was made to determine the minimum number of Iroquois servants, engagés, and freemen appearing in the Lesser Slave Lake, St Mary's, and Dunvegan records, 1818–21. The total number obtained was 68 distributed as follows: 14 under contract to the Hudson's Bay Company, 5 under contract to the North West Company on the Peace River, 35 free Iroquois attached to the Hudson's Bay Company on the Peace River or at Lesser Slave Lake, and 14 free Iroquois attached to the North West Company on the Peace (HBCA F 4/35; B 115/a/1–5; B 190/a/1–3).

In his 1821 Athabasca report, Simpson recommended a force of 80 officers and men for the Peace River posts of Fort St Mary's, Colville House, and Fort de Pinnette. Of these, 19 were to be Iroquois, a figure not out of line with the above count. However, the free Iroquois appear to be distributed in the wrong proportion as Simpson indicated most of these men were attached to the North West Company in the Athabasca district during the period considered (Rich ed *Journal of Occurrences in the Athabasca Department by George Simpson, 1820 and 1821, and Report* 380–1, 385–6).

17 Lamb ed *Sixteen Years in the Indian Country. The Journal of Daniel Williams Harmon, 1800–1816* 193

18 The members of these bands were almost invariably kinsmen. Bands usually consisted of the families of a man and his sons and/or sons-in-law, or the families of brothers. Although there seems to have been some preference for young men to join their father-in-law's group, residence arrangements were flexible and a new couple might reside with other kinsmen. Polygymous marriages are indicated by references to the 'wives' of individual (usually influential) men.

19 Ouellet 'Dualité économique et changement technologique au Québec (1760–1790)' 256–96: see appendix 'Les engagements pour L'Ouest: Acts Notariés et Actes Privés,' (294–5).

20 Contract with 'Amable Spenard du Lac Des Deux Montagnes,' 24 février 1797, ANQM

21 Johnson ed *Saskatchewan Journals* xcii

22 Thompson 'Journey'

23 Rich *Robertson's Correspondence* 56

24 The frequency of repeat contracts for Iroquois in the 'Répertoire' is low, about sixteen per cent. 1000 livres was paid to Jacques Ganawasa, Iroquois, from Sault Saint-Louis, an individual with several years' experience (contract dated 16 Dec. 1803, ANQM).

The wages given here are considerably above those cited by Innis for winterers in 1805 in the Athabasca department when a middleman received 300 to 550 livres per year. (Innis quotes a figure of 500 to 750 livres for a gouvernail in Athabasca.) The higher wages probably reflect the competition for manpower between opposition companies before 1804.

Innis lists equipment for winterers in 1805 as 2 blankets, 2 shirts, 2 pair of trousers, and tobacco. Extras for Athabasca winterers after 1806 included items such as knives, beads, and vermilion (Innis *The Fur Trade in Canada* 239–40).

25 Simon Yohatorie of Sault Saint-Louis signed contracts in February and April of 1800 (ANQM).

26 North West Company Servants Contracts, HBCA (1803–1826) F 5/2

27 The lists of North West Company contracts 1815–22 may include Iroquois who were hired to fulfill similar contracts in 1820. Thomas Tagouche (#90) and Jacque Tahontie (#91), for example, appear to be Iroquois names. Unfortunately, the lists provide no other clues to their identity (HBCA F 5/3).

28 North West Company Servants Contracts (1803–1826) HBCA F 5/2

29 'There are 80 or 100 Canadians and Iroquois Hunters with whom the North West Company have Contracts, but who are not considered Servants of the Company, ranging free over the Country wherever they find it convenient to Hunt' (G.C. Davidson *The North West Company* 281).

30 HBCA B 60/e/1, B 60/e/3

31 Masson ed *Les Bourgeois de la Compagnie du Nord-Ouest* I 109

32 Colin Robertson wrote from St Mary's fort on Peace River on Feb. 1820 to McDonald at Fort Wedderburn: 'I consider the Iroquois in the same light as they are considered by the Company: Voyageurs! and free on their arrival at their respective posts, which consideration is unfortunately warranted by their *engagements*' (HBCA B 190/a/2). See also Rich ed *Journal of Occurrences* 380–1.

33 Although the present discussion is concerned with Iroquois freemen, it should be remembered that the freeman class in the northwest included other immigrants from the east. William Connelly, master at Lesser Slave Lake post 1821–2, wrote: 'The People who go under the Denomination of Free ment [sic] Consist of Canadians, Halfbreeds, Iroquois, Sauteux, Courteorielles and Nipisingues' (HBCA B 115/e/3, Lesser Slave Lake Report on District 1821–22).

34 Rich ed *Journal of Occurrences* 380–1; Iroquois Accounts, HBCA F 4/35. The Iroquois concerned were Pierre Ticheronserac (Thisteronsenac, Thestironsura) and Eustace Araquatiron (Araquatison). The Hudson's Bay Company wished to hire them for the New Caledonia expedition. Pierre owed $100 to the North West Company (Rich ed *Robertson's Correspondence* 262). The Iroquois account book (HBCA F 4/35) shows his debt in 1819 as 161 3/4 skins and 45 livres NW Currency. Against his account is written 'deserted.'

35 Spry 'Routes Through the Rockies' 26–39

36 See, for example, Rich ed *Robertson's Correspondence* 60, 109, 213–14, 273–4; and Rich *Journal of Occurrences* 56, 62, 133, 176, 185–6, 191, 277, 338.

37 Rich ed *Journal of Occurrences* 277; see also page 56.

38 Ibid 17n, 62, 381

39 Johnson ed *Saskatchewan Journals* 311–17; Glover ed *Narrative* 231. Thompson states there was a party of 75 Iroquois of whom 25 were killed.

40 Ibid 315

41 Lamb ed *Journals of Mackenzie* 193; HBCA B 56/a/1

42 HBCA B 115/e/4

43 This picture emerges from a detailed analysis of the activities of freemen in post journals from St Mary' fort and Lesser Slave Lake prior to 1821 and Fort Dunvegan after 1821 (HBCA B 190/a/1–3; B 115/a/1–5; B 56/a/1–2).

44 HBCA B 115/e/1

45 HBCA B 115/a/5

46 Fleming ed *Minutes of Council of Northern Department of Rupert's Land, 1821–31* 120

47 A survey of the Hudson's Bay Company Northern Engagement Registers and lists of servants showed that between 1830 and 1860 only 33 new Iroquois recruits were brought inland. Of these, 17 returned to Canada or the Red

River settlement, 11 stayed in the northwest, and the fate of 7 was not indicated (HBCA B 239/u/1–3; B 60/f/1).

48 Father Lacombe reported at mid-century that the Iroquois dialect survived only among the old people who founded the population in the Jasper area. French and Cree were the predominant languages. Lacombe thought that the Jasper Iroquois derived from a group of 40 men brought from Montreal under contract to the Hudson's Bay Company in the post-1821 period. This population was much more likely founded during the period of competition (Lacombe, cited in MacRae *History of the Province of Alberta* 64).

49 Skinner postulated that the Plains-Ojibwa perhaps incorporated elements of the Iroquois false-face society into their own ceremonies. He cites Mackenzie's reference to Iroquois in the West as the source for diffusion of traits. It is unclear whether or not traditional ceremonial societies were active at the Roman Catholic mission villages in the east at the end of the eighteenth century, and so Skinner's hypothesis can only be considered very speculative. The Longhouse tradition now active at Caughnawaga and St Regis represents a more recent revitalization movement among eastern Iroquois (Skinner 'Political and Ceremonial Organization of the Plains Ojibway' 504–5).

Orkneymen in the HBC 1780–1821

JOHN NICKS

At the end of the eighteenth century almost eighty per cent of the employees of the Hudson's Bay Company were being recruited in the Orkneys, off the north coast of Scotland. In 1800, 390 of the company's 498 officers and servants were Orkneymen. Most of the rest, among whom were numbered nearly all of the officers, were English. Although Orcadians continued to constitute the largest single component of its manpower until 1821, they were never again to achieve such dominance. By 1812 they accounted for about two-thirds of the total, and by the time of union less than forty per cent (see figure 1).

Although a few Orcadians had been employed as early as 1701, the policy of hiring men in the Orkneys on a regular basis apparently began in 1727 on the recommendation of Joseph Myatt, governor at Albany.[1] Disillusioned with Londoners who had proved 'so well acquainted with the ways and debaucheries of the town'[2] he had written to the governor and committee of the company in London in the previous year suggesting that sober young Orkneymen should be entertained for the company's service. As he explained: 'When I was in the Orkneys there was several stout men that offered to serve you at £6 per annum and Mr. Baillie Grimes says he will procure any number of men for you that you may have occasion for.'[3] The Orcadian servants hired to work at Albany and the other factories at the Bay proved well suited to the needs of the company, and in the 1730s the recruitment there of most of their labouring servants and some craftsmen came to be the normal practice. By the second half of the century English labourers were becoming a rarity, although a fair number of Englishmen were still hired as tradesmen. The English continued to retain a virtual monopoly on positions as apprentices, writers, and officers.

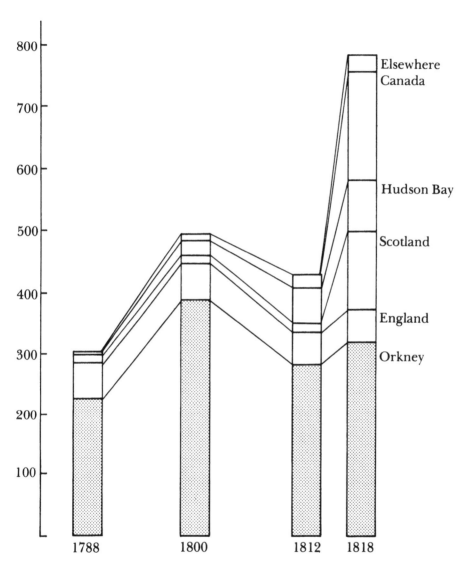

SOURCE: Lists of servants in HBCA A 32/4, 10, 11 and 16

Figure 1 Origins of Hudson's Bay Company employees

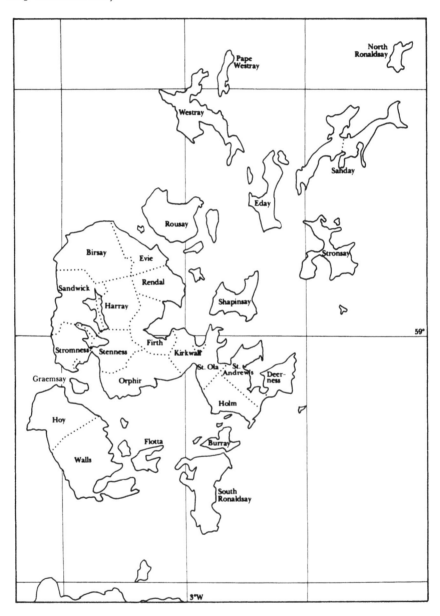

Figure 2 Orkney Islands ca. 1800

A number of excellent general accounts are available on the background of the Orkneymen and the contribution they made to the history of the Hudson's Bay Company.[4] However, no attempt has yet been made to examine the specific origins of these men in order to refine our understanding of them so that we may avoid easy stereotypes or generalizations. Were some parishes in the Orkneys more favoured sources of manpower than others? Did employees come mainly from the countryside or the port towns? Did they come from all ranks of Orkney society equally? Did their tendency to shun the society of employees from other lands reflect strong bonds of kinship as well as a sense of cultural exclusiveness? Did the recruiting system, which operated through the mediation of agents based in Stromness, lead to the development of an 'old boy' network? Were prominent or successful employees from the islands able to exercise any direct patronage in the hiring of their friends or relatives? Can we learn more about the reasons why so many young men were prepared to leave their families and native soil to seek employment on the frozen shores of Hudson Bay?

In order to answer any of these questions it is necessary to delve into the backgrounds of individual employees. Unfortunately, this is not possible on any systematic basis for employees whose careers ended before about 1780. Earlier employment contracts have not survived, and earlier lists of servants, where they exist, generally omit such information as age and parish of origin, essential data if one is to examine their Orcadian connections.[5] As a consequence, this study of the Orcadian employees of the Hudson's Bay Company prior to union in 1821 has been based on information assembled about servants active in the employ of the company between 1780 and 1821.

On the basis of lists of servants maintained by the Hudson's Bay Company it has been possible to look at the geographical distribution of the origins of recruits within the Orkneys (see map, figure 2).[6] Throughout most of the period between 1780 and 1821, men were hired through agents who lived in Stromness, the port of call for the company's ships. One might expect that ease of access to Stromness would have been a major factor determining who would come forward seeking employment at the bay. If that were true, the parish of Stromness, and those adjacent to it in the west mainland of Orkney should have provided most of the recruits. This does indeed appear to have been the case (see table 1). There was, however, a tendency for the distribution to become less concentrated in this region. This perhaps reflects a gradual depletion of the

TABLE 1

Distribution of employees among Orkney parishes

Parish	1788 No.	%	1800 No.	%	1812 No.	%	1818 No.	%
Birsay	29	15.3	65	17.1	32	11.3	39	13.8
Evie	8	4.2	20	5.3	17	6.0	17	6.0
Firth	10	5.3	12	3.2	25	8.9	12	4.2
Harray	16	8.4	34	8.9	35	12.4	25	8.9
Orphir	19	10.0	47	12.4	22	7.8	15	5.3
Rendall	2	1.1	7	1.8	4	1.4	5	1.8
Sandwick	23	12.1	18	4.7	8	2.8	31	11.0
Stenness	6	3.2	15	3.9	7	2.5	9	3.2
Stromness	31	16.3	34	8.9	34	12.1	25	8.9
West Mainland	144	75.8	252	66.3	184	65.2	178	63.1
Deerness	1	0.5	4	1.1	1	0.4	1	0.4
Holm	–	–	2	0.5	–	–	1	0.4
Kirkwall/St. Ola	19	10.0	25	6.6	30	10.6	29	10.3
St. Andrews	4	2.1	4	1.1	2	0.7	1	0.4
East Mainland	24	12.6	35	9.2	33	11.7	32	11.4
Hoy and Graemsay	–	–	2	0.5	1	0.4	5	1.8
South Ronaldsay	11	5.8	53	13.9	22	7.8	26	9.2
Walls and Flotta	6	3.2	13	3.4	5	1.8	8	2.8
South Islands	17	9.0	68	17.9	28	10.0	39	13.8
Eday	–	–	–	–	–	–	–	–
North Ronaldsay	1	0.5	–	–	–	–	–	–
Rousay	4	2.1	24	6.4	29	10.3	12	4.2
Sanday	–	–	–	–	–	–	4	1.4
Shapinsay	–	–	–	–	3	1,1	5	1,8
Stronsay	–	–	1	0.3	–	–	1	0.4
Westray	–	–	–	–	5	1.8	11	3.9
North Islands	5	2.6	25	6.6	37	13.2	33	11.7
Totals	190	100.0	380	100.0	282	100.0	282	100.0

TABLE 2
Distribution of employees in proportion to population

Parish	1788		1800		1812		1818	
	No.	%	No.	%	No.	%	No.	%
Birsay	1,350	2.1	1,450	4.5	1,430	2.2	1,520	2.6
Evie	890	0.9	810	2.5	680	2.5	810	2.1
Firth	570	1.8	630	1.9	500	5.0	540	2.2
Harray	660	2.4	720	4.7	690	5.1	720	3.5
Orphir	810	2.3	860	5.5	850	2.6	900	1.7
Rendall	670	0.3	600	1.2	550	0.7	600	0.8
Sandwick	870	2.6	970	1.9	920	0.9	930	3.3
Stenness	580	0.9	640	2.3	570	1.2	590	1.5
Stromness	2,140	1.4	2,220	1.5	2,300	1.5	2,940	0.9
West Mainland	8,540	1.7	8,900	2.8	8,490	2.2	9,550	1.9
Deerness	660	0.2	660	0.6	620	0.2	690	0.1
Holm	700	–	870	0.2	750	–	770	0.1
Kirkwall/St. Ola	2,550	0.7	2,620	1.0	2,280	1.3	3,240	0.9
St. Andrews	670	0.6	850	0.5	780	0.3	850	0.1
East Mainland	4,580	0.5	5,000	0.7	4,430	0.7	5,550	0.6
Hoy and Graemsay	410	–	420	0.5	470	0.2	500	1.0
South Ronaldsay	1,950	0.6	1,880	2.8	1,840	1.2	2,230	1.2
Walls and Flotta	990	0.6	990	1.3	1,080	0.5	1,240	0.6
South Islands	3,350	0.5	3,290	2.1	3,390	0.8	3,970	1.0
Eday	600	–	720	–	580	–	670	–
North Ronaldsay	420	0.2	400	–	380	–	420	–
Rousay	1,070	0.4	1,060	2.4	970	3.0	1,150	1.0
Sanday	1,770	–	1,750	–	1,800	–	1,860	0.2
Shapinsay	730	–	740	–	730	0.4	780	0.6
Stronsay	890	–	920	0.1	860	–	1,010	0.1
Westray	1,630	–	1,620	–	1,610	0.3	1,940	0.6
North Islands	7,110	0.1	7,210	0.3	6,930	0.5	7,830	0.4
Totals	23,580	0.9	24,400	1.6	23,240	1.2	26,900	1.2

Population figures are based on the census closest in time to the years indicated; see R.S. Barclay *The Population of Orkney, 1755–1961.*

traditional labour pool or the expansion of interest in employment with the company – probably both.[7]

Geographical patterns of distribution show up even more clearly when one cancels out the influence of population distribution by looking at recruitment levels as a percentage of population (see table 2). The predominance of the west mainland area is still apparent with about 2 per cent of its total population usually in the company's employ. However, proximity to Stromness is clearly not the only important variable. In most years the rural parishes in its vicinity were able to spare larger proportions of their population than the burgh of Stromness. This is a strong indication that employment opportunities at Hudson Bay held a greater attraction to rural residents than to urban dwellers.

It is also apparent that recruitment levels in most parishes varied a good deal from year to year, and that the variation followed no common pattern. In 1788, Sandwick was the most heavily represented parish; in 1800 it was Orphir; and after 1812 it was Harray. Frequently parishes showed sharp and temporary peaks in their participation rate, and for a time even some of the outlying islands such as Rousay and South Ronaldsay provided large numbers of recruits. Some of these shifts may have resulted from changing circumstances in the parishes affected. Others may perhaps be explained by changes in the recruitment network. Both of these possible factors deserve further examination with the help of local records. In some cases, temporary peaks almost certainly resulted from the influence of employees who became prominent enough to exercise some influence in favour of the employment of friends and relatives or to attract them through the example of a successful career. For example, this seems to be the most likely explanation for the large number of men who came from the island of South Ronaldsay near the end of the eighteenth century when William Tomison, a native of that island, was the senior officer in charge of the inland trade of York Factory.

More detailed examination of the individual backgrounds of the servants requires the linking of company records about them with such local documents as parish registers. The remainder of this paper consists of a preliminary report on a project to assemble biographical information about a representative sample of the Orcadian employees of the Hudson's Bay Company. In order to test the feasibility of linking records about them in the archives of the Hudson's Bay Company with parish registers and other related documents preserved in Scottish archives, I decided to start with a sample of all employees who were recorded as having come from a single parish. Although such a sample cannot be shown to be representative of all Orcadians in the company's employ, this strategy had the advantage of allowing more complete reconstruction of the family relationships of the men with greater economy of research time than would have been possible with a more geographically dispersed sample of similar size.[8] Furthermore, only a complete sample from a given area would be certain to include all members of the families in that area who participated in the trade. A more dispersed sample would underestimate the family concentration among the company's employees.

I decided to select the parish of Orphir, an area of agricultural settlement along the south coast of the mainland of Orkney about half-way between Stromness and Kirkwall. Not only was it a parish which provided a large number of employees, it also had the most complete set of parish registers for the period when most employees in the sample were born, an important consideration if a high rate of linkage was to be achieved.[9]

Between 1780 and 1821, 121 men were listed in the records of the Hudson's Bay Company as having come from the parish of Orphir. In most cases little is recorded about their personal background beyond age and parish of origin. Few of the men in this period left wills with the company, an important source of information often used by biographers of fur trade employees. In some cases, the basic information derived from the contracts and lists of servants could be supplemented by data derived from the servants' bills, documents drawn up to authorize withdrawals from the servants' accounts.[10] Many of these bills were made out to close relatives.

On the basis of these sources of information it was possible to link 95 employees with their baptismal entries (see table 3). A linkage was regarded as correct if the names were the same, if the age matched within a margin of three years, or if evidence from auxiliary sources like servants' bills confirmed an otherwise doubtful linkage. Of the 26 cases where no linkage was possible, 11 were probably born outside the parish. In most of the latter cases there was inconsistency in the company records with some indicating they were from Orphir and some identifying other parishes of origin. Another five could not be matched because more than one linkage was possible due to name duplication. The remaining 11 appear not to have had their baptisms recorded. This is not surprising. The register of baptisms was clearly defective at some periods, most notably between 1748 and 1758 and for shorter periods when a vacancy occurred in the ministry. In addition, dues appear to have been demanded by the clerks for the registration of baptisms and for part of the eighteenth century there was a tax on the registration of vital events.[11] It seems likely that some families either refused or were unable to meet such exactions. As a result it would be reasonable to conclude that some, especially at the lower end of the economic scale, were under-represented in the parish registers.

For the 95 men whose Orcadian connections have been identified, an attempt was made to compile information about the social and economic status of their families, their position in their families and relationships to other employees from the same parish. The main source of information was the parish register of baptisms, marriages, and burials. Unfortunately, records of deaths or burials were not systematically maintained before 1819. It was therefore difficult to achieve a high rate of linkage between 'nuclear' families and, as a result, kinship between employees could not usually be documented beyond members of the immediate family, i.e. brother–brother or father–son.

At their best, baptismal and marriage entries were very full and informative, providing much more than the bare demographic information. Place of residence for parents or marriage partners was frequently indicated. Names of witnesses or cautioners were also useful in providing information about circles of friendship and fictive kinship as well as family connections beyond the confines of the immediate circle. Entries in the Orphir parish registers relating to Magnus Tait (employed at York Factory 1786–1801) and his parents and brothers provide a good example:

1765   Magnus Tait, lawful son of Thomas Tait in Petertown and Kathairn
July 28 Sinclair his spouse was baptised.
        Witnesses. Peter Sinclair, grandfather to the child, and Magnus Bews.

Baptismal entries for his siblings, three of whom (James, Nicol, and William) also became employees of the company, revealed that his father, Thomas, occupied the farm of Orakirk which was located near the mouth of the Burn of Coubister in the township of Petertown. The marriage entry for Thomas and his wife indicated that the groom was the son of James Tait of Naversdale while the bride was a daughter of Patrick Sinclair of Padockpool.

Unfortunately, not all entries are equally informative. Some parish clerks were less conscientious and frequently omitted names of the witnesses or parents' place of residence in baptismal entries or of parents' names in marriage entries. Even the most assiduous record-keepers did not provide equivalent information in every entry. Indeed there appears to have been some correlation between the completeness of entries and the social status of the families involved. Events involving prominent landowners, church officers or elders, ministers, and school teachers were more

TABLE 3
Distribution of employees by cohort

	Total sample	Number linked	% linked
Cohort 1	48	36	75
Cohort 2	40	34	85
Cohort 3	33	25	76
Totals	121	95	79

TABLE 4
Proportions of labourers and tradesmen in total sample

	Labourers		Tradesmen	
	Number	Percentage	Number	Percentage
Cohort 1	36	75	12	25
Cohort 2	27	67.5	13	32.5
Cohort 3	22	66.7	11	33.3

fully recorded in most cases than those concerning small farmers, cottagers, or servants.

Similar problems are present with other classes of local records. Major changes in land occupancy were entered in the registers of sasines, but no comprehensive records of the movements of tenant farmers, cottagers, or servants appear to have survived. While there are records of the traditional rentals paid by the principal feuars for lands held of the earldom or bishopric, there is no detailed record of the services or rents they may have demanded of their tenants.[12]

On the basis of the information assembled about the employees who came from Orphir, certain patterns have emerged which merit some discussion. These concern the individual characteristics of the men hired and the motivations which led them to seek employment with the company. In order to see whether there were significant changes over time the employees have been divided into three cohorts based on the date of their first contract. Cohort 1 consists of all employees in the sample who were hired before 1790, cohort 2 of employees recruited between 1790 and 1804, and cohort 3 of those who started between 1805 and 1821 (table 3).

At all times the majority of the men were hired as labourers. However, the proportion of tradesmen and skilled labourers increased through time from a quarter to a third of the total (table 4). This undoubtedly reflected efforts to recruit more of the labourers from other areas.[13] The

TABLE 5
Categories of tradesmen employed

Occupation	Cohort 1	Cohort 2	Cohort 3	Totals
Blacksmiths	3	2	4	9
Boatbuilders	0	1	1	2
Carpenters	1	0	1	2
Coopers	0	2	0	2
Masons or bricklayers	3	3	3	9
Sailors	2	1	1	4
Sawyers	0	1	1	2
Tailors	3	3	0	6
Totals	12	13	11	36

TABLE 6
Age of employees at first contract

	Labourers				Tradesmen			
	sample	mean	median	mode	sample	mean	median	mode
Cohort 1	29	22.6	21	20	7	23.9	21	21
Cohort 2	21	21.0	21	20	13	23.2	22	22
Cohort 3	17	20.6	20	20	8	25.8	27	24,27

tradesmen hired in Orphir in the greatest numbers were masons, tailors, and blacksmiths; sawyers, boatbuilders, carpenters, and coopers constituted most of the remainder. Only a small number were hired as sailors to man the sloops used along the coasts of Hudson and James Bay (table 5).

The second characteristic considered was the age of the employees when they were first recruited (table 6).[14] The first conclusion reached was that both labourers and tradesmen tended to be very young. The modal age for labourers was only 20 and some were recruited as young as 15 although few were younger than 18. Men with a trade or special skills were understandably somewhat older. In contrast, studies of the Canadian voyageurs in the early eighteenth century have indicated a mean age of 26 and median of 24, and, on another sample, a modal age of 22.[15]

There was a tendency for the mean and median ages of labourers and tradesmen to diverge through time as the former became younger and the latter somewhat older. Both trends perhaps reflect a growing scarcity of labour supply in the preferred age categories. Clearly the company

TABLE 7
Distribution of employees by township of birth

Township	Percentage of population*	Number of employees	
		absolute	percentage
Cava	2.2	2	2.2
Clestran	18.9	15	16.9
Groundwater	7.2	0	0.0
Hobbister	7.1	7	7.9
Houton	6.5	4	4.5
Kirbister	4.8	3	3.4
Midland	7.7	4	4.5
Orphir	15.3	20	22.5
Petertown	6.3	4	4.5
Smoogro	4.8	6	6.7
Swanbister	11.5	18	20.5
Tuskerbister	7.8	6	6.7
Totals	100.1	89	100.0

*Based on population distribution as revealed in the manuscript returns for the census of 1841

desired to hire young men who were mature enough to have obtained full adult strength but flexible enough to adapt to the unfamiliar conditions they would have to face.

The geographical distribution of recruiting within the parish of Orphir was closely related to probable population distribution (table 7). Nevertheless, the distribution does not appear to have been simply proportional to population.[16] Proximity to the main road to Stromness appears to have been a factor (see figure 3). All of the townships located away from the main road, with the exception of the island of Cava, contributed fewer men than would have been expected if population was the only important variable. It is also observable that the townships of Orphir and Swanbister, which were closest to the church and parish school, had the highest rates of recruitment. This last circumstance suggests that the minister, and possibly the schoolmaster, may have played an important role in the recruitment process.

At least a part of the geographical concentration evident in table 7 could have resulted from a tendency for a limited number of families to monopolize available positions. More than 50 per cent of the employees in the first two cohorts had at least one brother who was or had been an

Parish of Orphir c. 1800

TABLE 8
Family concentration in the recruiting of employees

Labourers		No brothers	One or more brothers	Totals
Cohort 1	Labourers	13	16	29
	Tradesmen	4	3	7
	Percentage	47	53	100
Cohort 2	Labourers	9	12	21
	Tradesmen	7	6	13
	Percentage	47	53	100
Cohort 3	Labourers	12	5	17
	Tradesmen	3	5	8
	Percentage	60	40	100

employee of the company as well, but there was a dramatic change in the third cohort among servants employed as labourers (table 8). The drop in the degree of family concentration after 1805 probably reflects a broadening of the recruiting network as the labour supply became more restricted, fitting the pattern suggested by other changes already mentioned.

The sibling relationship was by far the most common that could be documented. In seven cases, three or four brothers worked for the company. Generally they did not all join up at the same time. The Tait family illustrates the most common sequence of events. James Tait, the eldest son in the family, joined the company in 1778. He proved to be exceptionally capable and rose rapidly from the rank of labourer to that of steersman and occasional trader by the end of his second contract in 1786. In the next six years, three of his younger brothers came out to join him. In the meantime he rose firmly into the officer class. All of the Taits served in the inland districts of York Factory. A similar pattern can be seen in the experience of Adam Snodie and his brothers. Adam, who had had the benefit of a good education, also rose rapidly from the servant into the officer class, and three of his brothers followed him into the service of the company although none did so with equal success. The Robertson family appears to illustrate a different process. The eldest son, Thomas, spent only eight years at the bay never rising above the level of labourer. At that point he returned home. Three of his younger brothers went out within a year or two of his return, and all stayed on to become long-service employees. While it is unlikely that their elder brother could have exerted any direct influence to ensure their selection, his experience, or necessity, may have motivated them to emigrate.

TABLE 9
Family sequence of employees

	First son	Second son	Subsequent son
Cohort 1	18	4	14
Cohort 2	12	12	10
Cohort 3	9	7	9
Totals	39	23	33
Percentage	41	24	35

Few documented cases of father-son continuity in the employ of the company can be produced. This may have been due to the shortness of the period studied and the difficulty in making inter-generational linkages with the parish data due to the lack of death or burial records. It would therefore be unwise to conclude that family traditions of service to the company were non-existent or even unimportant.

Evidence for connections beyond the nuclear family is equally slight. It is conceivable that successful employees like James Tait or Adam Snodie were able to exercise patronage on behalf of more distant kin, though there is no direct evidence that either did so. Nevertheless, in the absence of data necessary to test such a hypothesis, no firm conclusions can be reached.

One of the more interesting set of statistics concerns the number of eldest sons hired by the company (table 9). On average, more than 40 per cent of the employees were eldest sons. If one takes infant and child mortality into account, a substantial number of the second sons were probably the eldest surviving sons in their families. Thus it seems probable that eldest surviving sons made up the majority of the recruits. This is in marked contrast to the picture presented by Charbonneau for the Canadian voyageurs, where there appeared to be a marked preference for younger sons.[17] It is not clear, however, without an examination of the demography of the two societies, whether this difference derives from a deliberate process of selection or divergent demographic characteristics such as differences in family size or age-specific mortality.[18]

I considered finally, the economic and social status of the families which provided recruits. The basic measure used was the named place of residence, where this could be obtained.[19] Unfortunately, more than one-third of the employees came from families for which no place of residence was indicated (see table 10). In some cases, especially with the earlier

TABLE 10
Status as indicated by place of residence

	Farms	Cottages	Other	Not known	Sample
Cohort 1	19	2	0	15	36
Cohort 2	14	6	2	12	34
Cohort 3	10	6	2	7	25
Totals	43	14	4	34	95
Percentage	45	15	4	36	100

parish records, this may have been the result of inadequate or incomplete entries in the register. However, a persistent proportion of about one-quarter probably came from families at the lowest end of the social scale: the crofter families that constituted approximately that same proportion of the households in the parish near the end of the eighteenth century.[20] The largest identified component consisted of the families of the many small tenant farmers who worked most of the land in the parish. Four employees were the sons of the local schoolmaster, a position which carried more status than economic reward. The rest were born in named cottages, many of which appear to have been occupied by rural craftsmen or tradesmen.

The question of the motivation of the young men who sought employment with the company is difficult to answer as the evidence is largely anecdotal or indirect. According to the Rev. Mr William Clouston of the parish of Sandwick and Stromness, writing in the 1790s, the young men were attracted 'from a restlessness of disposition, a desire of change' and, although wages were low, they were better than the farmers in Orkney could give.[21] Possibly individual motives consisted of a complex of personal, sometimes frivolous notions as well as hard economic and social pressures. The former, however important they may have been in individual cases, are usually difficult to document. The latter can be tested more easily.

At the time that Clouston was writing, the company paid a minimum of £6 a year for labourers in their first contract, with room, board, and a basic set of clothing. After the first five years, and in all subsequent contracts, the level of compensation was progressively augmented, very substantially so if the employee learned special skills as a canoeman or merited advancement. In contrast, a farm servant in most Orkney parishes would receive from £2 10s to £3 10s per year with board. Similarly, a boatbuilder

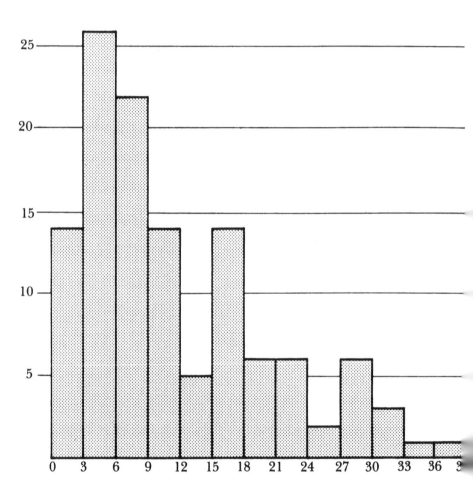

Lengths of service in groups of three years

Figure 4 Distribution of lengths of service of all employees in Orphir sample

would start with the company at £20 to £30 per year. In the port of Stromness he would be lucky to earn as much in gross income out of which he would have to find living expenses. There is little doubt that financial inducements were present for both labourers and tradesmen.[22]

According to Orkney critics of the company, many of the men saved enough to allow them to 'overbid the honest industrious farmer, who is incumbered with a number of small children,' and most of the men who returned, even those employed as tradesmen, were said to have 'generally set up as farmers on their return.' However, according to these critics, their skills as farmers were 'not improved by their absence, and their habits frequently not calculated to make them successful.' As a result, it was argued, they were soon reduced to a state of poverty and were forced to give way 'to another of his own tribe.[23]

To what degree is this picture supported by the experiences of the men in the Orphir sample? Unfortunately it has not been possible to obtain direct evidence about how many became farmers on their return, as tenancy records for the major estates in the parish do not appear to have survived. However, an indirect indication of the degree to which such a pattern may have prevailed can be provided by evidence about the length of time the men stayed with the company and the amounts of money they were able to save from their wages.

When one looks at the period as a whole, the majority of the men employed by the company served for eight years or less, the equivalent of one or two contracts. This would support the hypothesis that most of the men saw employment as a temporary episode in their lives. It is interesting to note, however, that there appear to be secondary peaks in the distribution of lengths of service at 15–17 years and at 27–29 years (see figure 4). These may represent the presence of two other categories of employees: long-service employees for whom employment with the company was to be something more than temporary but less than a lifetime commitment, and career employees.

There appear to have been significant shifts in this pattern through time. If one looks at the median length of service (see table 11),[24] one can see a significant decline, especially among those who were hired as labourers. Labourers in the first two cohorts tended to stay significantly longer than tradesmen. This pattern appears to have been reversed in the third cohort.

The reduction of the median length of service was at least partially caused by a change in the number of long-service and career employees (table 12). This trend probably reflects a hardening of class lines within

TABLE 11
Median lengths of employment in years

	Labourers		Tradesmen	
	sample	median(yrs)	sample	median(yrs)
Cohort 1	36	15	12	8/9
Cohort 2	27	8	13	6
Cohort 3	22	5	11	6

TABLE 12
Number of employees serving at least 15 years

	Labourers		Tradesmen		Totals	
	Number	%	Number	%	Number	%
Cohort 1	19	53	4	33	23	48
Cohort 2	9	33	4	31	13	32
Cohort 3	2	9	1	9	3	9

the fur trade society and a marked decline in opportunity for promotion from servant to officer status. Of the long-service and career employees in the first cohort, more than half rose at least into the lowest ranks of officer status as traders or occasional masters. Of those hired after 1790, only one became a master, and his case was clearly exceptional.[25]

It is interesting to note that some of the career employees, and even more of the long-service employees, returned home to Orkney after their second or third contract. After a hiatus of from one to several years they returned to Hudson Bay for an additional, sometimes lifelong period of service. Approximately one-third of the long-service employees and one-quarter of the career employees appear to have had this experience. Possibly at least some of them acted in this way because they could not readjust to life in their native land. Some undoubtedly missed the greater freedom of the fur trade society as it developed at the inland posts, or friends and family they had acquired there. Indeed some probably never intended their return to Orkney to be any more than a visit.

For a few, the return to Hudson Bay was a way of escaping from personal or domestic problems. At least two of the men from Orphir fled to escape responsibility for illegitimate children. One, Adam Mowat, returned two years later to be married. The other, Andrew Robertson,

TABLE 13
Rates of savings as a proportion of total earnings

	Labourers		Tradesmen		All servants	
	sample	%	sample	%	sample	%
Cohort 1	9	74	2	55	11	71
Cohort 2	20	69	11	77	31	72
Cohort 3	4	81	9	78	13	79
Totals	33	72	22	75	55	73

stayed in voluntary exile as a career employee of the company. Others may have been fleeing unhappy marriages as suggested by one of the parish ministers in the 1790's: 'when a man and his wife cannot live in peace together, the parties and the parish are relieved from such disquiets, by the husband's retreat to the Hudson's Bay settlements.'[26]

The second factor to consider is whether rates of savings were high enough so that men who stayed for no more than eight to eleven years would have been able to set themselves up as farmers. Unfortunately, the servants' account books kept by the company for this period have not all survived.[27] Enough remain, however, to illustrate the high savings rate that could be and often was attained. The majority of the men who stayed for more than two and fewer than twelve years managed to save more than 70 per cent of their total earnings (table 13).

With such a small sample it is hard to know whether there were any meaningful trends in savings rates during the study period. There is some indication that rates increased through time and that tradesmen saved at a marginally higher rate than labourers. Even if the savings rates were not significantly different for different categories of employees or at different times, the speed with which capital could be accumulated clearly varied directly with the level of wages. Tradesmen were able to save more in a shorter period of time than labourers; and both could accumulate capital more rapidly as wage rates rose in the early nineteenth century. Labourers in the first two cohorts usually had to work for eight years before their savings exceeded £60. Those in the third cohort could put by as much within four years. The wage rates of tradesmen were more variable so capital accumulation was more irregular. Nevertheless, on average, tradesmen from the first two cohorts could save over £65 in their first five years and those in the third cohort as much as £100 in the same period.

TABLE 14
Mean levels of capital accumulation

Years of service	Labourers			Tradesman		
	Sample	Savings		Sample	Savings	
3	6	£28 2 10		2	£50 9 4	
4	2	£39 9 4		3	£49 2 2	
5	8	£30 1 3		3	£65 9 11	
6	1	£41 1 11		2	£109 0 5	
7	2	£49 19 5		0		
8	3	£62 1 2		1	£170 14 7	
9	2	£71 1 3		1	£175 19 5	
10	3	£107 19 0		0		
11	1	£99 11 5		1	£264 0 6	

Mean levels of capital accumulation for employees in the first two cohorts are presented in table 14. Records are too fragmentary to warrant tabular presentation of similar figures for servants in the third cohort.[28]

The amount of capital required to set up as a farmer was probably quite variable. In Orphir, the average small holding consisted of about eight acres of arable land and sixteen of pasture.[29] The rent on such a holding was probably about £10 per year. In some cases, an entry fee or *grassum* was still exacted but it does not appear to have been a general practice. Where required it probably amounted to no more than two years' rental. The livestock for an average holding in Orphir would have been worth no more than £30.[30] When one includes other first year expenses, a minimum of £40 to £60 was probably required, depending on whether an entry fee was charged. On this basis, most returning servants could have afforded to become farmers if they had wished to do so.

Most of the Orkneymen who became employees of the Hudson's Bay Company seem to have been drawn from the middle and lower ranks of island society. Typically they were young, unmarried sons of small tenant farmers, craftsmen, and cottagers. Although many of the tradesmen were recruited from the urban centres, rural parishes like Orphir provided their fair share.

There was a marked tendency for recruitment to become more broadly based early in the nineteenth century. This was shown in an expansion of the geographical base, a reduction in family concentration, and changes in the age distribution of recruits. In the last quarter of the eighteenth century, employment with the company appears to have been considered desirable in many families. There is some evidence to suggest that the recruiting system favoured those favourably regarded by respected members of the community, such as the parish ministers, or those who had connections with someone already in the employ of the company. Further study is required to assess the importance of formal lines of kinship and informal bonds of friendship and patronage. In the early nineteenth century, service with the company appears to have been regarded with less favour, if one can judge by the decline in interest shown by the sons of farmers and by eldest sons.

Although a variety of personal reasons were probably involved, there is good reason to believe that the majority of the men who sought employment with the Hudson's Bay Company did so for economic reasons. Service with the company was an effective means of acquiring sufficient capital to allow them to take their place in the middle ranks of their native society. In the competition for land, returning employees were frequently in a position to outbid those who had stayed at home. In the eighteenth century, there were also many who found a satisfying way of life in the employ of the company. Most of these rose through the ranks and soon attained a status and level of income they could not hope to better, or even equal, if they returned home. However, as the possibility of such advancement faded, fewer men saw servitude to the company as a career opportunity. It seems likely that this strengthened the tendency of Orcadians to view their work in the fur trade as a means to an end: a way of accumulating capital so that they might realize ambitions within their own society. Is it any wonder that they should come to be regarded by their superiors as men with a low level of commitment to the interests of the company, but shrewdly attentive to their own welfare? It seems clear that attempts by the company after 1800 to lessen its dependence on Orkney as a recruiting ground were paralleled by a declining desire on the part of the Orcadians to enter its service or to stay in it for more than a few years.

NOTES AND REFERENCES

1 Probably a few served on company ships before 1700, but the first known to have been employed at one of the factories at the bay was Adam Isbister, a sailor who agreed to serve at Albany in 1701 to help man the *Knight* on its trading voyage to the Eastmain. A number of Orcadians were hired during the War of Spanish Succession, but with the return of peace in 1713, former

recruitment practices seem to have been resumed. By 1723, only 1 of the 36 men at Albany appears to have been from Orkney. See Davies ed *Letters from Hudson Bay 1703–40*, 13, 22, 27, 31, and 90.

2 Ibid 123

3 Ibid 116

4 The most extended accounts are in Clouston 'Orkney and the Hudson's Bay Company'; Glover 'Introduction' to Rich ed *Cumberland House Journals and Inland Journals 1775–82, Second Series, 1779–1782*; and E.A. Mitchell 'The Scot in the Fur Trade.'

5 The contracts consulted in HBCA are catalogued as A 30/1–19. Two series of lists of servants were used. The A 30 series consisted of lists kept in London on a yearly basis. Lists of servants assigned to individual posts and factories are found in the B series under the appropriate number. For example, York Factory lists were found under B 239/f. Only a fraction of the original contracts appear to have survived. There were none at all for the years 1785–9, 1793–1802, and 1807–12, and the files for some other years are incomplete. The A 30 lists started in 1785 and there was a lengthy gap in the series between 1801 and 1811. The post lists in the B series covered different periods, but in no case were they complete. Nevertheless, with these three sources it was possible to obtain a nearly complete coverage of the entire period.

6 Four years were chosen for which there were complete lists in HBCA A 30 series. 1788 was in A 30/4; 1800 in A 30/10; 1812 in A 30/11 and 1818 in A 30/16.

7 Most of the ministers from the west mainland of Orkney who contributed to the statistical account compiled by Sir John Sinclair complained of a serious shortage of labour (Sinclair *The Orkney Parishes: Containing the Statistical Account of Orkney, 1795–1798*).

8 Work is now in progress to expand the sample to include a cross-section of the parishes in Orkney including urban as well as rural areas.

9 Original parish registers are held by the SRO. Microfilm copies have been made by the Church of Jesus Christ of Latter-Day Saints which gave the author access to them through its EGL. The Orphir register was the only one in Orkney which had no gaps between 1710 and 1820, although there were some periods when the number of entries was suspiciously low. Between 1748 and 1758 at least one-third of the baptisms appear to have been unrecorded.

10 The main sources used were the lists of servants and servants' contracts already referred to. Wills were consulted in HBCA A 36 series. References to the bills, indicating the name of the payee, were found in the servants' accounts. Use was made of both the account books kept at individual posts now in HBCA B section and the ledgers kept in London and now in A 16 series.

11 This kind of inconsistency appears to be quite common in records of this

period and may reflect some variation in criteria for place of origin. In some cases, parish of birth may have been used, with parish of residence used in others.

There was a vacancy in the ministry for eight months in 1776 which led to a substantial reduction in entries for that year. Other years for which the entries appear to be deficient were 1787–88, 1796–97, and 1803.

Reference to the payment of dues is contained in the registers of baptisms but the amount levied is not indicated. Apparently church elders and officers were exempt. The tax was collected from 1783 to 1794. Although many felt that it deterred registration, this was not always true. In Orphir, the effect is hard to measure. The number of baptisms from 1784 to 1788 was below the average of preceding years but in the last six years of the tax, the number of registrations was, if anything, slightly above the average. For a general discussion of the impact of the tax see Flinn ed *Scottish Population History from the 17th Century to the 1930s* 208–9.

12 Registers of sasines are kept in the SRO. Use was made of EGL microfilm copies. Most of the extant rentals are published in Peterkin *Rentals of the Ancient Earldom and Bishopric of Orkney*.

13 These efforts are well documented in Rich *History of the Hudson's Bay Company 1670–1870* 2 vols.

14 Age in table 6 is based on date of baptism and 30 June as the date of engagement. In fact, contracts were often signed a few weeks earlier, but this probably only balances the fact that baptisms were probably performed a few days, and in some cases weeks, after birth.

15 Charbonneau et al 'Le comportement démographique des voyageurs sous le régime français' (results based on a sample of voyageurs born between 1640 and 1719); and Duchêne *Habitants et marchands de Montréal au XVIIᵉ siècle* 224–5 et le graphique 16 en annexe (age statistics based on a sample of voyageurs active between 1708 and 1717)

16 The probable population distribution for the period is based on the distribution in the 1841 census. This is the earliest census for which the ms enumerator's forms remain (microfilm, EGL). There was a close correlation between distribution and population. Using estimated population figures for the townships, a calculation was made of Pearson's coefficient of correlation with the result of $R = 0.8283$.

17 Charbonneau et al 'Le comportement démographique' 127

18 Estimates of the death rate in Scotland as a whole near the end of the eighteenth century suggest it was about 27 per thousand. See Flinn *Scottish Population* 269. If one uses the evidence for population structure adduced there and applies it to the appropriate Princeton Regional Life table (North

level 8, R = 9.75) one comes up with a survival rate for males to age 20 of about 58%. See Coale and Demeny *Regional Modal Life Tables and Stable Populations* 227.

Relatively minor shifts in average family size and rates of mortality could lead to major changes in the probability that one or more sons would live to maturity. A useful table illustrates this relationship in Goody 'Strategies of heirship' in Goody et al eds *Family and inheritance: Rural Society in Western Europe, 1200–1800* 16–18.

19 Assessment of the status of named places of residence was based on the annotated list of farm names in Marwick *Orkney Farm Names*. This was supplemented by information from the enumeration lists for the 1841 and 1851 censuses.

20 According to the statistical account of the parish of Orphir submitted about 1795, there were 46 cottagers and crofters out of a total of 188 heads of families, or 24.5% (Sinclair *Orkney Parishes* 74).

21 Ibid 123

22 A ship carpenter in Stromness could earn from 1s 3d to 2s per day, without board. Masons were paid at about the same rate. House carpenters would receive from 1s to 1s 8d per day and tailors were paid by the piece (ibid 112).

23 Ibid 75, 180

24 Data for Table 11 were drawn from a variety of files in HBCA as no single file contained the complete employment record of all employees. The most useful sources included lists of servants in both the A and B series and servants' accounts in both the A and B series.

25 The exception was Adam Snodie, son of the parish schoolmaster. Adam joined the company as a labourer. However, due to the quality of his education, he was almost immediately assigned to act as a writer. Subsequently he rose to become one of the inland masters.

26 Sinclair *Orkney Parishes* 180–1

27 The account books in HBCA A 16 series give good coverage for Albany but there are gaps in the records for all the other factories.

28 Complete records were available for only three labourers and nine tradesmen in this cohort.

29 Sinclair *Orkney Parishes* 78

30 This figure is based on a calculation of the average number of livestock for small farms in Orphir valued according to figures provided by the Rev. William Clouston (ibid 74, 112).

'Mixt Bands of Many Nations': 1821–70

CAROL M. JUDD

In the period after union of the North West Company and Hudson's Bay Company in 1821, a rich blend of diverse ethnic groups entered the northern department as employees of the Hudson's Bay Company. Some stayed for just a few years and then left; others served the company for many years before retiring to their homeland. Still others retired within the northern department. Thus the area now known as western Canada was formed and shaped from the outset of European occupation by a polyglot of ethnic groups which were continuously re-infused with new arrivals. Neither the diversity nor impact of these disparate groups in the society that developed in Rupert's Land has ever been systematically investigated. This paper will consider one aspect of the broad topic of ethnic participation in the fur trade. It will probe the ethnicity of annual recruitments to the servant classes of the Hudson's Bay Company from 1821 to 1870.

For the period under study, the records of the Hudson's Bay Company were not entirely consistent in their use of the term 'servant.' For formal purposes and in post accounts[1] all employees were usually called servants. Servant engagement registers[2] and contract records[3] listed only those employees below the level of shareholder. The minutes of the council of the northern department in its annual requisitions for servants,[4] however, also excluded clerks, apprentice clerks, postmasters, and interpreters. This paper will focus on the broad category of servants requested by the council of the northern department.

The largest number of servants were engaged at the lowest level of servitude, as middlemen or as labourers. These men performed a variety of manual tasks around the fur trade posts in winter and manned the company's boats and canoes in summer.[5] They fished and hunted, chopped and carried wood, packed furs, worked as unskilled carpenters, cleaned barns and byres, whitewashed buildings, and of course rowed boats (or paddled canoes), portaged cargo, and cooked their own food as well as that of officers.[6] Labourers and middlemen were usually hired at an annual salary of £17 to £20. Their three- to five-year contracts were subject to renewal upon the agreement of both contracting parties. They received room, board, and sometimes 'equipment' or gratuities[7] in addition to their salary. The labouring group had at least a limited range of career mobility. Middlemen could become bowsmen, steersmen, or guides. Labourers could specialize as hunters, fishermen, steersmen, or other upper-level voyageurs. They could, in exceptional circumstances, even become postmasters, the highest level of employment to which common servants could aspire.

Specialized servants also included tradesmen (often called mechanics)[8] such as blacksmiths, coopers, tailors, carpenters, boatbuilders, tinsmiths, and stonemasons. Tradesmen were hired at wages that varied from about £25 to £40 per annum to perform specific skilled tasks and were frequently recruited from areas not normally tapped for ordinary labouring servants. These men, in consideration of their specialized trades, were set apart from ordinary servants, receiving special allowances or exemptions from menial labour, and often allowed separate living quarters.[9] Thus the labouring classes of servants were stratified socially both in the eyes of the administrators of the fur trade and in the perceptions of the servants themselves.

An investigation of the ethnic identity of the members of the servant class of company employees is basic to an understanding of that segment of the labour force. Since the records do not indicate ethnic origins one must use other sources to deduce this information. This paper uses the ethnic labels provided by the letters and remarks of the officers of the company. The servant engagement registers, from which are drawn the statistics used in this paper, include a category of record entitled 'parish.' This record, being geographical, can be linked to the ethnic labels provided by the company to ascribe an ethnic background to each servant for whom a parish is given. However, the exact meaning of 'parish' is not recorded. It may have meant either the place of birth or the place where the employee spent his childhood. Less likely, it may simply have referred to the person's residence at the time of signing a contract. For the purposes of analysis, this paper assumes that 'parish' referred to the place from which the contracting employee derived his cultural traits.[10]

For about the first decade after its formation in 1670, the Hudson's Bay Company apparently hired all of its employees exclusively from the vicinity of London. By 1682 it was beginning to consider engaging Scots and shortly after the turn of the eighteenth century the company began to hire Orkneymen.[11] From then until the nineteenth century, the company engaged English, Scottish, and Orkney servants to run its overseas trade.

In the last quarter of the eighteenth century, competition from Canadian-based companies directly tapping the interior regions of the northwest forced the Hudson's Bay Company to expand inland and do likewise. This decision in its simplest terms meant that the company now had to maintain inland as well as coastal posts. It meant also that company servants who would transport trade goods to and from inland posts would replace Indian middlemen who had previously brought their furs to the bayside. Quite naturally, the company at first used Indians to operate its inland canoes,[12] but it soon began to train Orkneymen for this task.

From the outset it experienced serious difficulty recruiting suitable men and then enticing to re-enlist at reasonable wages those servants who were experienced inland canoeists and boatmen. By 1810 chronic man-power shortages forced the company to establish recruiting agents not only in the Orkneys but in Glasgow and on the Island of Coll. A year later the company also recruited rowdy Irishmen especially to intimidate the Nor'Westers. In 1814 several Norwegians also were sent to York Factory. Although Canadians occasionally deserted to the Hudson's Bay Company from its competitors, only in 1810 did the company seriously consider actively recruiting them. Canadians, engaged to the Hudson's Bay Company as voyageurs for Athabasca, first reached the northwest in 1815 and from then until 1820 were sent annually from Montreal. The Canadian group also included Iroquois who in 1818 were seen en route to Athabasca.[13]

During the period of competition with the North West Company, the Hudson's Bay Company suffered acute manpower shortages. To alleviate the problem, it diversified its hiring practices to include Irish, Norwegian, Canadian, and Iroquois. An old clerk much later succinctly summed up the result of this ethnic diversification among servants: 'First of all they had Orkney men – some good men among them. Then they got some Highlanders but they had the fear of God and would not break the Sabbath day they got Irish men to play the Shelila "a bit of timber" on the N.W. Company – but it was found that more than one party could play at the game and that *Pat* was more troublesome to his Master than to the opponents. Then they got Swedes [actually Norwegians], then Canadians when the Companys joined – but the Canadians worth keeping would not become "Esclave aux Anglais."[14] Thus the early ethnic diversification of hiring was seen in many ways as an unfortunate occurrence for the fur trade.

After the union in 1821, many of the formerly opposing posts and the manpower to run them became superfluous. Within three months of taking over direction of the northern department (itself a creation of the union), George Simpson had decided to reduce the burden of salaries by 25 per cent; to do this he would have to discharge immediately at least 250 men. Stating that each district had nearly double the number needed for maintaining it, Simpson intended to continue cutting back until the contingent of servants was suitably reduced.[15] With such an unprecedented opportunity at hand, Simpson might easily have reduced his staff by releasing ethnic groups that were considerably generally undesirable.

In fact, the reductions of staff after 1821 were made (at least as indicated by the surviving written record) without reference to ethnicity. Faced with salary cuts, and forced to work for a new company, some servants probably retired voluntarily. Others were discharged at the end of their contracts. The first forced reductions were imposed on older servants with large families. Since the company maintained families at posts by allowing dependents free rations and lodging, it believed that this measure would considerably reduce its overhead costs. Men with savings, or at least those who were not in debt, were then released. The company, however, retained men who were in debt (but not encumbered with large families) as the only means of recovering the amount owed. In addition, the 'leading turbulent characters' who were inciting mutiny against 'the new order of things' were let go free.[16]

In 1823, Simpson reported that initial servant reductions were complete, that most recruits for 1824 could be procured from among those whose contracts were expiring, but that fresh recruits would have to be introduced in 1825.[17] With its much reduced staff of young, active men without families, but inclined to indebtedness, as the nucleus of its labour force, the company was now able to formulate a coherent philosophy of hiring. Ethnicity was a key consideration in determining recruitments: 'The relative qualifications and merits of Canadians and Orkney men have been duly weighed and the preference is given to the former in so far as regards the duties and services to be performed, but in point of expense which is likewise a very important consideration the opinion is in favor of

the Orkney men. The Canadians, generally speaking are a volatile incon-
siderate race of people, but active, capable of undergoing great hardships
and easily managed by those who are accustomed to deal with them; the
Orkneymen on the contrary are slow and do not possess the same physical
strength, and spirits necessary on trying occasions; they are moreover
when not awed by force obstinate to an extreme and so gaurded [sic] that
it is a difficult matter to discover any plots or determinations they may
form until ready to be acted upon. If brought young into the Country
however say from 18 to 22 years of age they may be greatly improved; and
upon the whole we consider it good policy to have about an equal proportion of each, which will Keep up a spirit of competition and enable us to
deal with them on such terms as may be considered necessary and proper.
Scotch and Irish in any considerable numbers we have strong objections to
being quarrelsome independent and inclined to form leagues and cabals
which might be dangerous to the peace of the Country.'[18] As of 1823, then,
Simpson's stated policy was to maintain an even balance of Canadians
and Orcadians, in order to encourage competition and facilitate their
management. He wanted no more than a sprinkling of Scots and Irish
servants.

In 1824 and 1825 the company made additional cuts in staff by further
reducing the number of posts and tightening up the already revised
transportation system. Indeed, Simpson admitted that numbers were
'now as low as safety will allow.' Despite these cut-backs, in 1825 the
company was unable to get its full complement of recruits from either
Canada or Europe. A year earlier Simpson had considered that mixed
bloods in Rupert's Land were too proud and independent to enter the
service; they were also poor risks, being 'indolent and unsteady ... fit only
for voyaging.' Now, faced with shortages in his recruits, Simpson was
forced to reverse his position and consider engaging young 'halfbreeds
from Red River. ... If brought into the Service at a sufficiently early period
of life,' he rationalized, 'they will become useful steady Men and taking all
things into consideration I think they will be found the cheapest and best
servants we can get.'[19]

With this decision, Simpson and the company embraced a strategy of
hiring, within strict wage limits, from three areas: Britain, the St Lawrence, and Rupert's Land. The strategy included balancing recruitments
in an effort best to promote the interests of the fur trade. This quota
system remained in effect until external circumstances forced its abandonment. While in use, the quota system meant, for example, that recruits

from one region might have been substandard, being all that was available at the salary offered; or they might not have been available at all, thereby causing potential manpower shortages in the northern department.[20]

To counteract such difficulties the company usually employed one of three methods. Sometimes it offered higher wages to recruits. Although the higher wages were offset by higher prices being charged for purchases at fur trade posts, men coming into the country at higher salaries were considered to excite 'jealousy' among those working at lower wages.[21] Therefore, this measure was undertaken only as a last resort.

The company also encouraged retiring employees to re-engage. This would decrease the number of new recruits needed and provide a pool of experienced labour; it would also forestall retiring servants from becoming colonists in the struggling settlement of Red River.

The third alternative was by far the most popular. If men were difficult to procure in one region within a hiring area, the company would engage from another. This worked quite well in Europe where the recruitment base was generally in the Orkney Islands. Alternative regions included Lewis, the Shetlands, mainland Scotland, and even England and Ireland. In Canada, this alternative was less available. The company could attempt to tap different regions of the St Lawrence, but the labour pool remained basically unchanged. All Canadian men had similar employment options, usually lumbering, canal building, work with American fur trade companies, and, later, railway construction. People residing in the northern department and its environs helped to offset recruitment problems in other areas by providing a constant, readily available source of labour. During the decades under study, this important region contributed a large and increasing number of recruits.

In 1824 the northern department requested 'thirty stout young men' from Orkney on five-year contracts at £15 per annum. It also required the same number of Canadians. They would comprise the recruits of 1825. Here, then, is the first tangible evidence that servants were systematically recruited from several regions at once. The engagement registers for 1825, however, recorded a total of only 42 recruits beneath the level of clerk as having arrived in Rupert's Land. Of these 21 are known to have come from Canada, only 9 from the Orkneys, 1 from Ireland, and 1 from Scotland; 5 were hired from Rupert's Land and 5 were of unknown origin (see Table 1). According to Simpson's records, 12 men were sent from Orkney; therefore the company fell far short of its requested complement of Orcadians. Those who came were of poor quality. They complained about the climate and feigned illness. In fact 5 of the 12 were

TABLE 1
Recruits for the Northern Department *excluding clerks*

Year	Can	Nat	Scot	Ork	Lew	Sh	Ire	US	Eng	Unk	Total
1823	2	1		2							5
1824	1			9							10
1825	21	5	1	9			1			5	42
1826	26	20	1	10			1			12	70
1827	52	16	2	4				1	1	18	94
1828	10	11		18						12	51
1829	13	11	5	23						13	65
1830	25	10	2	30						5	72
1831	18	8		7	12		1			5	51
1832	12	19	1	1	26					14	73
1833	32	25	2	31					2	8	100
1834	9	4	2	15						4	35
1835	11	19	1	24			1			6	62
1836	14	10	3	21					13	2	64
1837	7	9	1		23		1			1	42
1838	13	10	2	27					2	2	56
1839	10	13	1	13						1	38
1840	6	12	1	4	26					2	51
1841	10	22	1	9	31						73
1842	3	10		19		16				2	50
1843	17	9		33						1	60
1844	10	13	1	19						4	47
1845	6	10		9						3	28
1846	4	18	3	9		4		1		2	41
1847	20	17	2	11	6	6				3	65
1848	13	17	2	12	1	16			1	2	64

Note:
Can = Canada   Sh = Shetlands
Nat = Native   Ire = Ireland
Scot = Scotland   us = United States
Ork = Orkneys   Eng = England
Lew = Lewis   Unk = Unknown
SOURCE: HBCA B 239/u/1-3

judged 'unfit for the duties of the Service ... and they are accordingly provided with a passage back.' Blaming John Rae, the company's hiring agent at Stromness, Simpson suggested that Rae either select candidates more carefully or that he be replaced by someone who would.[22]

As early as 1825, then, the company was experiencing some difficulty obtaining recruits. Especially in its expanding regions of MacKenzie River and west of the mountains the northern department again faced a shortage of manpower. In fact, Simpson appealed in 1828 to chief factor Ed Smith, in charge of Mackenzie River, to 're-engage as many [servants] as possible inland, owing to the very great demand for men.' That year the company requested and probably obtained its full complement of 20 Orcadians. The next year, despite offering a somewhat higher salary, Simpson instructed his agent to hire the required 30 labourers before the end of December, fearing that otherwise the agents for the Davis Strait fisheries would have the choice of men. Although the Orkney lads who arrived in those few years were by some accounts satisfactory,[23] Simpson apparently disagreed and in 1831 wrote: 'The European servants for next year I would recommend being got from Lewis, as those we have lately had from Orkney are by no means adapted for our work, being generally weak, soft & unhealthy.'[24]

In 1831, at least 12 Lewis men had arrived at York Factory. In 1832 a further 26 Lewis men and 3 mainland Scots, and only 1 Orkneyman, were included among the recruits.[25] Simpson, however, quickly changed his mind about the men from Lewis: 'The Lewis islanders are preferable in many points of view, being strong, hardy, active, and fit to be immediately employed on labourious service, but, although steady well behaved and generally of a serious turn of mind, we find them exceedingly stubborn and difficult of management and so clannish that it is scarcely possible to deal with them singly. Under those circumstances we are not desirous of having any more of them in the country at present, and highlanders are equally objectionable from the same cause.'[26]

Although a full complement of 30 promising Orkneymen reached the northern department in 1833, a contingent of Englishmen was also apparently sent out.[27] John Rowand noticed when they reached Edmonton, that although not small, the Englishmen were unable to carry 200-pound packages of grease as recommended. In 1836, a large group of English farmers was brought in, and a year later 24 more Lewis men came.[28] In 1842, 16 Shetlanders were recruited. From then on the company apparently gave up trying to recruit mainly in the Orkneys and began relying on several areas for its personnel.

The diversification of recruitment areas within a hiring region was not a decision based on preference, but rather was born of necessity. Orcadians were no longer easily obtained. In 1840, for example, the governor and committee described its continuing plight: 'The difficulty of procuring men in the Orkneys has again rendered it necessary for us to apply to the Lewis Islands for the Servants required for this years service: for altho' notice was given in the Orkneys as far back as November last only Eleven out of the Forty-six indented for have offered themselves. We cannot account for the unwillingness shewn by the Orkney people to enter the service as we have always heard they are well-treated and the wages allowed are fully as high as they could obtain in other quarters.'[29] According to a historian of the Orkneys, this phenomenon reflected a revolution in Orkney agriculture which improved conditions at home and made employment overseas less desirable.[30]

By 1842 the pattern of moving into ever new areas for recruits was well established. Most new groups were considered less than ideal: the English farm servants sent out in 1836 were so difficult to manage, being 'insolent, indolent, and mischievous' that four of the worst families were banished to the Columbia.[31] Other groups, especially in large numbers, also proved troublesome.

In addition, by the mid-1850s even the new areas were becoming less reliable sources, particularly when added to the general increase in the requirements.[32] As a solution, the company turned to Norwegians. Between 1854 and 1857, 94 Norwegians reached the northern department.[33] At this point complaints began to flood through Rupert's Land. The northern council at Norway House in 1858 discussed the problem thoroughly, and Simpson expressed its dilemma to the governor and committee: 'We sincerely regret to learn that almost insuperable difficulties are experienced in recruiting for the service in Orkney, Shetland, and the Highlands; and in consequence, you have again been obliged to have recourse to the North of Europe, for the Coy. of this Season. After giving the Norwegians a fair trial, we have come to the irresistable conclusion that they are not suited to the Company's service. We even consider it would be better to be short handed for a time, than to have the lives of our officers and servants and the safety of our establishments endangered by bringing to the country bodies of disorderly, impracticable men over whom we can exercise no controul and who virtually give us loss.[34] Indeed, so averse to this group of men was the northern council that it offered the whole of the 1858 contingent free passage home before it even got off the ship: 27 apparently left, and only 8 stayed to serve their contracts.[35] Such strong measures were unusual if not unique in the annals of the fur trade.

The problem of maintaining a constant supply of suitable recruits had only temporarily ended in 1821. As early as 1825 the company began to experience difficulty acquiring new European servants. Despite their perceived faults, Orcadians were preferred in the long run over all other

European groups: Lewis men, Highland Scots, Shetlanders, and even Norwegians were recruited to the northern department out of necessity rather than choice. But not all the company's servants were European.

Immediately after the coalition of 1821, George Simpson revealed that the northern council preferred Canadian servants: 'in regard to the description of menial servants, best calculated for the general business of the Country, we are disposed with few exceptions, to allow the preference to the Canadians, particularly as regarded activity and dispatch, and where much fatigue, hardship, and privations, were to be encountered.[36] Specifically, Canadians were deemed to be better canoemen and boatmen, better able to survive the rigours of long voyages, and better workers around the fort, especially as woodsmen.[37]

In 1824 the northern council ordered its first known group of Canadian recruits since coalition. It required 30 men. The Montreal agents, however, reported great difficulty attracting candidates, citing poor pay and reports of fines and harsh treatment as impediments.[38] Upon changing agents, the company began to have better luck hiring both tradesmen and voyageurs.

In Europe one could easily see ethnic patterns in the company's hiring strategy. In Canada, it is impossible to detect deliberate shifts in hiring regions. Neither Upper Canada nor the Maritimes were sources for recruits: presumably either people from these regions did not find service with the company attractive, or they did not possess the requisite skills. Lower Canada remained the focus for recruitment. Within this region employees tended to come from older, more closely settled centres such as Sorel, Maskinongé, and Montreal. They engaged from certain parishes (such as Berthier, Maskinongé, and Sault Saint-Louis), and counties.[39] Between 1823 and 1848 recruits for the Hudson's Bay Company came largely from the region between Montreal and Three Rivers, from the parishes on the banks of the St Lawrence.[40] In the earlier years many came from the counties of Berthier, Yamaska, and St Maurice further down the St Lawrence, but in the later years there was a decided shift toward Montreal and west. In the 1850s the trend to the west continued with recruits also beginning to come from along the Ottawa River as well as further down the St Lawrence, particularly near Quebec.

It is impossible at this stage to deal with these people as ethnic groups. Most of the Canadians were apparently French-speaking. Some were Iroquois from St Regis, Two Mountains, and Sault Saint-Louis. One cannot determine from the information at hand what proportion of recruits were of Iroquois descent. In 1835, for example, agent James Keith claimed to have 11 'whites' and 12 Iroquois ready to send west on contracts; however, on comparing Keith's figure with the company's engagement records, only 10 Canadians apparently came at all that year. Of these, 3 were probably Iroquois; of the 14 recruits from Canada in the following year, perhaps 4 were Iroquois.[41] The 'missing' voyageurs may have been sent straight through to the Columbia department and missed being recorded in the engagement register for the northern department.

Beginning in 1834 (see Table 1) the number of Canadians who signed on to work for the company dropped off sharply. Except for brief periods of recovery, Canadian quotas remained difficult to reach. In 1841, after requesting 40 Canadian recruits, Simpson lamented that the company had offered higher wages and should have had its pick of recruits. But hiring was as difficult that year as previously and among those obtained were very few good hands. 'Voyaging,' he complained, 'seems to be getting into disuse or out of fashion among the French Canadians.' Because the company had raised wages and still had not been able to hire good men, it determined no longer to deviate from its district standard salary (or prix du poste) 'even if we hire no one.' This stand caused at least temporary inconvenience as the company attempted to divert its hiring field more heavily to Europe. With this move can be seen the abandonment of the policy of balancing recruits from the two important areas. In 1845, for example, Simpson requested an increase in the number of recruits from Europe 'as far as such can be done without overburdening the York ship with passengers.'[42]

It would appear that French-Canadians never again engaged in ample numbers for the fur trade. The economy of Lower Canada was improving, and lumbering, railroad building, and other industries which offered higher salaries were more attractive to Canadians. Nevertheless, at least a trickle of recruits continued to flow from Lower Canada. Their geographic origins had changed, from Montreal and down river to Three Rivers, to encompass a broad area stretching from Pontiac in the northwest to beyond Quebec City in the east. The recruits also apparently derived in later years from somewhat different ethnic roots as Iroquois and mixed-blood Iroquois and French became more prominent.[43] In 1860 Sir George Simpson summed up the change that had taken place: 'The old class of Canadian Voyageurs, so long celebrated in this country, has disappeared as their occupation fell into desuetude, and we have now to depend almost exclusively on Iroquois for the little work we still do. Though excellent men for hard labor, they lack the dash, the vivacity and the song, which characterised the old voyageurs and were the chief attractions of canoeing.'[44]

In Canada as in Europe, the company apparently recruited from favourite places.[45] As the economy of an area fluctuated so too did the number of recruits it offered. In each region the company had relatively inflexible salary limits. It would not hire at all if the choice was to shift permanently its wage scale. This policy worked reasonably well as long as Rupert's Land remained the source of a constant supply of inexpensive labour.

Unfortunately, the company's engagement registers do not permit an accurate count of the people who engaged from Rupert's Land. They account only for those employees who worked under contracts of from one to seven years; in addition, the registers do not apparently include even all of these.[46] The bulk of the employees from the northern department engaged only for the season or for a trip in the company's boats and therefore did not fall within the purview of the registers. To date no complete record of casual or seasonal employees has come to light.[47]

The engagement registers also pose another difficulty: an employee from Rupert's Land was nearly always identified as 'native' in the record. Among the ethnic groups covered by this umbrella label were Indians, mixed bloods, and theoretically at least, also Europeans. Because very few natives of Rupert's Land at that time were of European descent, and fewer still probably worked for the Hudson's Bay Company, it is reasonable to assume that 'native' employees were either mixed bloods or Indians.

Indians were used as inland canoeists in the 1770s. Owing to chronic manpower shortages, they probably continued to participate in inland transport throughout the competition period. During that time the company also hired a limited number of half-breeds.[48] Two years after union, the first 'native' to appear in the new register engaged with the company. In 1825, unable to recruit its full complement of servants from Orkney or Canada, the company looked more seriously at Red River half-breeds. Indeed, Simpson anticipated that in a few years Red River would become the company's 'principal Nursery for voyageurs.'[49] The chief expressed advantages of local employees were their availability and cheap cost. That year at least five natives signed contracts with the company. In 1826, 20 more engaged (see Table 1).

Because so many had deserted the year before, Simpson announced in 1827 that he had hired no Red River half-breeds. 'But we mean to employ a few next year' he announced, 'and by distributing them throughout the country there will be less danger from their misconduct; as Boat and

Canoe men, and winter travellers they surpass both our European and Canadian Servants but they are not sufficiently steady for regular work at the Establishments until they attain a certain age when they become the most efficient men we have got.'[50] Obviously, then, his refusal to hire Red River mixed bloods in 1827 was a ploy to make them more manageable. In fact, his report reiterated 'in the course of a few years I think it [Red River] will be found the best nursery for the service.' Indeed a continuous and growing stream of local people continued to sign contracts with the Hudson's Bay Company. Many others worked for the season or for a single trip. The famous Portage La Loche brigade, dating from this period, was manned exclusively by Red River tripmen.

The company hired 'natives' primarily as voyageurs, but in 1830 gentlemen in charge of posts employing tradesmen were given permission also to hire half-breeds on seven-year contracts as apprentices. The boys, not to be younger than fourteen years, could not be employed with their fathers or in the districts in which their families lived.[51]

The company also employed Indians under contract, though more often they were seasonal employees. They were particularly prominent on the brigades of boats that shuttled up and down the important waterways between Red River and the coast. Simpson also intended to use Indians and half-breeds for the winter road which would follow the same route to Hudson Bay. In Athabasca and Mackenzie, Chipewyan Indians served in the brigades, and at Portage La Loche they transported cargo.[52] In fact, in 1832 Simpson recorded: 'I was at one time of opinion that very [few] of our Indians possessed sufficient physical strength for the severe duties of the voyage, but from the work I have seen them go through since we have employed them regularly as carriers, I am satisfied that if they are gradually broke in to labour they are fully equal to our voyaging service, and in many respects preferable to either European or Canadian servants, being more trustworthy when property is left under their own charge.[53]

Despite this glowing tribute, only those Indians who lived in barren country like York Factory, Norway House, and Berens River were really welcome as regular employees. Those Indians who began congregating at Portage La Loche to earn a livelihood by carrying goods across the gruelling twelve-mile portage were soon considered dangerous to the trade.[54] Indians were more usefully employed, from the company's perspective, in hunting furs or bringing in provisions.[55]

Yet as time went on the company began to rely more and more heavily on local Indians and mixed bloods to fill its recruitment quotas. By the mid-1850s these two groups of native people were the largest components of the company's labour force. This reliance was a direct result of increased employment options in Europe and Canada making service with the company a less desirable option at a time when larger numbers of recruits were required to meet the needs of the northern department.[56] In addition local people also had expanding employment options most notably trading on their own account to St Paul.

As a result good local recruits also became difficult to find. In 1853 James Anderson requested three boatmen from Red River for his Mackenzie district. He asked that 'Men with no families or small ones should be selected if possible; their characters should also be good.' The response he received was startling. 'The best men that can be procured within the prescribed limits as to wages shall be engaged but it is by no means easy to find Boutes at all who will engage much less single men or men whose character will bear close examination.[57]

A few years later the Company had become so dependent upon local people to man its boat brigades that it found itself in a delicate position regarding what it called 'Petty Traders': 'Your desire that steps should be taken against the Petty Traders who are at present opposing the Company, shall receive my best attention; but without the necessary force, to coerse the native population who side with them, I do not clearly see what is to be done. Threats, which would be disregarded, would be worse than useless, unless followed by active measures. There would be no difficulty in seizing the property and persons of any of the free Traders at a distance from Red River; but the consequences would be felt, the following summer at Depots when the Brigades from the interior were assembled. The crews consisting principally of semi savages halfbreeds and Indians, related to or connected with the Traders, would unquestionably retaliate on the Company and from their numerical superiority we should be unable to encounter the storm that would be raised. And vast destruction of life & property would be the first result, followed by the annihilation of the Company's Trade.'[58]

Later still 'native' employees exerted more direct pressure for better terms from the company. In 1863 James Grahame described the Indians of his boat crews as insubordinate, slow, and inordinately heavy eaters, who had successfully demanded an advanced rate of wages.[59] Therefore when Canadian and European sources became inadequate the company increasingly turned Rupert's Land, if not Red River, into its 'principal nursery for voyageurs.' When this occurred native employees achieved a new position of importance in the company's operations.

The expansion of the company's business inland in the 1770s had provoked chronic shortages of labour and forced the diversification from
traditional Orkney sources to include several ethnic groups. At union in
1821, the company suffered fleetingly from a surplus of labour. Within a
few years it began replacing with young recruits many of its older, experienced servants who, because of their large families or frugal habits, had
been forced to retire.[60]

In fact, the quest for healthy, energetic, but easily managed servants at a
reasonable price[61] did not end with the inauguration of the monopoly.
Ethnicity was an important factor in the selection of recruits. While the
council of the northern department preferred Canadian servants, the
governor and committee favoured Orcadians.[62] The blending of these two
perspectives produced a policy of balancing recruitments in the Orkneys
and Canada. In both areas suitable recruits were often hard to find.

The company's expansion into new areas of North America brought a
continuing heavy demand for labour to run its transport system. The
company was unable or unwilling to increase substantially the salaries of
labourers. At the same time increasing prosperity in Europe and Canada
brought more lucrative employment opportunities at home and made
employment abroad less desirable. The company was compelled to look
ever further afield for recruits. In Europe this meant utilizing men from
Lewis, mainland Scotland, England, and the Shetlands to augment the
Orcadian nucleus. In Canada, regions outside the preferred recruitment
areas had to be increasingly tapped until even these sources became
unreliable. In an effort to maintain a reasonable supply of recruits, the
company abandoned its policy of balanced hiring, and began to resort
more heavily to northern Europe. In the words of the old observer,
Charles McKenzie, 'They then had recourse to mixt bands of many
nations ... I only pity those who must do with such men in Inland posts.'[63]
This new venture in fact culminated in the return of 27 Norwegian
recruits in 1858. To complete its work force the company hired more and
more 'native' labourers. Eventually Indians and mixed bloods dominated
the servant class of contracted recruits in the northern department.
Themselves the sons of fur traders, the half-breed servants at least indirectly continued the blend of many diverse ethnic groups which had
comprised fur trade society for nearly a century.

This paper has demonstrated that many cultural groups leavened fur
trade society in the post-union period. In so doing it has raised questions
for further study. How and why did the Hudson's Bay Company develop

its hiring strategy? How effective was that strategy in terms of management tactics?

The paper has described the infusion of new recruits into the northern department. What happened after they arrived? Was there, for example, an ethnic basis for career patterns – were some groups more vertically mobile than others; did some groups concentrate on certain specializations; was ethnic background a consideration in geographical distribution or in retirement patterns; did some cultural groups re-engage more often than others; were some more manageable; conversely, was ethnicity a significant factor in mutiny and other expressions of labour unrest?

The study of ethnic groups in the fur trade is suited to both qualitative and quantitative approaches; indeed, historians can no longer overlook the fundamental question of ethnicity when examining social and labour aspects of fur trade society.

NOTES AND REFERENCES

1 HBCA B, record type d
2 HBCA B 239/u/1–3. Parishes taken from this source formed the basis of analysis undertaken in this paper. Philip Goldring, Wayne White, and I recorded them, along with all other data in that source, June to August, 1977.
3 HBCA A 32
4 HBCA B 239/k/2–3. Requisitions for servants were not made through the northern council until 1837 (for the year 1838).
5 It would appear that the terms middleman and labourer were interchangeable. Labourers usually came from Europe, while middlemen were recruited as a rule in Canada. Both groups were hired to engage in transport and in addition to perform other manual tasks.
6 See, for example, HBCA D 4/90, 57.
7 In 1822 the company attempted to eliminate the issuing of equipment, but with only partial success. Gratuities were given for performing duties beyond those enumerated in the servant's contract, and were recorded, at least in some cases, in the servant engagement registers cited above.
8 HBCA D 4/87, 90ff (minutes of temporary council held at York Factory, 1 July 1824, etc.)
9 McKenzie The Men of the Hudson's Bay Company, 1670–1920 21–2
10 The servant engagement registers, themselves based on servant contracts, provide in tabulated form several types of career information about individual servants. They include not only parish of birth or origin, but details of

individual contracts, gratuities, transfers between departments, retirement dates in many cases, and sometimes dates of birth and death.

To be useful, the several hundred parishes as provided by the registers had to be identified with a region or country. In many cases the parish name alone was the only clue necessary to place it within a country. Sorel, for example, was in Lower Canada; Stromness was in Orkney, and Stornoway was in Lewis. Other parishes were ambiguous. In nearly all cases where parish was included in the engagement register, the place of engagement was also recorded. Since most men engaged at established recruitment centres, the region or country of origin could be inferred. This did not eliminate the problem caused by some men apparently engaging at York Factory, by incorrect spelling or illegible handwriting, or by subsequent changes in parish boundaries.

I have used the company's own ethnic labels for European servants. Canadian servants were identified with counties. Wherever possible Iroquois settlements have been considered separately. No effort was made to separate ethnic groups from those who were listed as native. In this case I have relied· entirely on the comments and judgments of the qualitative record for discussing ethnic background.

11 Rich *Hudson's Bay Company: 1670–1870* I 146, 378–9
12 The company depended upon Indians as voyageurs until the 1780s, when its own servants began to be so engaged (Glover Intro. to *Cumberland House Journals and Inland Journals, 1775–82. Second Series, 1779–82* lxix).
13 HBCA A 5/5, 52; B 42/b/57, 19; Rich *History* II 334; HBCA B 22/a/21 4
14 PAC MG 19 A 44, Charles McKenzie Papers: Charles McKenzie to Hector McKenzie, Bonnie Point, Lac Seul, 28 Nov. 1853
15 HBCA D 4/1, 20; D 4/85, 3, Simpson's Official Reports, 1822
16 HBCA D 4/85, 43, Simpson's Official Reports, 1822; D 4/85, 65–6; D 4/86, 7, Simpson's Official Reports, 1823; D 4/85, 4, Simpson's Official Reports, 1822; Fleming ed *Minutes of Council Northern Department of Ruperts Land, 1821–31* 306, governor and committee to Simpson, 27 Feb. 1822. No complete records survive for servants for this period.
17 HBCA D 4/86, 13, Simpson's Official Reports, 1823
18 HBCA D 4/86, 14f–14
19 HBCA D 4/88, 29, Simpson's Official Reports, 1825; D 4/87, 27f, Simpson's Official Reports, 1824; D 4/87, 8; D 4/88, 57f, Simpson's Official Reports, 1825
20 HBCA D 4/96, 5, Simpson's Official Reports, 1829; PABC, Add. Mss 345, vol 2, file 93, James Hargrave to governor, chief factors & chief traders, northern department, York Factory, 28 Aug. 1839; HBCA B 235/c/1, 68, governor and committee to Thomas Simpson, 4 June 1840
21 HBCA D 4/100, 2, Simpson's Official Reports, 1834; D 4/100, 48f; D 4/100, 2

22 HBCA D 4/87, 33f, Simpson's Official Reports, 1824; B 239/u/1; D 4/88, 99, Simpson's Official Reports, 1825. The 1825 figure is perhaps inflated as it includes several people who may have been renewing contracts but appear in the contract book for the first time.

23 HBCA D 4/90, 115, Simpson to Edward Smith, in charge of Mackenzie River District, York Factory, 9 July 1827; D 4/92, 54, Simpson's Official Reports, 1828; D 4/125, 105f, Simpson's Correspondence Book Inwards, Edward Smith to Simpson, Portage La Loche, 28 July 1830

24 HBCA D 4/98, 44f, Simpson's Official Reports, 1831

25 HBCA B 239/u/1: The recruits include 14 of unknown origin; therefore this figure is approximate, as are all others.

26 HBCA D 4/99, 3f, Simpson's Official Reports, 1832

27 The quantitative record (see Table 1) indicates that only 2 were sent; however, it includes 8 of unknown origin as well as 2 mainland Scots.

28 HBCA D 4/126, 64, Simpson's Correspondence Book Inwards, Rowand to Simpson, Edmonton House, 10 Jan. 1834; B 239/u/1

29 HBCA B 235/c/1, 68

30 GAI Marwick 'Colonists & Adventurers' unpaged, 1963, D 971.201.M392

31 HBCA D 4/106, p. 36, Simpson's Official Reports, 1839

32 HBCA B 239/k/1–3 and B 239/u/1–3. Further research is required before reasons for this increased need can be provided.

33 HBCA B 239/u/2

34 HBCA D 4/78, 844, Simpson's Correspondence Books Outward (general)

35 HBCA B 239/g/38, 74; B 239/u/2

36 Fleming *Minutes* 416, Simpson to governor and council of southern department, York Factory, 30 Aug. 1822 (HBCA D 4/2, 3–6)

37 HBCA D 4/85, 4, Simpson's Official Reports, 1822; D 4/85, 14; Fleming *Minutes* 416; HBCA D 4/85, 44f

38 HBCA D 4/88, 74 Simpson's Official Reports, 1825. Simpson denied the charges: 'I beg leave most solemnly to assure Your Honors that they [the reports] are not founded on fact, [our fines are few, furthermore,] In regard to treatment, I moreover do not hesitate to say, and I say it with pride and satisfaction that the people never since the commencement of the fur trade were so well clothed, so well fed, so lightly Wrought so rarely maimed in maintaining proper discipline and subordination, in short so comfortable and well disposed as they have been during the last three years in the Northern Department.'

39 HBCA B 239/u/1. (Counties have been inferred from the 'parish' data.)

40 This observation is based on Bouchette *The British Dominions in North America* passim.

41 HBCA D 4/127, 73f, Simpson's Correspondence Book Inwards, 1833–35; B 239/u/1. The 36 recruits from Sorel included only two English names. Some Iroquois were métis; others may not have had Indian names. Several people engaging from Iroquois areas had French-Canadian names.

42 HBCA D 4/109, 22, Simpson's Official Reports, 1841; D 4/109, 23f; B 235/b/3, 8; A 12/2, 665; London Inward Correspondence from Simpson, 1845 (Lachine, 9 Dec. 1845): 'The price of labor is exceedingly high in this country at present and likely to continue so, arising from the demand for canals, railroads and other public works. I am, therefore, apprehensive we shall not be able to get the number of men required for the interior, unless a very considerable advance of wages be given; and as such advance might tend to raise the wages in the interior, I think it will be more politic, however inconvenient, to dispense with the recruits from Canada for next year, and to increase the number from Europe, as far as such can be done without overburdening the York ship with passengers.'

43 Spry *The Palliser Expedition: An Account of John Palliser's British North American Exploration Expedition, 1857–1860* 23

44 HBCA D 4/57, 116, Simpson Correspondence

45 HBCA D 4/25, 128, Simpson's Correspondence Outward, Simpson to James Keith (London, 18 Nov. 1840): 'The engagements of the Recruits to be for a term of 3 to 5 years, all to be taken from the Voyageur parishes, carefully excluding those who are brought up in the neighbourhood of Towns and as many of the favorite names, La Vallés, L'Esperances, Felixes, Convoyées etc. as possible.' Checking this statement against the quantitative record indicates that all of the families who are represented in that source came from Sorel.

46 Early indications are that employees from Rupert's Land may be under-recorded by about 30 per cent, but considerable research will be necessary before a more definite statement can be made.

47 The only source yet found which is at all useful is HBCA B 239/g which includes abstracts of the accounts of 'inland summer tripmen' and 'summermen' for most years.

48 This was drawn to my attention by John Nicks, Feb. 1978.

49 HBCA D 4/88, 54, Simpson's Official Reports, 1825

50 HBCA D 4/90, 9, Simpson's Official Reports, 1827; but see Table 1: 16 natives engaged in 1827. They may not have come from Red River, however.

51 HBCA D 4/97, 65, Simpson's Official Reports, 1830

52 HBCA D 4/97, 35, 39; PAC Selkirk Papers, 8404–05: G. Simpson 'Scheme of Improvement of R.R.S.' 10 Feb. 1826, Red River Colony; HBCA D 4/125, 13, Simpson's Correspondence Book Inwards, 1829–31, John Charles to George Simpson, Sturgeon Lodge, 14 Aug. 1830; D 4/24, 6, Simpson's Correspon-

dence Outwards, Simpson to Murdoch McPherson, London, 28 Feb. 1838; D 4/125, 106, Simpson's Correspondence Book Inwards, 1829–31, Edward Smith to governor, chief factors and chief traders, northern department, Portage La Loche, 28 July 1830

53 HBCA D 4/99, 52–3f. Isobel Finlayson also spoke highly of her Indian crew (Johnson, Intro. to 'York Boat Journal' 33).

54 HBCA D 4/103, 17, Simpson's Official Reports, 1836; D 4/24, 2, Simpson's Correspondence Outwards, Simpson to Alex. Rod. McLeod, 28 Feb. 1838

55 HBCA D 4/103, 2f

56 HBCA B 239/k/1–3

57 HBCA B 235/b/6, 41, Winnipeg district, Correspondence Books, memoranda from Mackenzie River for Red River by James Anderson, Portage La Loche, 18 July 1853

58 HBCA D 4/84b, 68, Simpson, Correspondence Outwards, Simpson to ? (unnamed) Lachine, 28 Nov. 1857, private

59 HBCA D 8/1, 360, A.G. Dallas Correspondence, James A. Grahame to governor, chief factors and chief traders, northern department

60 HBCA B 39/e/6, 6, Fort Chipewyan district report, 1824, by James Keith. Keith stated that this policy was detrimental to the fur trade as the new hands were not as efficient as the older, more experienced men.

61 Whether the company could have afforded to pay its men higher wages has never been investigated. Much detailed research will be needed before an answer to this important question can be obtained.

62 Fleming *Minutes* 307, governor and committee to George Simpson, London, 27 Feb. 1822; Innis, Intro. to Fleming *Minutes* xx–xxiv, discusses the debate between Simpson (and the northern council) and the governor and committee over this matter.

63 PAC MG 19 A 44, Charles McKenzie to Hector McKenzie, Bonnie Point, Lac Seul, 28 Nov. 1853

Linguistic Solitudes and Changing Social Categories

JENNIFER S.H. BROWN

No single word exists, within Canada itself, to designate with satisfaction to both races a native of the country. When those of the French language use the word Canadien, they nearly always refer to themselves. They know their English-speaking compatriots as les Anglais. English-speaking citizens act on the same principle. They call themselves Canadians; those of the French language French-Canadians.

HUGH MACLENNAN[1]

Canadians have long differed in their names for the various 'native' groups of their country, whether of European descent, Indian, or biracial. The solitudes go back a long way, and number more than two. Eighteenth-century fur traders did agree more than do present-day Canadians on some of their usages; for them, all 'French' fur traders or later, 'Canadian,' sprang from the Montreal fur trade (in essence, Quebec), while the 'English' comprised those traders not so affiliated, that is, those of the Hudson's Bay Company. Since then, the picture has become more complex. 'French-Canadian' is a more recent, and as MacLennan notes, anglophone term, which for English-speakers now parallels the persistent francophone usage, Anglais. But ne'er the twain shall meet, or so it seems. The eighteenth-century consensus on who a Canadian was has faded; now 'we' are the Canadians and 'they' are something slightly other.

Students of language are accustomed to thinking in terms of linguistic communities, and of course language is a social phenomenon. But communities imply boundaries and a degree of isolation and separateness. When changes, intrusions, or dispersals affect such a community, its members, jarred from their perhaps comfortable collective solitude, may confront individual loneliness, stereotyping, and labelling by outsiders who classify and objectify them as a category, taking perspectives very different from those the community had formulated within its own traditions. Canada has lived with this kind of process for a long time; its dynamics would appear to go back at least as far as the eighteenth-century fur trade and are vividly highlighted in changing fur trade social and ethnic categorizations, particularly in the stressful years from the late 1700s to the mid-1800s. The first two cultural and linguistic solitudes among fur traders were those of the Hudson's Bay Company and Montreal traders. These had hardly begun to blend after their companies' merger in 1821 when they were placed together in a newly sharpened isolation, expressed in a heightened sense of contrast between the 'Indian country' and the 'civilized world' – with all the social distance and misunderstandings that were associated with this polarity.

For these decades of western Canadian history, the presence or absence of particular terms, the contexts in which they were used, and their changing connotations, are subtle yet valuable indicators of the processes by which certain groups became identified as such, stereotyped, and ranked within a rapidly changing and diversifying social setting. The history of these emerging social groups – of the processes by which they acquired identities in both the minds of their members and the minds of others, and found or were assigned a place in a broader social context – is scarcely complete without some attention being given to the names they received and to their shifting meanings.

My interest in this matter developed from observing certain problems in terminology that writers on the fur trade face, with reference to the mixed Indian-European population which arose in the eighteenth and nineteenth centuries in the Canadian northwest. We have not usually been very sensitive to the traders' own vocabularies as indicators of cultural differences and social change. Yet Hudson's Bay Company and North West Company documents reveal some vivid contrasts between the vocabularies of the two companies, and some interesting changes from the period when the 'English' and 'Canadians' were separate and competing to the decades following their merger in 1821. Among the more visible contrasts are those between the English terms used by the Hudson's Bay Company and the heavily French-influenced vocabulary used by the Montreal-based Nor'Westers – *servant* versus *engagé*, for example. And some contrasts reflect the structural differences between the companies; long after the firms merged, the Nor'Westers still persisted in using their own organizational terms to some extent. Chief Factor George Keith, who served the combined company for many years, still evoked his North West background in his 1858 will by describing himself as a 'retired Wintering partner.'[2]

Other contrasts or shifts in word-use patterns reflect differing and changing perceptions of both Indians and the progeny of Indian-European unions in the two companies, and it is these usages upon which this paper focuses. Consider, for example, the words, 'halfbreed' and 'squaw' (squaw in the English lexicon, not as the widely distributed Algonkian word). By the 1770s, people who might readily have been described as 'squaws' and 'halfbreeds' (traders' Indian wives and the children of the same) were numerous in the social orbits of both the Hudson's Bay Company and the Montreal firms. But these terms (which became common nineteenth-century labels in northwestern Canada) were rare or absent in the eighteenth-century records of both fur trade groups. The Montrealers seem to have been the first users of the term 'squaw,' and Hudson's Bay men the occasional borrowers. Although Hudson's Bay men before 1821 typically did not describe their own Indian female companions as squaws (preferring the terms 'woman' or 'wife'), James Sutherland of that company, after a year of trading in opposition to Nor'Wester Duncan Cameron, used the term once in 1791 in reference to the Canadians' women, observing that at a spring rendezvous of these traders, 'the Indian Squaws are drest in Scarlot, Callicos, and Silk ribbands.'[3] The journal of Nor'Wester Donald McKay from Temiscaming partially covering the years 1799–1806 provides a few other early examples of the use of 'squaw' among the Nor'Westers; McKay occasionally used the term to describe his Indian companion and those of some of his colleagues.[4]

The *Oxford English Dictionary* gives some broader perspectives on the background of this term. The word entered English-language written records as early as the 1630s in New England, with the meaning of Indian woman or wife. Its apparent earlier appearance among Nor'Westers than among Hudson's Bay men perhaps reflects the formers' proximity to New England, and perhaps the influence of the numerous loyalists who left the northern American colonies to settle in adjacent parts of Canada during the American Revolution. Several men of this background later joined the North West Company. In contrast, the ties of the Hudson's Bay Company men were directly to Britain; most were hired there and sailed straight to Hudson Bay, having few cultural and linguistic contacts with areas farther south.

By the 1840s 'squaw' had become a more commonplace and apparently more pejorative term than formerly in the Canadian northwest. The correspondence of James and Letitia Hargrave from York Factory on Hudson Bay, for example, illustrates that this couple assigned it unfavourable connotations. (Letitia was the first European woman to reside at York Factory.) To a holiday dance, Letitia Hargrave wrote on 20 February 1841, there came 'forty squaws young and old with their hair plaited in long tails, nothing on their heads but their everlasting blankets smelling of smoke and everything obnoxious ... nursing their babies in the face of everyone.'[5] We may be able to trace a trend in the use of this term, from its occasional appearance in North West Company contexts in the 1790s to its more frequent and uncomplimentary use a few decades later, by Europeans setting themselves at a distance from Indian and part-Indian native women (whether or not these were traders' wives, as many still were). Changes in society and attitude in the fur trade country of this period seem to correspond closely with such a shift in terminology. (It is interesting to note, in this connection, the apparent absence or rarity in nineteenth-century Canada of the American phrase, 'squaw man,' to describe a white man with an Indian wife; comparisons of Canadian and American terminologies in this period could prove instructive regarding contrasts between their respective western social histories.)[6]

The term 'halfbreed' also seems mainly a nineteenth-century usage in the fur trade. And it too seems to become established early in North West Company contexts rather than being typical of Hudson's Bay traders' vocabularies. Its path to the northwest may have parallelled that of 'squaw,' since the earliest uses of the term in reference to the offspring of whites and Indians occur, according to the Oxford English Dictionary, in references to Florida and Carolina, in 1775 and 1791 respectively. And like 'squaw,' it did not at first appear to have the derogatory connotations it acquired in later years; North West Company men such as John Macdonell and David Thompson were using it between 1809 and 1812 as a neutral descriptive term.[7]

A few years later, Peter Fidler, a Hudson's Bay Company man embroiled in the intensifying struggle between the new Red River colony and the Nor'Westers, started to use the term. It is possible that Fidler in 1815 was the first Hudson's Bay man to use the term in writing. It would be reasonable to suppose that the Hudson's Bay men first acquired it from their Nor'Wester opponents in the transitional period of close and competitive contact.

Fidler's journal for 1814-15 indicates both that his own terminology was changing in that period, and that the Nor'Westers' terminology was still somewhat variable. On 12 and 18 October 1814, Fidler referred to Cuthbert Grant jr, son of an old Nor'Wester and an Indian woman, as 'Capt. Grant an Indian.' By late May and June of the following year, he was terming people of similar descent 'halfbreeds' and 'half breed Canadians.' In July 1815, the Nor'Westers sent him a document proposing 'articles of agreement' between the 'halfbreed Indians of the Indian Territory on one part and the Honorable HBC on the other.' The articles were signed by 'the four chiefs of the half Indians by the mutual consent of their Fellows'; Fidler recognized, however, the handwriting of a certain North West partner and observed that, of these chiefs, 'the two former are the sons of Partners and now serving their apprenticeship, and the other two are the sons of Partners of the North West Co. and are acting as interpreters.'[8] For political purposes and with the aim of driving the colonists away, the opposition was apparently emphasizing the independence and Indian-ness of its mixed-descent members with accompanying shifts in terminology; 'Half Indians' is not a typical term. These events would certainly have served to foster a sense among these native North West Company sons themselves of their own distinctive political identity and shared interests as a group – an experience not undergone by the Hudson's Bay Company native-born sons of this period.

The Nor'Westers of the time also naturally drew upon French racial terms – métis and (bois) brulé – from the older French fur trade. And by 1816 these words too began to find their way into some Hudson's Bay Company records, the writings of Colin Robertson, for example. Robertson, who had been a Nor'Wester for several years before 1810, was from 1816 until the 1821 union aiding the Hudson's Bay Company against his former colleagues, outfitting and leading expeditions from their own Montreal base into the interior to oppose them there. His letters of this period incorporated Canadian usages then current to describe persons of mixed parentage. On 12 November 1816, he reported to his London employers, 'Your European Servants and Metiss are in many places deserting over to the North West Company.' Another letter of June 1820 referred to his employers' opponents as the 'whole breeds and half breeds of the North West Company.'[9] Where Hudson's Bay men met Nor'Westers or, like Robertson, had previous connections with them, their vocabularies showed the influence of their opponents.

Where such close contacts did not occur, Hudson's Bay Company writers employed quite different ways of referring to the descendants of European traders and Indian women, revealing significant contrasts in terminology with writers of Montreal and North West Company origin. Conspicuous in the Hudson's Bay Company writings is the absence of any term specifically or exclusively denoting persons of mixed parentage. Hudson's Bay Company historians have sometimes unwittingly obscured this absence by implying the presence of later usages in periods (and places) where they were in fact not in use. E.E. Rich, for example, in his comprehensive history of the company, used James Isham's *Observations on Hudson's Bay*, written in 1743 at Fort Prince of Wales, as a basis for the comment: 'The English half-breed was therefore becoming a feature of life at the posts, and domestic ties to some extent explained the willingness with which men spent year after year at the posts ... Isham wrote of the half-breeds ... that he would "Venture to say ... that they are pretty Numerious" '[10] The comments are true enough. But 'half-breed' here is Rich's term; it occurs nowhere in Isham's own writings. Isham's son Charles, born of an Indian mother in Hudson Bay, was never so described in the records documenting his company service from the 1760s to 1814. Having had an English education which helped qualify him for the charge of inland posts, he was later known as Mr Isham, was implicitly ranked among the 'Englishmen' (a category that also subsumed Scots and Orkneymen), and eventually retired to England.[11] The York Factory servants' lists provided a column to list each employee's parish of origin; for Charles Isham and others of like parentage, the column, if filled in, carried the simple entry, 'Hudson's Bay.'[12]

Those Hudson's Bay offspring who did not receive English educations and contracts for company employment usually remained among their Indian maternal relatives and connections, and were commonly categorized as Indians themselves. On 7 February 1801, for example, John Ballenden at York Factory, recording a meeting with one of these youths, described him as 'the Indian Lad that came yesterday (and who is the Son of an Officer that holds a very high Station in Your Honours Service).'[13] A fairly extensive scanning of the Hudson's Bay records suggests that such children were typically categorized according to a binary system; rather than 'halfbreeds' they were 'English' or 'Indian' according to the cultural characteristics and social affiliations that they exhibited. Terms that emphasized their biracial descent as such were absent.

The Hudson's Bay records also show, however, the presence of another term, nonracial in meaning and broad enough to be of wide use. Both Indians and the offspring of fur traders and Indian women could be subsumed under the rubric *native*, and the absence of European women at the posts assured that all 'natives' were either Indian or part-Indian. On

14 February 1800, John Ballenden wrote in the York Factory journal of sending away about fifty 'Invalid natives ... necessity both on my side and theirs induced me to send them from the Factory to make a help to support themselves.' Conditions the next winter again being arduous, Ballenden noted on 19 December, 'The number of English and Natives that at present depends upon the Factory are far too many for what Provisions I have to support them.'[14] The term 'native,' from what is known of traders' numerous family connections, certainly covered in such usage persons of both Indian and mixed parentage.

Figure 1 compares racial terminologies of the Hudson's Bay and North West companies in the period between the late eighteenth century and 1821, and depicts the range of meaning of the Hudson's Bay Company term 'native.' Although intrinsically broader in scope than the Nor'Westers' 'halfbreed' or 'métis,' 'native' was occasionally used in Hudson's Bay Company contexts to refer implicitly only to men of mixed parentage. At York Factory in the 1821–2 season, for example, Governor George Simpson compiled a list of all clerks in the northern department, with brief notes on the origins and attributes of each. Among them were nine men described as native, none of whom was Indian.[15] Simpson, recently arrived from England, here used in this restricted sense an established company term that was soon frequently to be replaced in his writings by the narrower, more race-oriented, and potentially more derogatory term, 'halfbreed.'

The spread of this narrower term was already in evidence in the new colony of Red River at the time Simpson was compiling his list of clerks. In 1820, the Anglican clergyman John West arrived there to establish the Hudson's Bay Company's first permanent church ministry. This event, as well as the 1821 union of the two companies, had a considerable social impact, reflected to some extent in the terms in which West described the local population. By October, the second month of his work in the country, the term 'halfbreed' was being used in his Red River baptismal register, typically to refer to native-born wives of traders long isolated from churchly influences. Many entries read like number 16, the baptism of 'John, son of William Hall and a Half Breed Woman.' Such mothers, given the previous lack of clergy in the fur trade country, were assumed to be unbaptized and unmarried (since newcomers like West were hardly ready to grant Christian recognition to any marriage 'according to the custom of the country'). The registers thus generally left them nameless, described only as 'halfbreed,' or sometimes 'Indian,' if such were said to be the case. The effect of these usages was to reduce persons for the most

Hudson's Bay Company

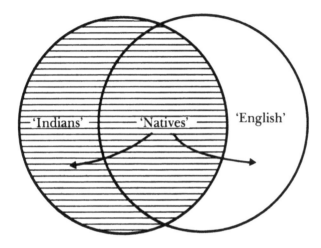

North West Company

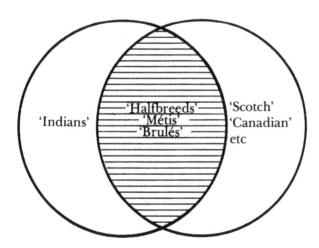

Figure 1 Two ways of classifying fur trade biracial groups before 1821. The arrows denote the possibility of HBC 'natives' passing to either the 'English' or 'Indian' category on the basis of cultural and social criteria.

part known and nameable (and to whom their offspring often had strong personal ties) to a generic class and racial category – a kind of verbal objectification reflecting the advent of new attitudes that were to dismay numerous fur trade families in the following few decades.

With baptismal entry 257, on 5 June 1823, an interesting variation in terms was introduced: 'half-caste' instead of 'halfbreed.' From there until entry 298 (1 October 1823), by which time West had been replaced by the Rev. David T. Jones, the term 'halfbreed' was not used. 'Half-caste' appears to be an intrusive term on the northern fur trade scene; the *Oxford English Dictionary* derives all earlier examples of its use from British writings about Asia, and cites the earliest known date of its occurrence as 1789. It was evidently in the vocabularies of West, Jones, and some others who were recent arrivals from England. But it failed to become standard usage in the northwest; from October 1823 on, 'halfbreed' again became the usual term to designate those of mixed descent in the church records, as it was becoming elsewhere.[16] The history and background of 'half-caste' may parallel those of another term used by some later clergy of Red River – 'country-born,' describing people of mixed descent born in the northwest. 'Country-born' was apparently also derived from the British Asian context,[17] and likewise failed to become widely established in the Canadian northwest.

The entrenchment of the term 'halfbreed' in Governor Simpson's administrative records in the mid-1820s, along with some of the connotations it was beginning to acquire, may readily be traced in the dossiers that Simpson compiled on native-born employees in the first decade of his administration. As this term tended to displace 'native,' his references to 'halfbreeds'' lack of success in the service became more frequent, while 'halfbreed' failures were increasingly judged a predictable feature of that group (conversely, their successes seemed matters for surprise). These men were ranked in a social order that during the 1820s appeared to become markedly more stratified and more prone to racial – descent- or 'blood'-based – discrimination. Along with this change emerged a complex of character traits regularly assigned to these people as a category: they were regarded as conceited, unsteady, untruthful, and lacking in propriety.

Those of European descent were also of course subject to the consequences of the increased stratification of company ranks that showed up, for example, in the sharpened lines drawn between gentlemen and servants, and clerks and postmasters.[18] Simpson's 'characters' of white employees were also frequently laced with strong criticisms; but although they might share some of the same vices as those of mixed descent, these men did not have to contend with the racial innuendoes and stereotypes that characterized Simpson's judgment from about 1827 on. They could escape being described in such terms as 'steady sober man although a halfbreed,' or 'a Halfbreed but steady correct and confidential,' or 'most steady and best conducted halfbreed I ever knew' – back-handed praise suggesting the obstacles facing these men who sought to follow their fathers into the fur trade.

Such developments as these amply explain why the term 'half-breed,' given such pejorative connotations in this period, fell into disrepute, in contrast to the term métis which was later used with pride by the mixed-bloods (usually those of North West Company background). Aside, however, from the effects of the uses that Simpson and his colleagues came to make of 'halfbreed,' its nineteenth-century history might be seen, in part, as a spinning out of logical possibilities in the term itself. Colin Robertson in 1820 (see above) played on the half-ness or incompleteness that the word suggests in his phrase, 'whole breeds and half breeds.' And occasionally a trader, perhaps unwittingly, would substitute for it another very similar English word, 'half-bred.'[19] This adjective, according to the *Oxford English Dictionary*, has two unflattering meanings, both older than 'half-breed.' The first, going back to 1701, is 'of mixed breed; born of parents of superior and inferior strain; mongrel'; the second, now obsolete, is dated 1732: 'imperfectly acquainted with the rules of good breeding; under-bred.' 'Half-breed,' which in the dictionary is free of such meanings, perhaps in actual usage tended to assimilate these connotations, at least by implication, from a word so similar to it; its semantic suggestiveness must itself be considered in examining the changing meanings and connotations of the word.

In short, the fur trade records suggest that 'halfbreed,' like several other social categories in the old northwest, was not a static term; its use patterns changed considerably from the time of its earliest introduction. And its spread corresponded to the dissemination of new value judgments and stereotypes ranking the biracial native population at a low level within a more highly structured and stratified social order than the fur trade country had previously seen.[20]

The above discussion raises some general questions of method regarding the semantics of social categories in fur trade studies. There has been some tendency in recent writings to continue Rich's inclination (noted above) to generalize social and racial terms that originally were fairly specific and/or localized. The word 'country-born,' for example, an apparently new term of fairly restricted usage in nineteenth-century Red River, has sometimes been applied to persons of mixed descent in general in the northwest.[21] Its capitalization in print further tends to reify or concretize this verbal category, implying the persistence or broad spread of some group self-labelled and labelled by others under that rubric. This extension of meaning needs to be examined, for the fur trade documents do not seem to justify such wide application of a term rather limited in its actual usage. The term métis is also at times overused, and with its heavy cultural and political baggage is better reserved for those who elected it themselves and were (or still are) thus known to their contemporaries. It is a controversial term now as in the past; its social and political connotations are still potent, for those who wish to espouse or reject them.

Semantic problems can also arise with terms used to describe Indian groups. It was noted earlier that numerous Hudson Bay 'Indians' were by the late eighteenth century of mixed descent and were defined as Indian on the basis of social and cultural attributes rather than strictly on the basis of race or 'blood.' It is possible that even those of European descent could be described as Indian if their character or behaviour seemed to justify it; just such a usage perhaps contributed to confusion regarding Hudson's Bay Company officer Moses Norton's possibly European parentage.[22] Correspondingly, the Hudson's Bay Company category, 'Home Indians' (referring to the largely Cree natives clustered about the bay posts), was a cultural rather than strictly racial category, comprising both Indians and persons of mixed descent. Once defined as 'Indians' they were not numbered among those who could be hired contractually among the company's 'English' and 'native' employees. Only those men defined as English or native received continuing contracts from London; 'Indians' served only as seasonal tripmen or hunters, or in other temporary capacities.

The whole subject of fur trade 'sociolinguistics,' as it might be called, deserves more attention, not just as a specialized sub-field but as a topic of interest and relevance to any researcher whose work touches on fur trade social life. It is constructive to question terms we apply to the past, whether we originate or borrow them.

The question of what labels to apply to the offspring of white and Indian parents seems to be one of the more vexing problems in terminology facing writers on the fur trade, and there is no single answer to this problem. It may be helpful, however, to keep in mind the fact that we commonly find ourselves using, and sometimes confusing, terminologies appropriate to two distinct levels of analysis. We often find it necessary or appropriate to resort at one level to the use of precise, dispassionate terms that describe rather than obscure or weigh down our subjects with historical baggage. When describing the biracial population of the northwest as a whole, for example, existing through time over broad areas, it seems useful to draw on ordinary words that carry no strong connotations and are hence not heavily culture-bound. 'Native-born,' for instance, is a term that in the fur trade context does very well for describing unambiguously the mixed native fur trade population until the 1830s or 1840s when significant numbers of native-born whites began to mature in the northwest. 'Biracial' or 'of mixed descent' will also do; 'mixed blood' is arguably a less attractive alternative.

At another level, we need to come to grips with the question of how to use and interpret 'the natives'' own categories. On this level, a useful litmus test is to imagine ourselves members of the group or category in question, and inquire how we would then respond to being designated in a particular way. How would Charles Isham, George Gladman jr, George Atkinson's descendants, or Cuthbert Grant's offspring, react to being called métis, halfbreed, Indian, or country-born – with puzzlement, anger, acceptance, pleasure? Their reactions would diverge, as we know, and we cannot always know what terms would have been intelligible, acceptable, or offensive. In instances of uncertainty, the only course is to apply to individuals those terms we judge most appropriate to their period, company background, or other social affiliations.

The Canadian fur trade was rather complex linguistically, not simply because of the presence of diverse native and European languages, but also because of the changing and different vocabularies of the fur companies, their followers and descendants, and the social groups surrounding them. There is much room in this setting for semantic analysis to achieve better understanding of past ordinary-language usages and their social significance.

In a quite real sense, fur trade documents of the past are written in a 'code' we must study and decipher. We realize that we must consciously translate the technical, obsolete, or foreign terms we encounter in these records. But the trickiest terms to decode may be those we assume we understand. We find ourselves, with respect to the past, in our own linguistic solitude – a solitude that requires a conscious recognition of our isolation and empathy with and understanding of past conditions if it is to be overcome. This situation recalls the anthropologist's ever present need to place data in their setting in the process of interpreting them – or in simpler terms, to 'listen to the natives.' We are all 'natives,' culture-bound, as we attempt to understand better the past through its always incomplete written records. Perhaps some sense of MacLennan's solitudes, of social groups as isolated today as in the often stressful conditions of the fur trade, is helpful in these studies – and particularly in examining those potent terms that various groups applied to themselves or to others as the population of the northwest grew and diversified.

REFERENCES

1 MacLennan *Two Solitudes* foreword
2 HBCA A 44/4, 45, will of George Keith
3 HBCA B 177/a/1, 31, Red Lake Journal, June 1791
4 OA Journal of Donald McKay (microfilm)
5 MacLeod *Letters of Letitia Hargrave* 94
6 Van Kirk 'The Role of Women in the Fur Trade Society of the Canadian West'; Brown 'Company Men and Native Families'
7 PAC Miles Macdonell papers, John Macdonell to brother Miles, 27 June 1812; Myers 'Jacques Raphael Finlay'
8 HBCA B 235/a/3 Fidler, Red River Journal
9 Rich *Colin Robertson's Letters, 1817–1822* 248, 121
10 Rich *History of the Hudson's Bay Company* 604–5
11 HBCA B 239/a/101, 99: Brown 'Charles Thomas Isham'
12 HBCA B 239/f/3, 11
13 HBCA B 239/a/105, 28
14 HBCA B 239/a/104, 24, and B 239/a/105 20
15 HBCA B 239/f/12, 3–8
16 Red River Anglican baptismal registers (St John's Cathedral, Winnipeg)
17 Louise E. Sweet, personal communication
18 For example, in HBCA A 34/2, 52–3
19 For example, Rich *Robertson's Letters* 65; and PAC Duncan Clarke papers, Donald McIntosh to Clarke, 20 July 1836
20 Brown 'Company Men' 411–25
21 For example, Pannekoek 'Rev. Griffiths Owen Corbett and the Red River Civil War of 1869–70'
22 Van Kirk 'Moses Norton'

Fur Trade Social History: Some Recent Trends

SYLVIA VAN KIRK

Since the last fur trade conference in 1970, the most important development in fur-trade history has perhaps been the significant growth in the area of social history. Between 1972 and 1976, four doctoral dissertations appeared in the field. As one of the functions of the fur-trade conferences is to provide a forum for researchers in the field, I will comment on the findings arising from these new works and suggest areas for further investigation.

Jennifer Brown's thesis, 'Company Men and Native Families' (1976) for the anthropology department of the University of Chicago, is the most comprehensive in scope.[1] Her approach centres on the importance of kinship connections in influencing the evolving personnel structures and domestic relations within the Hudson's Bay and North West companies. Brown's work underlines the valuable insights to be gained from an interdisciplinary approach; indeed the integration of interdisciplinary perspectives is a most encouraging trend in recent fur trade scholarship. The other three works, all in history, focus upon more specific aspects of fur trade social life. Van Kirk's thesis (1975) concentrated on the role played by women in the development of fur trade society; it traces the contribution and changing experience of Indian, mixed-blood and eventually white women over 150 years.[2] John Foster (1972) and Frits Pannekoek (1973) have completed substantial studies which focus on the experience of what they call the 'Country-Born' in the Red River Settlement. Both works expand upon, and in some respects modify, Marcel Giraud's pioneering book *Le Métis canadien*. Foster, in investigating the roots of the 'Country-Born', shows that they were inheritors of a 'Bay' tradition which differentiated them from their ethnic cousins, the métis.[3] In Red River, this differentiation between the two mixed-blood groups was exacerbated, Pannekoek argues, by the divisive influences of Anglican and Catholic missionaries. He develops his analysis up to the Red River resistance for which he provides a dramatic re-interpretation.[4]

In spite of different emphases, two basic themes underlie all these works. First, all the authors share a commitment to the idea that the fur trade produced an indigenous society in early western Canada. As Foster states, the fur trade was 'a socio-cultural complex' which lasted 200 years.[5] An appreciation of the complexities of the social interaction between European and Indian is essential to an understanding of the dynamics of the fur trade. Brown has brought forward a useful model (developed in other contexts) for defining what we mean by fur trade society. The fur trade can be conceptualized as 'a semi-autonomous social field.' While it overlaps with its parent societies, both Indian and European, it can generate its own rules, customs, and symbols internally, and induce compliance to them.[6] Both Brown and Van Kirk have been concerned to discover what constituted the norms of fur trade society.

The second theme is the important differences within the fur trade social field itself. Again to use Brown's terminology, the Hudson's Bay Company and the North West Company constitute two major sub-fields. A distinctive historical experience developed within each company, because of different organizational structures and background of company personnel. All these studies contribute to our understanding of the different traditions of these two companies. Significantly, however, the authors do not always agree on the nature and extent of these differences. These variations in interpretation raise a multitude of interesting questions, but this commentary will be limited to three major areas examined in these works. These are the differing organizational and personnel structures of the two companies; the nature of Hudson's Bay and North West Company interaction with the Indians, particularly intermarriage between traders and Indian women; and the different experience of the mixed-blood children of the Hudson's Bay Company tradition and those of the North West Company tradition.

Brown provides an analysis of the personnel structures of both companies. Her analysis of the Hudson's Bay Company contains some interesting similarities to Foster's recent work on the company. Both suggest that the model developed by Peter Laslett in his book *The World We Have Lost* is fundamental to an understanding of the organization of the company posts. The model is that of the patriarchal, hierarchical household of master and servants which, according to Laslett, constituted the basic socio-economic unit of seventeenth-century British society. The Laslett model certainly provides a helpful tool for understanding the social organization of company posts; one would like, however, to see a further elaboration of its applicability to the situation in Hudson Bay. Foster hints that aspects of this framework were modified on the bay, particularly with regard to the servants' marital relationships.[7] The extent to which European traders successfully transplanted their own social heritage to Rupert's Land is, of course, an important question. Brown does not see the Laslett model as being appropriate to the North West Company situation, but unfortunately there are no corresponding studies on the social antecedents of the Nor'Westers. One would suspect, for example, that a study of the social structure of the Highland clan would illuminate the structure of the North West Company.

Brown argues that the fundamental differences in the organization of the two companies was that the Hudson's Bay Company household structure provided for vertical integration whereas the North West Company lacked this, being sharply divided into horizontally extended components. Brown's study concentrates on the officer class of both companies. She presents an illuminating profile of the Hudson's Bay man which emphasizes the importance of kinship ties. He characteristically had very weak kinship ties in Britain; his kinship ties were therefore formed within the context of his experience on the bay; and he was part of a vertically integrated structure in which it was possible for him to progress through the ranks, especially if aided by the patronage of a senior man – In short his life and career were dominated by company membership.[8] Interestingly, Brown has found studies on the organization of modern Japanese companies useful for the elaboration of her two company models. The Japanese 'concept of frame,' whereby the company (or household) provides the structure for 'binding together and classifying heterogeneous individuals,' appears applicable to the Hudson's Bay Company.

An alternative 'concept of attribute' seems relevant to the analysis of the North West Company. Horizontally extended occupational, status, or kin groups provide the basis for unifying and classifying individuals.[9] The North West Company was essentially a series of Anglo-Scots partnerships, based on personal and familial associations. The Nor'Westers had extensive kinship connections, not only in Scotland, but also developing in Canada. They were notorious for recruiting their own relations, as witness Simon McTavish's employment of his McTavish and McGillivray relatives. Kinship connections were the key to advancement. Brown has made the perceptive observation that in the post-union period, Governor Simpson, with his highland Scots background, showed a greater affinity for the Nor'Westers than for his own Hudson's Bay men. He continued the Nor'Wester practice, securing places for quite a number of his own British relatives.

Although operative in the Indian Country, the concepts of vertical and horizontal integration need clarification when applied to the total company structures. The pinnacle of the Hudson's Bay Company man's achievement would have been a governorship on Hudson Bay – a position on the London committee, the management board of the Company, was virtually closed to him. In contrast, the clerk in the North West Company could become a wintering partner, attaining both managerial responsibility and a financial share in the company; ultimately he could become a Montreal agent. At this level, then, it would appear that the concept of vertical integration is more applicable to the North West Company than to the Hudson's Bay Company.

Brown's study does not focus on the servant class or labour force of the two companies. However, her placing of the French-Canadians and the Orkneymen within their respective company contexts does suggest some avenues for further research. According to Brown, the French-Canadians of the North West Company constitute a labouring class, ethnically and occupationally segregated from the officer class. There was little prospect of the servant progressing to the rank of officer. Building on her model of the North West Company organized along lines of class solidarity and ethnic homogeneity, Brown maintains that relations between the two groups were characterized by opposition and bargaining. This is an interesting hypothesis, but further evidence is required to confirm it. Indeed a serious study of the French-Canadian engagés and labour relations within the North West Company is much needed.

The question of mobility within the Hudson's Bay Company appears to be a more complex one. Although Englishmen dominated the officer class and Orkneymen the servant class, lines of ethnic and occupational stratification seem to have been blurred. Brown and Foster both emphasize the potential for vertical mobility within the company. Upon closer examination, however, promotional prospects, with a few exceptions, were not as bright as it might seem for the Orkneymen. Most of the men who became prominent officers in the eighteenth century entered the company's service as apprentices, destined to receive officer training in the field, or later in the category of writer. It is possible that these categories are the equivalents of the positions of apprentice clerk and clerk in the North West Company; as such they do not belong among the categories assigned to servants. Furthermore, the promotion of Orkneymen, which becomes noticeable with the company's move inland, seems to have arisen as a result of necessity rather than deliberate company policy. The company was under pressure to expand inland at a time when it was virtually impossible to recruit adequate personnel; most of the Orkneymen who became officers were restricted to the charge of small inland posts. Brown feels that the Orkneymen were not able to act very effectively as a group. But one suspects that further research may prove that the Orkneymen, with their extensive kinship links, developed a class and ethnic solidarity which will modify the model of a vertically integrated company structure (see John Nicks's preliminary study in this book).

The different background of company personnel and differences in company regulations very much affected the attitude of each company to the Indians. None of the studies under discussion focuses on the general question of Indian-European social relationships, with the exception of the issue of intermarriage. The time is ripe for a broader comparison of Indian relations with the personnel of the two companies. From Van Kirk's research, one gains a strong impression that in the Hudson's Bay Company there was a good deal more fraternization, particularly with the Home Guard, than the official regulations permitted. Company men seemed to possess a capacity for entering into relationships of respect and friendship with individual Indians; one thinks, for example, of Samuel Hearne and the Chipewyan leader Matonabbee or David Thompson and the Piegan war chief Kootenae Apee. Further studies, such as Charles Bishop's on Chief Kwah (in this book), which will give an individual dimension and personality to the Indians, are overdue.

The traditional emphasis on the Nor'Westers cordial relationship with the Indians is in need of modification.[10] There is evidence in the papers of an obscure Nor'Wester named George Nelson[11] that some of the western Indians were so resentful of the arbitrary treatment received at the hands of the pedlars in the 1770s that had they themselves not been decimated by the smallpox epidemic of 1780 they would have united to drive the traders out. Certainly relations between the Nor'Westers and Chipewyan in the 1790s were anything but cordial, the Nor'Westers maintaining their mastery through brute force and the lack of effective Hudson's Bay competition. Edward Umfreville, certainly no friend of the Hudson's Bay Company, declared during this period that the Indians had lost their respect for the French-Canadians and much preferred the sense of propriety shown by the Orkneymen. While it is true that relatively speaking the fur trade field does seem to be characterized by a lack of violence between Indians and Europeans, this very fact makes it doubly important to carefully analyse the reasons for the hostile incidents which did arise.

Foster has suggested[12] that an important reason for the generally peaceful relations between Indians and Europeans was the growth of familial ties between the two groups. Van Kirk and Brown's investigations into the nature of inter-racial marriage in fur trade society bear this out. It is not an exaggeration to claim that intermarriage between European traders and Indian women formed the basis of fur trade society; as Brown observes, these unions gave fur trade society its distinctive character and formed the basis for a self-perpetuating community. Western Canada presents us with a unique social situation. With the exception of one brief experiment in the 1680s, white women were excluded from the fur trade field until the early nineteenth century. From a variety of motives, both Indian and European, there was considerable pressure for the European woman's place to be taken by the Indian woman. The European trader took an Indian partner not only to satisfy his sexual needs, but because an Indian mate performed a variety of economic services necessary to the functioning of the fur trade. Van Kirk's investigation of the economic role played by native women leads to the conclusion that native women constituted an important, if unofficial, part of the labour force, particularly at the understaffed Hudson's Bay Company posts.[13] The traders soon understood that marriage alliances were conducive to better trade with the Indians, and it is most significant that the Indians encouraged the formation of these ties. A marital alliance served to integrate the trader (i.e. stranger) into the Indians' kinship network and brought with it greater prestige and economic security. According to Van Kirk, some Indian women themselves, desirous of an easier and richer life-style, actively sought a fur trader husband.[14] One point Brown, Foster, and Van Kirk emphasize is that these unions had to be contracted within the Indian frame of reference with regard to marriage and sexual mores. To the European traders, Indian attitudes often seemed lax and immoral, but failure to appreciate the social and economic context in which the Indians viewed these alliances could lead to hostility. An outstanding example is the Henley House massacre of 1755, where as Charles Bishop has emphasized in a recent article, the Europeans violated the contract; the master kept the Home Guard leader's women but would not accord him the expected economic privileges.[15]

Although the motives for forming marital alliances apply to both companies, actual unions evolved differently within the context of the two companies. According to official Hudson's Bay policy, unions with Indian women were strictly prohibited; company personnel were expected to follow a rule which Brown has aptly termed 'military monasticism.' By contrast, the North West Company sanctioned, perhaps even encouraged, intermarriage.

The official ruling of the Hudson's Bay Company presented its officers on the bay with a dilemma because it soon became obvious that it was not enforceable or even appropriate. The officers on the bay took the lead in bending the rules to fit the needs of the situation. According to Andrew Graham, by the mid-eighteenth century it had become customary for the chief factor to keep a woman; he might allow his officers some latitude, but servants were apparently required to adhere to official policy. Both Brown and Foster have suggested that the governor's prerogative of having a wife relates to the Laslett household model where only the master was allowed to have a family. It is difficult to know whether the governor rationalized his behaviour on these grounds or whether his action represents simply a compromise solution to the demands of the Indians who would put the greatest pressure on the officers in charge of the posts to take Indian mates. It is also questionable whether Graham's statement accurately reflects the state of affairs of the Bay. There is considerable evidence that the servants in the Bayside posts were anxious to form connections with Indian women, and that governors such as James Isham allowed their servants considerable leeway in forming what were coming to be regarded as marital unions.

The absence of concrete references in the Hudson's Bay Company journals makes it difficult to calculate the extent of Company-Indian unions and whether they were contracted according to a recognizable norm which can be termed 'the custom of the country.' It seems that Company men were considerably influenced by the Indian attitude toward marriage for it cannot be denied that many prominent Company officers practiced polygamy.[16] A question which requires further investigation then is whether monogamy, as Brown maintains, was the norm in Hudson's Bay Company unions. Certainly by the late eighteenth century, there is considerable evidence that Company men, especially officers, were forming stable, lasting relationships with their Indian wives and showed genuine concern for the welfare of their children. The stability of inter-racial marriages in the Company tradition was reinforced by the relative geographical immobility of personnel on the bay, the length of their tenure in Rupert's Land, and the lack of white kin connections which

could cause divided loyalties.[17] It also seems that the monogamous principle was largely re-affirmed when mixed-blood wives became common.

Brown sees a sharp distinction between the marital patterns of the
Hudson's Bay and North West companies; she describes the Nor'Wester
social scene as being characterized by a considerable 'trafficking' in
women and casualness in domestic relations.[18] Van Kirk's view differs
somewhat from this interpretation. While these patterns of behaviour
undoubtedly existed, she contends that they did not become the norm
which governed sexual relations between the Nor'Westers and the Indians: most Nor'Westers adhered to an indigenous marriage rite known
as 'marriage à la façon du pays.' The subject needs further investigation,
especially into the origins of the custom. It seems likely that marriage à la
façon du pays had its roots in the experience of the French colonial fur
trade. Evidence, from the Jesuit missionaries indicates that in the early
eighteenth century French-Canadian voyageurs were forming marital
unions with Indian women in the Great Lakes region. It is still not clear
whether the Nor'Westers simply adopted French custom or significantly
modified it and to what extent marriage à la façon du pays became
institutionalized within the structure of the North West Company.

Brown maintains that the North West Company made little effort to
regulate social behaviour, that it was largely a question of individual
conscience.[19] Van Kirk places more emphasis on evidence which suggests
that there was a widespread understanding as to what constituted marriage à la façon du pays, that the custom was reinforced by peer-group
pressure, and possibly regulation. For example, although an engagé was
allowed to take an Indian wife he could not do so without the consent of
his bourgeois. Furthermore, marriage à la façon du pays implied some
economic support on the part of the North West Company.[20] It was not
expected that employees pay for the provisioning of their wives and
children, and the company appears to have footed the bill for providing
employees' wives with basic apparel 'in the Canadian fashion.' By 1806,
these expenses had become so heavy that the Company attempted to
alleviate the situation by prohibiting its personnel from taking Indian
women 'after the fashion of the country.'

Hudson's Bay Company practice differed from this. Although the
committee eventually realized it was powerless to stop its servants from
forming unions with Indian women, it refused to assume any expense for
their maintenance. The onus was on the individual to provide for his
family as is shown in many company employees' wills.

While marriage à la façon du pays was contracted according to Indian custom, including the payment of a bride price, the Nor'Westers seem to have had a distinct aversion to polygamy. Among the bourgeois, there is no evidence of them maintaining more than one wife simultaneously. Van Kirk suggests it would be appropriate to characterize the Nor'Westers as practicing serial monogamy. The peripatetic ways of the Nor'Westers made it difficult for them to maintain permanent relationships; certainly several bourgeois had more than one Indian wife during the course of their stay in the Indian Country. It also seems to have been accepted that whatever the length of the union in the interior, the marriage, which by Indian definition did not imply a lifetime commitment, would not survive the trader's departure from the Indian Country. In order to ease the social dislocation caused by the severing of this tie, a custom arose, which Van Kirk has called 'turning off,' whereby the woman, often the children too, were placed under the protection of another Nor'Wester. As Brown emphasizes, the Nor'Westers with their strong familial and associational ties outside Rupert's Land felt a strong pull back to Canada or Britain; many had also amassed sizeable fortunes and were anxious to assume a 'civilized' life-style which included a white wife.

There were a number of Nor'Westers, however, who took their Indian wives with them when they retired; this trend becomes more noticeable when mixed-blood wives became the vogue. Again different patterns emerge between the two companies with regard to the marrying of mixed-blood daughters. In the Hudson's Bay Company, many of the first-known mixed-blood girls were daughters of officers. Their fathers, who became increasingly concerned to affirm the status of their offspring within the company structure, appear to have played an active role in marrying them off to incoming traders, even to the extent of providing a dowry. For the young Hudson's Bay man, marriage to the daughter of an officer was a useful means of assisting his advancement. In the North West Company, on the other hand, the largest pool of mixed-blood women was the daughters of French-Canadian voyageurs. Many of the bourgeois took métisses as wives, in unions which must have been motivated more by feelings of affection than the prospect of career advancement. It may be useful to speculate as to what extent these unions which cut across class and race affected the horizontal organization of the North West Company. By the early nineteenth century, fur trade marital relationships were characterized by widespread endogomy. Family trees became very intertwined, and the society of each company increasingly cohesive. It seems that within both companies as mixed-blood wives became common, marriage à la façon du pays evolved toward the European concept of marriage. It was celebrated by public recognition and festivities, often with the officer in charge of the post officiating; it was understood that it should be lasting and monogamous. Numerous Hudson's Bay men and Nor'Westers affirmed the validity of these unions and the legitimacy of their children.

After the union of the two companies, the 'custom of the country' suffered a double attack. Within the company structure, it was disregarded by Governor Simpson, who was immune to the socializing processes which had previously operated in the Indian Country. He regarded native women as casual mistresses, reserving the position of wife for an Englishwoman. The 'custom of the country' was also vigorously attacked by the missionaries whose impact was felt in Rupert's Land in the 1820s. Because of Simpson's influential position, it is not surprising that a number of officers followed his lead; a few such as J.G. McTavish and William Connolly renounced their country wives of long standing to marry European women. Brown attaches significance to the fact that these men were all Nor'Westers. It is true that the Hudson's Bay Company men showed little inclination to act in this way, but it should be pointed out that the majority of Nor'Westers also remained true to their native families. Brown has compiled an interesting table to show that there was a significantly greater tendency among Hudson's Bay Company men than among the Nor'Westers to submit to a church marriage when available.[21] These statistics are subject to various interpretations. They may signify that the Hudson's Bay men were more insecure about the morality and legality of their position, or it could be argued that the Nor'Westers were not prepared to make a permanent commitment. Further study is needed; the question underlies the difficulty of making generalizations. In the post-union period, however, especially among the rising generation, the church marriage became the accepted norm.

For the mixed-blood offspring of the fur traders, the post-union era was a period of adjustment and change. In spite of their common maternal ancestry, however, the differing company frameworks resulted in the emergence of two distinct mixed-blood traditions. These studies, particularly those by Brown and Foster, make it clear that it is inadequate to speak merely of English-speaking as opposed to French-speaking mixed-bloods. The basis of differentiation is the company background, whether the mixed-bloods are descended from Nor'Westers or Hudson's Bay men. Within the North West Company (or metis) group, for example, there are quite a number of individuals with British names, descendants of the bourgeois.

In tracing the Hudson's Bay Company experience, both Brown and

Foster have observed that the main pattern among the mixed-bloods in the eighteenth century was absorption into their mother's band. The category of half-breed is noticeably absent in the records, a fact which makes their numbers very difficult to determine. Instead a polarity developed. Most mixed bloods, especially the girls, were absorbed into the Home Guard Cree bands (although they might retain some sense of identification with their father's culture); a few children, however, remained under their father's influence, and if sent to England for education identified themselves as Englishmen. By the 1790s, the influence of the Hudson's Bay fathers had become dominant. By and large, they show considerable concern to reinforce the British heritage of their children and to integrate them into the company structure: the boys through employment in the company, the girls through marriage to an incoming trader or at least a mixed blood. The Hudson's Bay Company, in desperate straits for experienced personnel, began to apprentice young mixed bloods in 1794 and later provided the rudiments of education, in hopes that they might train 'a colony of useful hands.'[22] Emphasis was placed on the girls' education also, as it was considered imperative for them to learn the womanly virtues of European society.

Foster and, especially, Brown argue that paternal influence was a very important factor in shaping the subsequent history of the Country-Born. The Country-Born were a much more fractured group than the métis, who were able to develop a collective cultural identity. Brown contends that the paternal focus of the Country-Borns' social sphere resulted in mobility, dispersal, and ultimately assimilation.[23] The lack of a unified identity and purpose among the Country-Born is reflected in their inability to produce their own leaders. Pannekoek shows convincingly the sense of dependency ingrained in the Country-Born. In their search for an identity and a role they relied first on their company fathers, then on the Anglican missionaries, and ultimately, Pannekoek argues, upon the newcomers from Canada.[24] The métis, on the other hand, developed a strong sense of their place in the West and were able to produce articulate leaders to defend it. It seems that father-orientation and mother-orientation are useful concepts to apply to an analysis of the two mixed-blood groups and should be investigated further. Brown has suggested, for example, that the lack of paternal influence evident in the lives of many of the sons of the North West Company bourgeois resulted in their being absorbed into the larger métis group.[25]

The culture of the métis was based on an acceptance of their dual racial heritage; the aspirations of the Country-Born (essentially to become

British) necessitated a rejection of their Indian ancestry. Foster, and Pannekoek even more strongly, emphasize the formative influences which the Anglican missionaries exercised over the Country-Born in Red River. The missionaries built upon the British value system which had already begun to be inculcated within the company framework; they emphasized the civilizing virtues of Protestant religion, a sound education, and an agricultural life-style.

Ultimately, however, the Country-Born were probably betrayed by both their company and their church. Brown has documented convincingly the strong racist attitude which militated against the advancement of the mixed-blood sons of officers within the company after the union.[26] Governor Simpson had a very negative, stereotyped view of the capabilities of mixed bloods. Indeed Brown, in her illuminating chapters on the placing of mixed-blood children, shows that those who were sent to Britain and Canada for education and did not return faced less racial prejudice than those who remained in Rupert's Land.[27] Those of the Country-Born who looked to the church for advancement found that in reality their race would be held against them and they would always be regarded as inferior.

Mixed-blood girls also suffered from the growing racism of the post-union period. While expected to conform to the European ideals of chastity and piety, they were particularly victimized by the operation of a double standard upheld by company officers, notably Simpson, and the church. Native women, denied the status of wives, were now in danger of being reduced to mistresses or even prostitutes, while the European men excused their indulgence by blaming these women for not being able to curb the immoral tendencies inherent in their Indian blood. The status of native wives was also threatened by the appearance of white women in Rupert's Land. In the 1830s Simpson mounted a campaign to exclude mixed-blood wives from the fur trade elite. In this he had only limited success, partly because the early European wives failed to adapt to life in Red River, and a significant number of young officers continued to take highly acculturated mixed bloods as wives. Social rivalry between mixed-blood and European wives was an important factor in the social history of Red River, being most dramatically illustrated in the Foss-Pelly scandal of 1850.[28]

In analysing the role played in the 'Country-Born' in Red River, Foster and Pannekoek have arrived at different conclusions. Foster sees a positive role for the Country-Born. Their heritage, he claims, enabled them to co-operate with all the other ethnic groups in the settlement; they constituted a kind of cement which held the settlement together. Pannekoek, on the other hand, sees in the Country-Born a strong potential for discord, which was exacerbated by the Anglican clergy. Although he would acknowledge that there were occasions for co-operation between the métis and the Country-Born before 1850 (the point at which Foster's thesis concludes), he maintains that the divisive influence of religion had already set the two groups on divergent courses. During the Red River resistance, Pannekoek argues, the 'Country-Born' felt little sympathy with the cause of the métis; in fact, they were ready to take up arms against the métis who threatened to thwart their dream of finding their destiny in Canada. That two such divergent views of the 'Country-Born' can be presented indicates the complexity of Red River society. Further research and analysis are needed to test the validity of both views. In this, and in fur trade research in general, the use both of interdisciplinary models and concepts and of quantitative methods must be expanded and refined.

I hope this essay will serve to draw other researchers into the field. We are only just beginning to unravel the intricacies of the social world of the fur trade, which played such a significant part in the early development of Canada.

REFERENCES

1 Brown 'Company Men and Native Families: Fur Trade Social and Domestic Relations in Canada's Old Northwest'
2 Van Kirk 'The Role of Women in the Fur Trade Society of the Canadian West, 1700–1850'
3 Foster 'The Country-born in the Red River Settlement: 1820–1850'
4 Pannekoek 'The Churches and the Social Structure in the Red River Area, 1818–1870'
5 Foster 'Rupert's Land and the Red River Settlement, 1820–70'
6 Brown 'Company Men and Native Families' 14
7 Foster 'The Indian-Trader in the Hudson Bay Fur Trade Tradition' (paper presented to the Second Canadian Ethnological Society Annual Conference, Winnipeg, 1975) 7–9
8 Brown 'Company Men' 100
9 The model used here is based on ibid esp. 92, 123–4, 240.
10 See Morton *A History of the Canadian West to 1870–71* 349.
11 Toronto Public Library, George Nelson Papers, Baldwin Room
12 Foster 'The Home Guard Cree and the Hudson's Bay Company'

13 Van Kirk 'Role of Women' 123–42
14 For a study of the motivation of Indian women in the fur trade, see Van Kirk '"Women in Between": Indian Women in Fur Trade Society in Western Canada' 31–46.
15 Bishop 'Henley House Massacres'
16 Van Kirk 'Role of Women' 39
17 Brown 'Company Men' 224
18 Ibid 222
19 Ibid 187–9
20 See Van Kirk '"The Custom of the Country": An Examination of Fur Trade Marriage Practices.'
21 Brown 'Company Men' 277
22 See Brown 'A Colony of Very Useful Hands.'
23 Brown 'Company Men' 447
24 See Pannekoek 'The Anglican Church and the Disintegration of Red River Society, 1818–1870.'
25 Brown 'Company Men' 442
26 Ibid 415–20
27 See Brown 'Ultimate Respectability: Fur Trade Children in the "Civilized World."'
28 Van Kirk 'Role of Women' 397–410

PART IV ✧ PERSONALITIES

Angus Bethune

HILARY RUSSELL

Angus Bethune was a significant figure in fur trade history. He was a partner in the North West Company and, after the coalition of 1821, a chief factor in the Hudson's Bay Company. For these reasons alone, his career merits scholarly attention. A detailed biographical examination of the company elites to which Bethune belonged would, no doubt, reveal a great deal about the history of the fur trade.

But, in addition, Bethune's long career as a fur trader was wide-ranging and turbulent. He participated in controversial and important events. As a Nor'wester, he was involved in the take-over of Astoria, the company's adventure to China between 1814 and 1816, the 'rebellion' of the wintering partners, and the negotiations which led to the coalition of 1821. His career in the Hudson's Bay Company was less dramatic and adventurous, but continued to be marked by disturbances and conflict. From his postings as a chief factor in the southern department, he clashed repeatedly with Governor William Williams, pestered the governor and committee in London, thoroughly irritated Governor George Simpson, and often engaged in written and verbal battles with various officers and servants of the company. He also quarrelled with at least one missionary. His career was not crowned by many personal successes, in spite of his rank. Nevertheless, partly because of his rank, his failings and his failures could not help but influence the course of the fur trade.

The present level of published research on Bethune's career consists mainly of two thumb-nail sketches in Champlain Society volumes, an entry in *The Macmillan Dictionary of Canadian Biography*, the appraisals by Governor George Simpson and Dr Glyndwr Williams published in the summer 1976 issue of *The Beaver* and in *Hudson's Bay Miscellany 1670–1870*, my spring 1977 article in *The Beaver*, and a few notes by editors and annotators of fur trade documents.[1]

Angus Bethune was born in 1783 at Carleton Island (in present-day Ontario), the eldest child of the Reverend John Bethune and Véronique Wadden. His loyalist father was a chaplain of the Royal Highland Emigrants, and later became the first Presbyterian minister to settle in Ontario[2] – in Williamstown – a community which later fairly teemed with retired fur traders. This may have influenced Angus, as may have the North West Company career of his maternal grandfather, Jean Etienne Wadden.

Bethune is said to have entered the service of the North West Company at an early age, and was a clerk in the Red River department in 1804. The first detailed account of his activities was in the 1810 journal of Alexander Henry, the younger, where he figures in Henry's reports from Rocky Mountain House of attempts to reunite David Thompson and his brigade.[3] The Piegans were preventing the brigade from leaving the post to look for the explorer, and were determined that the arms and ammunition that the brigade carried should not fall into the hands of their enemies, the Flatheads. The fur traders tried to circumvent the vigilant Piegans by lying to them and bribing them with liquor; when finally the coast seemed clear, Thompson's men refused to embark unless Henry or Bethune accompanied them out of danger. Henry proposed that Bethune remain behind, risking the wrath of the Piegans. Aware of this possible consequence, Bethune refused. Henry took the rebuff rather badly, but bravely stayed behind, only to discover that he had sent the canoes in the wrong direction. They were recalled, and sent off again when the Indians had been made 'roaring drunk' once more.[3]

Thompson had hoped to reach the mouth of the Columbia before the Pacific Fur Company's expedition, but arrived four months after the American concern had founded the post of Astoria. Bethune's next appearance (in published accounts) was in the fall of 1813 at Astoria, where he acted as a witness to the bill of sale between Astor's concern and the North West Company.[4] He may have contributed nothing to the planning and negotiations leading to the take-over, but his presence illustrates his penchant for being implicated in controversial events. Many people were upset about the sale (Astor considered it a sell-out), and it continued to exercise Hubert Howe Bancroft and others decades later.

Bethune spent a rather hectic winter at the post (renamed Fort George). Its command was hotly disputed among the numerous North West Company partners there, the men were quarrelsome and insubordinate, and the women at the fort were disruptive. By the spring, about one-third of its inhabitants had contracted venereal disease, and Bethune suspected he was one of them.[5]

In 1814, at thirty years of age, he became a partner of the North West Company. That spring, he waited anxiously for the arrival of the *Isaac Todd*, a company vessel fitted out in England the previous spring to continue the trade from the Columbia to China. Bethune had been selected as the vessel's supercargo. During the next two years, he made two return voyages across the Pacific, mingling with Hawaiian royalty, spending about five months in China, and trading with Russians at Sitka and Spaniards at Monterey.[6]

The adventure to China was a disappointment to the company. It is difficult to say whether or not the supercargo was at fault. In the first place, the *Isaac Todd* was under license to the East India Company, and Bethune's efforts to turn a profit may have been completely hamstrung. (Simon McGillivray, no fan of Bethune's, reflected years later: 'the restrictions imposed on the private trade by the E.I.Co and the disadvantageous manner of remittance caused expenses which the trade could not bear.')[7] Further, the China market was a tricky one, being clogged with bureaucracy and fairly unpredictable by the time Angus arrived.

Still, William McGillivray had suspected in 1814 that Angus Bethune was not the most qualified person to conduct the business in China, and in 1816 he concluded: 'The expense attending the sending [of] our own vessels to China is too heavy – and the Partners of the North West Company do not understand the management of Ships and Captains.'[8] The London agents of the company also aimed some veiled barbs at Bethune, condemning the treatment that the ships' captains had received from North West Company partners.[9]

It is striking how few favourable judgments on Bethune's abilities as a fur trader and his qualities as a man occur in the documents available. He lacked rapport with top officials in both fur companies. William McGillivray's references to him in this period perhaps anticipate Bethune's public clash with the Montreal agents four years later.

In the interval between his return from China and the rebellion of the wintering partners, Bethune did not lack for excitement. Between 1817 and 1820 he apparently traversed half a continent three times, one of his journeys being marked by perils and violence, another with some mystery. He left Fort George in 1817 with an overland party destined for Fort William. The journey was a terrible one, visited with heavy rains, difficult and dangerous crossings (during one Bethune was nearly drowned), and losses of provisions and life. Ill and fatigued, seven of the party were sent back to Spokane by Bethune and Duncan McDougall. Only one of them arrived, and cannibalism had been resorted to en route. On the

Athabasca, friction between the officers led to force being threatened, guns loaded, and dirks exposed. Bethune and McDougall left the party a few weeks later.[10]

From this time until he showed up again at Fort George in November 1818, his whereabouts are not known. Furthermore, James Keith made a perplexing reference to Bethune's reappearance at the latter date at the post, which had just formally passed into the American government's hands, according to the terms of the Treaty of Ghent, though the North West Company continued to occupy it. Keith wrote to John George McTavish in February 1819 that McTavish's 'most welcome favour of last summer' was 'rather unexpectedly handed me p. Mr. Bethune 8 November.' Further, Bethune had 'brought along with him such an un-usual accession of Gentlemen of one kind or other as at first sight to induce me to infer that some permanent arrangements had been effected relative to the Country between our Agents and the United States Gov-ernment – but behold it was but a dream!!!'[11]

Bethune probably spent the winter of 1818–19 at Fort George. The following winter, spent at Ile à la Crosse, was full of contention and strife. There he met formidable opposition from John Clarke of the rival Hud-son's Bay Company post. Clarke left a partial account of their collision, though it is extremely one-sided, boastful, and possibly libellous. Bethune was physically prevented from kidnapping an ex-Nor'wester who had joined Clarke, and was exposed as 'a liar and a story teller' in front of some Indians whom he had tried to incite to violence against Clarke's post. (He had told them that Hudson's Bay Company servants had brought 'the sickness' and death to their people.) Further, Bethune supposedly ducked a contemptuous challenge to meet Clarke 'as a gentleman,' in spite of being threatened with a 'public horsewhipping' if he did not.[12]

The summer of 1820 and the winter of 1820–1 were the period of Angus Bethune's greatest prominence during his fur trade career. In July 1820, eighteen wintering partners, unwilling to renew their agreement with the Montreal agents, deputized Bethune and Dr John McLoughlin to pursue negotiations with the Hudson's Bay Company. To this purpose, Bethune would return to sea, this time crossing the Atlantic from New York City, and would hob-nob with Nicholas Garry and other eminent men.

McLoughlin was (and is) considered the 'senior' of the two spokesmen (though one year younger than Bethune and, incidentally, married to Marguerite, daughter of Jean Etienne Wadden, Angus's grandfather).[13] How or why the partnership between the two developed is not clear. Colin

Robertson described them as 'radicals,' and said he had predicted long before that they would lead the winterers in revolt.[14]

In this period, another assessment conveyed to Colvile by Samuel Gale, was that 'the most perfet reliance may be placed as well in the ability of Messrs. B&McL, in the affairs in question, notwithstanding their appearance may not announce the capacity which they actually possess: a complete knowledge of the business of the interior, a sound judgment as to consequences, and great weight with their constituents & others are perhaps better assurance of their capacity in the present matter than could be derived from higher qualifications which might have occasioned a less exclusive attention to their own particular line of business.'[15] This is one of the few favourable judgments found on Bethune's abilities and character. It is diluted, however, by being joined to an appraisal of McLoughlin.

How much impact McLoughlin and Bethune had on the negotiations which led to the coalition is disputed. E.E. Rich wrote that the agents proved to be better negotiators than the 'somewhat shame-faced winterers.'[16] One of McLoughlin's biographers, Richard G. Montgomery, made the dubious claim that the mission of the pair was a glorious success, and that McLoughlin was responsible for the union.[17] John McLean, among others, held that the split in their company revealed by the mission of McLoughlin and Bethune gave the Hudson's Bay Company the whip hand.[18]

In the spring of 1821, Bethune travelled from London to Liverpool and from there to New York in the company of Nicholas Garry. His travelling companion elicited but one substantive and unflattering comment in Garry's diary: 'A few days after we had been on Board Mr. Bethune had a violent attack of rheumatism, a little contradiction to the assurance he gave me in London that this affliction they were never exposed to; tho' on my laughing with him on the subject he assured me it was only to be imputed to the English climate, still it now came out from his other friends that it was a complaint of long standing.'[19] The identity of the 'other friends' was not stated. No indication was found in the documents of how McLoughlin and Bethune felt about each other, with the possible exception of McLoughlin's reference to Angus some years later as his son's cousin, 'Mr. Bethune,' and not as his old friend and colleague.[20]

If Colin Robertson's account of the July meeting at Fort William is accurate, certainly, Bethune was no equal of the doctor's. On hearing that McLoughlin was too ill to attend the meeting, Robertson predicted: 'Bethune I fear will be roughly handled in the absence of this honest fellow. He is particulary obnoxious to the agents. The Director ought to act with spirit in this case, as Bethune has actually some claim to his protection.'[21] Robertson's prophecy was substantially accurate, and, apparently, Bethune had a miserable time at the meeting. He was sent a challenge by winterer Thomas McMurray, and, as Robertson wrote gleefully: 'Poor Bethune has been dreadfully annoyed at this place, insulted by one party and neglected by the other. A sad change. I saw him, poor little fellow, when in London walking arm in arm with one whom William McGillivray would have been proud to acknowledge as an acquaintance – what a strange world this is.'[22] Why the winterers should have been so rude to him, their former spokesman, is not apparent; perhaps they considered he had botched the negotiations, or had, the year before, led them down a garden path.

The terms of the union were considered by some to be more generous than the wintering partners deserved, though some of the rebels may have had higher hopes and were upset by the inclusion of the Montreal agents in the agreement. According to Robertson, the price paid for the rebellion was that the attractive appointments went to the supporters of the agents, and 'those who espoused the cause of poor McLoughlin were thrown on the banks of Columbia, Lake Huron, and Hudsons Bay.'[23]

Bethune's first appointment as chief factor of the Hudson's Bay Company was to Moose Factory. He remained there only a year, and his correspondence and other documents at this post could not be found among microfilmed company papers.

The first documented clash between Bethune and Governor William Williams occurred in 1822. In this instance, Bethune was one of five chief factors in the southern council who had determined not to brook any interference from Williams or even from London in managing the business of the department. They wrote an imperious letter to London informing the governor, deputy governor and committee of their decisions and regulations. Perhaps characteristically, Bethune was singled out in this letter, having served, on one issue, as the 'medium' for 'Mr. McLoughlin and Mr Thain.'[24] (The letter did not meet with a grateful reception in London.)

Governor Simpson also singled him out in his analysis of the troubles in the southern council: 'Vincent and Bethune are at the bottom of it and Mr. Williams has not sufficient knowledge of the business to take a lead in the arrangements. The fact is they seem to have made a party against Williams, and are determined that he shall merely have the nominal management.'[25]

At the fractious 1822 meeting of the southern council, Bethune was put in charge of the Albany department. Thomas Vincent succeeded him at Moose Factory, over the shrill protests of Governor Williams.[26] Another collision with Williams was inspired by a January 1823 agreement between Bethune and James Keith, chief factor in charge of neighbouring Severn, in the northern department. In fairness to Bethune, the arrangements made were a result of Keith's initiative.

In order to discourage Severn and Albany Indians from trading at different posts and departments, these Indians were obliged to 'belong' to the district from which they had received their advances, and were to be forced to return to it by being denied spirits, gratuities, and remuneration. If they visited a different district without permission, their hunts were to be taken from them and accounted for 'to the place to which they belong.' Bethune predicted these rules would make the hunters 'more dependent and also more industrious' than they had been for some time. He differed with Keith only in the apportioning of the Indians. Keith suggested 'taking them as they stood' in the spring of 1821. Bethune preferred the fall of 1821, and, Keith's successor James Sutherland alleged, made 'sweeping claims' to the Indians of the inland posts.[27]

Williams was initially annoyed because the council's opinion had not been first sought. Bethune replied, in part, by lecturing the governor on the discretionary powers of chief factors, closing, 'Being aware that the Council cannot meet until the month of June or July next I cannot refrain from observing that your animadversions/in conclusion of your 3rd paragraph/is premature.'[28] Williams's temper was not improved by the resolve at the 1823 council meeting that Bethune had exercised no undue authority.[29]

Bethune did not remain at Albany long enough to witness the results of the agreement with Severn, as he was appointed to Sault Ste Marie in July 1824. Thomas Vincent was appointed to Albany.

This time Williams was pleased with Vincent's appointment, writing to London that he anticipated the returns of the 'almost ruined District' would improve. He continued with an obvious attack on Bethune, who had often referred to Albany's poverty in furs: 'the "exhausted state" of a Country implied much, sometimes this term is used to cover mismanagement, scheming, abandoning Posts and Indians, without considering the consequences likely to attach to change for the sake of novelty, without substantial reform.'[30] (Vincent concurred with this analysis in later district reports. He and Bethune had not rejoined forces against Williams.)

According to some 1824–25 documents, Albany's trade suffered from the Keith-Bethune agreement, and poor hunts, starvation, and, in one instance, robbery and murder had resulted. Bethune's determination not to allow Lac Sal and Osnaburgh Indians to take debt as usual had resulted in threatened attacks and consequent proposals to build blockhouses at these posts.[31] Simpson took a more jaundiced view of the change at Albany, complaining to London that its new management had not adhered to the Keith-Bethune agreement, and had 'put all the wiles of determined opposition in practice to draw the Indians from Severn.'[32]

At the Sault, Bethune was reduced from supervising the business of six posts to supervising a provision depot not involved in commerce with the natives. The depot probably did not rate or require a commissioned gentleman in charge; usually one clerk wintered there with two or three labourers under his direct supervision. Perhaps Williams engineered the appointment, hoping to get Bethune out of his hair – but he did not succeed in quelling the conflict.

Bethune precipitated a new battle by writing directly to William Smith, secretary of the governing committee in London, on a trivial matter. Williams had 'intimated,' he wrote, that 'wood' required to build a store at the Sault was 'on the spot,' and that the building was 'in a state of great forwardness.' But, he explained, 'no wood, not one stick,' was ready, and went on, 'I presume Governor Williams mistook some scattered decayed Logs for the Timber in question.'[33]

The tone of Bethune's letters to his governor is the same in 1825: 'The Mechanic, I suppose you mean Carpenter, is a Blacksmith also – who if I had employed to make the Nails required for the store as you insinuate, would have been adding an obstacle to in place of advancing the business, and have shewed a decided want of management on my part.'[34]

In his 1825 report, Bethune made an unusual proposal to shed himself of Williams: 'I think it would answer better, were the Governor and Committee to place this Post under their own direction, by this means these long and endless delays would be obviated, as their Honours could convey their instructions early in Spring, which would benefit and facilitate the business very much.'[35]

Bethune and Williams remained at loggerheads until the latter's recall in 1826. Their dispute even preoccupied the governor's last letter to London.[36] It may have played some part in his removal. The governor and committee may have been unimpressed with Williams's inability to handle Bethune (among others), and they must have resented receiving missives from the two requesting mediation in fairly inconsequential arguments.

Governor Simpson was more adept at keeping Bethune 'in his place,' but he did not find him much more palatable than Williams had. Bethune was judged very harshly in all areas in Simpson's 1832 character book: 'A very poor creature, vain, self sufficient and trifling, who makes his own comfort his principal study; possessing little Nerve and no decision in anything: of a snarling vindictive disposition, and neither liked nor respected by his associates, Servants or Indians. His Services would be overpaid by the victuals himself & Family consume. About 48 Years of Age.'[37]

Though, in some other cases, Simpson's character book portrayals are unfair and untrue, this judgment on Angus Bethune cannot be easily contradicted. Bethune's quarrels with his peers and superiors and his difficulties with the men under his supervision are easier to document.

At the Sault he was faced with at least two voyageur mutinies (though one of them was Lake Huron chief factor McBean's fault, in Simpson's opinion).[38] During the 1825–6 season, five men and one clerk under him left the service by desertion or dismissal.

John Corcoran, a clerk who had spent one winter with Bethune, reeled off a string of injustices he and five servants at the Sault had suffered, and blasted his former superior in a letter to London: 'Mr. Bethune is a person who attaches difficulties and importance to every thing he undertakes his treatment to those under him is beyond any thing I can describe, nothing short of the most abject submission will please him: God help those who winter with him at an Inland post, where even desertion the worst of alternatives is out of their power.'[39] Corcoran accused the chief factor of a number of serious offences, including smuggling, lying, and misappropriating the company's provisions.

Corcoran, however, was an unsavoury and violent character, an admirer of Governor Williams, and a pre-union Hudson's Bay Company man still prejudiced against former Nor'westers in 1826.[40] Simpson flatly denied Corcoran's allegations in a letter to London, accused the clerk of flagrant misconduct, and, in challenging Corcoran's assertion that he had been nearly worked to death, wrote: 'I cannot learn that he was put to any severe duty, in fact there is little or no employment even for one gentleman at the establishment.'[41]

In the summer of 1832 Bethune was appointed to the vacancy at Michipicoten which had occurred due to the ill health of chief factor George Keith. He may have rejoiced to have under his supervision three chief traders (all former Nor'westers): Thomas McMurray, who had 'challenged' him at the 1821 meeting, Donald McIntosh, and Alexander

McTavish. McTavish, who had made the dreadful journey from Fort George with Bethune in 1817, died suddenly in December 1832, and was referred to as 'my late friend and colleague' and 'one of the Honourable Company's best officers' in a letter from Bethune to Simpson.[42]

Bethune did not engage in documented disputes with McMurray, though he did with McIntosh. The chief trader's suggestion that Bethune was insufficiently acquainted with the business at Fort William elicited the retort: 'I do not pretend to be conversant with the Minutia of your Post, but I am as much so at least as my Predecessor ... I am fully as much disposed to further the Honble Compys affairs as others, but I do not say so much about it.'[43]

There is a carping and petty quality to other references to Keith in Bethune's Michipicoten documents. He seems to have been jealous of this popular officer, who was even somewhat admired by Simpson.[44]

At Michipicoten, Bethune was restrained twice by Simpson from deviating 'for the sake of change' from Keith's arrangements.[45] His response to the governor's check was a rather sarcastic and insolent letter: 'hoping that he [Keith] will excuse my freedom if this should ever meet his Eye, I cannot admit that he is infallible. You will, I make [?] no doubt, admit that I am at liberty (having no pretensions to infallibility) to act freely and to the best of my judgment.'[46] Bethune reacted adversely to the news of his reappointment to the Sault and Keith's return to Michipicoten in May of 1833, and apparently exchanged harsh words with Keith, the bearer of these tidings.[47]

The unhappy Bethune had suffered a personal tragedy only the month before – his wife and the mother of six of his children had died 'after a lingering and painful illness' from the effects of a miscarriage. Shortly after, his own health had failed.[48]

Some small consolation may have come from having the Lake Huron district added to his responsibilities that summer.[49] Except for short visits to LaCloche, Bethune nevertheless remained at the Sault, and, possibly because he was too preoccupied in his bereavement, he did not provoke any apparent controversy there.

In October of 1833 an Anglican missionary and his wife moved in with Angus, possibly to assist in the education and upbringing of his children, four of whom were under ten years of age. By the end of the winter, Bethune and the Reverend William McMurray (later archdeacon of Niagara) had fallen out bitterly. Each thought the other an obstacle to his duties, and McMurray wrote a long and hysterical letter to Simpson on the subject.[50] Sixteen years later, Simpson used this example as the reason a missionary should not live in a company establishment.[51]

Evidence in available documents indicates that the rest of Bethune's career in the Hudson's Bay Company was relatively free of dissension and débâcle. He availed himself of his rotation of furlough in 1834 and was slated to return to the Sault. Instead, in 1835, he was reappointed to Michipicoten. (Keith had been asked to relieve the dangerously ill John George McTavish at Moose.) In 1836 Bethune in turn was seriously indisposed, and requested a one-year leave of absence. He tried to extend this with a medical certificate, but was forced back into the service by Simpson.[52]

In 1837 he replaced John McBean as manager of the Lake Huron district. He incurred anew Simpson's disapprobation for importing too many provisions, and, apparently, the trade of the district suffered a substantial decline.[53] Lake Huron was Bethune's last known appointment with the company; he left LaCloche in the summer of 1839. Though company records state that he retired in 1841, no indication was found in them of his whereabouts between 1839 and his supposed retirement date.

According to other sources, he settled in Toronto either in 1839 or 1840, where he occupied himself by becoming a director of the Bank of Upper Canada, and, in 1845–6, an alderman for St David's Ward.[54]

He also nearly succeeded in depriving the world of Paul Kane's Indian art. In 1845 he met Kane, who was about to embark on his western tour. The artist sought Bethune's advice as to whether the company would assist his mission, and received such a chilling account of the 'inhospitality' of its officers that he was almost deterred from the undertaking.[55] Bethune did not mellow with age.

The last reference to him in fur trade papers, dated the year before his death, was penned by John Swanston and contained the melancholy intelligence: 'the late CF Angus Bethune I am told is quite an Idiot, this is a most [?] distressing state to linger through life in.'[56]

Angus Bethune died at his residence in Toronto on 13 November 1858, in his seventy-sixth year. He possessed an estate valued at $56,498.00, which included 1,500 acres left to him by his father, two houses, stocks, and mortgages.[57]

He had travelled more widely, and had perhaps caused more trouble than many, if not most, of his peers. He had participated in a number of significant events, and had encountered and occasionally quarrelled with some of the great men of his time. Perhaps if he had left behind a quantity of personal papers his biography would have already been written. Certainly his career had an impact on the fur trade, though perhaps not often a constructive one.

REFERENCES

1 Rich ed *Colin Robertson's Correspondence Book, September 1817 to September 1822* 206; Wallace ed *Documents Relating to the North West Company* 426; Wallace *The Macmillan Dictionary of Canadian Biography* 53; Williams 'Governor George Simpson's Character Book' 12; Williams ed *Hudson's Bay Miscellany 1670–1870* 178n; Russell 'The Chinese Voyages of Angus Bethune'; Cones *New Light on the Early History of the Greater Northwest: The Manuscript Journals of Alexander Henry ... and David Thompson ... 1799–1814* 774n; Thwaites ed *Early Western Travels 1748–1846* VI 294–5; Franchère *Journal of a Voyage on the North West Coast of North America during the Years 1811, 1812, 1813 and 1814* ed Lamb 128n

2 See MacKenzie 'John Bethune: The Founder of Presbyterianism in Upper Canada' 95–110; see also Campbell *A History of the Scotch Presbyterian Church, St. Gabriel Street, Montreal* 25–33.

3 Cones *New Light* 648–54

4 See Irving *Astoria, or Enterprise Beyond the Rocky Mountains* 293–323; Bancroft *The Works of Hubert Howe Bancroft* XXVIII; Bancroft *History of the Northwest Coast 1800–1846* II 209–22.

5 Cones *New Light* 911

6 For a more detailed account, see Russell 'Chinese Voyages.'

7 Gough '"Canada's Adventure to China", 1784–1821' 37

8 HBCA F 3/2, 129–129d, McGillivray to McTavish, 28 April 1816

9 PAC MG24 L3, Vol. 15, 9128, Inglis, Ellice & Co. to Sir Alexander Mackenzie & Co., 18 May 1816

10 Cox *The Columbia River* 258–328

11 HBCA F 3/2, 186, James Keith to J.G. McTavish, 6 Feb. 1819

12 Hargrave *Red River* 496

13 Elliott 'Marguerite Wadin McKay McLoughlin' 343–4

14 Rich ed *Robertson's Correspondence* 139; Rich *The History of the Hudson's Bay Company 1670–1870* II 392

15 PAC MG19 E1, Vol. 18, 6996–7, Gale to Colvile, 4 Sept. 1820

16 Rich *History* 30

17 Montgomery *The White Headed Eagle* 41–2. See also Davidson *The North West Company* 175.

18 McLean *Notes of a Twenty-Five Years Service in the Hudson Bay Territory* II 219. See also Wallace ed *Documents* ... 30; Sampson ed *John McLoughlin's Business Correspondence 1847–48* xxiv.

19 Garry *The Diary of Nicholas Garry* 12

20 Barker *The McLoughlin Empire and Its Rulers* 220–1

21 Rich ed *Robertson's Correspondence* 162

22 Ibid 171

23 Ibid 169

24 HBCA D 1/4, 26–30, Thomas Vincent, John Davis, Alexander Christie, Joseph Beioley and Angus Bethune to governor, deputy governor and committee, 10 Sept. 1822; see also 31, Williams to governor, deputy governor and committee, 18 Sept. 1822.

25 Quoted in Fleming and Rich eds *Minutes of Council Northern Department of Rupert Land, 1821–31* xlvi. See also HBCA D 2/1, 46–46d, governor, deputy governor and committee to Williams, 13 March 1823.

26 HBCA B 135/k/1, 2, minutes of council, Moose Factory, 1822; D 1/5, 21d–22, Williams to governor, deputy governor and committee, 14 Sept. 1823

27 See HBCA B 3/b/51b, 41–2, James Keith to chief factor superintending in Albany district, 27 Nov. 1822; B 3/b/51b, 46–8, Bethune to Keith, 8 Jan. 1823; B 3/b/52, 1, Bethune to Keith, 16 June 1823; B 3/b/52, 4–6, James Sutherland to Bethune, 12 Jan. 1824.

28 HBCA B 3/b/51b, 51, Bethune to Williams, 27 March 1823. See also B 3/b/51b, 50, Williams to Bethune, 29 Jan. 1823.

29 HBCA B 135/k/1, 12d, minutes of council, Moose Factory, 3 Sept. 1823; D 1/10, 21d–22, Williams to governor, deputy governor and committee, 5 Sept. 1823

30 HBCA D 1/6, 3, Williams to governor, deputy governor and committee, 17 Sept. 1824

31 HBCA B 3/b/53, 29, Sutherland to Angus Bethune or the gentleman in charge of Albany Factory, 26 Dec. 1824; B 3/e/10, 15d, Albany, report on district, 1824–5

32 HBCA D 4/88, 61d, Simpson to governor, deputy governor and committee, 1 Sept. 1825

33 HBCA B 194/b/1, 1, Bethune to William Smith, 5 Sept. 1824

34 HBCA B 194/b/2, 13, Bethune to Williams, 15 April 1825. See also B 194/b/3, 9, Williams to Bethune, 30 Jan. 1825. (Unfortunately, only one page of this letter is preserved on microfilm at the PAC; it can be partially reconstructed by reading Bethune's response.)

35 HBCA B 194/e/1, 4, Sault Ste Marie, report on district, 1825

36 HBCA D 1/9, 7d–8, Williams to governor, deputy governor and committee, 9 Sept. 1826

37 Williams ed *Miscellany* 178

38 Ibid 178n; see also HBCA D 4/18, 32, Simpson to McBean, 5 Jan. 1831.

39 HBCA A 10/2, 428b, John Corcoran to governor, deputy governor and committee, 18 Oct. 1826

40 See HBCA A 10/2, 428f; D 1/6, 9d–10, Williams to governor and committee, 17 Sept. 1824.

41 HBCA D 4/13, 50, Simpson to William Smith, 10 Jan. 1827

42 HBCA B 129/b/8, 1, Bethune to Simpson, 30 Jan. 1833. (Simpson did not share Bethune's opinion of McTavish; see Williams ed *Miscellany* 196–7.)

43 HBCA B 129/b/8, 41d, Bethune to Donald McIntosh, 7 May 1833

44 See HBCA B 129/a/17, 13, Michipicoten Post Journal, 6 Feb. 1833; B 129/b/8, 6d–7, Bethune to Simpson, 25 Feb. 1833.

45 See HBCA B 129/a/17, 2, Bethune to Simpson, 16 Feb. 1833.

46 HBCA B 129/a/17, 6–7, Bethune to Simpson, 25 Feb. 1833

47 See HBCA B 129/b/9, 1, Keith to Bethune, 15 May 1833.

48 PAC MG19 A21, Ser. 1, Vol. 3, 577, Thomas McMurray to James Hargrave, 10 May 1833

49 HBCA B 194/b/8, 11, Bethune to William Smith, 31 Oct. 1833; see also 4d, Bethune to George Keith, 3 August 1833; 7d, Bethune to McBean; 13, circular from LaCloche, Bethune to gentlemen in charge of posts, Lake Huron district, 5 Oct. 1833.

50 HBCA D 4/127, 19d–21, William McMurray to Simpson, 30 July 1834

51 HBCA D 4/70, 339–40d, Simpson to William McTavish, 1 Oct. 1849

52 HBCA D 4/23, 8–8d, Simpson to Bethune, 11 April 1837

53 HBCA D 4/23, 70d, Simpson to Bethune, 6 August 1837; 103, Simpson to Bethune, 28 Feb. 1838; A 11/46, 23, Joseph Beioley to governor, deputy governor and committee, 17 Sept. 1838

54 *History of Toronto and County of York* II 9; Cochrane ed *The Canadian Album, Men of Canada or Success by Example* I 40; Baskerville 'Donald Bethune's Steamboat Business: A Study of Upper Canadian Financial Practice' 138; *British Colonist* (Toronto) 7–10 Jan. 1845, 3

55 HBCA D 5/15, 300–300d, John Ballenden to Simpson, 29 Oct. 1845; see also Harper *Paul Kane's Frontier* 16.

56 PAC MG19 A21, Ser. 1, Vol. 18, 6267, John Swanston to James Hargrave, 1 June 1857

57 OA York County Surrogate Court Register Book 11, 393–9, will of Angus Bethune

Kwah: A Carrier Chief

CHARLES A. BISHOP

All our generalizations concerning a society are ultimately derived from our observation of the activities of its members. The lives of individuals are becoming increasingly useful because a chronological ordering permits us to observe the relations between a person and his culture over time, as each changes and modifies the other. This paper will present in such a manner the life of Kwah, chief of the Stuart Lake Carrier Indians.

I will consider the actions and decisions of Kwah in the light of both his own character and history, and the behaviour expected of a Carrier chief. 'Rational' actions and decisions would then be those normal for a Carrier chief *and* in keeping with what we know of Kwah's previous actions.

Everything that we know about Kwah has been filtered through the eyes of persons of an alien culture who either witnessed his behaviour, or retrieved information from others who knew him. All that we know about him is what the fur traders during his lifetime and one ethnologist priest, many years after his death, chose to write about him. Thus, there are huge gaps in his life which are usually detailed as a matter of course. The fur traders naturally tended to emphasize his relationship with the Fort St James trading post, but they also mentioned, all too briefly, other activities in which he engaged – such as hunting excursions, trading ventures, feasts, cremations, and potlatches.

Father A.G. Morice, the priest and ethnographer at Stuart Lake during the late nineteenth and early twentieth centuries, fleshed out, from Kwah's offspring and descendants, some of the bare bones of his life, and related these to Carrier culture and the changes of the times.[1] Thus, when information contained in the fur trade journals is supplemented by carefully scrutinized data on the Carrier obtained by later anthropologists, especially Morice,[2] a fairly complete picture of Carrier culture when Kwah was alive is available.

Kwah (spelled Qua, Quâ, or Quas in the fur trade journals), at the time of his death in 1840, was chief of all the Stuart Lake Carrier although there were lesser chiefs at other villages and other Carrier chiefs on lakes in interior British Columbia. For the European fur traders and the other Carrier Indians, he was probably the most important Indian in New Caledonia until his death. This paper will attempt to document and explain Kwah's role vis-à-vis the fur trade and his own society and in so doing indicate why he was the most important chief.

According to Father Morice (the only source on Kwah's early life), he was born about 1755 in a village on Stuart Lake.[3] The son of a nobleman named Tsalekulkye from Stuart Lake and a mother from Fraser Lake, he and his younger brother Oehulhtzoen (Hoolson in the fur trade journals) gained fame by avenging the murder of their father by the Naskhu'tin Carrier who lived on the Fraser River. With seven men, Kwah raided and killed the inhabitants of a Naskhu'tin village. Though Kwah's raid stood out in people's memories, such raids were not uncommon, often resulting from gambling rivalries or from quarrels over women since the Carrier were reported to have been both inveterate gamblers and jealous guardians of their wives. At this time, the Carrier resided semi-permanently in strategically located villages on waterways where salmon were abundant. On or near Stuart Lake alone there were five such villages, each numbering about 100 to 150 persons. Usually each village had a chief and several nobles who inherited their titles through the female line. There were many other Carrier villages, especially along the Fraser River, Fraser Lake, Francois Lake, and Babine Lake.[4]

While Kwah received a reputation for his bravery as a young man, he could not aspire to his father's position as a noble because of the rule of matrilineal succession. He gained his title from a noble relative on his mother's side – his mother's brother.[5] Gaining a title, however, was not automatic, for it involved giving a mortuary feast validating the claim; periodic feasts were required to maintain it. At the time of Kwah's deed of bravado about 1780, he had, according to folk history, just married the first of his four wives, and he seems to have taken up permanent residence in his father-in-law's village next to where Fort St James was later built.[6] His residence in this village was significant: had he married into any other village, he probably would not have achieved his great fame.

When Fort St James was built at the east end of Stuart Lake by the North West Company in 1806, the traders did not immediately recognize Kwah as chief of the adjacent village; it was some time before the post manager, James McDougall, dealt with him as head of the group. This may have been because of the traders' unfamiliarity with the Carrier whom they considered quite different from Indians east of the Rocky Mountains. As was the custom, both the North West and the Hudson's Bay companies had a policy of singling out people thought to be leaders and treating them deferentially. However, in the years following, Kwah demonstrated an ambivalent behaviour towards the traders which is well illustrated in the journals. This is not surprising: Indians during the early years of contact considered themselves in no way inferior to the traders whom they viewed as rather helpless despite their occasional arrogance.

The first insight into Kwah's character, apart from that derived from legend, is contained in Daniel Harmon's journal for 1811.[7] Harmon, although an experienced trader, had been in New Caledonia for less than a year when he found it necessary to give Kwah a sound beating, Kwah being, he claimed, the first Indian he ever struck. Kwah was apparently trying to demonstrate to the other Indians his influence over the traders, and testing Harmon. When Kwah attempted to acquire credit for another Indian, Harmon refused his request. Kwah who evidently considered himself equal to any trader, replied that the only difference between himself and Harmon was that the latter could read and write. Harmon reports Kwah's words in detail: 'Do not I manage my affairs as well, as you do yours? You keep your fort in order, and make your slaves (the post employees) obey you. You send a great way off for goods, and you are rich and want for nothing. But do not I manage my affairs as well as you do yours? When did you ever hear that Quâs was in danger of starving? When in the proper season to hunt the beaver, I kill them; and of their flesh I make feasts for my relations. I, often, feast all the Indians of my village; and sometimes, invite people from afar off, to come and partake of the fruits of my hunts. I know the season when fish spawn, and, then send my women, with the nets which they have made, to take them. I never want for any thing, and my family is always well clothed.'[8]

Harmon replied that he recognized this but could dispose of his property as he pleased. Kwah then, either to intimidate Harmon – which Harmon thought to be the case – or to demonstrate his prowess, began boasting that he had been to war and had taken many scalps. He then asked for cloth but refused the types which were offered to him at which point the exasperated Harmon hit him over the head with a stick and proceeded to beat him. Although Kwah called for help, his companions were apparently afraid to assist him, two other traders being present.

The following day Kwah sent one of his wives for medicines for his bruises which Harmon sent by her. A short time later, he made a feast of beaver meat, inviting Harmon who attended with his interpreter. Before serving the beaver meat, Kwah made a speech in which he mentioned his beating, adding that he now considered himself to be Harmon's wife, for that was how he treated his women when they misbehaved. He then thanked Harmon for knocking some sense into him though he warned the other Indians not to laugh at him for it. This curious incident, full of social and cultural peculiarities, was not reported further. But Morice used it as evidence that Kwah was neither vindictive nor above admitting a wrong.[9]

Kwah perhaps knew that in testing Harmon in front of the other Indians, he took a calculated risk of being put down: as with gambling, a favourite Carrier pastime, one could lose. Kwah realized that he would have to deal with Harmon again in future, and decided that an apology and a retribution feast at that point would in the long run be in his best interests. Actually, the apology may tell us little about Kwah's character. This was not the last time that Kwah angered or frustrated the traders. However, he learned to tread a narrow path between meeting his obligations as chief towards his own people and meeting the demands of the fur traders. When 'push came to shove,' however, his former obligations always came first. His excuse for not trapping was, on several occasions, his need to feed his family first.

Another example will illustrate his predicament. In September 1823, Kwah came to the post complaining that, because he was naked, he could not hunt beaver as the traders expected him to do. The fort St James manager, James McDougall, told him that it was his own fault – there were plenty of goods available for those who brought furs. Kwah replied that he had worked very hard at the salmon weir during the late summer in order to supply the post with fish and that without his aid the traders would have obtained few – which was unquestionably true. McDougall, after scolding him, relented and gave him a shirt since 'he was really pityful for a Chief.'[10]

Not mentioned in this journal entry is that Kwah, during late June, had made a great potlatch feast at which Indians from near and far were present. According to McDougall's entry for 2 July, after the presents were distributed by Kwah's family, 'if they follow their old custom they will remain with little.'[11] After the feast, Kwah was unable to hunt beaver because he had to go to another village to purchase food. Shortly after he returned he was employed building the fish weir. Thus it is little wonder that by September he was naked and had nothing to trade. And yet within a month after his scolding by McDougall he was able to clear his debt as if to show the trader (and perhaps the other Indians as well) that he could do it. He remarked then to McDougall that he thought this was the first time the trader was ever pleased with him.

But Kwah could become as annoyed with the traders as they with him. When chief factor John Stuart sent two high quality guns to be given to Kwah and another chief, Kwah returned the gun the day after he received it, saying that it was too expensive at sixty skins (made beaver, the standard of value), and that he would wait to see if Stuart would lower the price. McDougall told him that he should be pleased, since he was getting the gun 'on debt' instead of having to barter it directly for furs as was then the policy. But Kwah knew well his contributions to the post and did not hesitate to request other goods. McDougall refused him and lectured the chief and his brother Hoolson for asking for so many things free of charge. The trader complained that 'They are good Hunters but at the same time infamous Rascals – who are hardly ever Satisfied – They have done little this Year – yet expect more than they are worth – They find things too dear – but I told them that as long as they asked and got so many things for nothing as they did – The Tarif would not be lowered.'[12]

Kwah was apparently a hard worker and among the chief suppliers of furs to Fort St James, but he also periodically made threats he could not back up. In February 1826, for instance, he told William Connolly, McDougall's successor, that, unless goods were given in debt instead of by barter, he and his followers wouldn't trap any more. Connolly coolly replied that he did not care what Kwah did: 'they might depend upon getting nothing until they had the means of paying for it. They had therefore to chose either to be supplied as usual, or remain Naked.'[13] Kwah does not seem to have expected this reply and, in fact, was reproached by his band. Returning to Connolly, he wiggled out of the dilemma by saying that the interpreter had misunderstood him, that what he really had meant was that if he and his followers remained naked, they would be unable to trap. Connolly remained aloof, answering that each would be treated according to his own merits. Later he wrote in his journal: 'This old Man *Qua* has been in the habit of being much flattered, his Caprices and insolence have been more than once induced from an idea I presume of his great importance – but as I do not happen to entertain any favourable opinion of him, nor dread the effects of his bad humour – I shall lean neither one nor the other – He requires to be brought down – And the opportunity he now gives of doing it shall not be lost.'[14] Having reflected upon his conduct, Kwah returned yet again and apologized, but Connolly told him that he had to prove his good intentions by deeds, not words.

Kwah was constantly trying to enhance his position among the Carrier both by giving feasts and by impressing them with his extravagant demands upon the traders; but he also recognized the importance of hard work to achieving this end. The traders considered most Carrier lazy because of the ease with which they obtained their food and because they supposedly gambled and feasted instead of trapping furs for the post – Kwah was an exception. He did his share of feasting and gambling, but the journals clearly indicate that he was almost constantly employed in other activities as well, including trapping. During the 1820s and 1830s, there were only about ten beaver hunters attached to Fort St James although there were many more names on the account books. Kwah was among the best but he also acquired many of the furs which he traded from his relatives and sons whom he kept under his thumb, 'they being under his Immediate Influence, Pay Just what he pleases to allow them to do.'[15] Many of the furs and fish he brought or had sent to the post were undoubtedly caught by his subordinates. At this time, the land and its resources were, for the main, controlled by the nobles which explains why so few were classified as beaver hunters.

Besides furs, Kwah's most important contribution to the post was supervising and constructing the salmon weir. Indeed, without his help in this task, the supply of salmon for the post's needs would not have been met. His efforts perhaps explain why he could successfully make such extravagant demands of the traders – at least relatively often. His contributions to the provision quest were many: 'July 30, 1820: All the Indians here busy preparing to Dam the River, but I apprehend unless Qua comes to do that job well that it will be done very indifferently ... August 11, 1820: Quâ busy preparing for Salmon, he is never Idle but can hardly get any to follow his example ... April 17, 1821: [Qua] is the only Indian who can and Will give fish, and on whom we Must depend in a great Measure, It behoves us to endeavour to Keep friends with him, for Unfortunately he too well Knows our extreme Poverty.'[16] William Connolly reported that Fort St James required 36,450 salmon annually to carry on the business of the district.[17] The weir and traps built and managed by Kwah produced about 12,000 salmon.

Like most tribes in western British Columbia, the Carrier had a ranking system based upon differences in status, not wealth. While chiefs and nobles were no more wealthy than commoners, validation of their hereditary positions required great quantities of wealth for redistribution at potlatch and mortuary feasts. A chief had to work diligently to acquire the property needed for gifts. He had to demonstrate by example to his followers the virtue of hard work which might require a variety of seasonal activities. Kwah was no exception. A year in Kwah's life might have gone somewhat as follows.

Early in March, Kwah would begin to trap beaver; this would take up most of his time until late spring. The main beaver hunting seasons among the Carrier lasted from early March to the beginning of June, and again from the beginning of October to the end of November.[18] Kwah, however, did not devote all of his time to trapping. In March he might go caribou hunting in the mountains. On his hunting excursions he was often accompanied by a brother, son, or nephew.

Between expeditions he would return to the village and the trading post, for he was rarely away for more than a few weeks at a time except during the autumn. While at Stuart Lake, he would set his fish traps which he left to be attended by his women. During April and May, he would be off trapping or hunting waterfowl, but fish, furs, and waterfowl were frequently brought or sent to the post by his wives or sons. In April, the villagers would abandon their permanent winter homes to take up residence at locations where fish spawned. While Kwah did some beaver trapping in the summer, he more often set bear snares, visited other villages to trade, gamble, or participate in feasts, or held a feast himself. For instance, in July 1820, Kwah returned from Fon du Lac with 'a few Furs which he gained at play.' At one gambling feast held in June 1825, Kwah and his followers almost came to blows with other Indians.[19]

The remains of those who had died during the winter were kept in the houses or were temporarily buried until the summer when cremations and mortuary feasts took place. During the summer of 1823, Kwah held such a feast attended by Indians from many of the surrounding villages. When they arrived in their canoes 'they were received by Quâ and Party with every Kind of Attention and escorted to Quâs Lodge where they partook of what was put before them.'[20] On 2 July, the main feast, to which the trader, James McDougall went, took place; while the following day the presents were distributed to those Indians who had a right to expect them.

These feasts were held to commemorate the dead and to validate inherited titles. If the dead person being cremated or remembered had been a chief or prominent medicine man, many people from several villages might attend. Being a chief, Kwah was a regular participant as were most of the other nobles. On one occasion he went to the village of Noolah on Fraser Lake to witness the cremation of his sister. Due to the somewhat sensational nature of these cremations from the traders' perspective, there are some good descriptions of them in the journal records.

Prior to the salmon run in August, the summer offered ample opportunity for inter-village visiting and trade. Conflicts, desertions, and sexual liaisons were also most frequent at this time. For example, Kwah, who may have been a rather demanding husband with respect to his work expectations, had to chase after and retrieve one of his wives who ran away to Fraser Lake in August 1825 just before the salmon run began.[21] Perhaps she did not relish the thought of assisting her husband in maintaining the village and the trading post with salmon. Kwah, however, frequently acted as arbitrator in inter-village feuds and he certainly seems to have held sway in his own village.

In late July or early August, most of the Indians of the village, including Kwah, left to gather berries which they made into cakes. Or, if the log salmon trap needed to be built or repaired, Kwah would go to the mountains to get timber for it. Soon after, he would return to construct the weir, and once the salmon came, he helped empty the large log fish traps. The sighting of the first salmon called for a special celebration itself. James McDougall, for instance, alluded to this: 'This Afternoon by the rejoicing and Whooping of the Indians at the Village I was informed of Salmon having been seen in the River below the Village.' These salmon were the staple of Indians and traders alike, and once caught, were split open and dried in the sun on racks for winter use. Again in late August and early September, Kwah would collect berries further down the lake with the villagers, or he might set bear snares.[22] Usually Kwah spent the autumn hunting beaver, although upon request he would set his fish traps for whitefish to supply the trading post if it had been a poor year for salmon.

The snow and ice were too deep or thick to hunt beaver after early December, and Kwah generally spent most of the winter in the village as did the other Indians. In Kwah's time, Indians did not use ice chisels to break through beaver houses. In fact, not all Indians were eligible to trap beaver because use of the lands for beaver trapping was controlled by the chiefs and nobles of each village who themselves inherited them through the maternal line. These chiefs, including Kwah, prevented the others from trapping beaver except through express permission. Beaver at this date were important both for the mortuary feasts and as a means of acquiring trade goods, and so control by the nobles prevented others from giving feasts and thereby usurping their status. Marten trapping, however, could be done by anyone and so was encouraged by the traders. Feasting and gambling were common activities during the lax mid-winter period. These seasonal activities in which Kwah participated tended to repeat themselves year after year; and because it was important for the traders to know the whereabouts of Kwah and what he was doing, they are reported regularly in the post journals.

In the early years after the Fort St James post was opened, the traders frequently complained that Kwah was not trapping beaver as he had been instructed to do. No doubt this was because other matters took precedence. But as time passed, Kwah became a more regular trapper because trade goods were growing more important to the Indian economy and because these goods were attaining greater significance in the potlatch feasts. As their significance grew, so did proprietary rights pertaining to the lands from which fur bearers were obtained. As the years went by an increasing number of Kwah's male relatives, and especially his own offspring, came to engage in trapping under his guidance. After Kwah's death, his brother Hoolson came to control most of his lands, but when Hoolson died a few years later, the lands were partitioned among Kwah's offspring into family hunting territories not unlike those possessed by Algonkians in the eastern subarctic. Matrilineal inheritance rules pertaining to land gave way to patrilineal ones at this point.

Perhaps the single most important event remembered by Europeans about Kwah was his role in saving the life of James Douglas, later first governor of British Columbia. The episode stemmed from the murder of two Hudson's Bay Company employees by two Indians at Fort George on the Fraser River during the summer of 1823. One report suggested the murders were committed in revenge for the death of an Indian who had drowned when a Hudson's Bay Company employee accidently upset a canoe;[23] but in fact the murders resulted from a sexual union between the Fort George clerk, James Yale, and a Carrier woman who had been purchased by an Indian named Tree-aze.[24] When the interpreter discovered that the woman was secretly continuing her affair with the Indian while living with Yale, the interpreter and another employee were murdered by Tree-aze and an accomplice to prevent them from informing Yale who was then away from the post. No doubt Tree-aze believed that his woman had been stolen by Yale and perhaps thought that his actions were justified.[25]

Soon after the murders, Fort George was abandoned by the Hudson's

Bay Company as a means of punishment, but it was reported that this tactic hurt the traders more than the Indians since it disrupted the fur trade along the Fraser River. At first, the Fort George Carrier related to the murderers feared retribution through clan vengeance. They thus had to be convinced by the traders that they would not be punished for the deeds of the guilty. For instance, one rumour was spread among the Indians that James McDougall intended to 'take Quâ and his Brother Hoolson prisoners and Keep them tyed foot and hand.' There were other such rumours. Kwah, however, said that 'he Knows the Carriers to be such fabricators of falsehood – that he never puts faith in what they Say.'[26]

For several years the fur traders encouraged the Indians to kill the murderers but to no avail even though some acknowledged that the culprits should be punished. While to kill others not of one's tribe was not considered a crime (and certainly these European traders were aliens), to kill a relative was a most serious offence. Indians from the villages near Stuart Lake and Fraser Lake were not willing to risk clan antipathy should they follow the traders' instructions. In fact, Kwah himself was suspected of trying to dissuade the Fort George Indians from killing the culprits. James McDougall believed that both Kwah and his brother were ill disposed toward the Europeans and 'nothing but self-Interest has prevented them from committing themselves which they approve in others.'[27] McDougall thought that if Kwah really was interested in the welfare of the traders, he himself should have seen to it that the murderers were killed. If, in fact, Kwah did try to prevent other Indians from killing the murderers, it was more likely because, as a Carrier, he understood the consequences – further bloodshed. Also McDougall had not exactly endeared himself to Kwah.

Over the next few years the issue of the murderers was occasionally raised, but since they never showed themselves, the Europeans were unable to apply their system of justice. One of the murderers, however, seems to have been killed, perhaps by one of the traders while away from the post. The other remained at large until the summer of 1828 when he visited the village next to Fort St James. Since most of the Hudson's Bay Company employees were away during the summer, he made the mistake of assuming that it was safe to visit the Indian village quietly.[28] He hid in Kwah's house although Kwah was away at the time; the houses of chiefs were considered by the Carrier sanctuaries for persons who had committed crimes. The trader, James Douglas, probably neither knew, nor cared if he did, about this, since upon learning of the murderer's presence he, with a few post employees, promptly entered Kwah's house and killed him.

Several days later Kwah returned to the village and, after hearing about the killing, he gathered the men of the village and stormed into the Hudson's Bay Company post where he confronted Douglas. Douglas, upon seeing the angry mob, grabbed for a gun but was restrained by Kwah. Obviously Kwah was offended by the deed, especially since it had occurred in his house, a sanctuary, and so he demanded an explanation. Mob violence almost broke out when Douglas' wife grabbed a knife from the father of the man whom Douglas had killed. To retaliate, Kwah's nephew held a sword at Douglas' breast asking Kwah to say the word and he would kill him. Instead, however, Kwah, who literally held Douglas' life in his power, asked his followers to have pity on Douglas and not to shed any blood. At this moment, gifts were thrown to the Indians by the women of the post which distracted them from Douglas and which Kwah accepted as adequate compensation.[29] The Indians then went quietly home.

Although Kwah held no apparent malice towards the traders, the opposite was not the case. Since he was blamed for the confrontation with Douglas, he was not allowed entry into the post for several months. Actually, from the Carrier point of view, as chief, Kwah had little choice but to confront Douglas, especially since the deed had taken place in his own house. If he had ignored the killing, he would have lost face. Whether or not he actually meant Douglas any harm is difficult to say. He must have realized that if Douglas were killed, he himself could be killed. Even if he was not punished later by the traders (which is most unlikely), it is doubtful if he would ever have been able to regain his rapport with the traders. This ability to appraise quickly and while under pressure a situation and the long-term consequences of given actions made Kwah a great leader.

That the Europeans gave Kwah special treatment, which undoubtedly signalled their recognition of his important role in local affairs, is evidenced by various recorded events. Only two are given here. The first occurred during a visit to the fort by Sir George Simpson designed to impress the Indians and give them greater respect for the traders. Kwah was singled out for particular signs of friendship and respect by Simpson who gave him gifts, a handshake, and other personal attention. A second example occurred on New Year's Day 1829: post personnel for whatever reason determined to deliver beatings to the head men of the community after rendering them helpless through drink. Kwah, however, was again singled out and spared the ignominious treatment.[30]

Kwah died a very old man in the summer of 1840. That November a funeral feast was held in his honour but unlike his ancestors, he was buried instead of being cremated.[31] His grave can still be seen near Fort St James. On the plaque are inscribed the words:

HERE LIE THE REMAINS

OF

GREAT CHIEF

KWAH

BORN ABOUT 1755

DIED SPRING OF 1840

He once had in his hands the life of
(future Sir) James Douglas but was great
enough to refrain from taking it.

In his lifetime Kwah maintained with fish the Fort St James trading post, the headquarters of the New Caledonia fur emporium; spared the life of a future governor; and became the most important chief among the Carrier associated with Fort St James. Although he undoubtedly had inherited his title, and although he also had the good fortune to have been the chief of the village adjacent to the trading post, he possessed all of the necessary qualities of a leader. In addition to a prominent place in the history of the New Caledonia fur trade, he left a progeny of sixteen children so that today over half of the Stuart Lake Indians claim descent from him. Because of his importance, the traders dubbed him 'king' of the Carrier. Not inappropriately, his third son became known as 'prince,' and despite tradition, succeeded Kwah's brother Hoolson as chief of the Stuart Lake Indians. The surname Prince remained and is common even today among Stuart Lake Indians.

This brief biography of Kwah raises many questions. For example, it is still unclear whether Kwah was a chief in every traditional sense of the word, or whether he created new and innovative dimensions for that role.

We are also faced with having to see Kwah through the eyes of Europeans. What attitudes coloured the traders' reports of his behaviour? What attitudes biased the reports which Father Morice obtained about Kwah from Kwah's own offspring several decades later? Julian Steward and Morice differ on whether there were two kinds of chief or simply one. To what extent is this sharp disagreement[32] centred around the possible uniqueness of Kwah at a critical historical point? The techniques of collective biography can be applied to tribal figures only with great caution. The biographical data for persons such as Kwah is selective, biased, and far from complete. What the traders reported was relevant to Kwah in the trade situation; what his descendants told Morice was equally selective. Biographies such as this study should be seen, therefore, as tools with which to generate new avenues of exploration rather than as ends in themselves.

I would like to thank my wife, Dr M. Estellie Smith, who made many helpful comments while I was writing the paper. She cannot, however, be held responsible for any errors which may exist.

NOTES AND REFERENCES

1 *The History of the Northern Interior of British Columbia, Formerly New Caledonia* (*1660 to 1880*)
2 See especially Morice's paper, 'Are the Carrier Sociology and Mythology Indigenous or Exotic?' 109–26.
3 Morice *The History of the Northern Interior* 23
4 See HBCA B 188/e/1 Fort St James report on the district compiled by John Stuart for 1822–3; and Morice 'Carrier Sociology' 109. The term 'Carrier' was applied to the Indians of this area by the traders because of the custom whereby the widow carried around her neck a bag containing the ashes and bone fragments of her cremated husband.
5 See Steward 'Carrier Acculturation: The Direct Historical Approach' in Diamond ed *Culture in History: Essays in Honor of Paul Radin* 732–44.
6 Post-marital residence patterns for the early period of contact are not easy to discern. Kwah's father, Tsalekulyé, was a hereditary chief at the village of Pinche on Stuart Lake; perhaps Kwah upon marriage moved into his father-in-law's village near where Fort St James was later built (Morice *History* 20–3). Probably one or more of Kwah's wives were his mother's brother's daughters (Steward 'Carrier Acculturation' 736). This would have made sense given probable cross-cousin marriage among the Carrier and the fact that Kwah, an eldest son, inherited his title from his mother's brother. Kwah's mother, however, is said to have come from Fraser Lake, and Kwah's sister was cremated there.
7 See Harmon *Sixteen Years in the Indian Country: The Journal of Daniel Williams Harmon* ed Lamb 143–4.
8 Ibid
9 Morice *History* 88
10 HBCA B 188/a/2, Fort St James post journal (FSJPJ) 25 Sept. 1823
11 HBCA B 188/a/2, FSJPJ 2 July 1823
12 Ibid 26 Dec. 1823

13 HBCA B 188/a/5, FSJPJ 19 Feb. 1826

14 Ibid

15 HBCA B 188/a/1, FSJPJ George McDougall, 17 April 1821

16 HBCA B 188/a/1, FSJPJ

17 HBCA B 188/e/3, Fort St James report on the district, 1824–5

18 HBCA B 188/a/5, Fort St James report on the district contained in the post journal, 1826

19 HBCA B 188/a/1, FSJPJ James McDougall, 15 March 1821, and March and April entries, 1820; FSJPJ 10 May 1823, 2 May 1821, 31 July 1820; B 188/a/4, FSJPJ William Connolly, 18 June 1825

20 HBCA B 188/a/2, FSJPJ James McDougall, 28 June 1823

21 HBCA B 188/a/4, FSJPJ William Connoly, 15 August 1825

22 HBCA B 188/a/4, FSJPJ 27 July 1825; B 188/a/1, FSJPJ James McDougall, 6 August 1820; B 188/a/2, FSJPJ James McDougall, 9 August 1823, James McDougall, 29 August 1823; B 188/a/4 FSJPJ William Connolly, 31 August 1825

23 HBCA B 188/a/2, FSJPJ James McDougall, 13 Sept. 1823

24 HBCA B 119/a/1, Fort MacLeod post journal, 13 Feb. 1824. I am indebted to Professor Sylvia Van Kirk who kindly directed my attention to these sources.

25 Somewhat similar examples of cases involving the exploitation of Indian women by European traders can be found in other journal records. The traders at Henley House were killed by Indians for having kept Indian women belonging to Indian men. See Bishop 'The Henley House Massacres.'

26 HBCA B 188/a/2, FSJPJ James McDougall, 9 and 10 Nov. 1823

27 HBCA B 188/a/2, FSJPJ letter from James McDougall to John Stuart, 2 Jan. 1824

28 See Morice *History* 138. Morice, from oral testimony, has carefully evaluated the evidence (135–48).

29 HBCA B 188/a/12, FSJPJ 17 Sept. 1828; Morice *History* 140

30 Morice *History* 145, 147

31 HBCA B 188/a/19, FSJPJ 10 Nov. 1840

32 Steward states that a title of nobility and that of village chief could be held by the same person, as in Kwah's case, but that the two were separable. Titles were passed on through the matrilineal line to sister's sons while the title of village chief was 'strongly patrilineal, passing to the chief's brother or son' (Steward 'Carrier Acculturation' 735–6). Morice, however, makes no such distinction, simply stating that titles passed from 'uncle to nephew by a sister, and not from father to son' ('Carrier Sociology' 112). Probably the concept of a village chief independent of titles emerged when Prince succeeded Hoolson as chief – he could not have inherited his father's titles. The emergence of patrilineal succession no doubt reflects both European influence and the development of family hunting territories inherited through the patrilineal line after the middle of the nineteenth century.

PART V ✧ ON THE PACIFIC COAST

Wrangel and Simpson

STEPHEN M. JOHNSON

In June 1834, on the orders of Baron Ferdinand von Wrangel, the Russian-American Company prevented the Hudson's Bay Company brig *Dryad* from proceeding up the Stikine River. This confrontation brought together two able governors, one Russian and one British, of the fur trade in North America. As adversaries, they first earned each other's respect. How this event evolved into a close business and personal relationship in an era of Anglo-Russian tension is the topic of this paper.

During George Simpson's 1824–25 visit to the Columbia department he had determined to expand Hudson's Bay Company operations to include the Pacific northwest coast. Competition on the coast stemmed from the Americans and the Russians. Most of the American sea captains came from New England and traded for furs throughout the northwest coast and then bartered them for Chinese goods in Canton. They also sold supplies of manufactured goods and some provisions to the Russian-American Company in Russian America (Alaska). Simpson saw the Yankees as the strongest competitor of the two and sought to eliminate them first. He planned to extend British trading posts up the coast to the Russian boundary (established by the treaty of 1824–25), and ply the coastal waters to meet the American opposition. But he also regarded the American supply trade with the Russian colony as a source of profit for the Americans and sought to take their place by appealing directly to the Russian governor at Sitka in March 1829.[1]

The Russian-American Company, a joint-stock company that governed these Russian possessions for the Tsar by means of a charter, had found the supplying of its colony with the necessities of life to be a perennial problem. It could not afford to exclude the Americans who, with the

Mexicans, were their most regular suppliers at that time. Both the British and the Americans, by the treaty of 1824–5, were allowed to trade and fish in the 'panhandle' or straits of Russian America for ten years and the Russians could not exclude the Americans from their territory until 1834.

In the fall of 1829, Baron Wrangel, naval captain of the first rank, arrived in Sitka to begin his five-year tour of duty as governor. He had already gained some fame as a naval explorer of the north Pacific and begun a career as a scholar before his appointment to this post. In 1832 and 1833, the Hudson's Bay Company again appealed to the Russian governor to stop trading for supplies with the Americans and accept British supplies instead. The Hudson's Bay Company also warned that the Yankee traders bartered liquor, powder, and guns (prohibited items under the treaty) with the natives in Russian territory.

Governor Wrangel refused this offer both times, being unable and unwilling to rely on only one source for food and manufactured goods. He could not prevent the Americans from trading prohibited items and he knew that the Hudson's Bay Company also traded some of the same items in order to compete with the Americans. Wrangel was frustrated by the treaty provisions and the weakness of his company's trading power against its competitors.

Governor George Simpson knew that the furs bartered in the coastal trade came from the British interior, east of the Russian boundary, and were brought down to the coast for sale. He felt that the most efficient method of obtaining these 'British' furs and eliminating both the Americans and the Russians was to establish trading posts in the interior and capture the furs before they reached the coast.

The Russian-American Company had come to North America for the profits of the maritime fur trade. This trade had suffered a serious decline since the 1820s and Wrangel had considered the alternative of expanding Russian trade with the coastal natives for land furs, especially otter and beaver. Because of the Hudson's Bay Company competition and the profits to be made in whaling in the north Pacific, the Americans began to leave the coastal fur trade. Wrangel's main opponent for this trade was the powerful Hudson's Bay Company. By 1834, when the British company tried to exercise a treaty right, allowing it passage up the Stikine River through Russian territory into the British interior, to cut off the flow of furs to the coast, Wrangel took firm action and ordered his men at Redoubt St Dionysius and one ship to block the Hudson's Bay Company vessel.

This confrontation did not result in violence, for the Hudson's Bay company ship retreated and the governor and committee in London filed a claim for damages (£22,150) against the Russian-American Company through the British Foreign Office. In December 1838, after three years of fruitless correspondence, the Russian minister of foreign affairs ordered the Russian company's head office in St Petersburg to settle the *Dryad* dispute amicably. To both governments' surprise, the former protagonists, Baron Wrangel and George Simpson, had almost finalized such a settlement in their unofficial correspondence.

Wrangel, by then a rear-admiral and an adviser to the company's board of directors, first met Simpson in late August 1838, when the latter accompanied Sir John Pelly to St Petersburg. These two men came to Russia to help resolve the apparently deadlocked *Dryad* dispute and to talk about the American presence on the northwest coast. They hoped to appeal personally to the Russian minister of foreign affairs and to the Russian company. While in St Petersburg, they learned that the Russian government had refused to renew the American treaty article allowing them to trade and fish in Russian territory. They also learned from Baron Steaglitz, a banker, merchant, and shareholder in the Russian-American Company, about the Russian company's capital stock situation and that the minister of finance was in charge of their operations. Pelly and Simpson did not see the Russian minister, but they presented their ideas for supplying the Russian colony to the Russian-American Company's board of directors in early September. This body deferred all authority on this matter to Baron Wrangel, whom Pelly and Simpson saw as the 'principal councillor' and chief intermediary between the Russian government and this company.[2]

Simpson recorded a more candid opinion in his diary. He found the Russian-American Company 'secretly managed by old fashioned Russians who have a crafty illiberal system of management' which made them difficult to deal with. Andrei Severin, the only director who spoke English, was described as 'an old German' and a 'stupid old thief who professes to know everything about the country and trade, but really knows nothing.' Simpson's first impression of Wrangel characterized him as 'an extraordinary looking ferret Eyed, Red Whiskered and mustachioed little creature in full regimentals ... very thin, weak and delicate but evidently a sharp clever little creature.' He found all three directors 'stupid to a degree,' but Wrangel 'seems to have a controlling power, in short, he seems to have the principal management and I imagine represents the Government in their councils.'[3]

Meeting privately in their hotel, Pelly and Simpson convinced Wrangel that a supply arrangement would be worthwhile for the Russian-American Company particularly when they offered the option to purchase Hudson's Bay Company furs at Sitka for resale on the Russian market in northern China. Simpson stated that it was he who threw out the 'bait' concerning the sale of Fort Simpson furs to the Russians at Sitka, which the company could then import as their own produce. Simpson noted the effect this had on Baron Wrangel: 'little Baron opened his Eyes as if wakened from a Dream caught at the thing instantly.'[4] Pelly and Simpson felt that a co-operative agreement would be 'mutually beneficial' to both companies. Wrangel no longer saw the Hudson's Bay Company as a threat to the Russian company's interest and was now willing to consider a commercial bargain with them for provisions, manufactured goods, and furs. This deal would remove the high cost of competition in the fur trade.

Simpson's diary entry for the last day in St Petersburg, 13 September, recorded that, 'Wrangel and I are very thick, a nice intelligent clever little man, regret much we have not seen much of each other.' These words indicate that these two men, formerly antagonists, had formed a bond of mutual respect and esteem.

When Pelly and Simpson returned to London it was left to Wrangel and Simpson to work out the details of an agreement between the two companies through their correspondence. It was the beginning of a six-year period (1838–43) of extensive correspondence between them.[5]

Between mid-September 1838 and January 1839, the Wrangel-Simpson letters detail arguments over a number of topics involved in an agreement: the price of manufactured goods and provisions to be delivered on Hudson's Bay Company ships to the Russian colony; the price of Hudson's Bay Company land otter from the Columbia and Hudson's Bay to be sold to the Russian-American Company; and the cession of the Russian coastal strip to the British company for a specified rent and for a period of years in lieu of the *Dryad* claim. Simpson wanted three years rent-free to write off the claim for damages. Wrangel disagreed and convinced Simpson to accept one year's free rent (estimated at one-tenth of the claim). He likewise persuaded Simpson to agree to the transfer of only the mainland to the British, leaving the islands in the 'panhandle' under Russian control. Simpson was hopeful that an agreement could be drawn up, but, unknown to Wrangel and the Russian colonists in Russian America, the Hudson's Bay Company prepared an expedition to force its way up the Stikine River in 1840 should the agreement not succeed.

Chances of failure were slim as the agreement was practically an economic necessity for the Russian company. Simpson and Wrangel felt that enough common ground existed to sign a formal contract. Both petitioned successfully to their governments for authorization to do so, and they met for a second time in Hamburg in early February 1839.

The nine-article agreement was signed by Wrangel and Simpson on 6 February 1839 and attested by the Russian vice-consul. The contract was for ten years and called on the Hudson's Bay Company to pay an annual rent of two thousand Columbia land otter skins for the leased territory. It also provided for the sale to the Russian company of up to an additional five thousand land otter skins. The supply of British manufactured goods and provisions was settled and monetary and freight conditions agreed upon. Two articles dealt with the outbreak of war between Russia and Great Britain, and provided a mechanism to neutralize both companies' activity during the time of war. These clauses perhaps reflected the diplomatic tension between the two countries during 1838 and 1839. They also indicate how co-operative commercial interests could supersede the current St Petersburg–London climate of opinion. The contract officially adjusted all claims of the Hudson's Bay Company arising out of the *Dryad* affair. Typically, and in private, Wrangel still referred to the claim as vindictive damages, while Simpson called it fair compensation for a heavy loss.

Between 1839 and 1843, Wrangel and Simpson remained in close contact by means of correspondence and two more meetings. The first year and a half of the contract was filled with modifications, clarifications, and suggestions for its expansion. The two company representatives discussed a myriad of topics: a dispute concerning the trade boundary between the islands and mainland in the leased territory; supplies delivered to Sitka by American vessels contracted prior to their own agreement; the sale of Russian California and the use of its port facilities by the Hudson's Bay Company; the establishment of the Hudson's Bay Company's Fort Stikine at the site of the former Russian redoubt; and the recent Arctic exploration by a Russian-American Company servant compared with that of British explorers Dease and T. Simpson.

When Wrangel found out that Simpson was going to Norway in 1840, he invited him to come to St Petersburg again. Simpson agreed and during their third meeting, on Wrangel's estate outside St Petersburg in July 1840, the two business partners discussed current problems as well as a number of new topics and presented them in writing as formal proposals to their respective companies: an experimental purchase of lynx, black and silver fox, and other furs from the Hudson's Bay Company for resale on the Russian company's northern China market; the erection of another Hudson's Bay Company post within the leased territory at the mouth of the Taku River; the attitude of the Mexican government toward the Russian company and the sale of its California possessions; and Wrangel's fears of British expansion inland to establish a post in the interior.

In these and many subsequent letters, Wrangel reveals personal information about the health of his family, his country estate, as well as personal details on the habits and health of company board members. Wrangel certainly would never have spoken about company directors in such intimate terms unless he regarded Simpson as a close friend as well as business colleague.

During the period between the summer of 1840 and the spring of 1841, Simpson decided to journey around the world and return to England via Siberia and the Russian capital. Wrangel and Simpson's communications were filled with references to the distances involved, the passports needed, and the assistance that would be given to him along the way by the Russian-American Company's colonial office in Sitka and the various company agencies along the Siberian trek. Wrangel, a world traveller himself, persuaded Simpson to take along his nephew, Nicholas von Freiman, the new secretary for the Russian colony, en route from London to Sitka.

Wrangel and Simpson discussed two additional items that autumn of 1840. The Russian government contract for the supply of provisions to Kamchatka on Siberia's Pacific coast, was being sought by the Russian-American Company. Wrangel thought his company had a good chance of obtaining it and wanted to know if Simpson's company would be interested in supplying Columbia wheat to the Russian company for this purpose. Wrangel guaranteed Simpson that the Russian-American Company would have one hundred tons of goods annually as freight for the Hudson's Bay Company ships bound for the northwest coast every fall. Many of these would be British goods, which Wrangel assumed would be purchased for him by Pelly, Simpson, and Company,[6] the Russian-American Company's agents in London. This increase in shipping and freight brought profits to the Hudson's Bay Company and provided a cheaper mode of round-the-world transportation for the Russian company. In letters of the period, Simpson showed a particular concern for one of Wrangel's books, a narrative of his 1820–24 polar voyage, and sent him a review of it from the *Quarterly Review*. The letters also shared concerns for each other's health, wife, and family.

In 1842, on his round-the-world trip, Simpson met twice with the Russian governor, Adolf Etolin, at Sitka. Simpson accepted two of his ideas and brought them to Wrangel in St Petersburg: an exchange of Russian-American Company beaver from the Bering Strait area for the five thousand Hudson's Bay Company land otter usually purchased under the contract article; and the sale of Russian colonial products such as castorum and walrus tusks on the London market. Simpson and Etolin also signed tariff and liquor agreements for the improvement and regulation of the fur trade on the coast.

Wrangel (now chairman of the board of directors) and Simpson (now Sir George) met for the fourth and final time in October 1842. Simpson's journey through Siberia had been a tedious and exhausting one and he remained sick in bed for most of the eight days he spent in St Petersburg. Nevertheless, he and Wrangel covered a number of important topics, including means to relieve the financial burden on the Russian-American Company. Through this discussion and subsequent correspondence with John Pelly, Wrangel arranged for an insurance premium through a British firm to insure the fur cargo from Sitka across the North Pacific to Okhotsk. Wrangel was refused a year's credit on the payment due for the land otter skins purchased yearly by the Russian company. Simpson responded by offering a loan from a British bank which Wrangel declined. Simpson accepted the proposal for an equal exchange of Russian American beaver for the Hudson's Bay Company land otter (normally purchased) for the year 1844. Other topics discussed included Simpson's request for permission to abandon Fort Stikine when necessary, which Wrangel readily granted. This was an indication of a change in Simpson's estimation of the Pacific coastal trade. He decided to remove many posts and allow the Hudson's Bay Company shipping department to pick up the trade. The Kamchatka supply contract was mentioned but had still not been settled.

After leaving St Petersburg, Wrangel and Simpson exchanged during the rest of 1842 a series of letters that dealt with more practical items: the problems the British company was having in meeting the provisioning demands of the Russian-American Company, including late deliveries; the possibility of a Hudson's Bay Company vessel sailing direct from London to Sitka; a chart of the port of Sitka for English captains; the building of a lighter at the Sitka shipyard; and the murder of John McLoughlin jr at Fort Stikine.

By early 1843, Wrangel and Simpson had ceased to suggest any further means of enlarging or expanding the commercial arrangements between their companies. There were even some cut-backs. The lynx experiment was proving too costly to the Russian head office and was abandoned. The beaver-otter exchange was cancelled after one year by the Hudson's Bay Company. The Kamchatka contract was not given to the Russian-American Company. The last known effort to expand the arrangement was made in January 1845. Simpson suggested to Wrangel the opening of a market in Russia for Hudson's Bay Company furs. This Wrangel refused to grant because it infringed upon his company's monopoly of the fur trade in Russia.

Events after 1845 drew the two men and their companies gradually apart. Not only were additions to the contract arrangement modified or cancelled, but the Hudson's Bay Company was having trouble fulfilling the specified demands of the original contract itself. The Oregon Boundary Treaty of 1846 had clearly changed the British company's ability to fulfil certain articles of the contract. The Russian-American Company had found a cheaper method of transporting goods around the world in chartered vessels. This eliminated the option of the agreement most profitable to the Hudson's Bay Company. The 1848 gold rush had brought troubles for both companies, as well as high prices for supplies purchased in California and the Sandwich Islands.

Official exchanges between Wrangel and Pelly for the renewal of the contract began in 1847. The Hudson's Bay Company was seeking a reduction in rent and wished not to be bound to supply provisions from the Columbia River region. The Hudson's Bay Company's governor and committee in London, urged on by Simpson, sent instructions to the northwest coast to prepare to re-enter the Stikine River to explore its interior in case the renewal fell through. The Russian-American Company's position was articulated by Wrangel, who would accept no rent reduction, but freed the British company from the provisioning articles. Negotiations almost floundered over the number of land otter to be paid for the rent of the Russian territory. Probably the spectre of costly competition and possible open conflict in the fur trade, rather than commercial necessity, ensured the signing of the much revised document in 1849.

The possible abatement of the agreement brought out interesting reactions from Wrangel and Simpson. Wrangel defended the interests of his company above all else and remained firm about the price of the rent. He was so steadfast on this issue that he offered to a surprised Pelly to end the contract. Simpson conveyed his impressions of the contract correspondence to Pelly: 'notwithstanding the smooth and friendly tone of Baron Wrangell's letter, I feel satisfied in my own mind that, at the expiration of the agreement they will be prepared to enter on the possession of the country now occupied by us to the northward of 54°40′, and that they will give notice that we must discontinue our dealings with the Indians within their territory.' In fact, the Russians did send expeditions into the interior to expand their trade in 1847 and 1848.

However, Simpson felt that the renewal of the contract was important and desirable. He continued 'from what I know of Baron Wrangell and the RAC, I feel that we might place the most perfect confidence in the honorable fulfilment of any formal agreement, the terms of which were sufficiently clear and binding; but that none is to be placed in their smooth and plausible profession of friendship when unfettered by the strictest conditions.'[7] Simpson thus put little faith in the Russians should the contract expire, and advanced once again his competitive scheme of the 1830s to take control of the coastal fur trade from within the British interior.

After the renewal of 1849, the modified agreement was renewed continually until the Russians left North America in 1867. Simpson remained with the Hudson's Bay Company until his death. Wrangel retired from his company in 1849 to his country estate. He returned to the navy during the Crimean War, was promoted to the rank of admiral, and then served in the Russian government until the early 1860s.

Wrangel and Simpson worked with each other in the late 1830s and early 1840s to develop and expand their contract agreement to the benefit of their companies. The personal relationship formed between the formidable 'little emperor' of the Hudson's Bay Company and the equally able explorer-scholar-administrator of the Russian-American Company was unique. It was formed during an uneven conflict in the fur trade on the northwest coast. The resulting commercial agreement gave a breath of life to the troubled Russian colony and also gave the Hudson's Bay Company some control over its last competitor on the continent. Had Wrangel not confronted the Hudson's Bay Company in the 1830s, the British company probably would have driven the Russians off the coast and absorbed Russian America into their fur trade empire of North America. Thus Wrangel and Simpson's relationship in effect prolonged the existence of the Russian colony in North America.

NOTES AND REFERENCES

1 Lt Amelius Simpson on board the *Cadboro* delivered George Simpson's letter to the Russian governor Chistiakov in March 1829.

2 HBCA F 29/2

3 Johnson 'Simpson in Russia' 4–12, 58

4 Ibid

5 There are forty letters of the Wrangel-Simpson correspondence extant for the years 1838–43. There is one more letter in 1845. Much of this correspondence represents only one side, the other half being either lost or missing. All letters were found in HBCA. These archives also hold letters from Wrangel to Pelly during 1847 and 1848. The records of the Russian-American Company (in Russian) contain copies of some of this correspondence.

6 Sir John Pelly, George Simpson, and Andrew Colvile acted as the Russian-American Company's agent in London from 1839 to 1846, when Pelly's son Albert took over as Albert Pelly and Company.

7 HBCA D 4/69

The Russian Fur Trade

JAMES R. GIBSON

In vessels ... destitute of the instruments requisite for observing their course, and of any fixed notion concerning the conformation or extent of the earth, often even without a compass, ignorant Russian adventurers have embarked from Ochotsk, and rounding Kamtschatka, have discovered the Aleutian Islands, and attained to the north-west coast of America. Year after year, in more numerous parties, they repeated these expeditions, tempted by the beautiful furs which were procured in the newly-discovered countries. Many of their vessels were lost, – many of those who ventured in them were attacked and murdered by savages; yet still new adventurers were found yearly encountering all these risks, for the sake of the profitable traffic in these furs, especially that of the sea-otter.

CAPTAIN OTTO VON KOTZEBUE

Standard English-language treatments of the maritime fur trade of the Northwest Coast[1] in the late eighteenth and early nineteenth centuries have neglected or ignored Russian participation.[2] It is the purpose of this paper to publicize general aspects of Russian involvement. These can perhaps best be derived and demonstrated within a comparative framework. Indeed, the entire one hundred and twenty-five years of Russian mercantile activity along the shores of the far north Pacific – from the time of Vitus Bering's second expedition until the sale of Alaska in 1867 – were marked by two sets of contrasts of much significance to the security of tsarist tenure. The first contrast stemmed from fundamentally dissimilar environments and juxtaposed the continental fur trade of Siberia and the maritime fur trade of Alaska. The second contrast was culturally inspired and pitted Russian against American and British entrepreneurs on the Northwest Coast. In the first set nature was the variable and culture was the constant; in the second the opposite obtained. In both cases the Russian maritime fur trade came off second best.

Eastward expansion from the middle of the sixteenth century took Muscovy across the world's largest land mass. In the process Russia acquired the territorial bulk of its emerging empire, including most of Mackinder's Heartland, and it became the epitome of a continental power. But eastward expansion also brought Muscovy into the world's largest water body, a radically different environment to which it had to adjust if it wanted to successfully prosecute the sea otter and fur seal trade – the Muscovites being, in the words of the doomed La Pérouse, 'as greedy of furs as the Spaniards of gold and silver.'[3] Some land fur bearers, notably foxes, were also taken, but they were of negligible importance.[4] Sea otter fur was the golden fleece of the Russian argonauts; it has the densest pelage of all fur bearing animals. A marine mammal that seldom comes ashore (except at night, in winter, and during storms), the sea otter or 'sea beaver,' as it was termed by the Russians, had to be hunted by boat in the open sea. The chase was described by Ivan Veniaminov, a Russian Orthodox missionary who spent the second quarter of the nineteenth century in Russian America:

The hunting of [sea] otters is almost always done the same [way], i.e. by a [hunting] *party.* The time for hunting otters is from the first [middle] of May until [mid-] July, i.e., that time when there is least wind. Parties may not consist of fewer than 15 [one-hatched] kayaks or 15 hunters. The hunters in a party set out in late April [early May] or early [mid-] May for a certain place ...

Having chosen a very calm day, the hunters, after examining the coast, put out to sea at dawn *to find otters* at certain spots. At sea all of the kayaks in the party proceed in a line or formation, one beside the other at such a distance that an otter between them would be seen. In a large party this line stretches several miles. The first hunter to sight an otter or whose kayak is closest to an otter gives a signal by raising a paddle ... Having seen the signal, a section of the party, i.e., several kayaks, or sometimes the entire party, immediately surround the spot where the otter was first seen, forming a circle as large as possible, with harpoons at the ready. The otter, seeing its enemy, does not dive right away; rather, it examines and considers all of the circumstances and does various tricks and ruses under water in order to escape the danger. But no matter how long it stays under water, it finally has to surface. And then the nearest hunter, if he can, of course, shoots a harpoon at the otter and immediately raises his paddle; they surround it again but in a smaller circle because next time the otter cannot go far or stay long under water. And this is done as long as the otter has not been struck by a harpoon; an otter that has been hit can be considered bagged because the harpoon trailing after it in the water impedes its movement and indicates its location when the otter surfaces and hides.

After the first harpoon a second, third, and even more are shot. The otter always belongs to whomever shot it first; and if it has been struck simultaneously by two or more harpoons, it goes to the hunter whose harpoon is closest to the head.

If two or more otters are sighted at the same time, the party divides into groups and each group operates separately and orderly without any confusion.

The best time for hunting otters is when there is absolutely no wind and very few waves. With waves and wind otters are often lost, even wounded ones.[5]

Annually during the 1790s as many as 500 kayaks from Kodiak Island bagged up to 5,000 sea otter in the waters surrounding the islands and adjoining the coast of the Gulf of Alaska.[6] More experience, skill, and patience were required to hunt sea otter than the other game of the maritime fur trade – fur seals, sea lions, walruses, whales, and harbour seals, which, in spite of their greater size and strength, were caught more easily and more quickly.[7] Fur seals were far more numerous but much less widespread than sea otter, being confined mostly to the Pribilof Islands,[8] where, in the words of Martin Sauer, secretary of the Billings Expedition (1785–94), they 'swarm together in great herds on the low islands, and are killed by being struck just above the nose with a short bludgeon ... the largest,' he added, 'are about six feet long, covered with beautiful silvery grey hairs ... having a soft downy under fur, resembling brown silk.'[9] The meat (fresh and salted) of the young fur seals was eaten by the Russian traders; the fur was worn by the Russian lower classes.

Although fur seal skins were as little as one twenty-sixth as valuable as sea otter pelts to the Russians, they exported five times as many of the former from the colonies.[10] From 1786, when Russian hunting began on the Pribilofs, until 1833 a total of 3,178,562 fur seals – an average of 67,629 every fall – were taken. Sea lions, with their thick hide and wiry hair, were not killed for their pelts; rather, they were sought for the Aleut hunters, who utilized them thoroughly – hide for kayaks and umiaks, gut for kamleikas (rainproof capes), flippers for soles, whiskers for hats, and meat (fresh, dried, or salted) for food. Being stronger and fiercer than fur seals, sea lions were more dangerous to hunt, so rifles instead of clubs were used. On St George Island in the Pribilofs about 1,500 cured hides and up to 84,000 feet of gut were obtained yearly in the early 1830s. Walruses were hunted in summer for their tusks along the Alaskan coast of the

Bering Sea. The walrus slaughter was even bloodier than that of the fur seals. From 2,000 to 4,000 walruses were killed annually by the Russians during the early 1830s – and only for their tusks; the hide, meat, and blubber were discarded. Whales were hunted by Unalaska's Aleuts and Kodiak's Inuit, whose courage and agility were demonstrated in this perilous chase; they sought the whales alone in one-hatched kayaks in the open sea with slate spears. The whales were mortally wounded and washed ashore. Many were lost; for example, in the summer of 1831 only 43 of 118 kills were beached on Kodiak. Meat, blubber, oil, and spermaceti were derived from the carcasses. Finally, harbour seals were also hunted; they furnished the same products as sea lions.[11]

In contrast to all of these sea animals, various land fur bearers – sable, fox, squirrel, beaver, ermine, marten, river otter, wolverine, lynx, wolf – were the centre of economic attention in Siberia.[12] Sable was especially sought after. The most valuable of all furs, and virtually endemic to Siberia, this arboreal marten could be readily hunted on foot by Russian landsmen. The only maritime activity required by the continental fur trade was some river and coastal sailing in small craft. The advance to North America, however, necessitated oceanic navigation, which was much more demanding in terms of vessels and crews and hence capital. It was also much more dangerous.

Initially the Russians were able to succeed on the basis of their river and coastal experience because island-hopping along the Kurile and Aleutian chains hardly amounted to open-sea voyaging. Eventually, however, they had to cross the Bering Sea to exploit the Pribilofs, the Gulf of Alaska to reach the colonial capital of New Archangel (Sitka), the north Pacific to trade with the Sandwich Islands, and beginning in 1803 the entire Pacific, as well as the Atlantic and Indian oceans, to circumnavigate the globe. The sea otter was worth all of this effort and expense, for it became the most prized of all furs, outclassing even sable. By 1775 a sea otter skin was worth up to thirty-two times as much as a sable pelt at Okhotsk.[13] As a result, the sea otter came closer to extinction, and in fact one subspecies – the Northwest Coast – was exterminated. In 1825 Captain Otto von Kotzebue of the Russian navy declared: 'Its skin makes the finest fur in the world, and is as highly prized by the Chinese as by the Europeans. Its value advances yearly, with the increasing scarceness of the animal; it will soon entirely disappear, and exist only in description to decorate our zoological works.'[14] His prediction almost came true, thanks not only to overhunting but also to the animal's low fecundity. The most solicitous of all mammalian mothers, the sea otter dam is unable or unwilling to care for more than one pup at a time, and if two are born one is abandoned. The sable, on the other hand, bears several offspring annually, and, unlike the sea otter, moreover, is not a gregarious or diurnal creature. It was therefore more likely to survive.

It was more hazardous and expensive not only to obtain sea otter but also to market them. The chief markets for the soft and durable sable pelts were European Russia and western Europe, especially Leipzig, whither they were readily conveyed from Siberia. Lustrous sea otter skins were sold almost exclusively in China, where they were much in demand as trim. This market could have been reached directly from Alaska if China's ports had been open to Russian ships, but they were not. Kyakhta and Tsurukhaitu (especially the former) on the Russian-Mongolian frontier in the Asian interior were the sole ports of entry for Russian trade goods to China. So sea otter furs had to be shipped across the inclement north Pacific to Okhotsk and then trans-shipped via a long and rugged land and river route to Kyakhta, where they faced high tariffs and inscrutable buyers. So great were the difficulties of this second leg that profits were halved. It was not until the decline of Manchu power in the middle of the nineteenth century that Chinese ports were opened to Russian ships, but by then both the supply of, and demand for, furs had waned.[15]

The Russian sector of the Northwest Coast was farther removed not only from its market but also from its motherland. Siberia was considerably closer, so that what could not be produced locally could be brought from adjoining European Russia. Indeed, during the seventeenth century Siberia was supplied by means of the 'Siberian deliveries,' a transport system that carried freight from northeastern European Russia as far as the Pacific seaboard. In addition, Siberia, particularly western Siberia, contained arable land for the sustenance of the Russian occupants. Alaska, however, was woefully lacking in farmland, so it was acutely dependent upon external sources of provisions, as well as manufactured goods. Colonists were consequently also scarcer, and this weakened Russian tenure. Supplies were brought from Siberia via Okhotsk and from European Russia via St Petersburg and the Cape or the Horn but at great risk and high cost on account of the sheer distance, rough terrain, and oceanic storms and calms. Little could be produced in Alaska itself on account of the cool, damp climate and the limited soil cover. So the Russian-American Company, which monopolized the exploitation of Alaska from 1799 until 1867, turned to cheaper and readier foreign sources – Spanish missions in California, British posts in Oregon, and American ships on the Northwest Coast. Such reliance upon sources beyond its control (and indeed in opposition to its very presence) further undermined Russia's position.

The unfamiliar marine setting was yet another source of insecurity, but fortunately for the land-loving Russians they did not have to acquire very much seamanship in order to get sea otter, thanks to the Aleuts. Expert kayakers and harpooners who had hunted the animals before the arrival of the Russians, they were, in the words of Baron Ferdinand von Wrangel, governor of Russian America (1830–35), 'the most skilled hunters of sea otters.'[16] His second-in-command, Cyril Khlebnikov, remarked that the Aleuts were 'the only persons who have an innate passion for hunting sea otter.'[17] Consequently they were quickly and severely exploited by their conquerors. So were the Kodiak Inuit or Konyagas, who were almost as proficient as the Aleuts at hunting at sea.

At the beginning of the nineteenth century the Russian-American Company used up to 2,000 Aleuts and Konyagas every spring and summer to hunt in the Gulf of Alaska.[18] Wives and children were taken hostage to ensure that the men would hunt, and families were forcibly relocated near new hunting grounds. The resulting overwork, hunger, and disease took a heavy toll. So did hunting accidents and enemy attacks. From 1792 through 1805, 701 Aleuts were killed or captured by Tlingits, drowned, or poisoned. The Aleut population of Unalaska Island decreased by two-thirds within twenty-five years of Russian occupancy (1768–92), and Kodiak's Inuit population by half after forty years of Russian contact (1765–1805).[19] So dependent upon these so-called 'marine Cossacks' did the Russians become that they themselves did not even have to learn how to hunt sea otter.[20] Martin Sauer observed on Kodiak in 1790 that 'Foxes ... and the marmot are the only animals that the Russians can kill; for they are not capable of chasing the sea animals, which require particular agility in governing the small leather canoes [kayaks].'[21] Similarly, Lieutenant Alexis Lazarev of the Russian navy noted in 1820 on Unalaska that 'During our stay here we noticed that the Russians, going hunting or anywhere else in kayaks, always knew less about this matter than the Aleuts who live with them here.' He added that 'If the company should somehow lose the Aleuts, then it will completely forfeit the hunting of sea animals, because not one Russian knows how to hunt the animals, and none of our settlers has learned how in all the time that the company has had its possessions here.'[22] This was not the case in Siberia, where the Russians could hunt fur bearers as well as the natives. Being less useful to their conquerors – except to render an annual tribute of a few sable skins per man – Siberia's aborigines were exploited less and suffered less.

Although the Aleuts offered weak resistance, another group of natives – the Tlingits of the Alaskan panhandle – proved uncontrollable from the time of their initial contact with the Russians in 1783. Like other Northwest Coast Indians, whom Governor George Simpson of the Hudson's Bay Company described as 'numerous, treacherous, and fierce,'[23] the Tlingits had a cohesive society and a solid economy, owing largely to the rich fisheries and luxuriant forests of their coastal environment. They were thus able to oppose the Russians firmly, much more so than any native group in Siberia (with the possible exception of the Chukchi). The Russians even became dependent upon the Koloshes, as they called them, for some foodstuffs, namely wild goats, halibut, and potatoes. One of the basis weaknesses of the colonial capital of New Archangel was its location in the midst of the hostile Tlingits, who captured the settlement in 1802. Their fearsome opposition was not impaired until nearly half of their population succumbed to the great smallpox epidemic of the last half of the 1830s. They were further weakened by the withdrawal of their occasional allies – American traders – from the coastal trade after 1840. Thereafter the Tlingits turned to Russian suppliers. From 1842 the Russian-American Company hired from twenty to fifty Tlingits every summer as fishermen, woodcutters, carriers, and even sailors, paying them in money and kind.[24]

The Tlingits had long been abetted by American shipmasters, who represented even more formidable rivals for the Russians than the Indians. In Siberia the Russians had not been challenged by other great powers on account of the isolationism of China's Manchu dynasty and Japan's Tokugawa shogunate, both of which came to power just as Russia was conquering Siberia. On the Northwest Coast, however, Russia was less fortunate. Here was an area of keen international competition among the old powers, Russia, Spain, and Great Britain, and the new power, the United States. Americans and Englishmen were alerted to the fur wealth of the region by the publication in 1784 of Captain Cook's journal of his third voyage;[25] and before the end of the decade one of the earliest British traders, Nathaniel Portlock, was able to conclude that the coastal traffic was 'perhaps the most profitable and lucrative employ that the enterprising merchant can possibly engage in.'[26]

During the 1790s American and British vessels may have taken as many as 100,000 sea otter – more than one every hour![27] To the 'Boston men,' as to the Tsar's men, pelts were not an end in themselves but a means of exchange (in place of specie) for Chinese goods, which they obtained at Canton and sold in Europe and America. The Yankees traded shrewdly and ruthlessly, so much so that almost none of the British remained on the coast. The Americans offered the Indians better goods at lower prices, and some skippers were not above trading firearms, including even cannons, to the Tlingits, training them in their use, and inciting them against the Russians. In the mid-1820s Captain von Kotzebue remarked that 'No Kalush [Tlingit] is without one musket at least, of which he perfectly understands the use.' 'Bows and arrows,' he added, 'were formerly their only weapons; now, besides their muskets, they have daggers, and knives half a yard long.'[28] This threat did not diminish until the depletion of the sea otter rafts and fur seal herds and the advent of vigorous competition from the Hudson's Bay Company induced the American traders to abandon the Northwest Coast traffic after 1840.

This brings us to the second set of contrasts, a set of contrasting advantages and disadvantages between the Russians and their American and British rivals. The Russians profited from the sea otter trade longer than anyone else. The Spaniards became aware of Baja California's sea otters as early as 1733 but few pelts reached China via the Manila galleons because the peninsula's natives were unable to bag many specimens. Russian awareness of sea otter dates from the early 1740s, when the remnants of Bering's second expedition returned to Kamchatka with up to 1800 skins. By the mid-forties the Russians were regularly mounting trading expeditions to the nearby Commander, Kurile, and eventually Aleutian islands. By the time American and British merchants entered the trade in the late 1780s seventy-eight Russian maritime ventures had already obtained thousands of furs worth more than five million roubles.[29] That was a substantial head start. And the Russians continued to prosecute the sea otter trade – albeit much less profitably – for a quarter of a century after the Americans had abandoned it.

The Russians, unlike the Spaniards of Baja California, were able to get sea otter skins in quantity because they possessed the Aleuts, who were unequalled as hunters of sea otter. The Aleuts were, in a sense, serfs to their Russian masters, just as the peasants of European Russia were still bonded to their landlords. All Aleut adult males were obliged to work for the Russians; in effect this compulsory labour replaced fur tribute, which was banned in 1788. The Kodiak Inuit, who were nearly as skilful as the Aleuts, were likewise under the control of the Russians, who seldom hunted or trapped themselves. As La Pérouse noted, 'being more of soldiers than of huntsmen, it has appeared to them more commodious to subjugate the inhabitants, and impose on them a tribute, than to share with them the fatigues of the chace.'[30] Their Yankee and British competitors, on the other hand, had to be content with less certain and more dangerous barter alongside or aboard their ships. Indian customers drove hard bargains and did not always appear, and those who did sometimes attacked the trading vessels. Because they had less control over and contact with the natives, American and British traders had less effect on native numbers.

Perhaps as early as the mid-1770s the Russians had permanent posts on the Northwest Coast. The Americans had none (if their two-year occupancy of Astoria is excluded), and the British did not have any until the mid-1820s, when the maritime fur trade was in decline. These posts meant that the Russians could obtain furs year round, at least whenever the weather permitted, whereas the Americans had to sail from New England via the Horn and spend only the warmer half (or less) of the year on the coast before heading for Canton. And a post could hold more pelts than a ship. The posts also gave the Russians a stronger territorial claim than that of the American 'birds of passage,' as they were called by a Hudson's Bay Company servant.

The hunting grounds of the two best subspecies of sea otter – Kurilian-Kamchatkan and Aleutian – were under Russian control. Their pelts were dark and glossy. Foreign rivals had to be content with the Northwest Coast and New Albionian–Californian varieties, whose coats were browner, duller, and thinner and hence less valuable. Moreover, winter pelts were larger and had more sheen because by then the brownish pups had matured, so that the Russians with their year-round presence tended to get the best skins, even of the Northwest Coast sea otter, whose habitat they partly controlled.[31] In addition, the foremost rookery of the northern fur seal – the Pribilof Islands – was preempted by the Russians, who also owned the minor rookery of the Commander Islands. American sealers exploited the less valuable Californian subspecies; most of their take by far, however, consisted of skins obtained by bartering supplies at New Archangel.

In spite of these highly favourable circumstances, the Russians did not outcompete the Americans, who enjoyed several advantages of their own. For one thing, American vessels had quick access to the Chinese market through Canton. Russian traders were restricted by a treaty of 1727 to two border towns just south of Lake Baikal and far from the coast. The long and difficult transport of furs to these two inland markets from New Archangel via Okhotsk took up to two years and raised their price and made them less competitive with furs that reached Canton in American bottoms from the Northwest Coast in a couple of months. On several occasions the Russian-American Company even resorted to sending pelts to Canton on Yankee vessels, whose owners took a percentage of the sales. China's ports were not opened to Russian ships until the 1850s (in the wake of internal discord and foreign intrusion), but by then it was too late for the fur trade.

The American traders had better ships and better sailors. Captain von Kotzebue did not wonder that an American brig, despite the intoxication of the entire crew (including the captain), escaped shipwreck on a stopover at New Archangel in 1825 because, in his words, 'the North Americans are such clever sailors, that even when drunk they are capable of managing a ship.' He added that 'On my visit to the ship, I could not help remarking the great economy of all its arrangements: no such thing, for instance, as a looking-glass was to be seen, except the one kept for measuring the angle of the sextant, and that, small as it was, assisted the whole crew in the operation of shaving.'[32] The Russians had not yet fully adjusted to the sea, and Russian shipwrights and shipmasters alike had limited experience (partly because little was needed in view of the facts that the Aleuts did much of the boating and the Aleutians provided a land bridge between Asia and America). Shipwrecks, with their attendant loss of lives, furs, and supplies, were not uncommon. Russian vessels and crews were so unseaworthy that the Russian-American Company bought not a few foreign (mainly American) ships and hired foreign and especially Finnish seamen. Around 1830 Khlebnikov noted that American ships were better built, more versatile, longer lasting, and cheaper.[33] Russian shipping eventually improved, but this was long after the heyday of the maritime fur trade.

In addition, American (and British) trade goods were higher in quality and wider in variety on account of the inferior state of Russian manufacturing, farming, and transport, and the Americans could offer more for Indian furs. In the mid-1820s Yankee 'coasters' were paying the Tlingits five or six blankets plus some molasses, rusks, and groats for one sea otter pelt – twice as much as the Russians were offering.[34] So the latter got few furs from the Northwest Coast Indians, who were astute traders. The Russians were simply outbid by the American entrepreneurs, who, as a result of vigorous competition among themselves, were more ingenious and more efficient. Captain von Kotzebue asserted that 'no people in the world surpass the citizens of the United States in the boldness, activity, and perserverance of their mercantile speculations.'[35] By contrast, the monopolistic Russian-American Company was complacent and conservative.[36] To a lesser extent so was the Hudson's Bay Company monopoly in the late 1830s, when it claimed to have driven the 'Boston pedlars' from the coast. In fact, the latter had long before largely abandoned a business that had become increasingly unprofitable because of overhunting.

American traders turned to other ventures, which brings us to their remaining advantage – diversification. Unlike the Russians, their commercial risk was spread among several activities. To the fur trade they added smuggling along the western coast of New Spain and provisioning of New Archangel in the first decade of the 1800s, sandalwooding on the Sandwich Islands in the 1810s, and whaling in the North Pacific in the 1830s and 1840s, as well as fur sealing in the north and south Pacific and scouring the South Sea islands for such delicacies as bird nests and sea cucumbers. The Russians, on the other hand, restricted themselves to the fur trade, with its finite supply and capricious demand. Neither the sea otter nor the fur seal could endure the relentless hunting; both were simply too vulnerable. The fur seals were too concentrated and too defenceless, particularly on land. The annual Pribilof catch reached 100,000 skins in the 1790s but had fallen to 10,000 by the 1830s.[37] Although harder to bag, sea otter were likewise decimated, thanks to their low rate of reproduction and the higher value of the female's pelt, as well as the skill of the Aleuts. The animals' receding range took the Russians ever eastward and southward until they found no more rookeries and met stiff opposition. As Captain von Kotzebue put it:

At first the sea-otters were plentiful, even on the coast of Kamtschatka; but the unlimited pursuit of them diminished their numbers so rapidly, that the Company was obliged to extend their search for them over the Aleutian Islands, and even to the island of Kodiack, lying on the American coast, where they had fixed their chief settlement.

From thence the chase was continued to the bay of Tschugatsk [Prince William Sound] and Cook's river [Inlet]. The poor otters were severe sufferers, for the beauty of the skin nature had bestowed on them. They were pursued in every possible direction, and such numbers annually killed, that at length they became scarce, even in these quarters, having already almost wholly disappeared from Kamtschatka and the Aleutian Islands.

The Company therefore resolved to extend their settlements farther south; and thus ... arose the colony on the island of Sitka.[38]

Kodiak Island's annual catch of sea otter fell from 1000 in the early 1790s to 100 in the early 1830s.[39] By the mid-1850s the total colonial catch amounted to only a couple of thousand pelts yearly.

When the maritime fur trade ended, the Russians tried alternative pursuits – including coal mining and even the ice trade – but with little success because the limited and remote Alaskan resource base did not favour them. So there was little reason to stay. Besides, rosier prospects loomed in western Turkestan with its irrigated farmland and fabled commerce and in the Amur River valley with its prospective bread-basket and arterial waterway between the Siberian interior and the Orient. When Russia finally abandoned the Northwest Coast in 1867, the fur trade had long since ceased to matter. But for more than a century it had mattered a great deal, particularly to the Russians, so much so that its principal object – the handsome but hapless sea otter – was hunted to the verge of extinction. It is still an endangered species.

NOTES AND REFERENCES

1 The Northwest Coast stretched from at least the mouth of the Columbia River to the entrance to Cook Inlet, if not from Cape Mendocino to the tip of the Alaska Peninsula.

2 See, for example, Fisher *Contact and Conflict* ch. 1, and Howay 'An Outline Sketch of the Maritime Fur Trade.' These historians date the trade from 1785 to 1825, whereas in fact it was being plied on the Northwest Coast by the Russians from the late 1770s (and as early as the mid-1740s on the Aleutian Islands) and until 1867, albeit in a much reduced form.

3 La Pérouse *A Voyage Round the World* 108

4 More land furs were taken from the late 1820s in the wake of depletion of sea otter and fur seals.

5 Veniaminov *Zapiski ob ostrovakh* pt 2 342–4

6 [Khlebnikov] *Colonial Russian America* 1–2

7 Vrangel 'O pushnykh tovarakh severo-amerikanskikh rossiiskikh vladeny' [Concerning the Furs of Russia's North American Possessions] 501. For a German version of this account see Wrangell *Statistische und ethnographische Nachrichten über die Russischen Bestizungen an der Nordwestküste von Amerika* ch. 2.

8 The Russians also hunted fur seals on the Commander Islands off Kamchatka and the Farallon Islands off the Golden Gate. The latter, however, were smaller and had less silvery fur, so their skins were not as valuable.

9 Sauer *An Account of a Geographical and Astronomical Expedition to the Northern Parts of Russia* 180

10 Gibson *Imperial Russia in Frontier America* 35n, 36

11 Vrangel 'O pushnykh tovarakh' 510, 513, 515, 517

12 See Fisher *The Russian Fur Trade 1550–1799* and Pavlov *Pushnoy promysel v Sibiri* [*The Fur Trade in Siberia in the 17th Century*] XVII v.

13 Gibson *Feeding the Russian Fur Trade* 29
14 Von Kotzebue *A New Voyage Round the World in the Years 1823, 24, 25 and 26*
   II 46
15 At the same time in the European market beaver and sealskin hats were
   replaced by silk hats.
16 Vrangel 'O pushnykh tovarakh' 496
17 [Khlebnikov] *Russian America* 35
18 Davydov *Two Voyages to Russian America, 1802–1807* 194–5
19 Smallpox, for instance, reduced most of Russian America's native tribes by 75
   per cent in the last half of the 1830s (US General Services Administration,
   National Archives, 'Records of the Russian-American Company 1802–1867:
   Correspondence of Governors General,' File Microcopies of Records No. 11,
   reel 43, fos. 333–33v).
   [Khlebnikov] *Russian America* 145 gives the 1792–1805 figures for the
   Aleuts.
   According to Veniaminov, there were probably 1200 Aleuts in 24 villages on
   Unalaska in the early 1760s, 800 in 15 in 1805, and 470 in 10 in the mid-1830s;
   Zapiski ob ustrovakh Unalashkinskavo otdela [*Notes on the Islands of the Unalaska
   District*] pt 1 172–3.
   The native population of Kodiak and adjacent islands probably numbered
   8000 in the mid-1760s, 5000 in 1790, 4000 in 1805, and 3000 in 1818;
   Golovnin *Puteshestvie vokrug sveta ...* [*Voyage Around the World ...*] 134; Lisiansky
   A Voyage Round the World in the Years 1803, 4, 5, & 6 193; Sauer *An Account of a
   Geographical and Astronomical Expedition to the Northern Parts of Russia* 170.
   There may have been as few as 3000 in 1790; Sarychev *Puteshestvie po
   severovostochnoy chasti Sibiri, Ledovitomu moryu i Vostochnomu okeanu* [*Journey
   through the Northeastern Parts of Siberia, the Arctic Ocean, and the Pacific Ocean*] pt 2
   59; Von Langsdorff *Voyages and Travels in Various Parts of the World* II 59.
   There were perhaps as many as 6500 in 1795 and 4850 in 1804; Von
   Langsdorff *Voyages and Travels* II 60.
20 It should be pointed out in fairness to the Russian *promyshlenniks* (fur traders)
   that the hunting of elusive sea otters on the open sea from flimsy kayaks was an
   extremely difficult task that took years to master. As the German naturalist
   George Von Langsdorff reported in 1804, 'It requires a good deal of dexterity
   to manage such canoes ... Scarcely has a boy attained his eighth year, or even
   sometimes not more than his sixth, when he is instructed in the management
   of the canoes, and in aiming at a mark with the water javelin'; *Voyages and
   Travels* II 41.
21 Sauer *Account* 179
22 Lazarev *Zapiski o plavanii voyennovo shloopa Blagonamerennovo v Beringov proliv i
   vokrug sveta dlya otkryty v 1819, 1820, 1821 i 1822 godakh* [*Notes on the Voyage of*

the Naval Sloop Loyal *to Bering Strait and Around the World for Discoveries in 1819, 1820, 1821, and 1822*] 186, 235

23 Simpson *Narrative of a Voyage Round the World, During the Years 1841 and 1842* I 225

24 Sarafian 'Russian-American Company Employee Policies and Practices, 1799–1867' 209–10

25 Spanish navigators became aware of the Northwest Coast's peltry a decade earlier, when Juan Pérez in the *Santiago* obtained sea otter skins from some Haida in 1774, but the fact was not publicized by the secretive Spaniards.

26 Portlock *A Voyage Round the World* 382

27 [Khlebnikov] *Russian America* 3, 34

28 Von Kotzebue *New Voyage* II 54–5

29 Makarova *Russians on the Pacific 1743–1799* 209–17

30 La Pérouse *Voyage* 108

31 The only sea otter subspecies exterminated was the Northwest Coast, whose habitat was hunted by all nationalities. That of the New Albionian–Californian subspecies was also heavily hunted, but its pelt was only one-half to two-thirds as valuable.

32 Von Kotzebue *New Voyage* II 65

33 [Khlebnikov] *Russian America* 79–80

34 Ibid 68

35 Von Kotzebue *New Voyage* II 64

36 Particularly from the late 1810s, when the company came under increasing governmental control and naval officers rather than merchants were appointed to the post of governor of Russian America

37 Gibson *Imperial Russia* 35

38 Von Kotzebue *New Voyage* II 36–7

39 Gibson *Imperial Russia* 34

Outfitting New Caledonia 1821–58

MARY CULLEN

The Pacific slope fur trade district of New Caledonia was established between 1805 and 1808 in an effort to find a short supply route from the Pacific Ocean for the North West Company's far interior posts. Simon Fraser, the founder of New Caledonia, failed to discover a practicable highway inland from the Pacific but the five posts he established in north central British Columbia increased the pressure to find an efficient and economical line of supply. When David Thompson opened a usable route to the Pacific by the Columbia River the North West Company established posts around this river valley and supplied them from the Pacific. By the time the North West Company and the Hudson's Bay Company had merged a usable land-water communication had been inaugurated between the two Pacific fur trade districts, both receiving their outfits from Fort George at the mouth of the Columbia River. Despite this important breakthrough, 'distance from any Port of entry and the difficulty of getting the necessary supplies'[1] was seen as a major disadvantage of New Caledonia as the Hudson's Bay Company commenced trade there in 1821.

This paper examines how the Hudson's Bay Company handled the problem of supplying New Caledonia during the thirty-seven years it held an exclusive licence of trade from the British government for the area west of the Rockies. It discusses specifically the various routes adopted, the means of conveyance, the numbers of men and man hours employed, provisioning and volumes of goods transported. Essentially a survey, the paper will identify aspects of the operation of the New Caledonia supply system which require further research. At the same time it will demonstrate the difficulty and question the relevance of attempting to relate transportation on the Pacific slope in a precise way to the costs of trade.

During the years of Hudson's Bay Company monopoly control of the British fur trade on the Pacific slope (1821–58) transportation to New Caledonia operated within two main constraints. As in Rupert's Land, topography here played an important role in determining the flow of trade goods and furs. The vast district (almost 90,000 squares miles) was bounded on the east by the Rocky Mountains through which there was direct access at only two points – Pine Pass and Tête Jaune Cache Pass. Entering the district from the north was impracticable while, to the west, lay the coastal mountains whose only major river valley – the Skeena – was still unexplored. Southward, as its discoverer had found, long stretches of the Fraser River were useless as a supply route because of impassable rapids. The North West Company had established access to New Caledonia from the south by a difficult overland route which avoided the worst rapids of the Fraser and joined the Columbia River at Okanagan. Hudson's Bay Company options were limited to discovering new passes through the Rockies, exploring routes west, or finding alternate ways around the Fraser. Efficiency and cost were important considerations but evidently were not the only factors determining the choice of a supply line.

International competition acted as a second restraint on the Hudson's Bay Company's choice of a route for transporting goods to the northern interior of the Pacific slope. Joint occupancy of the Oregon Territory after 1818 meant the company monopoly there applied only to British trade rights and did not exclude American citizens who openly challenged the company throughout the Columbia valley and along the coast. The 1821 charter of the Russian-American Company extended Russian sovereignty just below 51° north latitude, establishing a protective corridor around this area. The Hudson's Bay Company's inland trade was directly affected by the American coasters and Russian coastal forts which drew off furs. Opening a short supply route west might annoy Russia and invite further inland competition. Geographic isolation and American and Russian competition therefore limited the company to lengthy eastern and southern accesses to New Caledonia.

Within weeks of Union in 1821 the Hudson's Bay Company rejected the southern line of supply established by John Stuart and planned a shift back to an eastern route, using Norway House as depot for New Caledonia.[2] The proximity of York Factory to the western interior had given the Hudson's Bay Company a strong advantage over the over-extended North West Company in the years of competition and it was

therefore natural that the company should be biased in favour of transporting the New Caledonia outfit from the bay. The Hudson's Bay Company's initial view of the fur trade of the Pacific slope also influenced this
decision. The governor and committee hoped to reap profit from the
Fraser valley northward but saw the posts of the ill-reputed Columbia
department simply 'as a buffer' to check opposition from the Americans.
Tying New Caledonia to the east for the purposes of supply thus not only
fitted the company's preference for the York Factory depot but also its
negative attitude to the Columbia. Its central position had hitherto made
Fort St James district headquarters; but in 1822 MacLeod's Lake, the post
to which supplies would come and returns leave, became the winter
residence of the officer-in-charge.

In the next two years efforts were made to improve the eastern supply
route by saving the heavy expense of the intermediate depot at Norway
House and having the New Caledonia brigade go directly to York Factory.
The shortcut investigated, by the Nelson-Burntwood-English rivers,[3] was
never employed, however, for the 1824 journey which took Simpson for
the first time to the Columbia department ended the company's brief
attempt to outfit New Caledonia from Rupert's Land. Simpson's journal
reference to the New Caledonia brigade route as 'the most tedious, ha-
rassing and expensive transport in the Indian Country'[4] indicates that the
supply of this district was a problem foremost in his mind as he travelled
west.

John Stuart may have influenced the governor's dissatisfaction with the
existing arrangement. The pioneer of the water-land communication
from New Caledonia to the Columbia, Stuart never fully accepted the
shift to York Factory and argued in his district reports in 1823 and 1824
that the company resort again to the Columbia route. Stuart saw two
principal disadvantages in the eastern line. First, MacLeod's Lake was
inconvenient as New Caledonia depot: since it was located at the end of
water transport from the east, distribution of supplies to the other posts
required winter-long overland trips with sledges and dogs, and collecting
provisions and conveying the returns back to embarkation point. With
Fort St James as depot four of the five district posts were accessible by
water. Second, a large number of men and months were required for the
trip east, 'more time and labour being required to convey the goods ...
from Fort Chipewyan to ... MacLeod's Lake, ... than from Norway House
to Fort Chipewyan.' Stuart reasoned that the Columbia line of supply
involved less time and could be conducted by the New Caledonians
themselves without any assistance from other districts.

Dissatisfied with the status quo and aware of the advantages to be gained by a change in transportation route, Simpson was finally convinced of the value of supplying New Caledonia from the west side of the mountains. The governor harshly criticized the poor management of the Columbia department but he became deeply impressed with the trade of the coast and its interior country which he felt 'if sufficiently extended and properly managed' could 'yield double the profit that any other part of North America does for the amount of capital employed.' A prerequisite of success in Simpson's opinion was that administration and supply of the whole Pacific fur trade should function as a unit. 'To turn it to the best advantage,' he stated, 'New Caledonia must be included and the Coasting trade must be carried on in conjunction with the inland business.'[5]

At the centre of Simpson's thinking was the replacement of the Fort George depot on the Columbia by a Pacific outlet at Fraser River and the use of this river as the main highway into the interior. Simpson realistically foresaw that a move north might be necessary if the Americans should settle around the Columbia. He also felt that the Fraser River was more conveniently situated for the joint supervision of the coast and interior trade. His vision of a unified Pacific trade managed from the Fraser River, however, coloured his assessment of its navigability and he misinterpreted both Fraser's 1808 journey down the river and James MacMillan's partial examination of it in November 1824 as endorsements for his conclusion that the Fraser should become the main supply line to New Caledonia.[6]

Simpson's plan had to be sanctioned by the governor and committee in London but his interim arrangements anticipated approval. For George depot was replaced by Fort Vancouver which was built on the north side of the Columbia. Though inconveniently situation 75 miles upstream and $1\frac{1}{4}$ miles from the river bank Simpson considered this post a secondary establishment which would serve temporarily as headquarters and whose main purpose would be farming.[7] Until the post at the mouth of the Fraser was established, Stuart's brigade route between New Caledonia and the Columbia was to be reemployed for the supply to the interior.[8]

The line of supply as worked out by Stuart involved canoe travel down the Fraser and its tributaries to Alexandria; here a change was made to horses for travel overland via Kamloops to Lake Okanagan; boats were then used for the journey down the Columbia to Fort Vancouver. In 1826, the first year of re-operation by this southern route, 70 of the 100 horses sent to Alexandria perished in the severe winter so that part of the New Caledonia returns had to be sent to York Factory. The remaining returns were successfully transported south proving Stuart's route practicable, despite difficulties. Plans were made to proceed to the Columbia again the following year which, for diplomatic purposes, Simpson admitted was still 'the only certain outlet for the Company's trade' west of the Rockies.[9]

Two reconnaissance expeditions on the Fraser were undertaken in the fall of 1826. The reports of J.M. Yale and Archibald McDonald were pessimistic, but Simpson presumed that travel would be safe at the proper season.[10] In the fall of 1828 Simpson descended the length of the river from Fort St James. The 600-mile journey was travelled smoothly with just three short portages between Alexandria and the forks. From this point however the character of the river totally changed, foaming waters churning between perpendicular mountains of rock. Even with three of the most skilful bowsmen, Simpson reluctantly concluded he could 'no longer talk of it as a navigable stream.'[11] Fort Vancouver remained Pacific headquarters and the Columbia River access to the Pacific now became essential for the supply of New Caledonia.

Although the indefinite extension in 1827 of the Treaty of Joint Occupancy assured Britain's continued use of the Columbia-Okanagan interior supply route, the clearly expressed boundary ambitions of the United States and encroaching American settlement never left the company free from pressure to find an alternate line. In 1834 the company directed Chief Factor Simon McGillivary to explore the Babine and Simpson (Nass) rivers with a view to discovering a new outlet to the coast. These explorations were not completed before coastal policy forced the company to withdraw. As long as the southern supply line was reasonably secure the governor and committee were not interested in a shorter route alienating the Russians and destroying company chances to eliminate the American coasters who depended for their profits on trade in supplies to Sitka.[12]

The company's thinking was explained in a letter of 4 March 1835 from the committee to Simpson: 'We do not think that under present circumstances any new access from the seacoast to New Caledonia would be of material advantage to our trade, which is supplied by the present route at a moderate cost; and it would be safer from opposition, and be less likely to excite any feeling on the part of the Russian Company if you endeavoured to intercept the trade of furs from the Interior to their ten leagues of country on the Coast, by extending your posts from the Interior, rather than by establishments supplied from the Coast.'[13] The decision to discontinue explorations west from New Caledonia and prevent Russian provocation paid off, for an 1839 commercial treaty with the Russian-American Company manoeuvred the Americans out of their market for supplies and effectively gave the Hudson's Bay Company a monopoly of the coastal trade.[14] The problem of supplying New Caledonia efficiently diminished in light of the stakes to be gained by the winner of the coastal contest.

While the company could claim after a decade of using the Columbia-Okanagan supply route that New Caledonia was being supplied at a 'moderate cost,' the exact cost of getting goods into the district was probably not known. Although the prime cost of goods sent to Fort Vancouver from London was advanced by one-third, district outfits throughout the Columbia department were valued at the same rate. Expenses in getting the outfits to the interior were expected to be charged to the fur trade but nowhere in the Columbia account books are freighting expenses computed as a separate item. There seems no way to compute complete transportation costs through analysis of the various accounts. The Columbia district transfer books debit the New Caledonia district to various posts along the route for such items as provisions, horses, and horse equipment. However the district transfers omit such freight expenses as boats for the Columbia which are listed elsewhere and include articles such as trade goods not available at the main depot. In the 'accounts current' the total owing to other districts is added to the value of the district inventory and the servants' wages to find the total district costs. These are then measured against the total returns to determine profit. Even by extracting transportation expenses from the district transfers and figuring the wages of the brigade men for the period away from the district, the combined result would not be an accurate reflection of the transportation cost. Many of the expenses for supplying New Caledonia, such as boats made at Fort Colville and provisions from Vancouver, were 'General Charges' which applied to the transport costs of other districts as well.[15]

Efficiency in time, labour, and means of transport were popular indices used by company personnel to measure the effectiveness of the process of supply even if they had no price equivalents. Thus a demonstrable advantage of the New Caledonia–Fort Vancouver line of supply over the York Factory route was its saving in time of nearly one and one-half months. The brigades usually left district headquarters the end of April or the first of May and returned in mid-September. Given about the same departure date for York Factory in 1825 and 1826 an end of October return was recorded.[16] The distance to the Columbia was about 1000 miles in contrast to the 2578 miles between Fort St James and York Factory.[17] The gain in time permitted distribution of the outfits to the posts before winter set in, thus equipping the natives for hunting at a much earlier period and freeing company manpower to undertake exploration and trading expeditions.

Fewer men transported the pieces inland from the Columbia than from Rupert's Land according to the available figures for the 1820s and 1830s. While 36 men brought in 130 pieces in 6 canoes in 1824, and 32 men transported 108 pieces in 6 canoes in 1825; by the Columbia route 26 men took in the New Caledonia outfit (size unknown) in 1826 and the same number transported 220 pieces inland in 1831.[18] The company's ability to reduce the personnel necessary for the New Caledonia transport service on its western route could not be solely attributed to the abandonment of the limited-capacity north canoe for this craft was still being used on the Alexandria–Fort St James leg of the journey until the mid-1830s. The organization of the transport was the key.

The valuable journal of the 1831 brigade journey to the Columbia kept by Peter W. Dease, then chief factor in charge of the New Caledonia district, considerably extends our hitherto scanty knowledge about the mechanics of the transport system. The brigades of three districts – New Caledonia, Fort Colville, and Thompson River – left Fort Vancouver together in 9 boats each manned by 7 men and evenly loaded with 46 to 48 pieces. About 275 miles upstream, Fort Nez Perces, on a branch of the Columbia, received its outfit and the loads were redistributed. At Fort Okanagan the Fort Colvile group departed for the upper Columbia with its outfit in 4 boats and the remaining pieces were packed on horses' backs for the overland trip. The small Thompson River section of the brigade stopped at Kamloops and after replacing 5 horses the New Caledonia train of 110 horses and 25 men continued on to Alexandria. Here some of the bales were untied to make up the outfit of this post, further lightening the loads which were now transferred to canoes. Due to the bad shape of the canoes 44 pieces were left in depot at Alexandria to be sent for later; 4 bark canoes were then loaded with 35 pieces each and a fifth weaker craft with 18. At Fort George another portion of the outfit was left and 2 wooden Indian canoes were hired to replace a wrecked bark canoe. Four bark and 2 wooden canoes travelled the remaining distance to headquarters on Stuart Lake.[19] Assistance in the difficult navigation of the Columbia River by the other brigades, lightening the outfit at Alexandria and Fort George, and finally the relatively short distance from Fort St James to

Alexandria (which made it possible to send for the oufit later or call for reinforcements from the district)[20] all contributed to the reduction of manpower necessary for the communication.

Boats gradually replaced canoes as cargo carriers on the upper Fraser. With the scarcity of bark in New Caledonia wooden canoes became important for a time; 6 to 10 appearing on the Fort St James inventories yearly from 1829 to 1838. Batteaux were also employed in the district and sometimes supplemented canoes for bringing out the outfits to Alexandria. Following the general disuse of the canoe for freight in the northern department in the 1820s, frequent complaints were made about the difficulty of getting good 'Boutes' for the Pacific slope. This labour problem and the small capacity of the wooden canoe led to the adoption of the Columbia boat, the type of craft used by the brigade on the Columbia River, for travel on the upper Fraser as well. Boats, batteaux, and canoes all appear on the 1836–37 and 1838 Fort St James inventories, but the 1839 inventory lists boats only.[21]

The distinction between a batteau and a Columbia boat is not clear from company records. In 1824 Simpson described the boats used on the Columbia as follows: 'they are called Boats but are more properly speaking Batteaux & wrought by Paddles instead of Oars, intended to carry 50 pieces Trading Goods besides Provisions for the Crew of Eight Men.'[22] The only extant detailed description was written by Lieutenant Charles Wilkes, who accompanied the brigade by boat as far as Walla Walla in 1842: 'They are thirty feet long and five and a half feet beam, sharp at both ends, clinker built and have no knees. In building them flat timbers of oak are bent to the requisite shape by steaming; they are bolted to a flat keel at distances of a foot from each other; the planks are of cedar and generally extend the whole length of the boat. The gunwhale is of the same kind of wood but the rowlocks are of birch ... [they] are so light as to be easily transported over the portages by their crews, and in case of accident are easily repaired.'[23]

The Columbia boat was apparently about the same length as the regular York boat, 30 ft. long but with a narrower beam – $5\frac{1}{2}$ ft in comparison with 7 or 8 ft. – and a smaller carrying capacity, 50 compared with 70 pieces. Like the York boat the Columbia boat also had sails and although paddles were intially used these were later replaced by oars.[24] The greater lightness of the Columbia boat for portaging may explain why no attempt was ever made to introduce the York boat on the Pacific slope.

About one-third to one-half of the New Caledonia servants made up the annual brigade to Fort Vancouver[25] and the arduous duties of that journey, combined with the task of redistributing supplies to the inland posts and the frequent poverty of food, made service in the district very unpopular. District servants of the North West Company period had received an extra allowance of stores[26] and the Hudson's Bay Company found it too had to provide some form of inducement to find employees for the area. Upon the recommendations of William Connolly and George Simpson, the New Caledonians were allowed a small addition to the wages of other districts.[27] The usual company stricture against liquor was waived for men in the transport service – on arrival and departure from the depot each received a regale or ½ pint of rum. Artist Paul Kane, travelling inland with the Columbia brigades in 1847, noted the departing regale was not distributed to the men until the end of the first day's journey 'where those who are entitled to get drunk may do so without interferring with the resident servants of the establishment.'[28] In 1831 brigade journey progress was slowed because of the intoxication of the crews.[29]

Engagements for the New Caledonia transport crews were usually renewed during the brief two weeks the men experienced the comforts of Fort Vancouver. Despite contract renewals the privations facing servants in the district drove them to desert along the route.[30] Six men left the New Caledonia brigade in 1846 because their food was worse than the Columbia fare. As settlement in the 1840s provided enticement for an alternate life-style and lessened opportunity for recapture, desertions from the brigade increased. Abandoning the service was seen as a serious offence and punished accordingly. The treatment of two Sandwich Islanders who left the inland bound brigade in 1847 is described by Paul Kane: 'The next thing was to punish the deserters ... Our guide, a tall, powerful Iroquois, took one of them and Mr. Lewis seized the other ... the punishment consisted in simply knocking the men down, kicking them until they got up, and knocking them down again until they could not get up any more, when they finished them off with a few more kicks.'[31] Reports of such harsh treatment for servants in the Columbia circulated throughout the northern department, making the service there, as Simpson wrote to McLoughlin, 'so unpopular with Canadians, Orkneymen & halfbreeds that it is a most difficult matter to get men for that part of the Country.'[32]

The best recruits for New Caledonia according to William Connolly were 'young Men from Canada.' Canadian recruits were sent from the

northern department to the Columbia in some years but it is not clear
from the minutes in what numbers they were sent to New Caledonia. The
quality of men recruited for the district was increasingly a subject of
complaint by the officers-in-charge. Connolly protested against the employment of convicts for New Caledonia in 1829, and in 1842 Ogden told
his successor that he had been sent from Canada in later years 'the refuse
of brothels and gaols.' As the use of York boats closed the training ground
for canoemen in the northern department the New Caledonians were told
to rear their own 'boutes' on the west side of the mountains.[33] Despite the
wide scale employment of Sandwich Islanders by the 1840s in the rest of
the Columbia,[34] the popularity of Canadians for the transport service
endured and New Caledonia continued to look to the northern department for its crews.

Provisioning of the brigade was an important part of the overhead cost
of transportation not only because of the cost of the supplies but also the
weight added to the loads. This logistical problem was handled by the
supply of provisions at three different points – Fort Vancouver for the
trip of Okanagan, Okanagan (provisions from Fort Colvile) for the trip to
Kamloops, and at Kamloops for the remaining journey to the district. The
mainstay, but far from favoured food of the crews, was dried salmon;
allowing a ration of three per day in 1826, Thompson River supplied 1500
for taking down the brigade (from Kamloops to Okanagan) and 2500 for
the ingoing journey (Kamloops to Fort St James).[35] As farming developed, especially at Colvile, flour, beef, and other foodstuffs were
supplied. 'The servants attached to the brigade,' noted Ogden in 1842,
'received their usual allowance of Flour at Okanagan in the following
proportions married men 100 lbs. each bachelors 50. Servants inland
married or single 25 lbs. each charged to their accounts.'[36]

Because the provisions supplied from Fort Vancouver were 'general
charges' not assigned to the district it is difficult to compute the total
amount of provisions consumed by the New Caledonians themselves on
an inbound trip. The provisions taken on at Fort St James and Fort Fraser
departing from the district were apparently absorbed as upkeep for these
posts, similarly obscuring the record of food consumed on the outward
journey. The district transfers provide data on the type of food supplied
from Kamloops and Fort Colvile, but often fail to distinguish between
outward or inward journeys, preventing assessment of quantity eaten.[37]
The proportion of boat or horse ladings occupied by provisions is not
evident from the extant bills of lading. One can only imagine that when
Dease in 1831 took 4000 salmon from Fort St James for the trip to the

'lower posts' and added another 1028 salmon at Kamloops,[38] several boats and horses were required to carry this load.

During the 1830s a fairly staple volume of returns and outfits was transported over the Columbia-Okanagan line. Invoices suggest little change in outfit volume, but its size in pieces does not appear in the various accounts. A total of 180 pieces including returns (162 packs), provisions, and baggage were brought out in 1831 and about 220 pieces including provisions and private accounts freighted inland. Fur returns fell off slightly in the early 1840s. A change in the number of men, boats, or horses employed for the transport could reflect changes in the size of the outfit or returns. That the volumes were relatively constant might thus be indicated by diverse sources observing that nine boats were employed on the Columbia River leg of the journey in 1831, 1841, and 1847.[39]

An additional 50 pieces of trade goods, mostly leather and grease, were annually sent into New Caledonia from the east. Moose and deerskins were used for leggings, shoes, and other items of clothing by the Indians and company servants and were also an important ritual artefact for such occasions as the funeral feasts of the Babines. Large animals were scarce in the north central interior. Since the company's closest sources of moose and deer skins were the Athabaska and Saskatchewan districts, when Fort Vancouver became depot for New Caledonia a second transport system had to be devised. In the fall of 1825 James McMillan had surveyed a track from Jasper House to the head of the Fraser River by the valley of the Miette to Buffalo Dung Lake and Moose Lake. This route was used to bring leather from the Saskatchewan district as far as Tête Jaune Cache at the source of the Fraser where a rendezvous was made with two canoes sent from New Caledonia headquarters to pick up the cargo. The company abandoned this route in 1831 and sent Athabaska leather over the Peace River route via Dunvegan and Findlay Forks. Each fall eight New Caledonians were sent to Dunvegan where they picked up 50 pieces of leather, the ladings of two canoes. The leather party travelled by water as far as MacLeod's Lake Post from where it freighted the leather by horse 83 miles overland to Fort St James. Eventually the company secured supplies one year in advance, keeping them in depot at MacLeod's Lake for distribution in the spring. When Peace River's supply of large animals became temporarily exhausted in the late 1830s, the Columbia portage to Okanagan was used to bring in Saskatchewan leather. Following the treaty with the Russian-American Company the company reserved the Athabaska Pass for freighting otter skins from the east side of the mountains for the Russians and again employed the Peace River route for New Caledonia's leather supply.[40]

The company seriously questioned Fort Vancouver as headquarters and principal depot during the early 1840s. Fort Vancouver was inconvenient for shipping and, in 1838, explorations were started for a depot site towards the south end of Vancouver Island. The establishment of British claims to the Columbia and the absence of effective inland communication to the north postponed change. After his Pacific visit in 1841, however, George Simpson concluded that 'the United States will insist on having a post on the North West Coast and that Great Britain will, for the sake of power, accept the straits of de Fuca as a boundary on the Coast.'[41] In 1843 Fort Victoria was built as general depot for Pacific trade. American immigration to the Columbia valley, combined with 'Oregon fever,' soon resulted in the British retreat anticipated by Simpson. Within three years the Oregon boundary had been settled at the 49th parallel.

Shifting company headquarters northwards carried as a corollary the opening of an all-British communication with the interior. Alexander C. Anderson, chief trader in charge of Alexandria, explored two routes from the interior to Fort Langley in the spring of 1846: north of the Fraser by the Anderson-Seton Lakes, to the Lillooet and Harrison rivers and then to the lower Fraser; and south of the Fraser through the valleys of the Coquihalla, Nicolum, and Sumallo rivers over the coastal mountain range, through open country to the Thompson. Anderson reported the first impassable for loaded boats but the latter practical if the brigades travelled out late enough to avoid the mountain snow.[42] Since 'accessibility ... at all seasons' was paramount, company officials relied on the Columbia to buy time for further explorations before deciding.[43]

Three more supply routes were explored between 1846 and 1848: the Fraser itself; a route by the banks of the Fraser to by-pass the rapids of Fraser Canyon; and a trail southeast of the river which avoided mountain and river travel and joined the Fraser 25 miles above Fort Langley.[44] Sceptical of Anderson's findings that the Fraser River was usable, company officials re-explored the river only to confirm Simpson's 1828 conclusion.[45] The southern route lacked food for horses, leaving only the banks of the Fraser. The New Caledonia brigade journey over this trail in the summer of 1848 was a disaster, with heavy losses of merchandise and horses. Donald Manson, officer-in-charge simply refused to use the route again, but the old Columbia-Okanagan route was now out of the question. The company had learned that duties had been placed on goods for the interior; and the Cayuse Indian war of 1848 effectively closed the Columbia as a commercial highway.[46] The Coquihalla route, with some changes, became within two years New Caledonia's supply line.

The company's all-British supply route inland was about three hundred miles shorter than the Columbia-Okanagan brigade trail. The three brigades travelled together in boats 70 miles up the Fraser River from Fort Langley. At Fort Hope, provisions were picked up for the overland journey and the outfit transferred to horses. Nearly 400 were used for the trip to Kamloops, an increase partly due to the accommodation of the Fort Colvile outfit which by the Columbia had been completely freighted by water. At Kamloops the New Caledonians separated from the other brigades and followed their usual route by horse to Alexandria, from there taking boats up the Fraser, Nechako, and Stuart rivers to headquarters at Fort St James. Initially a month longer, this route was painstakingly improved to bring travel time to the old schedule.

The type of craft used on the Fraser was the batteau. Before the first trial route the company sent Samuel Robertson, a Fort Vancouver boatbuilder, to Fort Langley to build four large batteaux. By 1848 seven 'boats' had been constructed.[47] How batteaux differed from Columbia boats is not clear, but the smaller number used suggests the former were slightly larger. Alterations were made in the design after several years' experience on the Fort Langley–Fort Hope line. Unfortunately, the adaptations for the boats built in 1852 are not mentioned. James Douglas noted they possessed 'many improvements in framing and modelling which will better adapt them to the navigation of Fraser's River.'[48]

Horse transport over the Fort Hope–Kamloops road was costly at first because of the many horses employed and the heavy losses incurred before the road was improved, and the shortage of horses during this period in the Columbia department. By 1850 the Clammatt and California mines had increased the demand for horses at Walla Walla, a traditional source of company supply. The Indians raised their prices from one blanket to six. The company decided to send breeding mares from Fort Vancouver and the Snake country to the stock farm at Thompson River. With more reinforcements from the Saskatchewan district the company eventually supplied the horse transport for the brigades entirely from Thompson River.[49]

In the 1850s mounting transportation expenses, coinciding with the decline in fur returns and the drop in the market for beaver, forced the company to assess the size of the New Caledonia outfits. About 250 to 260 pieces, or 130 horseloads, including servants' orders and provisions, constituted the district outfit in 1851. The volume of freight was too large according to Governor Simpson who complained that the increase arose from heavy demands on private account and 'from conveyance of families to and from Fort Langley.'[50] On 15 July 1851, James Douglas reported to Eden Colvile: 'I have this year commenced cutting down with a bold hand, the New Caledonia imports both on Company's and private account which I reduced to the old standard, when returns were larger than at present. Complaints will be rife, but to these I shall turn a deaf ear the necessity for a change for the better being too apparent to require proof beyond what is afforded by the state of returns and profits.'[51] There are no records of the impact of this reduction on profits or of its influence on the mode of transport; but clearly the volume of the outfit became crucial to the company as transportation costs increased and returns and markets declined.

The labour problems of the transport service intensified with the use of the Fort Langley–New Caledonia line, for its operation coincided with settlement and two major gold rushes on the Pacific slope. 'The men were troubled with visions of California' when they came out to Fort Langley in the summer of 1850; but although four deserted from the brigade on the return journey, they were all recaptured.[52] The district was severely shorthanded in 1853 with just 37 labourers; by 1855 the usual complement of 56 to 58 labourers had been restored by the addition of 'half white lads' brought up in the country. As news of gold discoveries around Thompson River spread in the summer of 1856 the company again experienced 'more than the usual difficulty in rehiring the interior servants.' The next year Douglas pleaded with Simpson that Canadian recruits were absolutely necessary 'as we cannot find a man in this part of the world, who could be induced, on any terms to winter in New Caledonia.' At the height of the Fraser River gold rush in the summer of 1858, when thousands swarmed into the lower British mainland, the annual pay of a brigade man compared unfavourably to one week's earnings at the gold mines, forcing the company to raise wages. Scarcely any white men were left in the district by 1858 and four of six Norwegian recruits sent from the northern department deserted. 'English half breeds' from Red River were now requested for the service of New Caledonia since they were 'more tractable and trust-worthy and better servants than other natives.'[53]

The Fraser River gold rush marked a turning point. The colony of British Columbia was proclaimed at Fort Langley in November 1858, and the exclusive trading privileges of the company were revoked. Fur resources and company policy had until then determined the logistics of supply; now competition and the creation of new routes opened up the inland fur preserve and lessened the company's control over such transportation costs as wages, provisioning, and the means of conveyance. In 1862 the last trip of the legendary brigade was made over the Alexandria-Kamloops–Fort Hope trail. Thereafter goods were forwarded by public pack train to Alexandria until 1864, when the company used its own wagons on the road from Yale to Alexandria.[54]

This survey raises questions about the early nineteenth-century fur trade on the Pacific slope and, in particular, its logistics. No one would reject transportation as a cost of the fur trade or its relevance to the success or failure of the Hudson's Bay Company's Pacific enterprise. The company's own views of the economics of supply are instructive, however. Freight expenses were charged to the fur trade in some form, though not always under the head of transportation. From the organization of the accounts of the Columbia department it would appear that the company felt this was sufficient.

Moreover, company action revealed that a shorter supply route to New Caledonia and the corresponding reduction of transportation cost simply did not rank against the object of attaining a monopoly of the Pacific coastal trade. The low prices and steady volume of furs guaranteed by a monopoly situation promised greater yield than the savings of improved inland transportation. Given the company's concern of eliminating rivalry as the means to profit and its willingness to undertake losses on that account, the historian must question the value of relating inland transportation costs more than very generally to the cost of trade. Only in the last decade of the Hudson's Bay Company's Pacific licence did transportation expenses become important as beaver declined and settlement introduced competition for labour and transportation. Exactly how crucial supply costs became to New Caledonia district profit in this period deserves further consideration; consideration which unfortunately may be hampered by the company's bookkeeping system and the dearth of post-1849 accounts.

It would be a pity if emphasis on the economics of logistics should discourage research on material and social themes, some of which have been suggested in the foregoing pages. By 1839 canoe freighting of supplies to New Caledonia had apparently ended, yet Governor Simpson's references in the 1840s to the Pacific slope as the 'nursery' for canoemen suggests the need for further investigation into the history of the canoe west of the Rockies. Moreover, despite the many articles on the York Boat, its Pacific coast counterpart, the Columbia Boat, has hardly been examined.

The men who operated the supply service are a fascinating subject in the labour history of the fur trade. If Canadians were preferred for the transport system of New Caledonia, was this bias evident throughout the country? Who were the labourers on the New Caledonia line of supply from 1821 to 1858? What role did ethnic origins play in the selection of servants for the transport? Examination of the operation of the brigades leads to many social questions. Did families travel with the brigades or remain in the district? Were single or married men preferred for the brigade service? While the transport service provided the occasion for desertion, was it generally the cause? What was the relative impact of dangerous travelling conditions, poor or scarce provisioning, and employee treatment on length of service? The material and human interpretation and the economic investigation of fur trade transportation on the Pacific slope have barely begun.

NOTES AND REFERENCES

1 HBCA B 188/a/1, 4–5, John Stuart to Nicolas Garry, 20 April 1822
2 Fleming and Rich Minutes of Council, Northern Department of Rupert Land, 1821–1831 8 July 1822, 17
3 Fleming and Rich Minutes of Council, Northern Department Resolution 38, 42–3, 5 July 1823; HBCA D 4/3, 23–4, Simpson to John Stuart, 17 Dec. 1823; Merk Fur Trade and Empire 12–15
4 Merk Fur Trade and Empire 37–8
5 Merk Fur Trade and Empire 71–2
6 Ibid 73–4, 114–18
7 Ibid 87–8, 123–4
8 HBCA D 4/5, 17–19, Simpson to William Brown, 4 April 1825
9 HBCA D 4/120, 8–9, Connolly to governor, chief factors and chief traders, 18 July 1826; D 4/119, 55–62, William Connolly to George Simpson, 30 April 1826; D 4/119, 62–6, William Connolly to governor and council of the northern department, 1 May 1826; D 4/120, 8–9, William Connolly to governor, chief factors and chief traders, 18 July 1826; Merk Fur Trade and Empire 264
10 HBCA B 97/a/2, 27–9, Archibald McDonald to McLoughlin, 30 Sept. 1826; D 4/120, 42–4, William Connolly to governor-in-chief and council, northern department, 15 March 1827; D 4/90, 105, Simpson to Connolly, 9 July 1827

11 Rich ed *Part of a Dispatch from George Simpson, Esqr., Governor of Ruperts Land to the Governor and Committee of the Hudson's Bay Company, London, March 1, 1829; continued and completed March 24 and June 5, 1829* 37–9

12 Rich *The Letters of John McLoughlin from Fort Vancouver to the Governor and Committee* ... I, first series, 1825–38, xci, xcii; HBCA D 4/126, 35–46, Simon McGillivary to George Simpson, 15 July 1833; 'According to his instructions to stop explorations towards discovering an outlet on the coast, McGillivary has been sent with the returns to the Coast' D 4/127, 53–4, P.W. Dease to governor and committee, 14 Feb. 1835

13 HBCA D 5/4, 104, governor and committee to Simpson, 4 March 1835

14 Galbraith *The Hudson's Bay Company as an Imperial Factor, 1821–1869* 141–55

15 Rich *Letters of John McLoughlin* I lxxvi, lxxvii; Fleming and Rich eds *Minutes of Council, Northern Department* 145, 26 June 1826. To see how the district transfers were set up, refer to HBCA B 223/d/35, 4; B 223/d/51, 15; B 223/d/114, 30; B 223/d/134, 44–5. See also HBCA B 223/d/137, 7.

16 HBCA B 188/a/8, 5 May, 23 Sept. 1826; B 188/a/10, 1 May, 8 Aug. 1827; B 188/a/12, 30 April, 1828; B 188/a/14, 2 May, 16 Sept. 1829; B 188/a/16, 7 May, 14 Sept. 1831; B 188/a/17, 7 May, 13 Sept. 1832; B 188/a/19, 23 April, 17 Sept. 1842; B 188/a/19, 19 April, 30 Sept. 1844; B 188/a/19, 21 April, 22 Sept. 1845; B 188/a/20, 23 April, 21 Sept. 1847; B 188/a/3, 7 May 1825; B 188/a/5, 30 Oct. 1825; B 188/a/8, 5 May 1826

17 McLeod ed *Peace River. A Canoe Voyage from Hudson's Bay to Pacific, by the late Sir George Simpson (Governor, Hon. Hudson's Bay Company), in 1828. Journal of the late Chief Factor, Archibald McDonald (Hon. Hudson's Bay Company) who accompanied him* xvii. The distance from Fort Vancouver to Fort St James has been figured from the Fort St James–Alexandria distance of 204 miles, Alexandria overland to Kamloops 215 miles, and my calculation of the remaining distance.

18 Fleming and Rich eds *Minutes of Council, Northern Department* 75, 1 July 1824; 105, 2 July 1825; HBCA B 188/e/4, report on district, 1826–27; B 188/a/17, 3, Fort St James Journal, 1831–32, 5 May–13 Sept. 1831

19 HBCA B 188/a/17, 3–52, Fort St James Journal, 1831–32, 5 May–13 Sept. 1831

20 According to Peter Skene Ogden the company had by 1842 regularized the practice of having a contingent from the district meet the New Caledonia Brigade at Alexandria. 'A boat from Frasers Lake instructions being left to that effect in the Spring comes down to meet the Brigade to Alexandria on or about the 15th August in charge of the Gentleman superintending at Frasers Lake, the crew consists of 6 men Canadians and Indians.' On the return 'at Chin Lac Forts [confluence of Stuart and Nechako Rivers] the Frasers Lake boat separates from the Brigade and proceeds to the latter place with its Outfit,

five men and an Indian is the crew of each boat and cargo from 50 to 56 pieces' Sage 'Peter Skene Ogden's Notes on Western Caledonia' 54.

21 HBCA D 4/119, 55–62, Connolly to Simpson, 30 April 1826; 62–6, Connolly to governor and council, 1 May 1826; B 188/a/17, Fort St James Journal, 1831–32, 20 Aug. 1831; B 223/d/22, 21–5; B 223/d/49, 41–5; B 223/d/59, 51–5; B 223/d/71, 41–3; B 223/d/80, 51; B 223/d/93, 73–7; B 223/d/105b, 63–7; B 188/a/17, May 6, 10–11, 1831; B 188/e/5, 1, report on district, 1834; D 4/20, 12–13, Simpson to P.W. Dease, 3 July 1834. The introduction of Columbia boats for use on the Upper Fraser was made by Peter Skene Ogden in 1836; HBCA D 4/22, 35d–37, Simpson to Ogden, 27 June 1836; D 4/23, 52–3, Simpson to Ogden, 30 June 1837. For 1839 inventory see HBCA B 223/d/80, 51; B 223/d/93, 73–7; B 223/d/105b, 63–7; B 223/d/115, 106–8.

22 Merk *Fur Trade and Empire* 38

23 Wilkes *Narrative of the United States Exploring Expedition during the years 1838, 1839, 1840, 1841, 1842* IV 371, 378

24 The regular York boat was estimated to be 28 ft long, 7 to 9 ft beam, although there were York boats as long as 40 ft. The capacity varied from 60 to 90 pieces with the size. The capacity stated here is based on the Standing Rules and Regulations 1836, No. 11, in Oliver ed *The Canadian North-West Its Early Development and Legislative Records: Minutes of the Councils of the Red River Colony and the Northern Department of Rupert's Land* II 746.

For information on York boat construction, see McDonald 'HBC Inland Transport; 1. Building the York Boat'; and Glover 'York Boats.'

'One of the Boats was broken considerably today by another coming in contact while under sail'; HBCA B 188/a/17, Fort St James Journal, 8 July 1831. Referring to the brigade on the Columbia River in 1847, Paul Kane noted 'the men plied their oars with unusual vigour' Kane *Wanderings of an Artist among the Indians of North America From Canada to Vancouver's Island and Oregon through the Hudson's Bay Company's Territory and Back Again* 179; see also General Charges debit to Fort Colville for '5 New Boats complete and 25 Extra Oars' HBCA B 223/d/90, 34.

25 This figure is based on labour distribution figures available for 1826 (42 total, 24 in brigade with leader), and for 1831 (67 total, 24 for transport), and a fairly consistent number of employees in the district from 1836 to 1856, between 57 and 62; Fleming and Rich eds *Minutes of Council, Northern Department*, 144, 26 June 1826; HBCA B 188/a/17, Fort St James Journal, 1831–32, 11 May 1831; B 223/d/37, 7; B 223/d/88, 2; B 223/d/100, 3; B 223/d/121, 3–4; B 223/d/152, 3–4; B 223/d/156, 3; B 223/d/162, 3–5.

26 HBCA B 188/b/5, 51–3, John Stuart to governor and committee, 27 April 1822

27 HBCA 188/b/5, 72, Connolly to McLoughlin, 6 Feb. 1827; D 4/120, 42–5,

Connolly to chief factors, chief traders, and governor, 15 March 1827; Rich *Part of a Dispatch, 1829*, 25. 'Boutes' and 'Mileux' were paid £24 and £19 respectively, an advance of £2 on most other districts and an augmentation of £3 each was allowed for the voyage to and from the depot. This advance was continued by the Rules and Regulations of 1836; Fleming and Rich eds *Minutes of Council, Northern Department* 227–8; Oliver *The Canadian North-West* II 749–50.

28 Kane *Wanderings* 178–9

29 HBCA B 188/a/17, Fort St James Journal, 1831–32, 28 June 1831

30 HBCA D 5/19, 366–72, Ogden to Simpson, 15 March 1847

31 Kane *Wanderings of an Artist* 181–2

32 HBCA D 4/28, 62d–74, Simpson to John McLoughlin, 21 June 1843

33 HBCA D 4/122, 30–4, Connolly to governor and committee, 28 Feb. 1829; *Minutes of Council, Northern Department*, 244, 2 June 1829; D 4/122, 30–4, W. Connolly to governor and council, 28 Feb. 1829; Sage 'Ogden's Notes' 53; D 4/28, 62d–74, Simpson to McLoughlin, 21 June 1843; D 4/29, 4–5d, Simpson to Ogden, 27 June 1843; D 4/31, 80–81d, Simpson to Donald Manson, 15 June 1844

34 Oliver *The Canadian North-West* II 785 6 June 1839

35 HBCA IM 224, 42, A. McDonald to Wm. Connolly, 14 March 1826

36 Sage 'Ogden's Notes' 54

37 See district transfers HBCA B 223/d/51, 15; B 223/d/114, 30; B 223/d/134, 44–5.

38 HBCA B 188/a/17, Fort St James Journal, 1831–32, 15 May 1831

39 HBCA B 223/d/65, 4; B 223/d/72, 3; B 223/d/85, 3; B 188/a/17, Fort St James Journal, 1831–32, 5 May, 77 packs left Fort St James, 19 packs from Fraser Lake picked up 7 May, 27 packs added from Fort George and then 38 from Alexandria. For sources on Columbia River leg see HBCA B 188/a/17, Fort St James Journal, 1831–32, 2 June 1831; Wilkes *Narrative* 329; Kane *Wanderings* 178.

40 HBCA B 11/e/2, 19–20, William Brown, Report on Babine Country & Countries to the Westward, 15 April 1826; B 188/e/3, 16, Report on district 1824–25; D 4/10, 22d–64d, Simpson to governor and committee, 31 Aug. 1825; B 188/b/4, 9–10, James McMillan to William Connolly, 24 Oct. 1825; B 188/b/4, Saskatchewan district, 5 Feb. 1826; B 188/b/4, 13, Connolly to McLoughlin, 30 Nov. 1825; Fleming and Rich eds *Minutes of Council, Northern Department* 144–5, 26 June 1826; 187, July 1827; 213, July 1828; 244, June 1829; Oliver *The Canadian North-West* I 643, 652–3, 3 July 1830; II 714 & 721, 3 June 1835; HBCA A 4–39, 72d–74, Simpson to Donald Manson, 3 June 1849; D 5/36 320–31, Donald Manson to governor and committee, 27 Feb. 1853; D 4/123, 83, Connolly to governor and council, 4 March 1830; D 4/123, 34, Connolly to

the gentlemen conducting the New Caledonia supplies, 3 Oct. 1829; Sage 'Ogden's Notes' 51; Oliver *The Canadian North-West* II 729, 21 June 1836; 762, 27 June 1837; 776, 6 June 1839; HBCA D 4/25, 36–7, Simpson to Ogen, 13 June 1839

41 HBCA D 4/110, 50, Simpson to governor and committee, 1 March 1842

42 PAC MG29 B35, Vol. 4, Alexander Caulfield Anderson, 'History of the Northwest Coast' (Victoria 1878), 73–98, 'Journal of an Expedition under command of Alex. C. Anderson of H.B.Co. undertaken with the view of ascertaining the practicability of a communication with the interior for the import of the annual supplies, 15 May to 9 June, 1846'; HBCA B 223/b/34, 1–13, Ogden, Work, and Douglas to governor and council, 2 Nov. 1846

43 HBCA B 223/b/34, 66–7, Ogden and Douglas to Simpson, 15 March 1847; PABC AB20, v20d, Ogden and Douglas to Yale, 28 April 1847

44 For further detail on these explorations see PAC Anderson 'History of the Northwest Coast' 99–108, 'Journal of an Expedition to Fort Langley via Thompson to Fraser River – Summer of 1847, Outward Journey'; HBCA D 5/20, 697–700, Yale to Simpson, 28 Dec. 1847; B 223/6/36, 85, Work and Douglas to Governor and Council, 6 Nov. 1847.

45 HBCA B 223/b/36, 85, Work and Douglas to governor and council, 6 Nov. 1827

46 HBCA D 5/20, 697–700, Yale to Simpson, 28 Dec. 1847; B 223/b/37, 46, Anderson to Donald Manson, 24 Aug. 1848, 45, Manson to board of management, 24 Aug. 1848; A 12/4, 533–4, Simpson to governor and committee, 30 June 1849, 547, Donald Manson to Simpson, 26 Feb. 1849; A 12/14, 523, Simpson to governor and committee 30 June 1849; D 4/40, 27d–32, Simpson to Ogden, Douglas, and Work, 20 Oct. 1849

47 PABC AB20, v20d, Ogden and Douglas to Yale, 28 April 1847; HBCA B 223/b/38, 62, Douglas and Work to governor and council, 5 Dec. 1848

48 HBCA B 226/b/7, 30–1, Douglas to Yale, 27 Oct. 1852

49 HBCA D 5/26, 286–27, Eden Colvile to Simpson, 15 Oct. 1849; D 5/27, 357–9, Donald Manson to governor, chief factors, and chief traders, 25 Feb. 1850; D 7/1, 49–50, Donald Manson to Eden Colvile, 1 March 1851; D 7/1, 246–62, James Douglas to Eden Colvile, 16 March 1852; D 5/28, 491, Peter S. Ogden to Simpson, 25 Aug. 1850; D 5/30, 443–6, Ogden to governor and council, northern department, 20 March 1851; D 5/28, 491; D 5/30, 443–6; D 7/1, 246–62, Douglas to Colvile, 16 March 1852; D 5/34, 484–5, Anderson to governor, chief factors, and chief traders, 28 Sept. 1852; B 226/b/10, 110–11, Douglas to Manson, 12 April 1854

50 HBCA B 226/c/1, 34, Simpson to Ogden, Douglas, and Work, 25 June 1850

51 HBCA D 7/1, 140–4, Douglas to Colvile, 15 July 1851

52 HBCA D 5/29, 56–9, James Douglas to Simpson, 15 Oct. 1850

53 HBCA B 226/b/10, 55–7, Douglas to Manson, 30 Nov. 1853; B 226/d/7, 96, Douglas to Yale, 23 April 1853; D 5/36, 394–402, Douglas to governor and council, 14 March 1853; B 226/b/13, 16–17, Douglas to Barclay, 10 July 1855; B 226/b/13, 66–8, Douglas to Smith, 8 July 1856; B 226/b/15, 24–5, Douglas to Simpson, 9 Dec. 1857; B 226/b/15, 69, Douglas to Smith, 23 July 1858; B 226/b/15, 40, Douglas to Simpson, 1 March 1858; D 5/49, 659–60 John Work to Simpson, 23 Aug. 1859

54 HBCA B 226/b/27, 18–25, R. Finlayson to board of management, 17 July 1862; B 226/b/23, 173–4, Finlayson to Ogden, 2 April 1864

PART VI ⬥ ECONOMIC ASPECTS

Indians as Consumers in the Eighteenth Century

ARTHUR J. RAY

You told me Last year to bring many Indians, you See I have not Lyd. here is a great many young men come with me, use them Kindly! use them Kindly I say! give them good goods, give them good Goods I say! – we Livd. hard Last winter and in want. the powder being short measure and bad, I say! – tell your Servants to fill the measure and not to put their finger's within the Brim, take pity of us, take pity of us, I say! – we come a Long way to See you, the french sends for us but we will not here, we Love the English, give us good black tobacco (brazl. tobacco) moist & hard twisted, Let us see itt before op'n'd, – take pity of us, take pity of us I say! – the Guns are bad, Let us trade Light guns small in the hand, and well shap'd, with Locks that will not freeze in the winter, and Red gun cases ... Let the young men have Roll tobacco cheap, Ketles thick high for the shape and size, strong Ears, and the Baile to Lap Just upon the side, – Give us Good measure, in cloth, – Let us see the old measures, Do you mind me!, the young men Loves you by comming to see you, take pity, take pity I say! ... they Love to Dress and be fine, do you understand me!—.

According to James Isham, a Hudson's Bay Company trader, the foregoing address was typical of those given by Indian trading leaders during the smoking of the calumet that preceded trade at the bayside posts in the early eighteenth century.[1] Isham's account of the Indian trading speech gives us a rare, fleeting picture of what the Indian was like as a consumer. While politely couching their demands in the form of a plea 'take pity of us,' and professing that they 'love the English,' the Indian leaders let the English traders know they expected favourable rates of exchange, good quality merchandise, items stylistically pleasing and well suited to their nomadic life-style in the harsh subarctic environment.

To what extent were the Indians able to press these demands? Did the

Hudson's Bay Company make a concerted effort to meet them? By seeking answers to these basic questions we should be able to fill out our sketchy image of the Indian as a consumer, and obtain a clearer picture of his English counterpart and of the nature of Indian-European exchange. This paper will consider the Indians' concern with the quality of merchandise offered by Europeans and its suitability for their needs[2] and the efforts of the Hudson's Bay Company during its first century of operations to develop an inventory of goods acceptable to the Indians.

When the Hudson's Bay Company was chartered in 1670, the founders addressed a number of difficult problems in their efforts to establish trade. In Europe, contacts had to be developed with reliable suppliers of suitable merchandise. In North America, the company faced the difficult task of luring the Indians away from the French. The Indians of the James Bay area and the shield uplands to the south toward the Great Lakes had been receiving French trade goods for a considerable period of time prior to 1668 when the first English trading expedition was sent into the bay.[3] Therefore, in the beginning the company was at a considerable disadvantage: the French had considerably more experience dealing with the Indians of central Canada, and the Indians had grown accustomed to their merchandise.

The English handicap was offset somewhat by the fact that the two famous French traders and explorers, Medard Chouart, Sieur des Groseillers, and Pierre Esprit Raddison, played active roles in the early history of the Hudson's Bay company. Both helped the company establish its policies for dealing with the Indians and helped set the first standards of trade for the exchange of goods and furs. Besides assisting the company in its early contact with the Indians, they helped the governor and committee in London select trade goods. Radisson appears to have played the more important role.[4]

At its meeting of 4 March 1671, the governor and committee ordered: 'Mr. Bailey with the Advise of Mr. Radisson & Mr. Groseleyer treate with such persons as they think fitt for Such goods as may bee needfull for Supplyeing a Cargo for the next years expedition for Hudson's Bay, that is to Say, two hundred fowleing pieces & foure hundred powder hornes, with a proportionable quantity of Shott fitt thereunto, first bringing patterns of the gunns to bee bought unto the next Committee & ... two Hundred Brass Kettles Sizeable of from two to Sixteene gallons a piece, twelve grosse of French knives & two Grosse of Arrow head & about five or Six hundred hatchets.' The order consisted of arms, ammunition, and metal goods, and at least the knives were said to be French. The hatchets were perhaps of French origin judging from instructions that Radisson received from the London committee the following year. On 21 May 1672 they ordered: 'that Mr. Raddison attende Mr. Millington forthwith with a pattern of biscay hatchetts to be provided for this Company, such as are usually sent from thence to France to Serve the Indians in & about Canada, & that Mr. Millington bee desired to give order for two thousand hatchetts to be brought from Biscay by the first opportunity.' Since the Biscay hatchet was an important trade item, the company's directors hoped to get them manufactured in England. On 4 December 1673 they instructed a Mr Rastell to: 'make enquiry among the mchants if hee can finde any Biscay hatchets to bee bought to the ende that by the Samples of them Such hatchets may be provided here as may be most agreeable to the minde of the Indians and that Mr. Millington gett patternes forthwith from Biscay of three ... Seizes, Vizt of 1¼, 1½ & 2 lb a piece.'[5]

This sequence of events with the Biscay hatchets highlights a pattern developed very early. The company attempted to obtain goods the Indians were already accustomed to in type, style, or pattern. They drew on the considerable experience of Radisson, who advised the company what to buy and assessed the quality of the merchandise obtained for shipment to the bay. Although several key items in the early inventories were of French origin, the company quickly turned to British manufacturers to produce copies. By 1679 an English ironmonger, Robert Carnor, was supplying most of the hatchets. In 1683, the company placed an order for knives with Samuel Bannor. Between that date and 1715, Bannor supplied the company with the bulk of its knives, hatchets, awls, and fire steels. As late as 1697, Bannor was still using French patterns to make some of the company's knives.[6]

English manufacturers also copied other French trade goods. For example, on 25 January 1682, the governor and committee ordered two of their suppliers to contact agents in France to buy samples of blankets so that the company could have similar ones made in England. Six French blankets were eventually bought at a cost of £4 13s. A wide variety of French goods were copied at various times, including awls, vermillion, ice chisels, firearms, and gunpowder.[7]

While the company was thus obtaining patterns for goods and developing contacts with suppliers in England, its men in the bay were gaining experience in the conduct of trade with the Indians. Increasingly these men were able to offer advice to augment that of Radisson and they were able to assess the degree to which the company was meeting Indian consumer demand. Indeed, at an early date the men in the bay were required to provide the governor and committee with this information. For example, in their letter to Governor John Nixon dated 29 May 1680 they informed him that he was supposed to: 'send us home by every return of our Ships all such goods as are either defective or not acceptable to the Natives and to inform us wherein they are deficient And also to direct us exactly as you can of what form, quality & conditions [of] every sort of goods wch is demanded there for the best satisfaction of the Indians, And wee will do our utmost that you shall be supplied with every species of Commodity in perfection.[8] This order became standing policy and it was often repeated in later letters with only slight revisions. The revisions were designed to give the governor and committee more precise information. For instance, the traders were ordered to give an exact accounting of the quantity of each good sold (including sizes, shapes, colours, etc., wherever appropriate); samples of goods the Indians disliked were to be sent back to London; and examples of items highly prized were also to be returned.[9]

In spite of its concerted effort, the company still fell short of achieving its objective of supplying the Indians with the variety and quality of goods demanded. In 1682, Governor Nixon filed a report to the governor and committee recommending a series of policies be implemented to improve trade. Many of the goods manufactured in England were of such poor quality that he believed the company should consider sending raw materials and tradesmen to the posts and manufacturing many trade goods in Hudson Bay. 'It is a great vexation to me,' Nixon wrote,

to see a poore Indiane with his coat all seem-rent, in less than 6 weeks tyme, and when they are torne, the poore rogues can not mend them, but must suffer could in winter, and just occasione have they to say we have stole their beaver, to my great shame and your loss, I humbly conceave that if yow had taylers in the country they would benefit yow ... The lyk of your smiths. It is a wonder to me that for all our wryting since the country hath been settled, that England can not furnish us with good edge toules, you have verry bad fortoun that you can find non, I have seen good edge tweles made in England, but I feare it is your fate to be cheated.

Wherefore it be a great deall better that they were to be made by the smithes in the country. I am sure that 5d worth of stuff will mak a hatchet ... as for the smith we must have hime (whither he make your iron worke or not) for the use of the factories ... so that I conclud the smiths will pay their wages by their worke, and the ware too the Indian's minds, the ice chissels nor indeed no other iron worke that yow send over is to their mindes, and that is the great cause that a great deall of beaver goeth to the frens which otherways would come to us;

Nixon considered the company's goods to be of such poor quality that he lowered the standard of trade without obtaining the prior approval of the governor and committee.[10]

The London directors were so upset by Nixon's actions that they met three times in June 1684 to discuss the matter. Soon after they wrote to Governor Henry Sergeant, Nixon's successor, and informed him:

We are heartily troubled that Governor Nixon has altered the Standard of Trade ... we have strickly examined him and finde that he gives us a very slender account of that alteration, take all those arguments he musters up in his Councell booke as he calls it & you will finde them but weake. Likewise we have examined Geo. Geyer (upon the premisses who was Chiefe at Rupert River, who assures us that the Indians he Traded wth ... (who Lye nerer the French then any factorey) were all pleased with the Goods they bought & the Quantety and no murmering amongst them or craveing more goods then at other times ... we have at this time sent you very good goods, choise goods as can be bought for money especially the Guns, Kettles, hatchets & knives in which we thinke we doe very much outvey the French ...

The Goods we have now sent you are very good cost us much more then formerly as we have mentioned in the former parte of our letter. Therefore, we wold have you indeavor what leyes in your power to bring our goods to the old Standard.[11]

For the time being, then, the governor and committee decided not to try to improve the quality of their merchandise by having some articles manufactured in the bay. Rather, they decided the best way to upgrade their trade goods was to offer higher prices to English suppliers. It was for this reason that the committee members took exception to Nixon's action of lowering the standard of trade. In fact, one committee member believed that Nixon's action was so prejudicial to the company's interest that he opposed the committee's decision to pay Nixon the £305 salary they owed him.[12]

Despite selling imitations of many French goods and paying higher prices for its commodities in England, the committee received an unabated stream of complaints from the bayside. Even George Geyer, who in 1682 had said the Indians were pleased with company goods, reported widespread dissatisfaction eight years later. This prompted the governor and committee to order that: 'all persons against whome Complaints has been Made by Governr Geyer in his Generall Letter [of 1690], shall not furnish the Compa with any goods, untill the Comittee are satisfied in that Matter & have otherwise determined it.'[13]

Judging from Indian complaints, of all of the goods sold in the early years of the company's operations, those manufactured from metal were the least satisfactory. Most of the Indians' basic tools had traditionally been fashioned from stone, bone, or wood, and if they broke, the hunter could easily repair or replace them. However, the situation was quite different when the Indian was using firearms, metal hatchets, knives, awls, firesteels, and kettles. If a blacksmith or gunsmith were not available, metal tools could not be repaired. Since few Indians lived near the posts in the seventeenth and early eighteenth centuries, tools could only be repaired or replaced once a year. The record clearly shows that the Indians for these reasons became very critical of the firearms, metal tools, and utensils the English and French offered them in trade. There is also reason to believe that European manufacturers did not have the technological capability to make metal goods that met exacting Indian requirements and local environmental conditions.

In the case of firearms, Indian complaints were most frequent in the 1670s and 1680s, but declined thereafter. Between 1700 and 1745 comparatively few criticisms were made. Thereafter, until the close of the period, they were more common. Complaints generally centered around apparent defects in the metal which the Indians believed caused gun barrels to burst. For example, on 22 August 1748 George Spence wrote from Fort Albany: 'Our armourer hath over hauld the Guns & can find no fault with them, but our Indians complain last Year that the Barrels are not so good as usual, they are full of flaws and apt to burst.' The governor and committee considered the matter and concluded that the fault did not lie with the guns, but with the Indians. Accordingly, on 16 May 1749 they responded: 'Upon examining Strictly into the Complaints made of the Guns We find it is chiefly the Indians Own faults by not puting Dry and Proper Wads in when they charge them or by firing them when the Muzzel is Slopt with Snow which will burst the best Gun that can be made, but as to the flaws, We have given such Strict Orders that We hope you will hear no farther complaints in that Head.'[14] The attitude of the London committee is understandable given that all of the guns were viewed by a gunsmith in London before they were packed. In addition, the gunsmiths at the posts were supposed to open the gun cases as soon as they arrived in the bay, examine the guns, immediately return those that were defective, and oil and repack the others.[15] Therefore, any guns the Indians received should have been inspected at least twice.

Most probably some of the problems the Indians experienced with firearms stemmed from harsh usage, given their life-style and their early stage in acquiring an iron-age technology. The Indians may not have fully appreciated that care and prescribed procedures had to be followed when they used their guns. However, the problems the Indians experienced with their firearms were more complicated than the governor and committee suspected. On 10 August 1749 Spence responded to the committee: 'We Agree with Your Hons in Opinion that the Guns proving bad is in a Great measure owing to the Carelessness of the Indians. we had Several Gun Barrels brought to us to mend this Summer that were Traded last Year and our Armourer thinks that it is owing to the Stuff [metals used in manufacture] and Likewise being filed too thin.' In their final comment to Spence on this subject the governor and committee replied on 21 May 1750: 'We are still not withstanding your Armourers Sentiments of Opinion that the Bursting of some of the Guns is entirely owing to the Indians Mismanagement either by Over charging, Improperly Wading, or Suffering Snow to get into them, and not to the Badness of the Shaft which is the same it allways was. And as to the Barrels being filed too thin it has been done by express desire of the Natives themselves to make them more portable if you are of the same opinion as your Armourer, you shall in future have the Barrels thick if you think it needfull, but then we are Convinced you will not be able to Trade them on account of their being To heavy, besides We have no Such Complaints from the Northward and your Guns are equall in strength and goodness to theirs.'[16]

This episode underscores the problems the company faced when trying to cater to Indian demands regarding metal goods. The Indians wanted goods as lightweight as possible, that could withstand hard usage and the severe climate. English manufacturers had had little prior experience designing for such conditions. Indeed, the patterns for some goods, such as firearms, were simply copied from those used by other exporting companies which often traded into temperate or tropical areas. For instance, the early firearms were patterned after those of the East India Company. However, goods well suited to those areas were often inadequate for the Canadian environment.

Experience had taught the Indians that even the most minute flaws in metal were potential sources of trouble during the winter when temperatures plummeted and made the iron very brittle. Accordingly, they would not accept any goods with cracks or other apparent defects no matter how minor they appeared to the traders. For instance, in 1750 James Isham returned a considerable number of guns from York Factory saying that they were untradeable. The governor and committee examined them and wrote back to Isham the following year: 'We were much concerned on reading your General Letter to find you had returned so many guns so defective as not fit for Trade ... but how great was our Surprize when on Strict Examination and the most close Inspection we could not find above four of the guns that had any thing like a fault to make them Untradeable the rest being altogether marked wherever there was a fire flaw/ a Scratch as tho made with the Point of a Pin/ which no Gun Barrel ever was or can be made without.' The following year Isham returned four more firearms saying that they were substandard because of 'fire flaws' in the barrels. Isham's action provoked the ire of the committee. In their 1752 letter to Isham, the governor and committee said they thought it extraordinary that he should have sent the guns back in view of their letter of the previous year and added: 'the Defects that you Condem them for are only Fire flaws as we said before which/were we to give ever so much for our Guns/ it is impossible to get them without, therefore we cannot still help imputing it to the Ignorance of your Armourer, more especially as the Guns sent to your Factory are equal in goodness to any we now send or ever did and it is Surprizing to us that the Trading Indians that came to York Fort should be more Curious than any of the other Natives, and more so within these two years then ever they were before.'[17]

The problem of 'fire flaws' was not limited to guns. Other metal goods were said to have the same defect. As with firearms, the governor and committee insisted these blemishes were not serious. In 1753 the traders at Fort Churchill returned some knives and firesteels as unacceptable to the Indians. The London committee considered the matter and the following year wrote Ferdinand Jacobs and the council at Fort Churchill telling them: 'the flaws you mention in the Knives and Steels we apprehend to be Fire Flaws which are not any real defect but a Mark of their Hardness.'[18] It is unclear what the 'fire flaws' were. Presumably they were small holes resulting from the casting processes used. It is uncertain whether they seriously affected the durability of arms and metal goods. Perhaps such minor defects were not a problem in England but were sources of difficulty in the subarctic. In any event, the company clearly had problems obtaining metal goods without them and the Indians tended to reject items with these flaws.

As early as 1682, Governor Nixon had suggested one solution would be to have some articles manufactured at company posts. Although the governor and committee did not accept Nixon's suggestion, they eventually decided to pursue this course after other traders made similar suggestions. For example, in his letter of 16 August 1724 from York Factory,

Thomas McCliesh informed the governor and committee: 'We desire that no more ice chisels nor scrapers be sent out of England, our smiths' making here being preferable and and more taken with [sic] the Indians.' The Governor and committee complied with McCliesh's request and sent bar iron in place of the chisels and scrapers.[19]

The company also confronted similar problems in its efforts to obtain other staple goods acceptable to the Indians. Only one other item, Brazil tobacco, will be considered here. Brazil tobacco ranked high on the Indians' list of priorities; therefore, it indicates the demanding consumer taste the Indian had, even for items not affecting his livelihood. The governor and committee devoted more attention to securing a suitable supply of this commodity than they did for any other item.

Initially the company shipped English tobacco (probably Virginia) to its posts. Its first order for Brazil tobacco, a twisted tobacco treated with molasses, was placed on 7 January 1684.[20] The shipment was received in February and placed on board the company's ships in May 1685. In their 22 May 1685 letter to Governor Sergeant, the governor and committee wrote: 'We are sorry the Tobacco last sent you proves so bad, we have made many yeares tryall of Engleish Tobacco, by several persons & whiles we have Traded, we have had yearly complaints thereof. We have made search, [of] what Tobacco the French vends to the Indians, which you doe so much extoll, and have this yeare bought the like (vizt) Brazeele Tobacco, of which we have sent for each Factorey a good Quantity, that if approved of we are resolved in the future to supply [you] with the like, as you have occation.'[21] The Indians heartily approved of this innovation and the company was soon engaged in a continuing search for the best Brazil tobacco that could be purchased in European markets. Initially the company ordered its tobacco from London merchants. Typical of these early orders was one that was placed with the firm of Brooke and Gulston on 27 February 1712. On that date the company's secretary, John Perry, indicated: 'The Hudsons Bay Compn will have ocasion for about one thousand weight of the Choicest Brazill Tobacco of the Sweetest Smell, but of A Small Role, about the Size of a Mans Little finger.'[22]

After receiving an unsatisfactory shipment of Brazil tobacco from their London supplier in 1722, the governor and committee decided to deal directly with Lisbon tobacco merchants. Since Lisbon was one of the leading Brazil tobacco importing cities, they believed they would have a better chance of getting the best tobacco available. The record suggests this was a wise decision. In 1735 the Lisbon firm of John and James Wats informed the company that 8335 rolls of Brazil tobacco had been landed in November and they intended to select twenty of the best for the company. Thereafter, the company had with its Lisbon suppliers a standing order for the twenty best rolls of tobacco as soon as the Bahia fleet arrived in port.[23]

Dealing directly with Lisbon merchants helped the company obtain better tobacco, but the governor and committee still had to check its tobacco cargoes closely to prevent abuses and maintain quality. For instance, Mawman and Company of Lisbon was a major supplier between 1735 and 1743. On 29 March 1743 the governor and committee wrote: 'the Tobacco is received, but find on looking into some of the Rolls, they are the worst they have had for some Years past, as being of a very bad Staple much of it wilted and to a great fault Loaded with Melosses which they are informed is done since it came from the Brazils together with a bad scent and too Large a twist for their Trade.'[24] The next year the company turned to a different merchant and apparently had no further dealings with Mawman and Company. Suppliers who failed to meet the company's rigid specifications lost its business.

The company closely watched Indian reactions to its goods, kept a watchful eye on the quality and variety of articles their French competitors were selling, and secured the best merchandise available in Europe; but the Indians were still not satisfied. In fact, judging from the record, Indian discontent was increasing toward the middle of the eighteenth century. For instance, on 8 August 1728, Thomas McCliesh wrote the governor and committee from York Factory informing them:

I have sent home two bath rings as samples, for of late most of the rings sent are too small, having now upon 216 that none of the Indians will Trade. I have likewise sent home 59 ivory combs that will not be traded, they having no great teeth, and 3900 large musket flints and small pistol flints, likewise one hatchet, finding at least 150 such in three casks that we opened this summer which causes great grumbling amongst the natives. We have likewise sent home 18 barrels of powder that came over in 1727, for badness I never saw the like, for it will not kill fowl nor beast at thirty yards distance: and as for kettles in general they are not fit to put into a Indian's hand being all of them thin, and eared with tender old brass that will not bear their weight full of liquid, and soldered in several places. Never was any man so upbraided with our powder, kettles and hatchets, than we have been this summer by all the natives, especially by those that borders near the French. Our cloth likewise is so stretched with the tenter-hooks, so as the selvedge is almost tore from one end of the pieces to the other. I hope that such care will be taken so as will prevent the like for the future, for the natives are grown so politic in their way of trade, so as they are not to be dealt by as formerly ... and I afirm that man is not fit to be entrusted with the Company's interest here or in any of their factories that does not make more profit to the Company in dealing in a good commodity than in a bad. For now is the time to oblige the natives before the French draws them to their settlement.[25]

In their response, the governor and committee indicated that steps had been taken to rectify the problems detailed.[26]

Writing from the same post eleven years later, James Isham sent a long list of Indian complaints. In a letter of 1739, Isham indicated that the Indians disliked the colour and size of the large pearl beads; complained that the kettles were too heavy for their size and the wrong shape; and claimed the gunpowder was very weak, foul smelling, and an objectionable ashy colour. Although they liked the shape, quality, and colour of the blankets, the Indians said they were too short. Cloth, on the other hand, was said to be of little service because it was too narrow, weak, and thin. Despite liking their design, the Indians also considered the buttons and combs to be too weak. The fire steels were faulty, giving little fire, the gun worms too big for the ramrods, the French flints the wrong shape, the yarn gloves useless, and the knives very displeasing, with bad blades and worse handles. The twine was weak and uneven, as thick as packthread in some places and as thin as sewing thread in others. Powder horns were the wrong shape and rings were too wide for womens' fingers. Isham concluded his list of Indian criticisms by remarking: 'Those are the only things of dislike of trading goods to the best of my knowledge, and according to your honours' desire, [I] have sent home samples of most part which is pleasing to the Indians, and most conducive to your honours' interest.' Isham must have sent home few examples of articles that pleased the Indians! Only the hatchets were said to be extraordinarily good.[27]

Indian dissatisfaction with many goods continued. Owing to the quantity and variety of goods imported, the governor and committee could not maintain complete control over all of their suppliers in any given year. Some defective merchandise probably slipped their notice every year. English manufacturers had probably still not come to grips with the problem of making light-weight durable goods. McCliesh said the Indians found the kettles thin and weak. Eleven years later Isham reported they thought them too heavy for their size. There was apparently some difficulty making articles stylistically pleasing and sturdy. Isham said the Indians found the combs and buttons pleasing in design but too weak; the governor and committee wrote: 'Buttons and Combs are made Neat but if made to Strong will look Clumsy and heavy.'[28]

Another aspect of Indian complaints cannot be overlooked. These criticisms were part of the bargaining ploys the Indians used to pressure the traders to lower the prices of goods. Since this strategy was most effective when European trading rivalries were strong, there should perhaps be some correlation between the frequency of Indian complaints and the intensity of English-French competition. This was probably the case.

French opposition was strongest between 1730 and 1755 when the company was forced to relax the standards of trade at all posts except Fort Churchill.[29] During this period Indian criticisms of company trade goods were most prevalent. McCliesh noted in his 1728 letter that it was particularly the Indians living near the French who 'upbraided' him for the poor quality of company merchandise; also, the Indians were becoming increasingly 'politic' in their way of trade as the French drew near.[30]

Besides holding McCliesh and other company traders up to ridicule for the 'substandard' trade goods offered for exchange, these 'Frenchified' Indians, as they were called, claimed that the French traded superior merchandise.[31] The governor and committee were puzzled as to why the Indians seemed to prefer French articles to those of the company – many company goods had been copied from French patterns and subsequently improved. Accordingly, on 18 May 1738 they wrote to Thomas Bird at Fort Albany: 'Wee Shall Expect by the return of the Ship this Year Samples of Such Sorts of Commodities which the French furnish the Indians ... that you not only say are better than ours but also more acceptable to the Natives, And also your remarks thereon.' Bird sent to London a variety of French goods obtained from the Indians. After inspecting these articles, the governor and committee wrote back in 1739: 'We have received the two pieces of Cloth and the Samples of other knives you sent us which you say are French, the worst piece is very coarse and loose and Narrow and not near so good or broad as what we have formerly & do now send, and therefore we do Expect you will write us the reasons why the Indians like the French better then ours which you have omitted to do, the Finest piece is also narrow. As to the knives the Difference is only in the Handles. Wherefore we have sent you Six hundred large Long Knives with box handles over and above ye Quantity you Indented for.'[32]

The governor and committee clearly believed the cloth they were shipping to the bay superior to that of the French; nonetheless they took steps to improve the quality. On 1 May 1740 they wrote to Rowland Waggoner at Moose Factory: 'we have taken very great care about the cloth for it is thick and Strong of good Wool and Spinning full Breadth & well dyed, much better then the french cloth, so do not Doubt but it will be very pleasing to the Indians ... The flannell now sent is thicker and better then what was sent heretofore, therefore let us know how it is approved of.'[33] Similar letters were sent to the factors at Fort Albany and York Factory. Thus the Indians not only successfully pressured the company to relax the standards of trade, but also brought about an improvement in the quality of goods offered to them. They effected change in this and many other instances even though company officials were convinced the merchandise they offered was the best available locally.

The Indians apparently used the same tactics in their dealings with the French. For example, the French were convinced that English woollens were better and cheaper than French and were preferred by the Indians. In the early eighteenth century over 21,000 yards of English strouds were imported into New France annually from New York for the Indian trade.[34] At mid-century, the governor and intendant of New France wrote to the French government: 'The English have the better of us in the quality of merchandise in two important articles. The first is kettles – the second is cloth. They [the traders] believe that up to the present the Indians wish only English cloth and they become so well accustomed to it that it would be difficult to introduce others.'[35] The governor's remarks are interesting given that French manufacturers had been producing imitations of English cloth for the Indian trade since the 1720s.[36] His comments were made during the very period when the Indians were telling company traders English woollens were not equal to French. Ironically, the cloth the Indians brought to the bay from the French posts may well have been made in England or copies of yard goods formerly sold by the company. The Indians were clearly successful in pitting the two European groups against each other, forcing them to lower prices, and getting them to make copies and improvements of each other's merchandise.

In conclusion, an examination of the early Hudson's Bay Company fur trade reveals the Indians as shrewd consumers who knew how to take full advantage of the economic opportunities offered to them. In this respect the Indians were clearly equal to their European counterparts. The old stereotype of the Indians being a people easily tricked by crafty Europeans and made to part with valuable furs for worthless trinkets obviously does not apply to the central subarctic before 1763.

In casting away the old stereotype and searching the rich historical record we find a consistent and logical pattern to Indian consumer demand. They wanted to barter their furs at the most favourable rates of exchange that competitive conditions permitted. They wanted light-weight durable goods well suited to the harsh subarctic environment. Given the widely scattered posts, Indians were usually unable to have their European manufactured tools repaired or replaced more than once a year. Therefore, they expected more from these tools than from those they traditionally made from local materials. Indeed, the Indians needed more reliable metal tools than did the European traders, who had access to blacksmiths and gunsmiths or to warehouses for replacements when the smiths could not effect needed repairs.

Perhaps we have dwelt too long on the sorry tale of the European abuse of Indians in the fur trade after 1763 – a well-known tale which usually casts the Indians as passive figures pushed around by different trading companies. By looking at an earlier period, when a more equal partner-ship existed between the Indian and the trader, the active role of the Indian is more readily apparent. In this instance, by recognizing that the Indians had well-defined demands and a critical eye to assess trade goods, we find that the Indian was probably an agent of technological change even though his culture was not as advanced technologically as that of his European partners. The latter were forced to make a number of changes in the manufacture of firearms and metal goods. The tempering and casting of metal had to be improved to produce knives, hatchets, kettles, ice chisels, and guns that were less prone to breaking in the severe cold. The record indicates that some of the craftsmen working at the trading posts were able to make certain tools that were more to the Indians' liking than those manufactured in Europe. The nature and importance of technological innovations resulting from attempts to meet the consumer demands of the Indian is a story that has yet to be told.

NOTES AND REFERENCES

1 Rich ed *James Isham's Observations and Notes, 1743–1749* 83–7
2 See also Ray and Freeman '*Give Us Good Measure*' 163–97.
3 For discussions of early trade into this region see: Bishop *The Northern Ojibwa and the Fur Trade*; Heidenrech and Ray *The Early Fur Trades: A Study in Cultural Interaction*; Ray *Indians in the Fur Trade* 3–26.
4 Rich ed *Copy-Booke of Letters Outward* 147
5 Rich ed *Minutes of the Hudson's Bay Company, 1671–74* 26–7, 58–9, 61
6 On 3 Feb. 1679 the company ordered 300 hatchets from Robert Carnor at a price of ten pennies per hatchet (ibid 32).

The first order with Bannor appears to have been placed on 7 Dec. 1683 (Rich ed *Minutes of the Hudson's Bay Company, 1679–84* 2nd part 171–2).

In a letter of 24 Feb. 1697 the company secretary informed Bannor that the company wanted him to make 1200 Jack Knives 'imitating the French' HBCA A 6/3, 37, Letters Outward.

7 Rich ed *Minutes 1679–84* 1st part 177, 2nd part 9. The common practice was to have the men buy French goods from the Indians. These goods would then be sent to London and used as samples. For evidence that French patterns were being followed, see the various minutes of the company edited by E.E. Rich. Other examples can be found in the unpublished minutes and outward correspondence books of the company.

8 Rich ed *Letters Outward* 8

9 The first order was sent to John Bridgar on 27 April 1683 and became standing policy (ibid 86–9). The second policy was implemented in 1680 (ibid 8). The governor and committee initiated the third policy to prevent confusion in the indents (HBCA A 6/3, 31, Letters Outward, 31 May 1697 to York Factory).

10 Rich *Minutes 1679–84* 1st part 251–2. The governor and committee questioned Nixon's right to take such action (Rich ed *Minutes 1679–84* 2nd part 251).

11 Rich ed *Letters Outward* 120–1. For the three meetings, see Rich ed *Minutes* 2nd part 251–2 and 256.

12 Rich ed *Minutes 1679–84* 2nd part, 256. Sir Edward Dering was in opposition.

13 Meeting of 3 Dec. 1690 (HBCA A 1/13, 4, Minutes)

14 HBCA A 11/2, 136, Letters Inward; A 6/8, 9, Letters Outward

15 The company had been doing these inspections since the early 1670s. On 24 March 1674 an attempt was made to enlist the services of the East India Company's gun surveyor (Rich ed *Minutes 1671–74* 91).

In their general letter of 3 May 1745, the governor and committee wrote: 'We do direct that you take all the Guns out of the Chests immediately [upon receipt] and that they be overlooked by the Armourer and then Oiled and repacked and in case of any Defect to give the Committee the number on the Case and the Name of the maker of the Gun and ... what the defects are that we may get them rectifyed' (HBCA A 6/7, 71, Letters Outward). This became a standing policy thereafter.

16 HBCA A 11/2, 140, Correspondence Inward, Fort Albany, 10 August 1749; A 6/8, 36, Correspondence Outward, 21 May 1750

17 HBCA A 6/8, 67 Correspondence Outward, 16 May 1751; A 6/8, 95, Correspondence Outward, 12 May 1752. When he sent the guns in question, Isham sent a covering letter in which he informed the committee, 'the reason of our

sending no others home have My self/ as I did those/ examined them very carefully & find several [4] that has flaws in the Barrells, which no Indian will trade' (A 11/114, 146–50, Correspondence Inward, York Factory, 8 August 1751).

18 HBCA A 6/8, 120, Correspondence Outward, 24 May 1753
19 Davies ed *Letters From Hudson Bay, 1703–40*, 99–100; HBCA A 6/4, 95–6, Correspondence Outward, 19 May 1725
20 Meeting of 7 Jan. 1684, HBCA A 1/8, 9
21 Rich ed *Letters Outward* 140–2
22 HBCA A 6/3, 120, Correspondence Outward, 27 Feb. 1712
23 The company had ordered the tobacco from a London merchant named Edward Bridgon. On 22 Nov. 1723 the company's secretary wrote Bridgon informing him: 'Complaint having been made to the Comitte that the Brazil Tobacco Imported last yeare by Mess Gutson Simens & Co of Lisbone for ye Comp account was not soe good as formerly I am ordered by them to acquaint you therewith, desiring you would Informe those Gent. of it' HBCA A 6/4, 82, Correspondence Outward. On 14 July 1724 the company began dealing with the firm of Lewsen, Gibbs and Potter of Lisbon (A 6/4, 82, Correspondence Outward, 14 July 1724).

The merchants, Lewsen, Gibbs and Potter, had suggested to the governor and committee that tobacco be specially ordered in Brazil to meet their requirements. However, the committee believed that this arrangement would not be as satisfactory as selecting from the best that was available in Lisbon (HBCA A 6/4, 94, Correspondence Outward, 27 Oct. 1724).

For John and James Wats see HBCA A 6/5, 103, Correspondence Outward, 25 Nov. 1735.

In their yearly letters to their tobacco suppliers, the governor and committee repeatedly stressed that the Brazil tobacco had to be the newest and freshest available or their Indian customers would refuse to buy it.

24 HBCA A 6/7, 13, Correspondence Outward, 29 March 1743. The London correspondence indicates that the company began dealing with Chase and Company of Lisbon (A 6/7, 32, Correspondence Outward, 22 Dec. 1743).
25 Davies *Letters* 136
26 The governor and committee responded to McCliesh saying: 'We take notice of the complaints mady by the Indians of ye unsizeableness and badness of some of our trading goods and have given such orders and directions to the persons that serve us with those goods that we hope will prevent the like complaints for the future' (HBCA A 6/5, Correspondence Outward, 21 May 1729, 26–8).
27 Davies *Letters* 278–80

28 HBCA A 6/6, 74–5, Correspondence Outward, 1 May 1740. The governor and committee added in their letter that they would again contact their suppliers to correct the defects in the other merchandise.

29 Ray and Freeman 'Give Us Good Measure' 163–97

30 Pierre Gaultier de Varennes de La Vérendrye had been placed in command of the northern posts of the French in 1728. Under his direction the French began pushing into the hinterland of York Factory in the late 1720s and the 1730s. Heidenreich and Ray Early Fur Trades 41–3. As noted earlier in the paper, guns were an exception to the escalation of complaints.

31 This term was used as early as 1703 to describe Indians who also traded with the French. In a letter from Fort Albany dated 2 August 1703, John Fullartine wrote 'there came an abundance of Indians down who used the French and were so much Frenchified that they asked for the goods which they traded in French' (Davies Letters 8).

32 HBCA A 6/6, 9–15, Correspondence Outward, 18 May 1738; A 6/6, 31–35, Correspondence Outward, 17 May 1739.

33 HBCA A 6/6, 66, Correspondence Outward, 1 May 1740. A letter to Richard Staunton at Moose Factory indicated that he had sent a French coat along with the French cloth the previous year. Many of the company goods were made in the bay and there is no indication that the Governor and Committee attempted to copy the coat Staunton sent (HBCA A 6/6, 71, Correspondence Outward, 1 May 1740).

34 Wraxall An Abridgement of the Indian Affairs Contained in Four Folio Volumes, Transacted in the Colony of New York From the Year 1678 to the Year 1751 ed McIlwain lxvii. According to Thomas E. Norton, Montreal-based traders had a preference for many English goods and French smugglers made their largest profits bringing strouds into Canada from New York (Norton The Fur Trade in Colonial New York 1686–1776 126).

35 Quoted in Innis The Fur Trade in Canada 85. According to Innis, English manufactured trade goods were generally cheaper and superior to those made in France in the early eighteenth century. For this reason a considerable trade developed between merchants in Montreal and the colony of New York (ibid 84–5).

36 Wraxall Indian Affairs lxxii

Agriculture and the Fur Trade

D.W. MOODIE

Agriculture has long served as a key to studies of regional and national development in Canada.[1] It provisioned the staple trades upon which Canadian economic development has been based and, as it expanded, offered incentives for the development of industry, as well as for increased trade and finance.[2] With few exceptions, however, agriculture has been dismissed as an insignificant appendage of the fur trade, the leading export staple of Canada until the early decades of the nineteenth century. Agriculture has received only passing mention in histories of the fur trade; while to the extent that relationships between agriculture and the fur trade have been explored in Canadian history, they have generally been described as competing, if not incompatible, economic enterprises.[3]

Thus, the fur trade has been seen as a negative force in New France that lured men into the wilderness and severely retarded the development of agriculture along the lower St Lawrence during the seventeenth and eighteenth centuries. Conversely, the establishment of agriculture provided a base and a haven for free traders, thereby disrupting the efficient prosecution of the French fur trade. In a colony where the only opportunity for the rapid accumulation of wealth lay in the fur trade, this was a problem that, despite many edicts against free trading, plagued colonial officials until the end of the French regime. Nowhere, perhaps, have the negative effects of agriculture upon the fur trade been more strongly emphasized than in Galbraith's study of the Hudson's Bay Company's monopoly trade in the nineteenth century.[4] During this period, the company was least successful in defending its trade against the encroachments of agricultural settlers, and against rivals in Rupert's Land who were agriculturally based. Galbraith has argued that the company's trade in the Red River valley, where its competitors were farmers as well as traders, was crippled from within, while in the frontierlands of the Oregon, its operations were obliterated when the American settlement frontier leap-frogged the Great Plains to the Pacific northwest.

These views are consistent with Turner's view of American history wherein the fur trade and agriculture have been depicted as mutually exclusive and successive enterprises in the course of Anglo-American expansion across the continent.[5] In Turner's thesis, agriculture advanced steadily in the form of a settlement frontier, destroying the forest as it progressed and driving the fur trade and the Indians into the uncivilized reaches of the farther west. In Canada, agriculture did not advance steadily westward; and it did not destroy the wilderness resource base of the Indian and the fur trader. If the plough, like a cancerous growth, was devastating for the Indian and the fur trade in America, in Canada it was benign, and the world of the Indian and the trader was destroyed, not by agriculture, but ultimately by the industrial revolution and the market economy of Europe. In the end, the Canadian fur trade was the engine of its own destruction, for the resource base was depleted, the Indian an industrial dependent, and the trade in demise long before agricultural settlers advanced into the southern margins of the fur trade domain.

In Canada agriculture did not destroy the fur trade as it apparently did in America. Canadian historians, however, with the major exceptions of Harold Innis and W.L. Morton, have emphasized the conflicts rather than the complementarities between these two pioneering enterprises. In interpreting Canadian history Innis and Morton looked to agriculture to explain fur trade history at both the regional and national levels. Innis recognized incompatabilities between them, but thought agriculture essential to the expansion of the fur trade to continental proportions. He attributed this dependence to the limited transport technology of the trade and the immense distances over which it was conducted:

The extension of the trade across the northern half of the continent and the transportation of furs and goods over great distances involved the elaboration of an extensive organization of transport, of personnel, and of food supply ... The organization of food supplies depended on agricultural development in the more favourable areas to the south and on the abundant fauna of the plains area. Limited transport facilities, such as the canoe afforded, accentuated the organization and production of food supply in these areas. The extension of the fur trade was supported at convenient intervals by agricultural development as in the lower St. Lawrence basin, in southeastern Ontario, and areas centring about Detroit, and in Michilimackinac and Lake Michigan territory, in the west at Red River, though the buffalo were more important in the plains area in the beginning, and eventually in Peace River. On the Pacific coast an agricultural base was established in the Columbia.[6]

Morton examined fur trade agriculture to explain the emergence of a distinct way of life in early Manitoba and the northwest. In his work on the Red River Colony, Morton focused upon the complex interplay between agriculture and the buffalo hunt to elucidate not only the economy of a colony dependent upon the fur trade for its commerce, but also the very nature of Red River society, its institutions, and its ultimate destiny.[7] In exploiting earlier work by Giraud, Morton showed how neither farming nor buffalo hunting could displace one another in the life of the Red River Colony. The river lot farmer was frequently in need of plains provisions while the colony hunter depended in varying degree upon agricultural produce. Moreover, each depressed the price of the other's produce in the fur trade market, the only external market and a market which neither could be relied upon to fill. Thus, in the fur trade economy of the colony, agriculture played a compromise but nonetheless essential role. It was perhaps for this reason that Morton came to regard agriculture as the indispensable enemy of the fur trade and was the first to emphasize its importance in the trade of the western interior.

In revising Burpee's earlier views about the beginnings of the western trade, Morton demonstrated how provisioning problems complicated and delayed the French penetration of the west as they expanded beyond the Indian agricultural lands of the St Lawrence – Great Lakes. He has also shown how the fur trade initiated not only the pemmican trade but also the first agriculture in the prairie-parkland west. Although he did not underestimate the value of pemmican as a staple food of the western trade, Morton also wrote that: 'It was, however, a last resource rather than the preferred item of the traders' simple menu. They supplemented their diet by hunting, fishing and gardening. These pursuits were often, indeed, the only means of subsistence. The solitary trader who had to buy fish and game for his table found in gardening a considerable aid to survival and a welcome addition to his diet. The great companies also, seeking to check costs mounting with the extension of the trade, encouraged their efforts at horticulture and even more ambitious attempts at agriculture.'[8] Thus Morton described how even in the heart of the buffalo country the fur trade called agriculture into being both at the fur posts and at the Red River Colony.

Despite this work by Innis and Morton, it is only recently that studies specifically concerned with fur trade agriculture have begun to emerge. For the most part, this research has focused upon Indian agriculture and that established by the fur companies in western Canada and Alaska. The remainder of this paper draws upon some of this recent work, but its main purpose is to call attention to agriculture as a neglected but worthwhile field for fur trade research.

Three main types of agriculture supported the fur trade: company agriculture, colonial agriculture, and Indian agriculture. That begun by the fur companies and practised by their personnel developed exclusively in response to the needs of the fur trade. Confined to the trading settlements, company agriculture developed in step with the expansion of the European component of the fur trade. Thus when de Monts and Champlain planted gardens at the first fur trade settlements on the Bay of Fundy and later at Quebec,[9] they began a practice subsequently extended almost everywhere that fur trade posts were built. Although inauspicious at the time, these first plantings also presaged the beginnings of agricultural colonization in Acadia and in the St Lawerence valley. Colonial agriculture in these areas, and elsewhere, however, emerged subsequent to the fur trade and, unlike company agriculture, was only partially a response to fur trade needs. Colonial agriculture was also highly localized and, throughout the fur trade period, remained confined to four major regions: the Bay of Fundy, the lower St Lawrence, peninsular Ontario, and the Red River valley.

Indian agriculture antedated the fur trade and provided a pre-existing agricultural base for the development of the European trade in eastern Canada. In penetrating along the axis of the St Lawrence and the Great Lakes, the French trade expanded along the transition zone between agricultural and hunting Indians in eastern North America. In this zone the complementarity in trade was high and the exchange of Indian corn and tobacco for hides, furs, and other commodities had long antedated the advent of the French. In this way, the ground was prepared for the European trade which, in its westward advance, followed pre-existing trade routes and used the corn supplies of the south to exploit the richer fur bearing lands of the north. Here Indian agriculture played its most important role in the Canadian fur trade, a role that did not disappear with the collapse of Huronia, but persisted among the Indians of the Great Lakes until the beginning of American and Loyalist settlement in this region in the later eighteenth century.

Commenting upon the neglect of agricultural studies in North American Indian history, Wessel has recently observed that 'from the time of the earliest meetings between Europeans and Indians north of the Rio Grande, agriculture played a fundamental role linking Indian and white destinies on the continent.'[10] More than any other enterprise, the fur trade forged the first contacts between North American Indians and Europeans and, as it developed throughout most of the United States and much of eastern Canada, the system was largely fuelled by native agriculture. Prior to 1650, the value of Indian agriculture to the French fur trade, and to the Huron middlemen upon whom it depended heavily, can scarcely be exaggerated. As Innis observed:

The opening of the St. Lawrence route to the Hurons facilitated the spread of European goods to the country tributary to the Ottawa and beyond. But expansion of trade to Georgian Bay and the Interior necessitated the development of a technique by which trade could be carried on over long distances. An important feature of this technique was the existence of a base of supplies in the interior. The semi-agricultural activities of the Indians of the interior, and especially of the Hurons, gave them a decided advantage in the trade. The raising of corn by the Hurons and, to a less extent by the Algonquins, gave them a commodity of high food value, easily cultivated, of heavy yields, and of light weight which could be carried long distances in canoes and which, used with fish and game taken on the journey, gave them sufficient strength to overcome the difficulties of long voyages ... Moreover, because of the position of the Hurons at the edge of the Canadian shield, they rapidly extended the trade in foodstuffs with the northern hunting Indians ... These people in turn became traders.[11]

Recent research by Heidenreich[12] and Trigger[13] has so expanded the literature on the Huron that more is now known about their agriculture and its role in the fur trade than about that of any other aboriginal group in North America. Prior to the beginning of the European trade, there existed a widespread commerce centred upon Huronia and involving a variety of sedentary, semi-sedentary, and purely nomadic groups. Included in this commerce was the trade that developed directly between the agricultural Huron and the hunting Algonkin of Lake Nipissing. This trade was centred upon an exchange of Huron corn and tobacco for Nipissing skins and dried fish. The advent of the European trade intensified this commerce, bringing the trade in furs to the fore, and increasing the value of Huron corn, not only for voyaging and subsistence, but also as a commodity for which iron goods, or the furs necessary for their purchase, could readily be acquired. In the middleman trade of the Nipissing, corn figured prominently in both these roles. The Nipissing regularly visisted Huronia in winter to acquire corn in exchange for fish and furs. In spring, some of the Nipissing voyaged northward where they traded corn and other commodities with the Cree and the more distant Algonkin bands for their prime northern pelts. The Nipissing then traded these furs, either directly to the French or, as was more frequently the case, to the Huron for ironware and corn, usually at their Lake Nipissing rendezvous. In proceeding to Huronia in autumn, the Nipissing caught and dried fish which they later sold for corn at the Huron villages.

The exchange in corn was therefore scarcely less important than that of furs and European trade goods. The products of their cornfields, together with their strategic location as the northernmost sedentary agriculturalists, permitted the Huron to dominate, if not control, much of the French trade in the interior. Corn eased the subsistence of the different Algonkin bands who wintered over and traded their furs at the Huron villages. It also afforded the Algonkin a valuable, if not unrivalled, commodity with which to victual their canoes on their middleman trading expeditions of summer. Although not to the same extent as ironware, corn was also in demand among the more distant hunting groups from whom traders such as the Nipissing procured furs at a profit. The amount of corn that eventually filtered through to the more distant hunting groups, such as the Cree, was probably very small and its attraction as a trade item to these northern hunters did not lie solely in the amount of food it contributed. It also seems to have had an attraction as an exotic food, one for which there may have been a craving among the purely hunting and gathering populations. In this context, Perrot remarked that: 'The kinds of food that the savages like best, and which they make most effort to obtain, are the Indian corn, the kidneybean, and the squash. If they are without these, they think they are fasting, no matter what abundance of meat and fish they may have in their stores, the Indian corn being to them what bread is to Frenchman. The Algonkins, however, and all the northern tribes, who do not cultivate the soil, do not lay up corn; but when it is given to them ... they regard it as a [special] treat.'[14]

Likewise, La Vérendrye, the first European to observe the trade between the hunting Assiniboine and the Mandan agriculturalists of the upper Missouri, witnessed a commerce not unlike that between the Huron and Nipissing. In this case, plains provisions and European wares were traded by the Assiniboine for Mandan corn, tobacco, and other commodities. From La Vérendrye's accounts, Will and Hyde have concluded that the Assiniboine valued the Mandan corn more highly than European goods and that the hunting tribes generally had a craving for the vegetable produce of the upper Missouri agriculturalists.[15] From Father Aulneau, it is known that the Assiniboine regularly traded for Mandan corn prior to European contact,[16] and it is highly likely that this trade intensified following the opening of English trading posts on James Bay in the later seventeenth century. During this period, the Assiniboine, along with the Cree, came to monopolize the middleman trade with the English, and a regular supply of corn in the western interior, like that of the Huron in the east, would have greatly enhanced the position of the Assiniboine in this trade. However, the role of Indian corn in this theatre of middleman trading awaits further investigation.

Like the different Indian groups, the French could not break the Huron monopoly upon either the fur trade or the provision supply base around which it revolved. Fully aware that groups such as the Nipissing preferred to trade for merchandise and corn at the Huron villages rather than directly with the French, the latter attempted to cultivate Indian corn and thereby compete with the Huron. Thus, Father Sagard wrote that the French 'sow every year Indian corn and pease which they trade with the Indians for furs.'[17] Although in his first planting at Quebec, Champlain found that Indian corn grew well, early efforts to develop agriculture at Quebec failed to even render the French agriculturally self-sufficient. As late as 1625, only 15 acres were under cultivation at Quebec, and it was almost another twenty years before the small French outpost in America was capable of feeding itself, let alone able to generate surplus foodstuffs for the fur trade. Although the Company of New France encouraged agricultural settlement with this objective in mind, Trigger has pointed out that:

the total amount of food available to the French for trade was insufficient to undercut the Huron. Throughout this period the Algonkin, although better located for trade with the French than with the Huron, continued to rely on the latter for supplies of corn. The cost of transporting goods to the New World ensured that French trading in agricultural produce was only with hunting groups, like the Micmac and Montagnais, who lived too far away to make the large scale transport of corn from the horticultural tribes living in the interior a practical proposition. The Huron country remained the granary for the Ottawa Valley Algonkin, as well as for the semi or nonagricultural peoples of the upper Great Lakes and central Quebec.[18]

It would appear, however, that the tentacles of the Huron trading empire even extended at times to the remote Montagnais. On their annual trading expeditions to Three Rivers and Quebec the Huron carried agricultural produce in addition to that required for voyaging, which they were able to trade to advantage with the hunting tribes gathered at the French settlements. According to the Jesuit relation of 1634, this included exchanging corn and tobacco for moose skins from the Montagnais.[19]

Until the 1640s the French colony frequently faced starvation in winter and remained dependent on the annual supply ships from France. Symptomatic of this problem was Champlain's proposal to send some of his men to winter for their subsistence among the far-off agricultural Abenaki on the Atlantic coast; he also endeavoured to persuade the Abenaki to transport and sell their corn to the French at Quebec.[20] By this time, however, warfare had so disrupted the Abenaki way of life that they were purchasing extra corn from the Indians of southern New England and, as early as 1625, had begun trading their furs for food from the Plymouth colonists in Massachusetts.[21]

The trade in food for furs that had emerged in New England by this time was perhaps part of the French trade from the beginning, although unlike that of the English, it was more expensive and dependent upon imports from France. In 1626, for example, the ships sent to Quebec contained 'all the merchandise which these Gentlemen use in trading to the Savages' which, in addition to iron and cloth goods, included 'prunes, raisins, Indian corn, peas, crackers or sea biscuits, and tobacco; and what is necessary for the sustenance of the French in this country besides.' Ten years earlier, Father Biard stressed the importance of bread, peas, beans, and prunes, in addition to European manufactures, in the Micmac trade of the Maritimes.[22] Bailey has suggested that the eastern Algonkians in this manner lost a measure of self-reliance and that the new foods promoted disease and higher infant mortality among the Indians involved in the trade.[23] When did this trade begin and how essential was it? Did it intensify among the impoverished Micmac, Montagnais, and Algonkin when the heyday of the middleman trade had passed them by? When did colonial foodstuffs replace those from Europe and did the Indian in this way furnish a significant market for the habitant of Quebec or Acadia? Just as the Home Guard Cree in the English trade of Hudson Bay came to rely on imported foods, so it would seem that agricultural produce, both imported and locally grown, became a conspicuous part of the fur trade as it wore on in Canada and game resources could no longer entirely support the Indian way of life. Unlike the trade in manufactured goods, that in food has virtually been ignored, although it would appear to have been an important part of the trade at the beginning, and vital at its conclusion.

Except for the period of Huron hegemony, very little is known about the role of Indian agriculture in the Canadian fur trade. There is even debate as to whether the Huron increased their corn production, or were incapable of doing so as they rose to dominance in the French trade. In America, where Indian agriculture was ubiquitous to the east of the Great Plains, it has been suggested that Indian farming suffered greatly following European contact. Increased warfare with other Indian groups and with whites, frequent crop destruction, population declines and displacements, an unprecedented focus upon fur hunting, and a growing trade with Europeans for gunpowder, clothing, and food all worked toward a breakdown of traditional agricultural systems.[24] In Canada, the fortunes of war induced by the fur trade led directly to the collapse of Huronia, but there is little evidence that the Huron agricultural system had been seriously weakened prior to the Iroquois onslaught. Wessel has recently postulated that Iroquois warfare was directed against not only the Huron but also agricultural tribes generally because of their ability to dominate the trade at Iroquois expense.[25] At the same time, he has stressed the commercial advantages that accrued to Indian groups such as the Huron living along the continental areas between hunting and agricultural populations, and therefore the exceptional nature of their agriculture in the development of the fur trade.

This transition zone in the Canadian trade lay along the northern frontier of aboriginal agriculture. The northeastern limit of native agriculture was at the villages of the Malecite Indians in New Brunswick; the northwestern limit at the villages of the Mandan and Hidatsa in North Dakota. Unlike the Huron, who almost perished as a result of the economic advantages they had won in this zone, the Mandan prospered under similar circumstances until the demise of the fur trade, profiting from both Indian middlemen and the French, British, and American fur traders who followed in their wake. Unfortunately, little or nothing is known of equivalent circumstances in the northeast. Did the Malecite employ their agriculture to commercial advantage in their relations with hunting Indians, or did it lanquish in the face of turbulent conditions induced by the fur trade? What was the extent and nature of Micmac agriculture in the fur trade of the Maritimes and when and how did it originate?

Following the collapse of Huronia in the centre of this zone, neighbouring tribes, including refugee Huron, continued to supply the corn needs of the upper lakes trade. Unlike the previous Huron system, agricultural produce at this time was traded both to Indians and to the Europeans now directly involved in the trade. Production also became concentrated at places such as Green Bay, Mackinac Island, and Detroit. It would seem that, in the initial phases at least, the fur trade did not cause the Indians in this region to neglect or abandon their agriculture. Rather, it would appear that agriculture expanded into areas and among peoples where hitherto it had been unknown.

A major gap in this context is the role of agriculture among the Ottawa who came to dominate the middleman trade of the upper lakes. About the time of contact, Champlain wrote 'Most of them plant Indian corn and other crops. They are hunters who go in bands into various regions and districts where they trade with other tribes more than four or five hundred leagues distant.'[26] During the period of Huron supremacy, the corn supplies of the Ottawa secured them advantages both in trading and in voyaging among the more remote tribes to the west of Huronia. When the Huron were eliminated, some of the Ottawa, along with other groups, sought refuge from the Iroquois at Chequamegon Bay on the south shore of Lake Superior. The corn produced by the Ottawa and other refugee agriculturalists at Chequamegon quickly assumed a prominent role in the developing trade of Lake Superior. In Huron fashion, it provisioned the Indian canoe brigades that renewed direct trading links with the St Lawrence, while the corn and European merchandise available at Chequamegon soon attracted the northern hunting Indians. In 1669, for example, Father Dablon reported that the Cree from the north had called at Chequamegon 'to the number of two hundred canoes coming to buy merchandise and Corn.' In the same year, Dablon further remarked that, at Chequamegon, 'More than fifty Villages can be counted, which comprise diverse peoples, either nomadic or stationary ... they live there on fish and corn and rarely by hunting, and number more than fifteen hundred souls.'[27] Thus, with its rich fishery and cornfields, Chequamegon functioned for a brief period as a small scale Huronia in the new French trade of the upper lakes.

Although the history of the Ottawa is known only in sketchy fashion, they continued to profit in the trade from their agriculture long after their middleman role as fur traders had been usurped by tribes to the west. Thus, Alexander Henry the elder, in commenting on the pivotal role of the maize of this region in provisioning the trade of the Ohio, the Mississippi, and the northwest, remarked that 'It is the Ottawas, it will be remembered, who grow this grain, for the market of Michilimackinac.'[28]

Still less is known about the Ojibwa, who had been solely engaged in hunting and gathering at the time of contact, but commenced to cultivate on the south shore of Lake Superior following the collapse of Huronia and the development of the European trade in this region.[29] Through subsequent migration and conquest, the Ojibwa expanded from the shorelands of Lake Superior and Georgian Bay to occupy an immense territory which, by the middle of the nineteenth century, stretched from southern Ontario in the southeast to the grasslands of Saskatchewan in the northwest. The easternmost of the Ojibwa bands, the Amikwa and Mississauga, were by 1710 cultivating corn on the shores and islands of Georgian Bay and, as the Iroquois threat passed, the Mississauga occupied the old Huron lands of peninsular Ontario and there some of them, like neighbouring bands of Huron and Ottawa, raised corn for the French trade at Detroit.

At the height of their territorial extent in the mid–nineteenth century, four main divisions of the Ojibwa can be recognized: the Southeastern, the Northern, the Southwestern, and the Plains Ojibwa. Of the different lands occupied by these people, those of the Southeastern Ojibwa in southern Ontario and in the lower peninsula of Michigan were best suited for corn cultivation. There, living to the south of their rugged homeland in the Canadian Shield, many of the Southeastern Ojibwa continued to cultivate among other agricultural groups and in the milder lands vacated by the Huron and their allies. The Southwestern Ojibwa occupied the south shore of Lake Superior and the northern interior of Wisconsin and Minnesota, including the entire headwater region of the upper Mississippi. They inhabited a country rich in wild rice but not equally suited to maize cultivation. Nevertheless, they introduced corn into areas that lay beyond the prehistoric aboriginal agricultural frontier and, during the first half of the nineteenth century, a small-scale agriculture based largely on this crop became a regular feature of the village way of life that emerged among the Ojibwa of this region.

The most expansive of the Ojibwa territories was that occupied by the Northern Ojibwa, who lived in the agriculturally hostile forest and Shield country to the north and west of Lake Superior. From the Red River valley west to the grasslands of eastern Saskatchewan were the Plains Ojibwa or Bungi. In the early nineteenth century, some of the Plains Ojibwa commenced a desultory agriculture along the northeastern margins of the grasslands. About the same time, agriculture appeared among some of the southernmost of the Northern Ojibwa living in the vicinity of the border lakes of Ontario and Minnesota. The limited and often ephemeral agriculture of the Plains and Northern Ojibwa, in contrast to that of the Southwestern Ojibwa, was not associated with a village way of life. However, it was distinctive in carrying native agriculture to its northern limit in North America, reaching its outer limits in north-western Ontario at Eagle Lake and Lac Seul, and achieving its northward extreme on the continent in Manitoba along the Dauphin River at latitude 51° 30′ north.

The spread of agriculture among the Ojibwa ushered in the final stage in the northward diffusion of Indian domesticated plants (or cultigens) in North America, a process that had begun several millenia before the arrival of Europeans. The antecedents of this diffusion occurred in prehistoric time and are known only indirectly and in limited detail from the surviving archaeological evidence. The poleward thrust of Ojibwa agriculture, in contrast, occurred in historical time and lends itself to the more comprehensive procedures of documentary investigation, thus affording a potentially unique perspective from which to view the general processes of agricultural diffusion in aboriginal North America.

Ojibwa agriculture was also a product of its time and therefore of the fur trade milieu in which it emerged. Their corn and dried squash facilitated fur hunting when the larger food animals were in decline and corn was also sold to the European traders. Henry Schoolcraft, for example, reported in the early 1830s that the Red Lake Ojibwa were supplying corn 'to the posts on the Upper Mississippi, and even as far east as Fond du Lac.'[30] Ojibwa agriculture profoundly affected their culture as well as their commerce with Europeans and, like Indian agriculture elsewhere, can be highly revealing of the workings of both.

It would seem, for example, that the Ojibwa exchange in corn during the first half of the nineteenth century involved characteristics of both the European and Indian cultures, so that a dual economy was in effect among them at this time. In the Lake of the Woods, Ojibwa agriculture strongly reflected the impact of the European market system upon their economic behaviour. From the outset, corn production in this region was commercial in nature, and traders from both the North West and Hudson's Bay Companies vied with one another for the corn supply to ensure greater mobility in the competition for furs. After union in 1821, Indian agriculture at Lake of the Woods declined, largely because of the drop in price brought on by the cessation of competition. The chief factor at Rainy Lake reported in 1822–23 that during the period of competition the

Indians 'would never give more than 2 bushels for a three point blanket, which traders, some from competition & some from necessity were obliged to give; as soon as the junction was affected the exorbitant price was reduced to a pint of powder for a bushel. On this, the Indians in great part discontinued their cultivation.'[31]

This trade, clearly within a market framework, contrasts with patterns observed among the Ojibwa at both the individual and band levels. The bands, it seems, operated on a reciprocal exchange basis wherein status accrued to those who gave away the most. Thus, it was observed that the Red Lake Ojibwa would live well from their corn and fish, 'were it not for the habit of giving it away to any and every one who may have, from laziness or any other cause, failed to secure the necessary store of food for the long winter.' Likewise, it was remarked that: 'This band would be well supplied with food, if other bands did not pour in upon them during the fall and winter, to live by begging, and thus consume their supplies. Most of the men assist their wives in cultivating their gardens; but some are not only too indolent to assist, but give away very liberally what their wives and daughters raise, and then, as soon as spring opens, leave them to live as best they can while raising another crop.'[32]

Like Indian agriculture, the history of European agriculture in the fur trade largely remains to be written and, ultimately, the significance of both will be known only in terms of the overall provision requirements of the fur trade. Morton has observed that the provisioning of the fur trade is a much neglected subject, but described it as a central theme in the history of Manitoba.[33] It is also a central theme in Canadian history and, until further research is conducted, the role of agriculture in the fur trade and in early Canada will not be adequately understood.

Although agricultural foodstuffs were secondary to the products of the hunt and the fishery in provisioning the Canadian fur trade, they were nonetheless indispensable to the trade. From the outset, food was imported from both France and Britain to secure the subsistence of the European personnel against the often extreme vagaries of the hunt and the fishery. As the fur trade expanded inland, agricultural produce, in the same way as pemmican and wild rice, was essential over wide areas to provision the men engaged in the transport of furs and trade goods. Food of this nature relieved the monotonous diets at the trading settlements and was important and at times vital to the health of the Europeans engaged in the trade. Agricultural products were also traded to the Indians for furs, a role that was most conspicuous in the dying days of the trade when the Indian, long accustomed to exchanging his furs for gunpowder and clothing, was reduced to trapping for the food he needed in the company stores. Food was also given to the Indians in lavish trade ceremonies, and frequently without any ceremony at all in times of distress, for the trader, like the Indian, quickly learned to accommodate the needs and expectations of his trading partner in the vital business of provisioning as he did in the exchange of other commodities. When the fishery failed and the hunt was poor, oatmeal from Britain, Indian corn from Michilimackinac, or the potato crop from the traders' gardens was often as vital to the Indian enmeshed in the trade as it was to the European who conducted it.

With the major exception of pemmican, the wild foods that provisioned the fur trade were generally gathered and consumed locally. The demand for agricultural produce, in contrast, generated a widespread commerce that had far-reaching effects in Canada. It afforded a market for the colonial farmer and for the Indian agriculturalist of the Great Lakes, both of whom produced surplus foodstuffs in demand in the fur trade lands to the north. Each of these agricultural systems also sustained a large labour force upon which the fur trade of the north could draw. For both of these reasons, the fur trade spawned agricultural colonization in Canada, first in the east in New France and later in the west at Red River. For the same reasons, company agriculture everywhere preceded the settlement frontier. It was thus an incipient farming frontier beyond the permanent frontier of agricultural colonization in Canada, first in Acadia and the St Lawrence – Great Lakes lowlands, later in the west in what was to be the agricultural heartland of the new dominion, and finally in the Fraser delta and in the east coast lowland of Vancouver Island. Thus the fur trade carved out not only the political boundaries of Canada but also the agricultural areas of present-day Canada and, as Innis concluded, thereby established the basic geographical framework for subsequent economic growth in Canada: 'The economic organization of the fur trade was dependent on the Canadian Shield for a supply of furs and on the development of agriculture at convenient intervals to support the heavy cost of transportation. The economic organization of modern industrial Canada has depended on these agriculturally developed areas and more recently on the Canadian Shield. Agriculture and other lines of economic activity were started in suitable territory south of the Canadian Shield under the direction of the trade.'[34]

Much of this story, however, remains to be written. Little is known of the agriculture developed by the French traders living beyond the frontiers of permanent settlement, and still less of the demands of the fur trade for the agricultural produce of New France. The fur trade, however, remained the sole agent of economic growth in New France and, directly or indirectly, provided the only unsubsidized market for surplus agricultural production during the French regime. It thus fostered rather than inhibited the development of agriculture in the colony, a view that conflicts with earlier interpretations. In Eccles' view, for example, French colonial agriculture suffered mainly from chronic labour shortages imposed by the manpower requirements of the fur trade.[35] Innis was of the opinion that the expansion of the fur trade exacerbated this problem because 'The population of New France during the open season of navigation was increasingly engaged in carrying on the trade over longer distances to the neglect of agriculture and other phases of economic development.'[36]

If the labour demands of the fur trade retarded agricultural development, they did so only in the early years of the colony when the struggle for agricultural self-sufficiency was being waged. Otherwise, the sorry state of French-Canadian agriculture was owing to a surplus rather than to a dearth of labour which, in the face of rapid population increase and limited alternative employment, drifted into a dominantly subsistence agricultural way of life. As for the later labour requirements of the fur trade, Harris has recently concluded that: 'The fur trade's requirements for white manpower were small and relatively fixed, and as the colony grew, the trade required a steadily smaller percentage of its men. By the early eighteenth century few men living east of Trois-Rivières had ever participated in it, and in any given season no more than two percent of Canadian men were in the west.'[37] Thus, the plight of French-Canadian agriculture did not lie in any inherent conflicts with the fur trade. Rather, it was owing to the lack of external markets and to a population which, for imperial reasons, had expanded beyond both the needs of the fur trade and the agricultural system required to support it.

Similar circumstances lay behind the languishing agriculture of the Red River Colony, where a growing population and lack of economic opportunity led to the freeing of trade which broke the commercial monopoly of the Hudson's Bay Company in the West. Although this damaged the company's trade, it merely accelerated more powerful forces that had long been at work throughout the fur trade lands of the West. Of the many changes in the western interior at this time, Morton has written that: 'the decline of the fur trade was the most significant. The swarming free traders, whose activities had brought Winnipeg into being and who kept the commerce of the colony thriving, were in fact the scavengers of the trade. They were sweeping up the last remnants of the once great trade of the Winnipeg basin, the westward plains, and the Saskatchewan valley ... The trade of the great Company suffered from this competition, but its great resources of capital and skill, still fed by the vast preserves of the north and of the Mackenzie basin, little touched by the free traders, were not lightly to be overcome, and sustained it.'[38]

Of equal and related significance at this time was the decline in the ability of the land to support the Indian way of life. Just as the free traders fanning out from Red River had heralded the end of the trade in the West, so the steady drift of Indians into the Red River Settlement in search of food, shelter, and employment signalled the beginning of the end of the Indian way of life throughout the region. This was a process that was complete among the Indians of the prairie-parkland and the southern forests by 1876, by which time their old ways could no longer support them and their lands had been ceded to the Canadian government. Thus, the advent of the agricultural frontier to western Canada did not displace the Indian economically nor did it destroy his way of life. Rather, the development of agriculture in this region, as elsewhere in Canada during the fur trade period, served as a buffer between the Indian and starvation, affording him food when his lands would no longer yield and succouring him as his way of life underwent drastic and irreversible change. Finally, as the fur trade retreated into the north, it was increasingly sustained by the products of the expanding agriculture of the south.

As we have seen, Heidenreich and Trigger have elucidated the nature of Huron agriculture and its significance in the changing relations between Europeans and Indians during the first half of the seventeenth century. Elsewhere, I have investigated the agriculture and resource assessments of the Hudson's Bay Company during its confinement to the shores of Hudson Bay (1670-1774).[39] Kaye has described company, colonial, and Indian agriculture and the complex interrelations among them in the northwest between 1774 and 1830.[40] In what is undoubtedly the most important published work on company agriculture, Gibson has elucidated the symbiotic relation that developed between agriculture and the fur trade west of the Rocky Mountains; he has also analysed the overall provision requirements of the Russian-American trade as well as the commerce in agricultural foodstuffs that ensued between the Hudson's Bay Company and the Russian-American Company.[41]

Although large gaps exist and many themes remain to be explored, from these and related studies it has become increasingly apparent that there were few aspects of the fur trade in which agriculture was not involved, just as there were few areas of Canada in which fur trade agriculture was not the pioneer form of agriculture. Agricultural production for the fur trade involved not only the fur traders themselves but also at different times French, British, and even American agricultural settlers. In the seventeenth and eighteenth centuries, large areas of the fur trade were also dependent upon Indian agriculture so that, as a supporting enterprise of the trade, agriculture spawned a complex set of relations that directly involved Indians, fur traders, and settlers and indirectly soldiers, missionaries, and colonial officials. Thus the agricultural component of the fur trade affords not only another perspective from which the long and varied history of the trade can be studied but also a distinct vantage point from which to view the colonial societies to which it was linked and, more especially, the Indian upon whom the fur trade was entirely dependent.

I am indebted to Dr Barry Kaye, Department of Geography, University of Manitoba, for freely given assistance and much valued advice in the course of writing this paper. I would also like to acknowledge the permission of the Hudson's Bay Company to consult and quote from its archives.

NOTES AND REFERENCES

1 Easterbrook 'Recent Contributions to Economic History: Canada' 267
2 Fowke *Canadian Agricultural Policy, The Historical Patterns*
3 Jones, in his *History of Agriculture in Ontario, 1663–1880*, has accorded cursory recognition to the role of the fur trade market in initiating commercial agriculture in southern Ontario but, with the major exception of H.A. Innis, Canadian economic historians have either ignored or deemed inconsequential agriculture as a supporting enterprise of the fur trade. See, for example, Easterbrook 'Recent Contributions' 266–7. Most histories of the Canadian fur trade acknowledge that the fur traders planted gardens and kept a few livestock, but this aspect of the trade has not been researched systematically. See Morton *A History of the Canadian West to 1870–71*; Rich *The Hudson's Bay Company, 1670–1870*; Rich *The Fur Trade and the Northwest to 1857*; Phillips *The Fur Trade*; Davidson *The North West Company*. It should be noted that the relations between agriculture and the fur trade in other areas have received much closer scrutiny. Gibson, for example, has examined agriculture as part

of the general problem of provisioning the Russian fur trade (*Feeding the Russian Fur Trade*), and Wishart has studied agriculture and its role at the American trading posts on the upper Missouri ('Agriculture at the Trading Posts on the Upper Missouri Prior to 1843').

4 Galbraith *The Hudson's Bay Company as an Imperial Factor, 1821–69*
5 Turner '*The Significance of the Frontier in American History*'
6 Innis *The Fur Trade in Canada, An Introduction to Canadian Economic History* 389
7 See Morton's 'The Red River Parish: Its Place in the Development of Manitoba', his 'Agriculture in the Red River Colony,' his 'Introduction' in E.E. Rich ed *London Correspondence Inward from Eden Colvile, 1849*, and his *Manitoba, A History*.
8 Morton *Manitoba* 41
9 For an excellent account of early French attempts at agriculture, see Saunders 'The First Introduction of European Plants and Animals into Canada.'
10 Wessel 'Agriculture, Indians, and American History'
11 Innis *Fur Trade* 26
12 Heidenreich *Huronia, A History and Geography of the Huron Indians 1600–1650*
13 Trigger *The Huron, Farmers of the North* and *The Children of Aataentsic: A History of the Huron People to 1660*
14 Perrot in E.H. Blair ed *The Indian Tribes of the Upper Mississippi Valley and the Region of the Great Lakes* I 102
15 Will and Hyde *Corn Among the Indians of the Upper Missouri* 172, 180
16 Aulneau in Thwaites ed *The Jesuit Relations and Allied Documents* LXVIII 293
17 Sagard in Wrong ed *The Long Journey to the Country of the Hurons* 50
18 Trigger *Children* I 359
19 Le Jeune in Thwaites ed *Jesuit Relations* VI 273
20 Champlain in *The Works of Samuel de Champlain* ed Biggar V 314, VI 43–4
21 Snow 'Abenaki Fur Trade in the Sixteenth Century' 7–9
22 Lalemant in Thwaites ed *Jesuit Relations* IV 207; Biard in ibid III 69
23 Bailey *The Conflict of European and Eastern Algonkian Cultures 1504–1700* 56–9
24 Martin 'Ethnohistory: A Better Way to Write Indian History' 49
25 Wessel 'Agriculture' 12
26 Champlain *Works* IV 280–1
27 Dablon in Thwaites ed *Jesuit Relations* LIV 195, and 165, 167
28 Henry *Travels and Adventures in Canada and the Indian Territories Between the Years 1760 and 1776* 122
29 The only publication on Ojibwa agriculture is Moodie and Kaye 'The Northern Limit of Indian Agriculture in North America.' The discussion that follows is based upon both this paper and more recent unpublished research by the authors.

30 Schoolcraft in Mason ed *Expedition to Lake Itasca* 21
31 HBCA B 105/e/2, 3, Lac la Pluie report on district
32 Minnesota Historical Society, St Paul, Division of Archives and Manuscripts: Extracts from Sela G. Wright's Sketch of the Red Lake Mission, 26 Jan. 1852, in Mss Relating to Northwest Missions, Grace Lee Nute, compiler; and J.P. Bardwell to the American Missionary Association [Red Lake], August 1851
33 Morton *Manitoba* 27n
34 Innis *Fur Trade* 398
35 Eccles *The Canadian Frontier 1534–1760* 88
36 Innis *Fur Trade* 390
37 Harris and Guelke 'Land and Society in Canada and South Africa' 141
38 Morton *Manitoba* 104
39 Moodie 'An Historical Geography of Agricultural Patterns and Resource Appraisals in Rupert's Land 1670–1774'
40 Kaye 'The Historical Geography of Agriculture and Agricultural Settlement in the Canadian Northwest 1774–ca. 1830'
41 Gibson 'Food for the Fur Traders: The First Farmers in the Pacific Northwest, 1805–1846' 18–30; Gibson *Imperial Russia in Frontier America*

Innis, the Fur Trade, and Modern Economic Problems

IRENE M. SPRY

Harold Adams Innis wrote his great book, *The Fur Trade in Canada*, fifty years ago. Since then much new work on the fur trade has been done[1] but Innis' pioneer analysis remains of basic importance, not only in relation to the fur trade itself, but for the light it throws on many current social and economic problems. This paper explores the relevance of Innis' study to some major issues faced by Canada today. Limits of space make it impossible to discuss its wider implications in other parts of the world and especially in the development of Third World countries.[2]

Innis showed that much that is characteristic of Canadian development may be traced back to the fur trade. He demonstrated that, contrary to a common contention,[3] Canada 'emerged not in spite of Geography but because of it. The significance of the fur trade consisted in its determination of the geographic framework' of the country. 'By 1821 the Northwest Company had built up an organization which extended from the Atlantic to the Pacific. The foundations of the present Dominion of Canada had been securely laid.' Innis wrote '"The lords of the lakes and forests have passed away" but their work will endure in the boundaries of the Dominion of Canada and in Canadian institutional life.'[4]

The position of the St Lawrence, with its waterway to the West, made it the basis of Canadian unity. The fur trade (before 1821) had created and the wheat economy after 1896 had confirmed the east-west axis of the Canadian economy, but already in the 1930s Innis foresaw that, with control by the St Lawrence waterway 'slightly but definitely on the ebb,' the second unity of Canada, based on wheat, was 'beginning to drift in the direction of the first' when in 1821 the St Lawrence lost the fur trade to Hudson Bay. The exploitation of new resources, forests, and minerals fractured the east-west link and developed north-south ties that have increased regional dislocations, as well as Canadian dependence on the United States. The growth of regionalism, as Innis pointed out, has been paralleled by the 'increasing strength of the provinces in contrast to the Dominion.'[5]

Innis saw, also, that 'We have not yet realized that the Indian and his culture were fundamental to the growth of Canadian institutions.' Like later students of the fur trade, he was deeply impressed by the culture shock created by the encounter of European civilization and technology with the civilization of the native peoples of the country that is now Canada. He wrote: 'The history of the fur trade is the history of contact between two civilizations, the European and the North American ... The supply of European goods, the product of a more advanced and specialized technology, enabled the Indians to gain a livelihood more easily.' The technical superiority of firearms over bows and arrows, of steel tools and weapons over bone and flint implements, of kettles over bark containers was so great as to give rise to an insistent demand for them. The price that the native peoples paid for them was not just furs; it was the loss of their independence and their own way of life and, indeed, in many cases, of life itself. 'The new technology with its radical innovations brought about such a rapid shift in the prevailing Indian culture as to lead to wholesale destruction of the peoples concerned by warfare and disease.' The 'rapid destruction of the food supply and the revolution in the methods of living accompanied by the increasing attention to the fur trade ... disturbed the balance which had grown up previous to the coming of the European.'[6]

This disruptive contact of unlike civilizations is not yet at an end. Resistance by native peoples to the James Bay project and to the Mackenzie Valley Pipeline are dramatic examples of the continued disturbances engendered by the impact of a technologically sophisticated culture on simpler cultures based on a balance between the people of the country and its living, renewable resources. Many submissions to the Berger Inquiry illustrate the problem in its modern aspect. Judge Berger said: 'We look upon the north as our last frontier. It is natural for us to think of developing the north, of subduing the land, populating it with people from southern Canada, and extracting its resources to fuel Canada's industry and heat our homes. Our whole inclination is to think in terms of expanding our industrial machine to the limit of our country's frontiers. But the native people are saying to us, why do you say the north is your last frontier? Why should you develop it? They feel it is their homeland, that they should determine what is to happen there.'[7] He gave to his report the title *Northern Frontier, Northern Homeland*. 'Pipelines are only the latest assault on the north, following the explorers, whalers, fur traders, white trappers, missionaries, highway-builders, DEW-line workers, gold diggers, assorted anthropologists, geologists, and archeologists, as well as a few hippies and intrepid tourists.'[8]

The wrenching effect on native societies that Innis described continues. Although the Indian was an essential partner in the fur trade, this did not save him or his culture. In modern clashes of sophisticated and simple technology, and the accompanying struggle between centralized authority and local, egalitarian self-determination, there is no such ameliorating partnership; massive exploitation by outside interests of mineral resources in lands long occupied by Indian and Inuit imposes a 'sudden change of cultural traits' which, as Innis observed in relation to European newcomers, 'can be made only with great difficulty ... Depreciation of the social heritage is serious.'[9]

Loss of independence[10] by the local population is the counterpart of domination by a metropolis whose expansive energy and enterprise gave rise in the first place to the encounter of cultures. 'The fur trade was necessarily carried on through the production of manufactured commodities in Europe and the transportation of those commodities to native populations who demanded them to an increasing extent as older cultural traits disappeared.' 'The organization [of the fur trade] never took an independent position from the old world such as an organization with diversified economic growth could afford. Canada remained in the first instance subordinate to France and in the second place subordinate to Great Britain chiefly through the importance of the fur trade and its weak economic development.'[11]

The economic pattern of dependence on a metropolis has recurred throughout Canadian history in the development and displacement of successive staple exports. His study of the fur trade gave Innis the key to this aspect of Canadian development: 'The economic history of Canada has been dominated by the discrepancy between the center and the margin of western civilization.'[12] The industrialization of Great Britain in the nineteenth century and of the United States in the twentieth century has involved Canada as a hinterland supplying new staple products, just as New France was earlier involved in supplying *castor gras* and *castor sec* to old France. 'Canada moved from colony to nation to colony' with the influx of American capital.[13]

Lumber, wheat, pulp and paper, and minerals have, in turn, succeeded fur as staple exports linking the Canadian economy to external metropolitan centres to whose economic fortunes and policies the Canadian economy has been inescapably tied. The dependence of the Indians on the fur trade has been followed by dependence of Canadians of every type of ancestry on the activities of foreign enterprise, the supply of foreign capital, the demands of foreign markets, and imports of foreign products. 'Energy has been directed toward the exploitation of staple products and the tendency has been cumulative ... Population was involved directly in the production of the staple and indirectly in the production of facilities promoting production'. Agriculture, industry, transportation, trade, finance, and governmental activities tend to become subordinate to the production of the staple for a more highly specialized manufacturing community.'[14] In the search for profit-making opportunities and to supply the needs of their people and of their home industries, entrepreneurs in France, Britain, and the United States have provided capital and advanced technology to develop production in Canada of the raw material and foodstuffs they needed. Canada's role, like that of the Indian fur trappers and middlemen, has been largely to assist in the massive exploitation of the country's virgin resources, extracting, collecting, and bringing out produce in demand in the metropolitan market.

For each staple in turn the organization required to get production going, on a remote frontier, to mobilize the product, and to transport it over immense distances to the metropolitan market had to be highly specialized and complex. That specialized and complex organization itself became an obstacle to flexible adjustment when conditions changed.

As the fur trade moved from the sea coast and the St Lawrence estuary further and further inland, meetings of Indians with sea-faring ships gave way to trade to the interior organized and carried on by Europeans in place of Indian middlemen. Synchronized meetings and exchanges of trade goods and furs and the establishment of provision posts made it possible for the trade to move westward and, eventually, to penetrate to the far northwest. The French trade was supported by a military organization. When this collapsed, the 'institutional organization of the colony adapted to the characteristics of the trade failed to adjust itself with sufficient rapidity to the demands of a diversified economic growth essential to independent survival.'[15]

On the foundations the French had laid, their successors built a canoe route from Lachine to the mouth of the Columbia River, with a northward feeder that tapped the resources of the Mackenzie River country and northern British Columbia. The North West Company emerged as an organization superbly efficient in opening up new sources of supply in more and more remote, as yet unexploited, regions. When the Nor' Westers reached the limits of new territory, when there were no more frontiers to be explored, their organization, so brilliantly successful in expansion, found it impossible to adjust to stability.[16]

The Nor'Westers' great rival, the Hudson's Bay Company, had, in its first hundred years, organized an efficient system of trade based on Indian middlemen bringing pelts down to the bay and taking back trade goods to the inland country from which came the supplies of fur. Challenged first by the French coureurs de bois and later by the Nor'Westers, the Honourable Company was forced to push inland to face the competition in the Indian country, taking over the responsibilities of the Indian middlemen. 'In its expansion to the interior the Hudson's Bay Company suffered materially through the rigidity of the organization which had been adapted to Hudson Bay.' 'The technique of conducting the trade under such conditions as the Bay imposed had been elaborately worked out, and the limitations of this technique for the conduct of the trade in the interior were striking.' After reorganization, however, "the growing effectiveness of the Hudson's Bay Company's competition ... and the inability of the Northwest Company to adapt its organization to permanent conditions and its consequent demand for new territory led to increased hostility between the two Companies.'[17]

The result in 1821 was the union of the two companies. Under the ruthless drive of 'the little emperor,' Sir George Simpson, the consolidated company forged from the legacies of the Northwest Company and the old Hudson's Bay Company a still more effectively integrated system of trading posts, transportation, and provisioning services, supplementing canoe traffic with brigades of York boats, Columbia boats,[18] Red River carts, and, eventually, with steam boats on Red River, Lake Winnipeg, and the Saskatchewan.

The Sayer[19] trial of 1849 established that 'le commerce est libre!' Thereafter, the company ceased to attempt to enforce its charter rights, and petty traders, from Red River Settlement and elsewhere, increasingly eroded its monopoly position. After the acquisition of its stock in 1863 by the International Financial Society, and especially after the sale of its lands and privileges in 1869, fundamental reorganization became necessary once again to provide for the company's new interests in real estate and in a general retail business, and also to make it possible for the fur trade to survive under the new conditions of competition.

At each of these turning points in the history of the fur trade the danger became apparent of dependence on an elaborate and highly expensive organization focused on a single, dominant economic activity. Extreme difficulty was experienced in readjusting that organization to a drastic change in the economic situation.

The problem has been a recurrent one in Canada's history: The more elaborate and complex the institutions and infrastructures developed to facilitate and improve the efficiency of a great staple trade, the greater is the difficulty of reconstruction to allow the economy to adjust to any fundamental change in conditions. This is the 'staple trap' so ably analysed by Mel Watkins in relation to problems of economic development.[20] The system of transportation and finance, supply and marketing institutions built up in relation to the expanding wheat economy of the first three decades of this century faced this familiar crisis in the drought and depression of the 'thirties.[21] Perhaps it is this type of crisis that is at the root of the current troubles of the nickel and other mining industries. Indeed, it is disturbingly possible that the present malaise of the Canadian economy as a whole may arise from a need to achieve a fundamental change in pattern from dependence on massive exports of raw products to a more diversified type of economy. Any such readjustment cannot help but be immensely difficult, demanding, as it does, new ideas, new institutions, and a new alignment of people and of property rights.

The Fur Trade in Canada made abundantly apparent the extreme vulnerability of an economy dependent on a single, dominant staple export. The originator of the idea of staple exports, an American, Guy S. Callender, laid stress in his *Selections from the Economic History of the United States, 1765–1860* on the importance of the development of a staple export to make possible economic growth and prosperity in any colony.[22] In like vein, the late W.A. Mackintosh wrote: 'The prime requisite of colonial prosperity is the colonial staple. Other factors connected with the staple industry may turn it to advantage or disadvantage, but the staple itself is the basis of prosperity.'[23] Innis was led by his study of the fur trade and subsequent study of the wheat economy, the pulp and paper industry, and mining, rather to emphasize the dangers of concentration on one dominant export, especially one derived from the exploitation of virgin natural resources. His studies gave him a lively awareness of the problems that resulted from the 'close dependence of the colony on the fur trade' during the French régime,[24] as well as in later stages of development.

These problems included the uncertain and uncontrollable fluctuations in the yield of a product dependent on nature-given stocks of a resource. The exhaustion of easily accessible stocks compelled a search for new sources of supply. The discovery of a new source released a sudden upsurge in the flow of furs until, in its turn, it was worked out, necessitating exploration yet further afield for as yet untapped new resources. To bring into production each progressively more distant source of supply meant progressively heavier transportation costs and capital expenditures without providing a lasting solution to the problem of procuring stable and dependable supplies.

This pattern of discovery, rapid exploitation, and exhaustion of natural stocks[25] has been repeated in other staples that have successively dominated Canada's economic fortunes. It is still evident in Canada's mineral industry with its expansion into frontier areas, experimental technology, and extraction of low-grade deposits, all entailing heavy capital expenditures and increasing vulnerability in an uncertain world market, as well as an ultimate limit to the possibility of indefinitely continuing expansion of discovery of new resources.

To limitations of and fluctuations in supplies are added limits to and fluctuations in the market to be supplied. Innis traced market difficulties in the fur trade, from the inability in the seventeenth century of the French hat-makers to absorb increasing quantities of *castor sec*, to the displacement in the mid–nineteenth century of beaver hats by silk hats. Market difficulties have at times been severe in each of the staple exports that have followed the fur trade, as a result of changes in taste, changes in technology, the appearance of competing sources of supply, and the contraction of demand in periods of depression. The present difficulties of Sudbury and Thompson have much in common with difficulties experienced in the fur trade. Changes in technology have made possible the opening up of competing laterite deposits of nickel, while future possibilities include the substitution of nickel from manganese nodules from the bed of the ocean for nickel recovered from land mines.[26]

The impact of market limitations and market fluctuations is intensified, just as it was in the fur trade, as a result of the dependence of our successive basic staples on foreign capital and foreign enterprise. From its beginnings, the fur trade in Canada was dependent on credit provided by merchants in France and later in Britain. Progressively heavier capital requirements were met by an extension of commercial credit and by the proprietors of stock in the Hudson's Bay Company. Innis quotes, for instance, a letter dated 1790 from John Inglis in London: 'the merchants in this country and in Canada, who are engaged in this adventurous

Traffick, have generally a property embarked, and chiefly in the Indian Country equal to two years returns, and there is besides fixed property of considerable value at the Posts.' Flexibility was maintained by the principle of partnership which 'characterised the history of the Northwest Company.' This principle 'was to persist as the dominant type of organization of the fur trade practically until the end of the nineteenth century. It was the device with which the trade could be prosecuted with greatest effectiveness over great distances in which the central authority could exercise no direct control over the individual trader. On the other hand amalgamation marked in a definite way the beginning of control exercised by capital interests with headquarters in London.'[27]

Inflows of foreign capital and foreign enterprise have been a persistent characteristic of the Canadian economy and one that, with industrialization and increasing capital intensity, has intensified the centralization of control in foreign hands. Since the Second World War the influx of foreign capital and the related increase of foreign control has assumed such proportions that public concern has found expression in a series of government inquiries (*Watkins Report*, 1968; *Wahn Report*, 1970; *Gray Report*, 1971); in the disclosure requirements of the Corporations and Labour Unions Returns Act (CALURA) of 1962; and in the creation of the Foreign Investment Review Agency in 1974.

Whether foreign capital and enterprise are beneficial or detrimental to the Canadian economy is a matter of continuing controversy. It seems clear at least that ultimately they exacerbate balance of payments difficulties inherent in dependence on natural resource–based staple exports. Noting that the 'highly developed militaristic organization in erecting fortified posts and in carrying on effective campaigns' in support of centralized monopoly control of the fur trade imposed heavy drains 'on the resources of the home government, and more especially on the resources of the colony,' Innis said that this had 'been brought out very clearly' by Adam Shortt's work on currency, finance, and exchanges in the French period.[28] Such 'drains' continue today. 'During 1974 the deficit on interest and dividends, at $1,555 million, was the single largest component of the deficit on non-merchandise transactions ... Payments of interest and dividends on direct investment advanced by 31% to $1,192 million in 1974 following an increase of 32% the previous year. Income payments on portfolio investment ... rose by 9% to $1,243 million for 1974.' By 1977 the deficit had risen to $3,413 million.[29]

The outflow of fur trade earnings to foreign creditors, merchants, and monopolists during the French regime was paralleled by the outflow (however intermittent) of profits to the proprietors of the Hudson's Bay Company. We owe to Innis' study of the fur trade a pioneer analysis of the structure and policy of this three-hundred-year-old multi-national – surely the doyen of all multi-nationals in existence today. Innis showed how the ingenious combination of individual initiative and independence on the trading frontier with centralized co-ordination, that had characterized the North West Company and the Hudson's Bay Company during the period of desperate competition between them, gave way to an increasing concentration of authority in the period of monopoly that followed the merger of 1821. The 'effectiveness with which the trading territory was brought under the control of the central authorities was the cause of dissatisfaction among the partners of the interior who had been accustomed to Northwest Company methods,' but the trend to centralization continued.

After the shares of the company were acquired in 1863 by the International Financial Society and the company had in 1869 surrendered its Charter privileges and lands (without consultation with or warning to the company's officers in the interior), the company was reorganized in relation to its new interests in real estate and in a general retail business. In 1871 a new deed poll was arranged with the commissioned officers, but in 1893 this was acquired by the home board. 'The disappearance of the partnership arrangements in the Deed Poll contributed to the general decline of initiative in the service.' Tightening control from the central headquarters was made more effective by the spread of the price system and changes in accounting.[30] The pattern of corporate centralization had developed in relation to changing conditions in the trade along lines that today have become increasingly familiar with the emergence of corporate complexes organized for the exploitation of forest and mineral resources in Canada and elsewhere in the world.

Modern multi-national corporations, like the old Hudson's Bay Company, are, as a *Financial Post* study notes, distinguished, 'thanks to jet transport, computers, and telecommunications,' by 'the capacity centrally to direct a scattered empire according to long-range plans.' Perhaps, as Daniel P. Moynihan, former us ambassador to the United Nations, is reported to have said, 'The multinational company is conceivably the most creative institution of our civilization ... the most effective wealth producer ever devised.'[31] Perhaps, however, such giant corporate complexes, Canadian as well as foreign, 'these self-determining, self-propelling, perpetual money-making machines,' are a challenge to political democracy, as Eric Kierans has recently urged. Such a challenge can be met only through politics which need 'a strong defence against those who would seek to substitute their aims and values for the wider cultural, social, spiritual and economic aspirations that define the character and nature of each of us.'[32]

Whichever of these views may be valid, there can be no doubt about the importance of the multi-national corporation in the 1970s. Innis' analysis of the development of the Hudson's Bay Company gives useful insights into the emergence of the corporate complexes that dominate today's industrial scene.

The key to understanding these corporate giants, as Innis stated, is the effect of the cost structure on the pattern of competition and combination: 'Large overhead costs in this industry [the fur trade], as in other industries, involved severe competition in the beginning and a combination in the end.'[33]

The term 'overhead costs,' which Innis uses so often in analysing the development of the fur trade, covers a complex set of problems which give rise to 'rigidities' in supply and demand that engender situations of disequilibrium and instability. From 1610, when 'Champlain complained that he had taken the most active part in the fight with the Iroquois but that his competitors got most of the furs,'[34] Innis traced the imperatives of the cost structure of the trade in shaping competitive pressures and the resulting responses of combination and monopoly.

European merchants seeking a profit from the fur trade had to commit themselves to what was for the time a heavy expenditure on trade goods and their shipment across the Atlantic. Once the kettles, knives, blankets, and guns were at the rendezvous at Tadoussac or Hochelaga, that expenditure was irrevocable. The Indians bringng down peltries from the interior faced the same problem. Time and exhausting effort had to be spent irreversibly on the long and difficult journey to the rendezvous. 'It was unprofitable for either party to return with the goods brought.' The supply of both trade goods and furs at the rendezvous was, in technical terms, absolutely inelastic. Competition on either side was ruinous. Already in 1611 at Tadoussac the Indians wanted to wait until several ships had arrived in order to get the European wares more cheaply. Co-operation, accordingly, gradually developed among the French traders, providing in 1613 a basis for monopoly control in what Innis describes as the first trust in North America. He added that 'the honour of being the first successful trust promoter must be given to Champlain.' Monopoly control made it possible to cut down expenditure on transportation, with only two ships bringing out trade goods, according to a report in 1626, in contrast to as many as twenty in earlier years. On the other hand, heavy costs were involved in maintaining the monopoly against would-be competitors attracted by the improved profits.[35] This is a text book case illustrating modern monopoly theory and barriers to entry into a market!

The trade in furs penetrated progressively further into the interior in response to the combined pressures of the exhaustion of accessible beaver stocks and the development of competition from the south, from the Dutch and later the English through Iroquois middlemen, and from the north, after the founding of the Hudson's Bay Company. As the distances covered lengthened, the time span between the initial outlays on goods, transport, and provisions and the realization of returns grew ever greater. Expenditures on defence, with a cordon of military posts, became necessary. The heavy cost of the long journey into the interior became heavier as the journey grew longer still. There was no way of adjusting that cost to fluctuating returns, or of using the unused capacity, on the return trip downstream with a light cargo of furs, of the canoes and voyageurs that had been needed to haul upstream the heavy cargo of trade goods for the pays d'en haut. Since the entire journey had to be made, if it was made at all, there was great pressure to spread the indivisible cost over the largest possible volume of pelts. In addition, inland posts had to be maintained, especially in the period of feverish competition. They were subject to fluctuations of activity with peaks of 'busy-ness' when Indians came in to trade and slack intervals between times. Dwindling fur resources, combined with competition, forced the traders to search for untapped sources of fur and of Indian hunters. The initial cost of exploration was, again, an irreversible and indivisible commitment of funds on a scale which created further pressures for expansion of the trade.

After 1763 the 'pedlars from Canada' took over the system of trade, transportation, and provisioning that the French had established. With that system, they inherited the whole pattern of inflexible costs and fluctuating, uncertain, and uncontrollable trade returns. The ruinous results of competition became increasingly clear. Despite recurrent outbreaks of new competition, notably in the case of the xy Company, the North West Company eventually solved the problem of co-ordination among traders from the St Lawrence. The problems inherent in competition persisted, however, in the opposition of American traders to the south and the Hudson's Bay Company to the north. Expansion by the Nor'Westers provoked defensive expansion by their rivals. As the duel between the North West Company and the Hudson's Bay Company grew more intense, costs increased still further with duplication of trading posts and proliferation of personnel to withstand the opposition. The literally cut-throat competition between the giant duopolists became intolerable and the two companies merged in 1821. The combined company enjoyed a short period of effective monopoly in which the advantages of monopoly control were evident in centralized planning of operations, whittling down of costs, and programs of conservation and rehabilitation of depleted fur resources. It also became apparent that there were dangers in loss of flexibility and of independent initiative in the interior as authority became increasingly centralized.

The consolidated company made tremendous efforts to defend the monopoly rights bestowed by the Charter of 1670 in Rupert's Land and by licence in the Indian Territories beyond Rupert's Land. It negotiated agreements with the American Fur Company in the Rainy River district. Elsewhere, notably in the Snake River country west of the Rocky Mountains, it sought to trap out the beaver, creating a 'fur desert' which would insulate richer territory in the north from intrusive competitors. Inevitably, as settlement increased and steamboats and then railroads opened up the country, the company's monopoly position grew weaker. It withdrew further into the north, but, as transport facilities improved still further, it entered a period in which it faced, even in the far north, challenges from 'large competitive organizations,' such as the Lamson-Hubbard Company.[36]

The pattern of competition which Innis traced was very different from the flexible, atomistic competition envisaged in the economic theorist's model of perfect competition. 'Competition in western Canada from the French and later the Anglo-American merchants and the North West Company from the St Lawrence with the Hudson's Bay Company from Hudson Bay assumed an intense form, characteristic of duopoly, and led to monopoly in 1821.'[37] In periods of competition heavy capital requirements combined with inflexibilities of cost and capacity, as well as uncertainties of yields and of market outlets, resulted in an oligopolistic market structure dominated by concern with the activities of the opposition and offensive and defensive measures. Defensive measures included persistent efforts to attach Indians to the company concerned, not only by better terms of trade and provision of goods of the type and quality that the Indians wanted,[38] but also by means of alliances and military and other support, by 'connubial alliances' which, Sir George Simpson wrote, 'are the best security we can have of the good will of the natives,'[39] by appropriate rituals and gift giving, and by 'long experience in dealing with native populations, knowledge of Indian economy and Indian life' which 'were of crucial importance in checking outside competition.'[40] Such measures are akin to those adopted by modern corporations in their efforts to build up customer loyalty.

The history of the fur trade convinced Innis that such 'imperfect competition' was more likely to generate violent disequilibrium situations than the smooth adjustment of demand to supply in the kind of equilibrium that is possible only in markets in which there are many small sellers and buyers dealing in a homogeneous product and using mobile resources easily transferred in minute increments from one market to another. He thought it was necessary to modify equilibrium analysis, to turn to the study of 'the meeting of economic masses' and monopoly theory. 'The study of the Canadian economy becomes of crucial significance to an understanding of cyclical and secular disturbances not only within Canada but without. In a sense, the economics of frontier countries are storm centres to the modern international economy.'[41]

Innis' later studies made abundantly apparent the increasing importance of these problems in an industrialized economy in which massive capital is tied up, not merely for two or three or even seven years, but for decades. The problems of rigid costs and capacities combined with great uncertainty which Innis identified in the fur trade have multiplied and intensified with the expansion and deepening of industrialization and an increasingly complex and sophisticated technology. No wonder, then, that the tendencies to combination and centralization of control which Innis found at work in the fur trade have become increasingly urgent today.

His second great study of a staple export industry, *The Cod Fisheries*, led Innis to contrast the flexibility and decentralizing effect of small units of investment and mobile capital equipment characteristic of the fishing industry in its commercial phase with the cost and market structure of the fur trade. The dispersed and atomistic flexibility of the fishing industry 'made for decentralization. Unity of structure in the economic organization of the St. Lawrence was in strong contrast with the lack of unity in the fishing regions.' Moreover, 'competition between small units, together with flexibility of organization, weakened government control.'[42] This was in sharp contrast to the fur trade in which the 'tendency toward centralization was responsible for the development of paternalistic government' during the French régime,[43] just as in later stages of Canada's development the 'key position of the St. Lawrence necessitated dependence on government support.' 'Government ownership in Canada has

assumed a crucial position and has developed as a result of strong underlying forces with a drift toward economic planning.'[44] This was one reason
for Innis' plea for political economy instead of economics.

Innis complained that 'the textbooks of the United States and England
pay little attention to the problems of conservation and of government
ownership which are of foremost importance in a new country such as
Canada.' His work on the fur trade had shown him how important was the
problem of the progressive exhaustion of virgin stocks of natural resources. He followed this problem up through the history of successive
staples: 'Concentration on staples involved exhaustion of resources, increasing costs of transportation, and shifts to new staples.' Exhaustion sets
limits to growth based on each successive type of raw material and the
system of transportation, finance, and related institutions developed to
make possible its exploitation. Already in 1934 Innis wrote: 'The last
regions of expansion have been staked,'[45] a statement which has a familiar
ring today.

Not only those concerned with conservation but also students of Marx
have found Innis' fur trade studies of interest in giving clues to possible
solutions of some unresolved problems, notably Danny Drache in two
papers: 'Canadian capitalism: Sticking with staples' and 'Rediscovering
Canadian political economy'; Russell Rothney's study of mercantile capital and the people of the Hudson Bay basin; and Ian Parker's 'Harold
Innis, Karl Marx and Canadian Political Economy.' William Christian has
shown the importance of Innis as a political theorist. 'His studies of the fur
trade and the cod fisheries were manifestations of Innis's attempt to
transcend the intellectual biases of training and membership in distinct
professional groups.' 'He drew his theory from the facts that he studied;
but there was always an interpenetration of facts and theory, each refining
and modifying the other.' 'Innis's concern for the condition of Western
civilization' reached back to his concern with the impact of European and
Indian civilizations on each other in the fur trade. Preoccupied at the
outset of his career with Canada and with its special problems, he went on
to examine the rise and fall of civilizations and their dependence on
means of communication, a dependence which had impressed him in his
study of the fur trade. No optimist, Innis extended his work on the fur
trade to later phases of Canadian development during the gloomy period
of depression in the 1930s when the weaknesses of an economy dependent on a dominant staple export were sharply emphasized. Nonetheless,
he continued to hope that human creativity would find solutions for

Canada's – and, indeed, for the world's – pressing problems. As William Christian points out, 'his intense faith in human creativity and the power of thought to transcend circumstances' had already been suggested in his 'admiration for the adaptability of the fur traders in the woods beyond the control of their monopolist would-be directors.'[46]

Innis died a quarter of a century ago. This is therefore an especially suitable time and occasion to look back at his work on the fur trade in Canada, the foundation on which he built his remarkable and highly original contribution to our understanding of some of the problems that beset the world we live in and threaten the survival of the civilization which is our heritage.

NOTES AND REFERENCES

1 Recent work includes Ray *Indians in the Fur Trade* and Ray and Freeman '*Give Us Good Measure.*'
2 For example, the important role of staple exports in the economic history of the United States is made clear in North *The Economic Growth of the United States, 1790–1860*. There is much discussion in the literature of current development of staple exports and the attendant problems. Examples drawn to my attention by my colleague, Otto Wadsted, include: Baldwin 'Export Technology and Development from a Subsistence Level'; De Bulhöes 'Agriculture and Economic Development'; Hla Myint 'The Gains from International Trade and the Backward Countries'; Nurkse *Equilibrium and Growth in the World Economy* especially essay 7: 'International Investment Today in the Light of Nineteenth Century Experience' originally published in *The Economic Journal* Dec. 1954; Prebisch *Towards a New Trade Policy for Development*. Specific reference is made to Innis' work by Higgins *Economic Development: Problems, Principles, and Policies* 176 and Kindleberger *International Economics* ch. 5 'Trade and Growth in Developing Countries'; ch. 21 on direct investment is also relevant.
3 For example: 'Canada is a nation created in defiance of geography'; Mackintosh 'Economic Factors in Canadian History,' reprinted in Easterbrook and Watkins *Approaches to Canadian Economic History* 1–15. The quotation is from p. 15 of the reprinted source.
4 Innis *Fur Trade* 265, 397
5 Innis and Innis *Essays in Canadian Economic History* 74
6 Innis *Fur Trade* 392, 397. In contrast, the paper by Morantz in this volume suggests that in the James Bay area the fur trade had not produced any violent disturbance. Similarly, Fisher's *Contact and Conflict: Indian-European Relations*

in British Columbia, 1774–1890 shows the fur trade brought only minimal cultural change to the Indians.

7 A lecture at Queen's University given in Nov. 1975, quoted in O'Malley *The Past and Future Land: An Account of the Berger Inquiry into the Mackenzie Valley Pipeline* 7

8 O'Malley *Past and Future Land* 13

9 Innis *Fur Trade* 386

10 That the metropolitan centre also becomes to some extent reciprocally dependent on the population of the hinterland does not reduce the importance of the new dependence of the hinterland population. 'Those who take advantage of the market adapt to it, and finally become its creatures, under its sovereignty and incapable of separation' (Afriat 'The Collective Optimum').

11 Innis *Fur Trade* 118, 122–3

12 Ibid 388

13 Innis *Essays* 405

14 Innis *Fur Trade* 388

15 Ibid 115

16 Ibid 262–5

17 Ibid 158, 159, 265

18 For the importance of the Columbia boats, see Cullen's paper in this volume.

19 Guillaume Sayer was the son of John Sayer (who wrote the supposed O'Connor Journal). In a personal communication, M. Lionel Dorge, of La Société historique de Saint-Boniface, very kindly, in answer to my query at the fur trade conference, sent me a transcript from Guillaume Sayer's dossier and a xerox of 'l'acte de mariage' of Guillaume (sometimes known as Pierre-Guillaume) Sayer to Josephte Frobisher, 2 March 1835, at Saint-François Xavier. This identifies his father as 'John Serre.' As M. Dorge points out, the name 'Sayer' (pronounced 'Sair') has been spelled phonetically by the curé who recorded the marriage.

20 Watkins 'A Staple Theory of Economic Growth,' reprinted in Easterbrook and Watkins *Approaches* 49–73

21 Innis *Essays* 263–4

22 Callender *Selections from the Economic History of the United States, 1765–1860*

23 Mackintosh 'Economic Factors' 4 (citation from reprinted source)

24 Innis *Fur Trade* 63

25 The classic case of this 'boom and bust' pattern of economic expansion is the Yukon Gold Rush described by Innis in *Settlement and the Mining Frontier* 179–269.

26 The fact that the new technology and the new sources of supply are both controlled by the same multi-national corporation that owns the mines in

Sudbury and Thompson does not lessen the severity of the impact of the changes on these mining communities.

27 Innis *Fur Trade* 251–252, 283–4

28 Ibid 118; Shortt *Documents Relating to Canadian Currency, Exchange and Finance during the French Period*

29 Statistics Canada *Canada's International Investment Position, 1974* 44; Statistics Canada *Quarterly Estimates of the Canadian Balance of International Payments, Fourth Quarter, 1977* 33 (Table 1)

30 Innis *Fur Trade* 325–330, 360, 361, 366–7

31 *Financial Post* 'What exactly Is a Multinational?' 12, and 'The March of the Multinationals' 8

32 Kierans 'The Corporate Challenge to Government' 24, 26

33 Innis *Fur Trade* 29

34 Ibid

35 Ibid, 29, 31, 32

36 Ibid 362

37 Innis *Essays* 377–8

38 See Ray's paper in this volume.

39 Innis *Essays* 257

40 Innis *Fur Trade* 118

41 Innis *Essays* 130, 270, 272, 382

42 Innis *The Cod Fisheries: The History of an International Economy* 484–506, *Fur Trade* 117, *Essays* 80, 84. (The contrast between the two industries does not, of course, mean that there was perfect competition at all times and places in the cod fisheries. There were, for example, oligopsonistic merchants at St John's, Newfoundland, and elsewhere.)

43 Innis *Fur Trade* 117

44 Innis *Essays* 80, 84

45 Innis *Essays* 3, 124, 173

46 Christian 'Harold Innis as Political Theorist' 21, 22, 30

EPILOGUE
Old trails and new directions

GLYNDWR WILLIAMS

Gatherings such as the Third North American Fur Trade Conference have two main purposes. They bring together scholars working in a particular field and provide them with opportunities for discussion, formal and informal, of each other's work; and they help to indicate and bring before a wider public the shape and direction of current research in the subject. I shall consider here this second aspect, and although the stately pace of historical scholarship rules out any dramatic developments in the eight years since the second conference (1970), some new trends in fur trade studies can be clearly discerned alongside the continuing process of research which is conventional and traditional in approach – and none the worse for that. It would indeed be wrong to suggest that tension exists between the old and the new. Co-operation among historians, economists, and geographers has been a feature of research into the fur trade for half a century, and the growing interest in the subject among scholars from other, and sometimes newer, disciplines is to be greeted with enthusiasm rather than suspicion.

For most students of the fur trade, the documentary confines of their work are those of the Hudson's Bay Company Archives. There are exceptions of course: a thin deposit of North West Company materials; a rather larger body of material on the American fur traders; some British and French official records; missionary sources; and a scattering of private papers in Europe and America. But the Hudson's Bay Company Archives are at the heart of fur trade scholarship, and since the 1970 conference two developments of consequence have affected them. First, the decision was taken at the time of the tercentenary of the parent Hudson's Bay Company to lift the restrictions on the use of company records, which hitherto had been available only to 1870. Like a creeping artillery barrage, the limit was to move forward in stages, to 1900, and then to 1914, with – it was anticipated – eager infantrymen from the ranks of scholarship pressed hard against the new line. Secondly, the archives were moved from London to Winnipeg in 1974, and there they sit in the austerely modern building of the Provincial Archives of Manitoba. A first visit to the new location (a meeting-place for participants second only to the Hotel Fort Garry) during the conference brought a sense of sharp, almost poignant, contrast with the cramped, homely quarters of Beaver House, London, where four researchers had made a crowd, six an unruly mob. Now there was space and light, and all the supporting aids of a modern archive. Uniquely, company documents are available on microfilm in Ottawa and London, and in their original form in Winnipeg. The physical moving of the archives and the lifting of restrictions on post-1870 records have already brought a marked expansion of fur trade studies; but the changes are too recent to be reflected in the conference proceedings. There, no paper rested on the post-1870 documentation, and the familiar roll-call of the sources cited – the fort journals, the correspondence books, the early accounts – was a constant reminder of the finite nature of company records before 1870. Too numerous for any one scholar to encompass, they may be too slender to bear the weight of research teams and computers, if that is to be their fate.

The conference proceedings were stamped with the imprint of younger scholars, who in the fields of economic and social history in particular are adding much to older interpretations. It is true that there were papers, of the highest scholarly standards, which could have been delivered to such a conference twenty-five years ago; but probably half those given followed newer fashions. A few, notably Irene Spry's paper on Harold Innis, Cornelius Jaenen's survey of French attitudes towards the Indian, and Calvin Martin's study of Indian attitudes towards game resources, were timeless in the best sense of the term, and defy this simplistic classification into the old and the new. If we are to pursue the path of categorization, then there were papers in most sessions which took a traditional approach: Richard Ruggles 'Hudson's Bay Company Maps'; Hilary Russell 'Angus Bethune'; James Gibson 'The Russian Fur Trade'; and Stephen Johnson 'Wrangel and Simpson.' All were balanced in the same session, in varying degree, by papers with radically different approaches; and I found the resulting sense of contrast my most enduring memory of the conference.

In his paper Richard Ruggles drew on his massive researches as a historical cartographer (which in 1970 produced, in collaboration with John Warkentin, *The Historical Atlas of Manitoba*) to show the purpose, extent, and limitations of the Hudson's Bay Company maps up to the early nineteenth century. It reflects the divided feelings of most scholars who have studied this subject: realization of the malevolent inaccuracy of those critics who accused the company of neglecting all exploration, and regret that for many years a policy of commercial secrecy prevented the company maps from being known to the outside world. Towards the end of his paper Ruggles touches on the maps drawn at Churchill in the 1760s from Chipewyan Indian information, and these form the centre-piece of the paper on Indian maps presented by Malcolm Lewis. In it he pursues a detailed and sophisticated analysis of these and other Indian maps which goes some way towards refuting the assertion, not heard as often nowadays as it once was, that in North America the European was the true discoverer of the land because he, and he alone, drew recognizable maps of the region. Lewis's insistence on the topological character of Indian mapping – a concept he illustrated by producing a map containing the schematic outline of the London underground system – shows that the accusations of gross inaccuracy often levelled at 'native maps' spring from an inability to decode Indian cartographic conventions. In one of the most interesting speculations of the conference, Lewis went on to surmise that the very differences between Indian maps and the geometrical maps of the Europeans may illustrate Indian thought processes. The source material may prove too limited for examining this hypothesis, but the effort is well worth making, and it is to be hoped that the essential preliminary project of a 'carto-bibliography' of Indian and Eskimo maps will come to fruition.

Several papers were biographical. Two followed well-established precedents in fur trade historiography. Hilary Russell investigated the career of Angus Bethune, one of the Nor'Westers who joined the Hudson's Bay Company in 1821. She makes no high claims for one described by Colin Robertson as a 'poor little fellow,' a trader outstanding only for the amount of adverse criticism he attracted. Her paper does, though, raise indirectly a wider issue which in due course the volumes of the *Dictionary of Canadian Biography* may help to settle: the general calibre of the servants of the fur trading companies. If Simpson's 'Character Book' of 1832 is to be believed, most of his chief factors and chief traders were knaves or fools even in the years when the company was enjoying its greatest geographical sway and commercial dominance. One would welcome a more detached and balanced estimate of this than Simpson's, and an attempt at collective biography is now overdue. Simpson himself is bound to figure somewhere in a conference of this nature, and if Stephen Johnson's paper did not have the impact of Elaine Mitchell's at the 1970 conference, where the 'Man of Feeling' tried to show a side of Simpson which historians had missed, his account of the negotiations between Simpson and Wrangel proves that on occasion the company's overseas governor could cultivate a relationship which was harmonious both at a personal and professional level.

For biography of a less conventional nature we turn to Charles Bishop's paper on Chief Kwah. When the editors of the first volume of the *Dictionary of Canadian Biography* defended their selection of only 65 Indians out of 594 entries for the period of Canadian history before 1700, they explained that 'For almost all of them the information is fragmentary. Like fireflies, they glimmer for a moment before disappearing again into the dark forest of unrecorded history.' This problem of evidence has also beset Bishop, though he largely overcame it in his book on *The Northern Ojibwa and the Fur Trade* (1974). Recently he and Arthur Ray have argued strongly in favour of a combination of the anthropologist's field-work and archaeological approach and the historian's archival methods ('Ethnohistoric Research in the Central Subarctic: some conceptual and methodological problems' *West. Can. J. Anthro.* VI 1976). Properly used, they maintain, the documents will set the probings of the anthropologists in their correct historical perspective. It is an approach more difficult to apply to the study of an individual Indian, as Bishop's investigation of Kwah shows: 'Everything that we know about him has been filtered through the eyes of persons of an alien nature.' And because these witnesses were, with one exception, traders, the information they relay about Kwah relates to his abilities as a provider of furs. We are left with a flat, one-dimensional image of one of the leading Indians of New Caledonia in the first half of the nineteenth century, and only with difficulty can other sources be found to round out our perception. It is an extension of a problem familiar to historians elsewhere – that of having to rely on the literate or the elevated for an account of the doings of the illiterate or the unknown. It confronts scholars searching the chronicles of a medieval monk for a glimpse of the life of the peasantry, or the memoirs of a fastidious philosophe for an explanation of the motives of an eighteenth-century revolutionary crowd. In the fur trade country the gulf of language and culture which has to be crossed is even wider, and it conceals pitfalls of daunting depth and danger.

When we move from the trading career of one Indian to the trade of many, we find the conventional orthodoxy of fur trade history represented by James Gibson's paper on the Russian fur trade. If we stretch the definition of European a little further than usual, then this is Eurocentric history; the Indians, Aleuts, and Eskimos appear here only in their guise of agents of the Russian promyshlennik. The one-sidedness of the approach is deliberate: Gibson has used his knowledge of the Russian sources to concentrate on the European power whose activities in the fur trade are least familiar to us. In an earlier work, *Feeding the Russian Fur Trade* (1969), Gibson studied the agriculture of the west coast and its relationship to the Pacific fur trade. It was a pioneer work whose approach has been extended to the heartland of the fur trade by two doctoral theses, D.W. Moodie 'An Historical Geography of Agricultural Patterns and Resource Appraisals in Rupert's Land, 1670–1774' (University of Alberta 1972), and Barry Kaye 'The Historical Geography of Agriculture and Agricultural Settlement in the Canadian Northwest, 1774–c. 1830' (University of London 1976). In his paper 'Agriculture and the Fur Trade,' Moodie summarizes the most important aspects of his and Kaye's work on a subject which has been regarded by most as lurking on the fringes of the fur trade – marginal in both location and importance. Moodie's definition embraces Indian, company, and settler agriculture, and he argues that agriculture was neither an insignificant nor a rival force as far as the Canadian fur trade was concerned. Rather, by provisioning the fur trade, agriculture played a complementary and essential role.

At the centre of fur trade studies lies the relationship between European and Indian, and several papers illustrate current reinterpretations of the subject. It is a warning against the dangers of postulating too sharp a division between the old scholarship and the new, between orthodoxy and revisionism, that the process in this area of the trade relationship began with E.E. Rich's article 'Trade Habits and Economic Motivation among the Indians of North America' (*Can. J. Econ. Pol. Sci.* XXVI 1960). Rich, architect of some of the most imposing monuments of fur trade history, drew on his earlier work to point out that by European standards Indian behaviour in trade matters was unconventional and often inexplicable. The price mechanism, laws of supply and demand, and other features of the market economy simply did not apply. The problem was examined at the second conference by Abraham Rotstein, whose paper 'The Two Economies of the Hudson's Bay Company,' together with his article, 'Trade and Politics: An Institutional Approach' (*West. Can. J. Anthro.* III 1972), offered an alternative explanation of competition and agreement in the fur trade. Away from his main argument, that for the Indians the fur trade operated in a political, institutionalized fashion,

Rotstein's study of the eighteenth-century post account books revealed a bewildering adaptability of the supposedly immutable trade standard by the factors' application of the 'overplus,' the 'double standard,' and 'presents.' His work drew attention at one level to the strength of the Indian position in the fur trade, and at another to the information that could be wrested from company account books.

At both these levels intensive mining and some speculation have been carried out in the last few years, as the trio of papers by Toby Morantz, Trudy Nicks, and Arthur Ray all reveal. Morantz's paper on the James Bay Cree contains some forthright criticism of the inadequacy of both historians and anthropologists who have viewed the fur trade from behind their own particular ramparts, and have not come out from behind their defences to mingle, and to learn from each other's techniques and findings. Her paper is a clear rebuttal of the older historiography which saw the 'dependence' of the Indian as almost a sine-qua non of the fur trade; it supplies reinforcement from James Bay for Robin Fisher's view of the northwest coast Indians as 'intelligent and energetic traders, quite capable of driving a hard bargain ... The Indians met the maritime fur trade and moulded it to serve their own ends' (*Contact and Conflict: Indian-European Relations in British Columbia 1774–1890* [1977] 23).

But Morantz goes beyond the trading relationship, and by insisting that the Indians did not become slaves to the new technology throws doubt on the impact of the European intrusion on the life-style of the Indians, at least before the twentieth century. This may be a difficult argument to sustain in its entirety, but substantiation of another of her points, that there were many fur trades, not just one, comes in Trudy Nicks's paper on the Iroquois and the fur trade in western Canada. This shows the Iroquois moving across the plains and northern forests as bands of itinerant trappers, much in demand by European traders, and much resented by the local Indian population.

The same problems, but in a different geographical environment from Fisher's, and within a more rigid economic framework than Nicks's, are discussed in Arthur Ray's paper 'Indians as Consumers in the Eighteenth Century.' Here Ray continues the research of his earlier books, *Indians in the Fur Trade* (1974) and (with Conrad Heidenreich) *The Early Fur Trades: A Study in Cultural Interaction* (1976), with a scrutiny of the early post accounts. These reveal that the Indians who came down to the bay posts, far from being innocents ripe for exploitation, were in fact pernickety customers ready to complain when dissatisfied with the quality or type of trade goods offered to them. In the period before 1763, it was the Indians who set the standard of what was and was not acceptable – not the European. They played off British against French, used defective goods as bargaining ploys, and were generally as shrewd and hard-headed as the European factors.

In the years between the second and third conferences research has produced and refined new interpretations of the economic relations between European and Indian, but most noticeable advances have taken place in the contiguous area of social history. The papers presented by Jennifer Brown, John Nicks, Carol Judd, and Sylvia Van Kirk have few parallels with earlier fur trade studies, and both their subject-matter and their techniques have more in common with the work of scholars in the wider pastures of European and North American social history than with the long-respected names of fur trade history. There is a question of definition of course. The limits of social history can be stretched so far that one becomes more aware of its elasticity than its centre of interest, but the present focal points of the subject in the context of the fur trade stand out with some clarity. The social historians are interested in the type and background of men who joined the fur trade; their life-style and its relation to their previous existence; and the impact, both short- and long-term, of the traders on the indigenous population. The papers of John Nicks and Carol Judd fall within the first category.

In his case-study of a single Orkney parish John Nicks gives us an intriguing insight into the working methods of the historical demographer, the information they can be expected to produce, and their limitations. Generalizations about Orkneymen in company service are common enough: we are told (usually by Simpson) that they were dour, reliable, unenterprising, clannish, and so on. Nicks eschews this subjective approach, in which fast-moving value judgments collide noisily with each other, for a more dispassionate analysis of the company servants from Orphir: their age on joining the service, the nature of their first appointment, length of service, salary and rate of saving, status of family, and distribution within the parish.

John Nicks's continuing research on the Orkney traders is set within a wider context by Carol Judd, who surveys the various ethnic groups employed by the company after 1821. Factual information is provided to substantiate what has long been known in outline, that the two largest groups were Canadians and Orkneymen, but that new areas, or old areas rediscovered, were also supplying recruits. A mixture of Orkneymen, Shetlanders, Highland Scots, Irish, French-Canadians, Norwegians, Indians, and mixed bloods was the result of conflicting or changing policies and of recurrent labour shortages. It was an ethnic rag-bag which posed teasing problems of management, and Judd's paper suggests that in future the ethnic origins of individuals and groups should be taken into account as a matter of course by students investigating patterns of behaviour, promotion, and distribution in the fur trade service. Ethnic origins, she argues convincingly, constitute a 'fundamental question.'

Jennifer Brown's paper on naming and classifying, and Sylvia Van Kirk's on recent historiographical trends are concerned less with the ethnic origins of the traders than with the domestic relationships they established in their new abodes. Their papers extend into the fur trade country proper the earlier doctoral studies on Red River by John Foster, 'The Country-Born in the Red River Settlement, 1820–1850' (University of Alberta 1972), and Frits Pannekoek, 'The Churches and the Social Structure in the Red River Area, 1818–1870' (Queen's University 1973). These stressed the division in the settlement between the two main mixed-blood groups, corresponding roughly to the servants, or former servants, of the Hudson's Bay Company and of the old North West Company. This division lies at the root of the quest to define and characterize 'fur trade society'; but their research into the structures of the two companies, and the different attitudes within each, at several overlapping levels, to the perennial question of relations with Indian women, has taken this group of historians and anthropologists well beyond their original starting point.

In Jennifer Brown's doctoral thesis, 'Company Men and Native Families: Fur Trade Society and Domestic Relations in Canada's Old Northwest' (University of Chicago 1976), kinship groups and ties were shown to be important in the North West Company, negligible in the Hudson's Bay Company. Like Carol Judd's, her work implies that explanations of mobility and promotion within the two companies are more complex than was once thought, and the tentative generalizations of scholars currently working in this field are beginning to look very different from the confident ones of an earlier generation. Also open to question is the traditional assumption that the Nor'Westers had closer and more amicable relations with the Indians than did the Hudson's Bay men, an assumption gently queried by Rich many years ago, but only now coming under critical scrutiny of a more general kind. This scrutiny has also cast doubt on the conscientiousness with which the Hudson's Bay Company's standard directives prohibiting liaisons with Indian women were in fact observed, and Van Kirk's thesis, 'The Role of Women in the Fur Trade Society of the Canadian West, 1700–1850' (University of

London 1975), has shown that traders took Indian women not only for sexual reasons but because they fulfilled an important economic role in the fur trade.

Once more, the union of 1821 is seen as a watershed, not because it marked a fusion of racial attitudes comparable to the union of material interests, but because it put power into the hands of Simpson, with his prejudices against mixed bloods and his determination to dismiss redundant servants, and because it was followed by the arrival at Red River and elsewhere of white women and missionaries. In brief, the work of the social historians is providing information not only on the life-style of the traders, their partners and their offspring, but also on the internal structures and trade rivalries of the main competing organizations.

What of the future? The examination of the records up to 1870 by scholars asking fresh questions, using different research methods, and hoping for new answers, will clearly continue. It would be wrong to consider this work as significant only in detail; some of the re-evaluations presented at the conference are of fundamental importance. The incursion into the area of economic historians using more sophisticated devices than their forbears, the collaboration of anthropologists and historians in 'ethnohistory,' and the specialized work undertaken by historical geographers and cartographers all promise well for the future, though the work of synthesis will not be easy. But the most notable advances are likely to come in the post-1870 period, where the documentation is still largely untapped.

The problems will be as great as the opportunities. A glance at the development of fur trade scholarship reminds us how much it owed to the volumes of the Hudson's Bay Record Society, particularly to that great spurt of editorial and publishing activity which produced twenty-two volumes between 1938 and 1959. It will be difficult for the Record Society to play as major a part for the post-1870 period: its obligation to continue publishing volumes from the earlier materials, and the growth of company affairs and records after 1870, will surely confine its role to the driving of trial shafts into the mounds of company documentation.

There will be problems of definition. Before 1870 the Hudson's Bay Company was identified with the fur trade, and for much of the period the fur trade with the company. In the decades following the deed of surrender the company went into land sales, railway construction, government finance, retailing, and all the familiar activities of an international corporation. The fur trade remains after 1870, but it is not the same; it is a dwindling element in the northern economy, and government officials, police, and missionaries are as likely to be found with the Indian or Eskimo as the once-ubiquitous trader. It is not mere sentimental nostalgia which will continue to attract scholars back to the fur trade in the period when it was one of the formative influences in Canada's development, but a recognition that the subject provides within manageable compass all the ingredients of human motivation and accomplishment which historians and their public seek.

Bibliography of Published Works Cited

Adair, E.R. 'France and the Beginnings of New France' *Canadian Historical Review* xxv 3 (1944)

Adams, A.T. ed *The Explorations of Pierre Esprit Radisson* Minneapolis 1961

Adler, Bruno F. 'Karty Piervobytnyh Narodov' [Maps of Primitive Peoples]. *Isviestia Impieratorskavo Obshchestva Lubitielei Estiestvoznania, Antropologii i Etnografi, sostoyaszchavo pri Impieratorskom Moskovskom Universitietie* Tom 119 *Trudy Geografisheskavo Otdielienia* Vypusk 2, St Petersburg 1910

Afrait, S.N. 'The Collective Optimum' Research Paper No. 7409, University of Ottawa 1974

Alarchon, Fernando 'The relation of the Navigation and discovery which Captaine Fernando Alarchon made ...' in Richard Hakluyt *The Third and Last Volume of the Voyages, Navigations, Traffiques, and Discoveries* London 1600

Anderson, James *Fur Trader's Story* Toronto 1961

Anon. 'Narrative of a Journey into Mohawk and Oneida Country, 1634–1635' in John F. Jameson ed *Narratives of New Netherland, 1609–1664* New York 1909

Arbor, Edward ed *The First Three Books on America* Birmingham 1885

Atkinson, Geoffrey *The Extraordinary Voyage in French Literature before 1700* New York 1900

– *Les Nouveaux horizons de la Renaissance* Paris 1935

– *Les Relations de voyages du XVIIe siècle et l'évolution des idées* New York and Paris 1924

Aulneau, Father J.P. in R. Thwaites ed *The Jesuit Relations and Allied Documents* LXVIII New York 1959

Bailey, A.G. *The Conflict of European and Eastern Algonkian Cultures, 1504–1700* 2nd ed, Toronto 1969

Baker, Burt Brown *The McLoughlin Empire and Its Rulers* Glendale, Calif. 1959

Baldwin, R.E. 'Export Technology and Development from a Subsistence Level'
  The Economic Journal LXXIII 289 (1963) 80–92
Bancroft, Hubert Howe *The Works of Hubert Howe Bancroft* XXVIII *History of the
  Northwest Coast 1800–1846* II San Francisco 1884
Barclay, R.S. *The Population of Orkney, 1775–1961* Kirkwall 1965
Baskerville, Peter 'Donald Bethune's Steamboat Practice' *Ontario History* LXVII
  (1975)
Baudet, Henri *Paradise on Earth. Some Thoughts on European Images of Non-European
  Man* New Haven 1965
Bausum, Henry S. 'Edenic Images of the Western World: A Reappraisal' *South
  Atlantic Quarterly* LXVII 4 (1968)
Belleforest, François de *La Cosmographie universelle de tout le Monde* 2 vols, Paris
  1575
Benson, Adolph B. ed *Peter Kalm's Travels in North America* 2 vols, New York 1965
Bergeron, Pierre *Histoire de la nouvelle découverte* Paris 1630
Berry, J.W. 'Multiculturism and Intergroup Attitudes' *Conference on Multi-
  culturalism in Education* Toronto 1977
Biard, Father Pierre in R. Thwaites ed *Jesuit Relations and Allied Documents* III
  New York 1959
Biggar, Henry P. ed *The Works of Samuel de Champlain* 6 vols, Toronto 1922–36
Bishop, Charles A. 'The Emergence of Hunting Territories Among the Northern
  Ojibwa' *Ethnology* IX (1970) 1–15
– 'The Henley House Massacres' *The Beaver* (autumn 1976)
– *The Northern Ojibwa and the Fur Trade. An Historical and Ecological Study* Toronto
  1974
Blackned, John and Brian Craik 'Rupert House: Cree Way Project' *The Beaver*
  (1975)
Blair, Emma H. ed *The Indian Tribes of the Upper Mississippi Valley and region of the
  Great Lakes, as described by Nicolas Perrot, etc.* 2 vols, Cleveland 1911–12
Boas, George and Arthur O. Lovejoy *Primitivism and Related Ideas* Baltimore 1935
Bochert, Samuel *Opera Omnia. Hierozicon* London 1663
Bogoras, Waldemar 'Ideas of Space and Time in the Conception of Primitive
  Religion' *American Anthropologist* n.s. XXVII (April 1925)
Boucher, Philip 'France Discovers America: The Image of Tropical America in
  Sixteenth and Seventeenth Century France and its Impact on Early French
  Colonialism' doctoral dissertation, University of Connecticut, 1974
Bouchette, Joseph *The British Dominions in North America; Or a Topographical and
  Statistical Description of the Provinces of Lower and Upper Canada ... and a Topo-
  graphical Dictionary of Lower Canada ... in two Volumes* London 1831
Brown, Jennifer S.H. 'Charles Thomas Isham' *Dictionary of Canadian Biography* V
  (in press)

- 'A Colony of very Useful Hands' *The Beaver* (spring 1977) 39–45
- 'Company Men and Native Families: Fur Trade Social and Domestic Relations in Canada's Old Northwest, doctoral dissertation, University of Chicago, 1976
- 'Ultimate Respectability: Fur Trade Children in the "Civilized World"' *The Beaver* (winter 1977) 4–10, (spring 1978) 48–55

Brun, Christian 'Dobbs and the Passage' *The Beaver* (autumn 1958)

Buffon, Georges-Louis Leclerc de *Œuvres Complètes* 32 vols, Paris 1824–8

Callender, Guy S. *Selections from the Economic History of the United States, 1765–1860* New York 1965

Campbell, Rev. Robert *A History of the Scotch Presbyterian Church, St. Gabriel Street, Montreal* Montreal 1887

Cartier, Jacques 'The Third Voyage of Discovery ...' in Richard Hakluyt *The Third and Last Volume of the Voyages, Navigations, and Discoveries ...* London 1600

Chailley Bert, Joseph 'La politique indigène' *Revue économique internationale* ii (juin 1904)

Champlain, Samuel de in H.P. Biggar *The Works of Samuel de Champlain* v and vi Toronto 1933

- in William L. Grant ed *Voyages of Samuel de Champlain* New York 1907

Charbonneau, Hubert, Bertrand Desjardins, et Pierre Beauchamp 'Le Comportement démographique des voyageurs sous le régime français' *Histoire Sociale/Social History* xi 21 (May 1978)

Charlevoix, P.F-X. *Histoire de l'isle Espagnole de S. Domingue* 2 vols, Paris 1730

- *Histoire et description generale de la Nouvelle-France* 6 vols, Paris 1744

Chinard, Gilbert *L'Amérique et le rêve exotique dans la littérature française au XVIIe et XVIIIe siècles* Paris 1913

- *L'Exotisme américain dans la littérature française au XVIe siècle* Paris 1911

Christian, William 'Harold Innis as Political Theorist' *Canadian Journal of Political Science* x (1977) 21–42

Clouston, J.S. 'Orkney and the Hudson's Bay Company' *The Beaver* (1936–37)

Coale, Ansley J. and Paul Demeny *Regional Modal Life Tables and Stable Populations* Princeton 1966

Cochrane, Rev. William C. *The Canadian Album, Men of Canada or Success by Example* Brantford 1891

Cohn, Norman *The Pursuit of the Millennium* London 1957

Cole, Richard G. 'Sixteenth-Century Travel Books as a Source of European attitudes towards non-white and non-Western cultures' *Proceedings of the American Philosophical Society* xvi (1972)

Cones, Elliott ed *New Light on the Early History of the Greater Northwest: The Manuscript Journals of Alexander Henry ... and David Thompson ... 1799–1814* 2 vols, New York 1897

Cox, Ross *The Columbia River* ed Edgar I. Stewart and Jane R. Stewart, Norman 1957

Cumming, William P. et al *The Exploration of North America 1630–1776* London 1974

Dablon, Father Claude in R. Thwaites ed *Jesuit Relations and Allied Documents* LIV New York 1959

Dalrymple, Alexander *Memoir of a Map of the Lands Around the North Pole* London 1789

Davidson, George 'Explanation of an Indian map made of the rivers, lakes, trails and mountains from the Chilkaht to the Yukon drawn by the Chilkaht Chief, Kohklux, in 1869' *Mazama* (April 1901) 1–8

Davidson, Gordon Charles *The North West Company* New York 1918, rpt 1967

Davies, K.G. ed *Letters from Hudson Bay, 1703–40* London 1965

d'Avity, Pierre *Description générale de l'Amérique, troisième partie du monde* Paris 1637

– *The Estates, Empires and Principalities of the World* London 1615

Davydov, G.I. *Two Voyages to Russian America, 1802–1807* Colin Bearne, Kingston 1977

De Bulhões, O.G. 'Agriculture and Economic Development' in W.W. Rostow ed *The Economics of Take-off into Sustained Growth: Proceedings of a Conference Held by the International Economic Association* London 1963

de Laguna, Frederica 'The Atna of the Copper River, Alaska: The World of Men and Animals' *Folk* 11/12 (1969/70)

Delanglez, Jean ed *The Journal of Jean Cavelier, The Account of a Survivor of La Salle's Texas Expedition 1684–1688* tr Jean Delanglez, Chicago 1938

de La Peyrère, Isaac *Preadamitae. Sive Exercitatio super Epistolae ad Romanos* [*Pre-Adamites, Commentary on the Epistle to the Romans*] Paris 1655

Dempsey, Hugh A. 'David Thompson on the Peace River, Part II' *Alberta Historical Review* 14 (1966)

Denys, Nicolas *Description geographique et historique des costes de l'Amérique septentrionale* 2 vols, Paris 1670

De Pauw, Corneille *Defence de recherches philosophiques sur les américains* Berlin 1790

– *Recherches philosophiques sur les américains* Berlin 1768

Deschamps, Hubert *Les Méthodes et les doctrines coloniales de la France* Paris 1953

Deschamps, Léon *Histoire de la question coloniale en France* Paris 1885

– 'La Question coloniale en France' *Revue de Géographie* XVI nov. 1885

Devine, E.J. *Historic Caughnawaga* Montreal 1922

Dewdney, Selwyn *The Sacred Scrolls of the Southern Ojibway* Toronto 1975

Dickason, Olive P. 'The Myth of the Savage and Early French Colonization in the Americas' doctoral dissertation, University of Ottawa, 1976

Diereville, sieur de *Relation du Voyage de Port-Royal de l'Acadie ou de la Nouvelle-France* Rouen 1708

Dobbs, Arthur *An Account of the Countries Adjoining to Hudson's Bay* London 1744

Doob, Leonard W. *Becoming More Civilized: A Psychological Exploration* Westport, Conn. 1973

Douay, Fr Anastasius 'Narrative of La Salle's Attempt to Ascend the Mississippi in 1687' in John G. Shea *Discovery and Exploration of the Mississippi Valley* New York 1852

Drache, Danny 'Canadian Capitalism: Sticking with Staples' *This Magazine* IX 3 (1975) 7–10

– 'Rediscovering Canadian Political Economy' *Journal of Canadian Studies* IX 3 (1976) 3–18

Drober, Wolfgang *Kartographie bei den Naturvölken* Erlangen 1903

Du Bartus, Guillaume *La Seconde sepmaine* Anvers 1591

Duchêne, Louise *Habitants et marchands de Montréal au XVIIᵉ siècle* Paris 1974

Dudley, Edward and Maximilien E. Novak eds *The Wild Man Within: An Image in Western Thought from the Renaissance to Romanticism* Pittsburgh 1972

Du Teritre, Jean-Baptiste *Histoire générale des Antilles habitées par les françois* 4 vols, Paris 1667–71

– *Histoire générale des Isles de S. Christophe et autres dans l'Amérique* Paris 1654

Easterbrook, W.T. 'Recent Contributions to Economic History: Canada' in W.T. Easterbrook and M.H. Watkins *Approaches to Canadian Economic History* Toronto 1967

Easterbrook, W.T. and M.H. Watkins *Approaches to Canadian Economic History* Toronto 1967

Eccles, W.J. *The Canadian Frontier, 1534–1760* Toronto 1969

– *France in America* New York 1972

Echeverra, Durand *Mirage in the West. A History of the French Image of America to 1815* Princeton 1957

Elliot, John H. 'Discovery of America and the Discovery of Man' *Proceedings of the British Academy* LII (1972)

– *The Old World and the New, 1492–1650* Cambridge 1970

Elliot, Robert *The Shape of Utopia: Studies in a Literary Genre* Chicago 1970

Elliot, T.C. 'Marguerite Wadin McKay McLoughlin' *Oregon Historical Quarterly* XXXVI 4 (1935)

Engel, Samuel *Essai sur cette question: Quand et comment l'Amérique a-t-elle été peuplé d'hommes et d'animaux?* 5 vols, Amsterdam 1767

Estienne, Henri *L'Introduction au traité de la conformité des merveilles anciennes avec les modernes* Genève 1566

Fairchild, Hoxie *The Noble Savage: A Study in Romantic Naturalism* New York 1928
Feit, Harvey A. 'The Ethno-Ecology of the Waswanipi Cree; or How Hunters Can
    Manage Their Resources' in Bruce Cox ed *Cultural Ecology: Readings on the
    Canadian Indians and Eskimos* 115–25 Toronto 1973
– 'Twilight of the Cree Hunting Nation' *Natural History* LXXXII (Aug.–Sept. 1973)
Financial Post 'The March of the Multinationals' *The 1977 Ranking of Canada's
    Largest Companies* Toronto 1977
– 'What Exactly Is a Multinational?' *The 1977 Ranking of Canada's Largest Companies*
    Toronto 1977
Fisher, Raymond H. *The Russian Fur Trade 1550–1799* Berkeley and Los Angeles
    1943
Fisher, Robin *Contact and Conflict: Indian-European Relations in British Columbia,
    1774–1890* Vancouver 1977
Fleming, R. Harvey ed *Minutes of Council of Northern Department of Rupert's Land,
    1821–31* Introduction by H.A. Innis, Hudson's Bay Record Society III London
    1940
Flinn, Michael ed *Scottish Population History from the 17th Century to the 1930's*
    Cambridge 1977
Fontaine, Charles *La Description des terres trouvée de notre temps* Lyon 1559
Fontenelle, Bernard de *Œuvres de Monsieur de Fontenelle* 8 vols, Paris 1752
Foster, John E. 'The Country-born in the Red River Settlement: 1820–1850'
    doctoral dissertation, University of Alberta, 1972
– 'The Home Guard Cree and the Hudson's Bay Company, the First Hundred
    Years' in D. Muise ed *Approaches to Native History in Canada: Papers of a Conference
    Held at the National Museum of Man, October, 1975* National Musuem of Man,
    Mercury Series, History Division, Pape No. 25, Ottawa 1975
– 'The Indian-Trader in the Hudson Bay Fur Trade Tradition' Paper presented
    to the Second Canadian Ethnological Society Annual Conference, Winnipeg,
    1975
– 'Rupert's Land and the Red River Settlement, 1820–1870' in L.G. Thomas ed
    The Prairie West to 1905 Toronto 1975
Fowke, Vernon *Canadian Agricultural Policy: the Historical Patterns* Toronto 1946
Frame, Donald M. ed *The Complete Works of Montaigne* Stanford 1957
– ed *Montaigne's Essays and Selected Writings* New York 1963
Francis, Daniel and Toby Morantz *Partners in Furs: A History of the Fur Trade in
    Eastern James Bay, 1600–1870* Quebec, forthcoming
Fraser, Simon *Letters and Journals, 1806–1808* ed W. Kaye Lamb, Toronto 1960
Friederici, Georg *Der Charakter der Entdeckung und Eroberung Amerikas durch die
    Europiäer* 3 vols, Stuttgart 1936

Frisch, Jack 'Some Ethnological and Ethnohistoric Notes on the Iroquois in
Alberta' *Man in the Northeast* XII (1976)
Furtado, Celso *Economic Development of Latin America: A Survey from Colonial Times to
the Cuban Revolution* Cambridge 1970

Galbraith, J.S. *The Hudson's Bay Company as an Imperial Factor, 1821–69* Toronto
1957
Garry, Francis N.A. and W.J. Noxon eds *The Diary of Nicolas Garry* Toronto 1973
Gerbi, Antonelli *The Dispute of the New World: A History of a Polemic, 1750–1900*
Pittsburgh 1973
Giamatti, A.B. *The Earthly Paradise and the Renaissance Epic* Princeton 1966
Gibson, James R. *Feeding the Russian Fur Trade* Madison 1969
– 'Food for the Fur Trades: The First Farmers in the Pacific Northwest,
1805–1946' *Journal of the West* VIII (1968) 18–30
– *Imperial Russia in Frontier America* New York 1976
Glacken, Clarence J. *Traces on the Rhodian Shore. Nature and Culture in Western
Thought* Berkeley 1967
Glover, Richard ed *David Thompson's Narrative 1784–1812* Toronto 1962
– Introduction to K.G. Davies ed *Letters from Hudson Bay, 1730–40* London 1965
– Introduction to E.E. Rich and A.M. Johnson eds *Cumberland and Hudson House
Journals 1775–82, Second Series 1779–82* London 1952
– 'York Boats' *The Beaver* (March 1949)
Golovinin, Fleet Captain *Puteshestvie vokrug sveta ...* [Voyage Around the World ...]
Moscow 1965
Gonnard, René *La Légende du bon sauvage* Paris 1946
Goody, Jack 'Strategies of Heirship' in Jack Goody, Joan Thirsk, and E.P.
Thompson eds *Family and Inheritance: Rural Society in Western Europe, 1200–1800*
Cambridge 1976
Gough, Barry M. 'Canada's Adventure to China, 1784–1821' *Canadian Geo-
graphical Journal* XCIII 3 (Dec. 1976/Jan. 1977)

Hallowell, A. Irving *Culture and Experience* Philadelphia 1955
– 'Ojibwa Ontology, Behavior, and World View,' in Stanley Diamond ed *Culture in
History: Essays in Honor of Paul Radin* New York 1960, 19–52
– 'Ojibwa World View and Disease' in Iago Galdston ed *Man's Image in Medicine
and Anthropology* Institute of Social and Historical Medicine, New York
Academy of Medicine, Monograph 4, New York 1963
Halot, Alexandre 'Aptitude des français à coloniser' *Questions diplomatiques et
coloniales* IV mai-août 1898

Hammond, George P. and Agapito Rey 'Don Juan de Oñate Colonizer of New Mexico 1595–1628' *Cornado Cuarto Centennial Publications, 1540–1940* VI Albuquerque 1900

Hanke, Lewis *Aristotle and the American Indians: A Study in Race Prejudice in the Modern World* London 1959

Hanotaux, Gariel 'L'Amérique du Nord et la France' *Revue des deux mondes* V (1912)

– 'La Leçon du Canada' *Revue des deux mondes* i (1913)

Hardouin, Jean *Nouveau traité sur la situation du Paradis terrestre* La Haye 1730

Hardy, Georges *Histoire de la colonisation française* Paris 1931

Hargrave, Joseph James *Red River* Montreal 1871

Harmon, Daniel Williams *A Journal of Voyages and Travels in the Interior of North America* New York 1903

– *Sixteen Years in the Indian Country: The Journal of Daniel William Harmon* Toronto 1957

Harper, J. Russell *Paul Kane's Frontier* Toronto 1971

Harris, D.A. and G.C. Ingram 'New Caledonia and the Fur Trade: A Status Report' *The Western Canadian Journal of Anthropology* III (1972) 179–96

Harris, R. Cole and Leonard Guelke 'Land and Society in Canada and South Africa' *Journal of Historical Geography* III (1977)

Hazard, Paul *European Thought in the Eighteenth Century. From Montesquieu to Lessing* Cleveland 1967

Hearne, Samuel *A Journey from Prince of Wale's Fort in Hudson's Bay to the Northern Ocean* ed Richard Glover, Toronto 1958

Heidenreich, Conrad *Huronia, A History and Geography of the Huron Indians, 1650–1660* Toronto 1971

Hennepin, Louis *Description de la Louisiane nouvellement découverte* Paris 1683

– *A New Discovery of a Vast Country in America* 2 vols, London 1698

Henry, Alexander *Travels and Adventures in Canada and the Indian Territories Between the Years 1760 and 1776* Edmonton 1969

Hervé, Georges 'Débuts de l'Ethnographie au XVIIIe siècle (1701–1765)' *Revue de l'Ecole d'Anthropologie* xi (nov-déc 1907)

Higgins, Benjamin *Economic Development: Problems, Principles and Policies* New York 1968

Hinks, Arthur R. *Maps and Surveys* Cambridge 1913

History of Toronto and County of York Toronto 1885

Hla Myint, U. 'The Gains from International Trade and the Backward Countries' *The Review of Economic Studies*, 58 (1954–55) 129–42

Hodgen, Margaret T. *Early Anthropology in the Sixteenth and Seventeenth Centuries* Philadelphia 1964

Howay, F.W. 'An Outline Sketch of the Maritime Fur Trade' *Annual Report of the Canadian Historical Association* (1932)
Huet, Pierre-Daniel *Traité sur la situation du Paradis terrestre* Paris 1691
Humbolt, Alexander von *Kritische Untersuchungen uber die Historische Entwickelung der geographischen Kenntnisse von der Neuen Welt ...* Berlin 1836

Innis, Harold A. *The Cod Fisheries: The History of an International Economy* New Haven 1940
– *The Fur Trade in Canada, An Introduction to Canadian Economic History* revised ed, Toronto 1956
– *Settlement and the Mining Frontier* Toronto 1936
Innis, Harold A. and Mary Q. Innis eds *Essays in Canadian Economic History* Toronto 1956
Irving, Washington *Astoria, or Enterprise Beyond the Rocky Mountains* Paris 1836

Jaenen, Cornelius J. 'Amerindian Views of French Culture in the Seventeenth Century,' *Canadian Historical Review* LV (1974)
– 'Concepts of America, Amerindians and Acculturation' paper read at 9th Annual Algonquian Studies Conference, Worcester, 1977
– *Friend and Foe. Aspects of French-Amerindian Cultural Contact in the Sixteenth and Seventeenth Centuries* Toronto 1976
– 'The Meeting of the French and Amerindians: A Reinterpretation of Cultural Contact in the Seventeenth Century' *Revue de l'Université d'Ottawa* xliii 1 (1973)
Jenness, Diamond *The Ojibwa Indians of Parry Island: Their Social and Religious Life* National Museum of Canada, Anthropological Series, Paper no. 17, Ottawa 1935
Jennings, Francis *The Invasion of America: Indians, Colonials and the Cant of Conquest* Chapel Hill 1975
Johnson, Alice M. ed *Saskatchewan Journals and Correspondence Edmonton House 1795–1800; Chesterfield House 1800–1802* Hudson's Bay Record Society xxvi London 1967
– 'Simpson in Russia' *The Beaver* (autumn 1960)
– 'York Boat Journal' *The Beaver* (Sept. 1951)
Jones, H. Mumford *O Strange New World* New York 1952
Jones, R.L. *History of Agriculture in Ontario, 1663–1880* Toronto 1946
Journal des savants pour l'année MDCXXIV Paris 1724
Julien, André *Les Voyages de découvertes et les premiers établissements* Paris 1948
Justel, Henri *Recueil de divers voyages faits en Afrique et en Amérique* Paris 1674

Kane, Paul *Wanderings of an Artist Among the Indians of North America from Canada to Vancouver's Island and Oregon through Hudson's Bay Company's Territories and Back Again* Toronto 1925

Kaye, Barry 'The Historical Geography of Agriculture and Agricultural Settlement in the Canadian Northwest 1774 ca 1830' doctoral dissertation, University of London, 1976

[Khlebnikov] K.T. *Colonial Russian America* tr Basil Dmytryshyn and E.A.P. Crownhart-Vaughan, Portland 1976

Kierans, Eric 'The Corporate Challenge to Government' *The Role of Government in Canadian Society* Walter L. Gordon Lecture Series 1 Toronto 1977

Kindleberger, Charles P. *International Economics* 4th ed, Homewood 1968

Lafitau, Jean-François *Les Mœurs des sauvages amériquains comparées aux mœurs des premiers temps* 2 vols, Paris 1724

Lahontan, Baron de *Dialogues curieux entre l'auteur et un sauvage de bon sens* Paris 1703

– *Voyages du Baron de LaHontan dans l'Amérique septentrionale* 2 vols, Amsterdam 1705

Lalemant, Father Charles in R.G. Thwaites ed *Jesuit Relations and Allied Documents* New York 1959

Lamb, W. Kaye 'The Founding of Fort Victoria' *British Columbia Historical Quarterly* VII (April 1943) 71–92

– ed *Journal of a Voyage on the North West Coast of North America during the Years 1811, 1812, 1813, and 1814* tr Wessie Tipping Lamb, Toronto 1969

– ed *The Journals and Letters of Sir Alexander Mackenzie* Cambridge 1970

– ed *Letters and Journals of Simon Fraser, 1806–1808* Toronto 1960

– ed *Sixteen Years in the Indian Country: The Journal of Daniel William Harmon, 1800–1816* Toronto 1957

Landes, Ruth *Ojibwa Religion and the Midewiwin* Madison 1968

Larrabee, Edward 'Recurrent Themes and Sequences in North American Indian-European Culture Contact' *Transactions of the American Philosophical Society* n.s. LXVI 7 (1976)

Laslett, Peter *The World We Have Lost* New York 1965

Laudonniere, René Goulaine de *L'Histoire notable de la Floride* Paris 1586

Lazarev, A. *Zapiski o Plavanii voyennovo shlvopa Blagonamerennovo v Beringov proliv i vokrug sveta dlya otkryty v 1819, 1820, 1821 i 1822 godakh* [*Notes on the Voyage of the Naval Sloop* Loyal *to Bering Strait and around the World for Discoveries in 1819, 1820, 1821, and 1822*] Moscow 1950

Leacock, Eleanor 'The Montagnais "Hunting Territory" and the Fur Trade' *American Anthropological Association Memoir* LXXVIII (1900)

Le Clerq, Chrestien *Nouvelle Relation de la Gaspésie* Paris 1691
LeFevre de la Barre, Joseph-Antoine *Description de la France équinoctiale* Paris 1666
Le June, Father Paul in R.G. Thwaites ed *Jesuit Relations and Allied Documents* VI
    New York 1959
Le Roy, Louis *De la Vicissitude ou variété des choses en l'univers* Paris 1576
Leroy-Beaulieu, Paul *De la colonisation chez les peuples modernes* Paris 1891
Lery, Jean de *Histoire d'un voyage fait en la terre du Brésil* Paris 1585
Lescarbot, Marc *La Conversion des sauvages qui ont esté baptisez en la Nouvelle France*
    Paris 1610
Levesque, Pierre-Charles *L'Homme morale, ou l'homme considéré tant dans l'état de pure*
    nature que dans la société Amsterdam 1775
Levin, Harry *The Myth of the Golden Age in the Renaissance* Bloomington 1969
Lewis, Malcolm G. 'The Recognition and Delimitation of the Northern Interior
    Grasslands during the Eighteenth Century' in Brian W. Blouet and Merlin P.
    Lawson eds *Images of the Plains* Lincoln 1975
Lips, Julius 'Notes on Montagnain-Naskapi Economy' *Ethnos* XII (1947)
Lisiansky, Urey *A Voyage Round the World in the Years 1803, 4, 5, & 6* tr author,
    London 1814
Lovejoy, Arthur O. *The Great Chain of Being. A Study of the History of an Idea*
    Cambridge, Mass. 1957
Lunn, Jean 'The Illegal Fur Trade out of New France, 1713–60' *Canadian*
    Historical Association Papers (1939) 61–76

McDonald, A.A. 'H.B.C. Inland Transport; 1. Building the York Boat' *The Beaver*
    (Oct. 1923)
Mackenzie, Alexander *Voyages from Montreal on the River St. Laurence through the*
    Continent of North America ... London 1801
MacKenzie, James 'John Bethune: the Founder of Presbyterianism in Upper
    Canada' in *Called to Witness: Profiles of Canadian Presbyterians* ed W. Standford
    Reid, Toronto 1975
McKenzie, N.M.W.J. *The Men of the Hudson's Bay Company 1670–1920* Fort William
    1921
Mackintosh, W.A. 'Economic Factors in Canadian History' *Canadian Historical*
    Review IV (1923) 12–25
McLean, John *Notes of a Twenty-five Years Service in the Hudson Bay Territory* London
    1849
MacLennan, Hugh *Two Solitudes* Toronto 1945
McLeod, Margaret A. *The Letters of Letitia Hargrave* Champlain Society XXVIII
    Toronto 1947
McLeod, Malcolm ed *Peace River. A Canoe Voyage from Hudson's Bay to the Pacific, by*

the late Sir George Simpson (Governor, Hon. Hudson's Bay Company), in 1828. Journal of the late Chief Factor, Archibald McDonald (Hon. Hudson's Bay Company) who accompanied him Ottawa 1872

MacRae, A.O. *History of the Province of Alberta* 1912

Magne, Emile *Scarron et son milieu* Paris 1905

Mair, L.P. *Studies in Applied Anthropology* London 1957

Makarova, Raisa V. *Russians on the Pacific 1743–1799* tr Richard A. Pierce and Alton S. Donnelly, Kingston 1975

Martin, Calvin 'Ethnohistory, a Better Way to Write Indian History' *Western Historical Quarterly* IX (1978)

– *Keepers of the Game: Indian-Animal Relationships and the Fur Trade* Berkeley 1978

Marwick, Hugh *Orkney Farm Names* Kirkwall 1952

Mason, Philip *Patterns of Dominance* London 1970

Masson, L.R. ed *Les Bourgeois de la Compagnie du Nord-Ouest* I Quebec 1889

Means, Philip *The Spanish Main* New York 1965

Mesnard, Pierre ed *Jean Bodin: La Methode de l'histoire* Paris 1941

– *Œuvres philosophiques de Jean Bodin* 3 vols, Paris 1951

Mitchell, E.A. 'The Scot in the Fur Trade' in W.S. Reid ed *The Scottish Tradition in Canada* Toronto 1976

Montesquieu, Baron de *Œuvres* 7 vols, Amsterdam 1785

Montgomery, Richard G. *The White Headed Eagle* New York 1934

Moodie, D.W. 'An Historical Geography of Agricultural Patterns and Resource Appraisals in Rupert's Land, 1670–1774' doctoral dissertation, University of Alberta, 1972

Moodie, D.W. and Barry Kaye 'The Northern Limit of Indian Argiculture in North America' *Geographical Review* LIX (1969) 513–29

Morantz, Toby 'James Bay Social Organization, 1730–1850' Paper presented to Direction de l'Archéologie et de l'Ethnologie, Ministère des Affaires Culturelles, Québec 1977

– 'James Bay Trading Captains of the Eighteenth Century: New Perspectives on Algonquian Social Organization' in *Actes du Huitième Congress des Algonquinistes* ed W. Cowan, Ottawa 1977

– 'The Probability of Family Hunting Territories in Eighteenth Century James Bay: Old Evidence Newly Presented' *Proceedings of the Ninth Algonquian Conference* ed W. Cowan, Ottawa 1978

Morice, A.G. 'Are the Carrier Sociology and Mythology Indigenous or Exotic?' *Proceedings and Transactions of the Royal Society of Canada, for the Year 1892* x (1893)

– *The History of the Northern Interior of British Columbia, Formerly New Caledonia (1660–1880)* Toronto 1904

Morton, A.S. *A History of the Canadian West to 1870–71* London 1939
– ed *The Journal of Ducan M'Gillivray of the North West Company at Fort George on the Saskatchewan, 1794–5* Toronto 1929
Morton, W.L. 'Agriculture in the Red River Colony' *Canadian Historical Review* xxx (1949) 305–22
– in E.E. Rich ed *London Correspondence Inward from Eden Colvile, 1849* London 1956
– *Manitoba, A History* 2nd ed, Toronto 1967
– 'The Red River Parish: Its Place in the Development of Manitoba' in R.C. Lodge ed *Manitoba Essays* Toronto 1937, 89–105
Mury, François 'Le Génie colonisateur de la France' *La Nouvelle revue* cxx (oct 1899)
Myers, J.A. 'Jacques Raphael Finlay' *Washington Historical Quarterly* x (1919) 163–7

North, Douglass C. *The Economic Growth of the United States, 1790–1860* Englewood Cliffs 1961
Norton, T.E. *The Fur Trade in Colonial New York 1686–1776* Madison 1974
Nurkse, Ragnar *Equilibrium and Growth in the World Economy* Cambridge 1962

Oldmixon, John 'The History of Hudson's Bay' in J.B. Tyrrell ed *Documents Relating to the Early History of Hudson Bay* Toronto 1931
Oliver, E.H. ed *The Canadian North-West; Its Early Development and Legislative Records: Minutes of the Councils of the Red River Colony and the Northern Department of Rupert's Land* Ottawa 1914–15
O'Malley, Martin *The Past and Future Land: An Account of the Berger Inquiry into the Mackenzie Valley Pipeline* Toronto 1976
Ouellet, Fernand 'Dualité économique et changement technologique au Québec (1760–1790)' *Histoire Sociale/Social History* ix (1976) 256–96
Oury, Dom Guy *Marie de l'Incarnation, Ursuline (1599–1672) Correspondance* Solesmes 1971

Pannekoek, Frits 'The Anglican Church and the Disintegration of Red River Society, 1818–1870' in Carl Berger and Ramsay Cook eds *The West and the Nation* Toronto 1976, 133–49
– 'The Churches and the Social Structure in the Red River Area, 1818–1870' doctoral dissertation, Queen's University, 1973
– 'The Rev. Griffiths Owen Corbett and the Red River Civil War of 1869–70' *Canadian Historical Review* lvii (1976) 133–49
Parker, Ian 'Harold Innis, Karl Marx and Canadian Political Economy' *Queen's Quarterly* liv (1977) 545–63

Parkman, Francis *France and England in America. A Series of Historical Narratives* 1 Boston 1871
- *The Jesuits in North America in the Seventeenth Century* 2 vols, Toronto 1899
- *Pioneers of France in the New World* 2 vols, New York 1969
Pavlov, P.N. *Pushnoy Promysel v Siberi XVII* [*The Fur Trade in Siberia in the Seventeenth Century*] Krasnoyarsk 1972
Peckham, Howard et al *Attitudes of Colonial Powers towards the American Indian* Salt Lake City 1969
Pelleprat, Pierre *Relation des missions dans les isles et terre ferme de l'Amérique* Paris 1655
Perrot, Nicholas in E.H. Blair ed *The Indian Tribes of the Upper Mississippi Valley and the Region of the Great Lakes* 1 Cleveland 1911
Peterkin, Alexander *Rentals of the Ancient Earldom and Bishopric of Orkney* Edinburgh 1820
Phillips, C.P. *The Fur Trade* 2 vols, Norman 1961
Piollet, J.B. 'Que nous sommes un peuple colonisateur' *Etudes* lxxxii (jan-mars 1900)
Poncelin de la Roche-Tilhac, J.C. *Almanack Américain* Paris 1784
Portlock, Captain Nathaniel *A Voyage Round the World ...* London 1789
Prebisch, Raul *Towards a New Trade Policy for Development* New York 1964
Preston, Richard J. *Cree Narrative: Expressing the Personal Meaning of Events. Canadian Ethnology Service Paper #30* Ottawa
Prévost, A.F. *Le Philosophe anglais* 5 vols, Paris 1783–5

Quaife, Milton ed *The Western Country in the 17th Century. The Memoirs of Antoine Lamothe Cadillac and Pierre Liette* New York 1962

Ray, Arthur J. 'The Factor and the Trading Captain in the Hudson's Bay Company Fur Trade Before 1763' *Proceedings of the Second Congress, Canadian Ethnology Society* ed J. Freedman and J. Barkow, Ottawa 1975, 586–602
- 'Some Conservation Schemes of the Hudson's Bay Company, 1821–50' *Journal of Historical Geography* (1975) 49–68
Ray, Arthur J. and D.B. Freeman *'Give Us Good Measure': An Economic Analysis of Relations Between the Indians and the Hudson's Bay Company Before 1763* Toronto 1978
'Répertoire des engagements pour l'ouest conservés dans les archives judiciares de Montréal' *Rapport de l'archiviste de la Province de Québec* (1942–43; 1943–44; 1944–45; 1945–46)
Rich, E.E. ed *Colin Robertson's Correspondence Book, September 1817 to September 1822* Toronto 1939

- ed *Cumberland House Journals and Inland Journals 1775–82 Second Series 1779–1782* London 1952
- *The Fur Trade and the Northwest to 1857* Toronto 1967
- *History of the Hudson's Bay Company 1670–1870* 2 vols, London 1959
- ed *Hudson's Bay Copy-Book of Letters Outward etc., Begins 29th May, Ends 5 July 1687* Toronto 1948
- ed *James Isham's Observations on Hudson's Bay, 1743* Toronto 1949
- ed *Journal of Occurrences in the Athabasca Department by George Simpson, 1820 and 1821, and Report* Toronto 1938
- ed *The Letters of John McLoughlin from Fort Vancouver to the Governor and Committee* ... I First Series, 1825–38, Introduction by W. Kaye Lamb, Toronto 1941–4
- ed *Minutes of the Hudson's Bay Company 1671–1674* Toronto 1942
- ed *Minutes of the Hudson's Bay Company 1679–1684, First Part, 1679–1682* Toronto 1945
- ed *Minutes of the Hudson's Bay Company, 1679–1684, Second Part, 1682–1684* Toronto 1946
- ed *Part of a Dispatch from George Simpson, Esqr., Governor of Rupert's Land to the Governor and Committee of the Hudson's Bay Company, London, March 1, 1829; continued and Completed March 24 and June 5, 1829* Toronto 1947
- 'Trade Habits and Economic Motivation Among the Indians of North America' *Canadian Journal of Economics and Political Science* XXVI (1960) 35–53
Ridington, Robin 'Beaver Dreaming and Singing' in Pat Lotz and Jim Lotz eds *Essays in Memory of Diamond Jenness. Anthropologica, Special Issue* n. s. XIII (1971) 115–28
Ritzenthaler, Robert E. 'Chippewa Preoccupation with Health: Change in a Traditional Attitude Resulting from Modern Health Problems' *Bulletin of the Public Museum of Milwaukee* XIX (Dec. 1953)
Rogers, Edward S. *The Material Culture of the Mistassini* Nat. Museum of Man, Bull. No. 218, Ottawa 1967
Rothney, Russell 'Mercantile Capital and the Livelihood of Residents of the Hudson Bay Basin' master's thesis, University of Manitoba, 1975
Ruggles, Richard 'Governor Samuel Wegg, Intelligent Layman of the Royal Society, 1732–1802' *Notes and Records of the Royal Society of London* XXXII 2 (1978)
- 'Governor Samuel Wegg "The Winds of Change"' *The Beaver* (autumn 1976) 10–20
- 'Hospital Boys of the Bay' *The Beaver* (autumn 1977) 4–11
Russell, Hilary 'The Chinese Voyages of Angus Bethune' *The Beaver* (spring 1977) 22–31

Sagard, Father Gabriel in G.M. Wrong ed *The Long Journey to the Country of the Hurons* Toronto 1939

Sage, W.N. ed 'Peter Skene Ogden's Notes on Western Caledonia' *British Columbia Historical Quarterly* I (Jan. 1937)

Sampson, William R. ed *John McLoughlin's Business Correspondence, 1847–48* Seattle 1973

Sarafian, Winston Lee 'Russian-American Company Employee Practices, 1799–1867' doctoral dissertation, University of California at Los Angeles, 1970

Sarychev, G.A. *Puteshtvie po severo-vostachnoy chasti Sibiri, Dedovitomu moryer i Vostochnomu Okeanu* [*Journey through the Northeastern Parts of Siberia, the Arctic Ocean, and the Pacific Ocean*] Moscow 1952

Sauer, Carl O. *Sixteenth Century North America: The Land and the People as seen by the Europeans* Berkeley 1971

Sauer, Martin *An Account of a Geographical and Astronomical Expedition to the Northern Parts of Russia* London 1802

Schoolcraft, Henry in Philip P. Mason ed *Expedition to Lake Itasca* East Lansing 1958

Sheehan, Bernard W. 'Indian-White Relations in Early America: A Review Essay' *William and Mary Quarterly* 3rd series XXVII (1969)

Shortt, Adam *Documents relating to Canadian Currency, Exchange, and Finance during the French Period* 2 vols, Ottawa 1925

Simpson, Sir George *Narrative of a Voyage Round the World, During the Years 1841 and 1842* I London 1847

Sinclair, Sir John *The Orkney Parishes: Containing the Statistical Account of Orkney 1795–1798* Kirkwall 1927

Skinner, Alanson Buck 'Notes on the Eastern Cree and Northern Saulteaux' *Anthropological Papers of the American Museum of Natural History* IX 1 (1911)

– 'Political and Ceremonial Organization of the Plains Ojibway' *Anthropological Papers of the American Museum of Natural History* XI (1914) 504–5

Smith, David Merril *Ikonze: Magico-Religious Beliefs of Contract – Traditional Chipewyan Trading at Fort Resolution, NWT, Canada* National Museum of Man, Mercury Series, Ethnology Div., Paper No. 6, Ottawa 1973

Smith, Donald B. *Le Sauvage. The Native People in Quebec Historical Writing in the Heroic Period (1534–1663) of New France* Ottawa 1974

Snow, Dean R. 'Abenaki Fur Trade in the Sixteenth Century' *Western Canadian Journal of Anthropology* VI (1976) 7–9

Speck, Frank G. 'Mistassini Hunting Territories in the Labrador Peninsula' *American Anthropologist* XXV (1939) 452–71

– *Naskapi: The Savage Hunters of the Labrador Peninsula* Norman 1935

Spencer, Robert F. 'Shamanism in Northwestern North America' in Raymond D. Fogelson and Richard N. Adams eds *The Anthropology of Power; Ethnographic Studies from Asia, Oceania, and the New World* New York 1977, 351–63

Spry, Irene *The Palliser Expedition: An Account of John Palliser's British North American Exploration Expedition* Toronto 1963
- 'Routes through the Rockies' *The Beaver* (1963) 26–39
Statistics Canada *Canada's International Investment Position, 1974* Catalogue No. 67–202, Ottawa 1978
- *Quarterly Estimates of the Canadian Balance of International Payments, Fourth Quarter 1977* Catalogue No. 67–001, Ottawa 1978
Steward, Julian H. 'Carrier Acculturation: The Direct Historical Approach' in Stanley Diamond ed *Culture in History: Essays in Honor of Paul Radin* New York 1960
Sullivan, Robert J., SJ *The Ten'a Food Quest* Catholic University of America, Anthropological Series, No. 11, Washington, DC 1942

Tanner, Adrian 'Bringing Home Animals. Religious Ideology and Mode of Production of the Mistassini Cree Hunters' doctoral dissertation, University of Toronto, 1976
- 'The Significance of Hunting Territory Systems of the Algonkian in Social Theory' *American Anthropologist* n.s. XLI (1973) 269–80
Ternaux-Compans, Charles-Henri ed *Voyages, relations et mémoires originaux pour servir à l'histoire de la découverte de l'Amérique* 10 vols, Paris 1837–40
Thevet, André *La Cosmographie universelle* 2 vols, Paris 1575
- *Les Singularités de la France antarcticque* Paris 1556
Thompson, David 'Journey to the Bow River and Rocky Mountains Nov. 1800' in *Journals of Travel and Observation in Canada 1790–1825* microfilm copy at Glenbow-Alberta Institute
Thorman, G.E. 'An Early Map of James Bay' *The Beaver* (spring 1961) 18–22
Thwaites, Reuben Gold ed *Early Western Travels 1748–1846* Cleveland 1904
- ed *The Jesuit Relations and Allied Documents* 72 vols, Cleveland 1896–1901
Trelease, Allen W. 'The Iroquois and the Western Fur Trade: a Problem in Interpretation' *Mississippi Valley Historical Review* XLIX (1962–3) 32–51
Triggar, Bruce *The Children of Aataensic: A History of the Huron People to 1660* 2 vols, Montreal 1976
- *The Huron Farmers of the North* Toronto 1969
Turner, Frederick Jackson 'The Significance of the Frontier in American History' in *Frontier American History*, New York 1920, 1–38

Van Kirk, Sylvia 'The Custom of the Country: An Examination of Fur Trade Marriage Practices' in L.H. Thomas ed *Essays on Western History* Edmonton 1976
- 'Moses Norton' *Dictionary of Canadian Biography* IV (in press)

- 'The Role of Women in the Fur Trade Society of the Canadian West, 1700–1850' doctoral dissertation, University of London, 1975
- '"Women in Between": Indian Women in Fur Trade Society in Western Canada' *Canadian Historical Association Papers* (1977)

VanStone, James W. *Athapaskan Adaptations: Hunters and Fishermen of the Subarctic Forests* Chicago 1974

Velat, B. and Y. Champailler eds *Œuvres de Boussuet* Tours 1961

Veniaminov, I. *Zapiski ob ostrovakh Unalashkinskavo otdela* [*Notes on the Islands of Unalaska District*] St Petersburg 1840

Vignon, Louis *L'Expansion de la France* Paris 1891

Voltaire *Essai sur les mœurs* 2 vols, Paris 1735–6

Von Kotzebue *A New Voyage Round the World in the Years 1823, 24, 25 and 26* II London 1830

Von Langsdorff, G.H. *Voyages and Travels in Various Parts of the World* II London 1814

Vrangel, F. 'O pushaykh tovarakh severoamerikanskikh rossüskikh vladeny' ['Concerning the Furs of Russia's North American Possessions'] *Teleskop* XXVIII 16 (1835)

Wallace, Stewart ed *Documents Relating to the North West Company* Toronto 1934
- *The Macmillan Dictionary of Canadian Biography* 3rd ed, Toronto 1963

Watkins, M.H. 'A Staple Theory of Economic Growth' *Canadian Journal of Economics and Political Science* XXIX (1963) 141–8

Wauchope, Robert *Lost Tribes and Sunken Continents: Myth and Methodology in the Study of American Indians* Chicago 1962

Wax, Rosalie and Murray Wax 'The Magical World View' *Journal for the Scientific Study of Religion* I (spring 1962)

Wessel, Thomas 'Agriculture, Indians and American History' *Agricultural History* L (1976) 9–20

Wilkes, Charles *Narrative of the United States Exploring Expedition during the years 1838, 1839, 1840, 1841, 1842* IV Philadelphia 1845

Will, George and George Hyde *Corn Among the Indians of the Upper Missouri* Lincoln 1917

Williams, Glyndwr ed *Andrew Graham's Observations on Hudson's Bay 1767–91* London 1969
- 'Governor George Simpson's Character Book' *The Beaver* (summer 1975)
- *Hudson's Bay Miscellany 1670–1870* Winnipeg 1975

Wishart, D. 'Agriculture at the Trading Posts on the Upper Missouri Prior to 1843' *Agricultural History* XLVII (1973) 56–62

Wissler, Clark 'The Excess of Females among the Cree Indians' *Proceedings of the National Academy of Sciences* XXII (1936) 151–3

Wrangell, Count Admiral von *Statistische und ethnographische Nachrichten über die Russichen Bestizungen an der Nordwestküste von Amerika* St Petersburg 1839; rpt Osnabruck 1968

Wraxall, Peter *An Abridgement of the Indian Affairs Contained in Four Folio Volumes, Transacted in the Colony of New York From the Year 1678 to the Year 1751* ed C.H. McIlwain, Cambridge 1915

Lightning Source UK Ltd.
Milton Keynes UK
UKHW012355200722
406167UK00001B/398

9 781487 592165